Archaeologies of Cultural Contact

Archaeologies of Cultural Contact

At the Interface

Edited by
TIMOTHY CLACK
and
MARCUS BRITTAIN

OXFORD
UNIVERSITY PRESS

Great Clarendon Street, Oxford, OX2 6DP,
United Kingdom

Oxford University Press is a department of the University of Oxford.
It furthers the University's objective of excellence in research, scholarship,
and education by publishing worldwide. Oxford is a registered trade mark of
Oxford University Press in the UK and in certain other countries

© Oxford University Press 2022

The moral rights of the author have been asserted

First Edition published in 2022

Impression: 1

All rights reserved. No part of this publication may be reproduced, stored in
a retrieval system, or transmitted, in any form or by any means, without the
prior permission in writing of Oxford University Press, or as expressly permitted
by law, by licence or under terms agreed with the appropriate reprographics
rights organization. Enquiries concerning reproduction outside the scope of the
above should be sent to the Rights Department, Oxford University Press, at the
address above

You must not circulate this work in any other form
and you must impose this same condition on any acquirer

Published in the United States of America by Oxford University Press
198 Madison Avenue, New York, NY 10016, United States of America

British Library Cataloguing in Publication Data
Data available

Library of Congress Control Number: 2022935508

ISBN 978–0–19–969394–8

DOI: 10.1093/oso/9780199693948.001.0001

Printed and bound in the UK by
TJ Books Limited

Links to third party websites are provided by Oxford in good faith and
for information only. Oxford disclaims any responsibility for the materials
contained in any third party website referenced in this work.

Acknowledgements

As editors, we would like to thank the contributors for their support, patience, and commitment throughout the project. Hilary O'Shea and Jenny King from Oxford University Press helped tremendously in shepherding the collection through the commissioning, review, and production process and are owed thanks.

For use of the epigraphs from *Oryx and Crake* in Chapter 5, we are grateful to Margaret Atwood, Penguin Random House (US), Penguin Random House (Canada), and Curtis Brown. Permission to reproduce images was provided from the Stuttgart State Office for Historic Preservation (front cover and Fig. 5.2), Natural History Museum London (Fig. 4.1), La Valette Military Museum (Fig. 6.1), Henrik Pihl (Fig. 9.2), Mark Horton (Fig. 11.4), National Archaeological-Anthropological Museum Netherlands Antilles (Fig. 12.1), and UK National Archives (Fig. 12.2).

During the final stages of this book's production, we received the incredibly sad news that one of the book's authors, Mary Beaudry, had died. Held in great affection by so many, her passing is a great loss to archaeology.

TC and MB
Cambridge, May 2022

Contents

List of Figures	ix
List of Contributors	xiii
Archaeologies of Cultural Contact: An Introduction *Marcus Brittain and Timothy Clack*	1

I. DEALING WITH DIFFERENCE

1. The Domestication of Difference: Globalization, Hybridity, and Material Culture in Archaeological Perspective *Nicole Boivin*	25
2. Nodes of Interaction: Changing Rock Paintings in the Eastern Cape Mountains of South Africa *Lara Mallen and David G. Pearce*	44
3. Becoming One or Many: Material Mediation of Difference in Honduras *Rosemary A. Joyce and Russell N. Sheptak*	62
4. Other than Human Hybridity? *Timothy Clack*	84
5. Disentangling Neanderthal-Modern Human Interactions in Western Europe: A Heuristic Odyssey *Brad Gravina, Francesco d'Errico, and François Bachellerie*	110

II. CONFLICT, POWER, AND BELIEF

6. The Biographies of Resistant Material Culture in Occupied Landscapes: The Channel Islands and World War II *Gilly Carr*	159
7. Unblended America: Contesting Race and Place in Nineteenth-Century New England *Karen Ann Hutchins-Keim and Mary C. Beaudry*	178
8. 'Such Was the End of Their Feast': Violence, Intimacy, and Mimetic Practice in Early Modern Ireland *Audrey Horning*	196

viii   CONTENTS

9. Tacit Knowing of Thralls: Style Negotiation and Hybridization
among the Unfree in Eleventh- and Twelfth-Century Sweden   211
Mats Roslund

10. Cultural Interaction at Palmares: An Archaeology of South
American Maroons   237
Pedro Funari and Aline de Carvalho

11. Creole Identity and Syncretism in the Archaeology of Islam   253
Andrew Petersen

12. Syncretism and Cognition: African and European Religious
and Aesthetic Expressions in the Caribbean   267
Jay B. Haviser

III. CONCLUDING THOUGHTS

13. Observations of a Diverse Discussion on Power and Diversity   297
Jeb Card

Index   309

List of Figures

2.1. The area historically known as Nomansland, in which the paintings we describe are found, lies below the Drakensberg escarpment in the eastern part of South Africa.   45

2.2. Examples of hunter-gatherer paintings from the case study area, showing the attention to detail and artistic skill characteristic of this tradition: (a) eland antelope, (b) running human figure, (c) therianthrope that conflates human and antelope features.   46

2.3. Type 3 paintings are typically finger painted and include human figures, often carrying bows and arrows, and quadrupeds, most of which seem to be horses. Black represents red, stipple represents faded red.   51

2.4. Several of the Type 3 human figures wear European-style dresses with bustle pads. Black represents white, stipple represents yellow.   53

3.1. Map showing *pueblos de indios* (grey) and Spanish towns in the San Pedro district of northern Honduras *c.*1780.   64

3.2. Brushed, red slipped jar rim from Omoa, *c.*1770–1800.   75

3.3. Unslipped bowl rim from Omoa, *c.*1770–1800. (a) Exterior showing groove and punched marks made using punch. (b) Interior showing facet from forming with paddle.   75

4.1. Photograph of four hominin endocasts: (from left to right) Neanderthal, AMH, *Homo erectus* and *Australopithecus africanus* (photo: T. Clack and Natural History Museum London).   89

4.2. The löwenmensch ('lion-man') figurine photographed from two angles. The statuette is carved mammoth ivory (height 311 mm, width 73 mm) from Hohlenstein-Stadel Cave, Asselfingen, Baden-Württemberg, Germany (photo: Y. Mühleis © Stuttgart State Office for Historic Preservation).   91

5.1. Distribution of the Châtelperronian including main sites mentioned in the text.   111

5.2. Diagnostic stone tools of the final Mousterian (1–5), Châtelperronian (6–12), and Proto-Aurignacia (13–22) industries of southwestern France; (1) MTA backed knife, (2) large sidescraper, (3) pseudo Levallois point, (4) scraper on a Levallois flake, (5) biface, (6–9) Châtelperronian point, (10) oblique truncation, (11) circular endscraper, (12) blade core

X LIST OF FIGURES

on a flake, (13–15) bladelets with a point created by direct bilateral retouch, (16–21) Dufour bladelets, (22) nucleiform burin (modified after Bachellerie 2011; Bordes 1972; Bordes 2002; Thiébaut 2005; Mazière 1978; Primault 2003).   117

5.3. Bayesian models of ^{14}C ages obtained by (a) Higham et al. 2011b and (b) Hublin et al. 2012 on bone samples from the Châtelperronian levels of the Grotte du Renne, Arcy-sur-Cure. Note the absence of 'outliers' and the merging of levels IX and X into a single stratigraphic unit in the Hublin et al. model.   129

5.4. Refitting of Châtelperronian blades onto their core (after Bachellerie et al. 2007).   133

5.5. Bone tools, ornaments, and pigments from the Châtelperronian levels of Grotte du Renne, Arcy-sur-Cure (after Caron et al. 2011). Personal ornaments made of perforated and grooved teeth (1–6, 11), bones (7–8, 10), and a fossil (9); red (12–14) and black (15–16) colorants bearing facets produced by grinding; bone awls (17–23).   135

6.1. (a) V-sign badge, La Valette Military Museum; (b) cigarette lighter, La Valette Military Museum; (c) German bread bowl featuring Guernsey crest, La Valette Military Museum; (d) crested badge, La Valette Military Museum.   167

7.1. Map of Massachusetts showing location of sites discussed in the text.   184

9.1. (a) Indigenous late Viking Age pottery from Sigtuna, (b) Baltic ware from Lund, Skåne, (c) Baltic ware from Sigtuna, Uppland, and (d) Baltic ware from Skara, Västergötland. All dated to the eleventh century. Scale 1:4.   212

9.2. Distribution of Baltic ware in Scandinavia. Occasional vessels have been found in other parts of the Nordic countries but were of little significance for pottery consumption. (a) In eastern Denmark and Gotland the production of indigenous late Viking Age pots ceased in the first half of the eleventh century when people switched to Baltic ware. (b) In northern Halland, Småland, Västergötland, and Östergötland the older tradition was continued parallel to the new Baltic ware. (c) In the eastern part of the Mälaren Valley Baltic ware was present in central places while a significant proportion of late Viking Age vessels continued to be manufactured there. Only a few vessels of simple Baltic ware were used in the countryside, which retained the older tradition. Between Götaland and eastern Denmark was a zone with a varied pattern of consumption, which is indistinct because of the lack of source material. The manufacture of Baltic ware stopped around 1,200 CE in eastern Denmark and in the mid-thirteenth century in the other areas. Map by Henrik Pihl (Roslund 2007).   218

LIST OF FIGURES   xi

9.3. Sigtuna. (a) Indigenous late Viking Age pottery, (b) late Slavic pottery imported from the Novgorod area, locally manufactured Baltic ware of (c) simple variant and (d) normal variant. Arrows indicate tradition influences. Scale 1:4.   224

9.4. Sigtuna. Percentage of early black earthenware in each period. A weak presence of Finno-Ugrian pottery (eleven units) during the first half of the eleventh century and weiche Grauware (thirteen units) around 1,100 testifies to the presence of people from the Gulf of Finland and the southwest Baltic (n = 10,594).   225

9.5. Novgorod, the Troitski excavation. Large storage vessels from the twelfth century. Scale 1:4.   227

9.6. Lund. Early black earthenware distributed by ware group over time. Percentage of units of each group in relation to the others within each period (n = 593).   229

9.7. Lund. Baltic ware from (a) the eleventh century and (b) the twelfth century. Scale 1:4.   230

9.8. Lund. Late Baltic ware from the twelfth and thirteenth century. Scale 1:4.   232

10.1. Map showing the location of Palmares. The maroons were situated between the states of Alagoas and Pernambuco.   241

11.1. Map of the Islamic world showing places mentioned in the text.   255

11.2. Arab Sassanian coin. This silver dirham was minted on the orders of Ziyad ibn Abi Sufyan, the Arab governor of Southern Iran. It bears a portrait of Khusrau II (Sassanian emperor 590–628) as well as inscriptions in Middle Persian. However, on the edge of the coin there is an Arabic Islamic inscription 'in the name of Allah the Lord' indicating that this is an example of the Sassanian-style coins that continued to be produced for more than a hundred years after the Arab Islamic conquest of Iran.   258

11.3. Bronze lion excavated at Shanga, Kenya (photo: Mark Horton).   259

11.4. Plan of the Umayyad city of 'Anjar in Lebanon. This site, which has many similarities to a Roman town, was built by the Umayyad caliph al-Walid in 714–15.   263

12.1. Nanny and her charge, Barbados, 1880 (left); Nanny 'Yaya' with children on Curacao, 1907 (right).   272

12.2. African-descendant prisoners for Obeah violations in the Caribbean, Antigua, 1905 (UK National Archives, CO 152/287, Knollys to Lyttelton no. 208, 12 May 1905, London).   275

12.3. Photograph of Father Onderwater.   276

12.4. Father Onderwater excavation with in situ African-Creole fetish objects from the early to mid-twentieth century.   278

xii LIST OF FIGURES

12.5. Bone buttons and a brass clasp, direct association with the priest skeleton (left); rosary beads and crucifix, direct association with the priest skeleton (right). 278

12.6. One of many altar contexts at the grave site; note the candles, cigars, coins, and food offerings (top right); coins found in both surface and sub-surface contexts at the site (523 total, 65.6 percent copper coins) (top left); rag-thread bundles and honey-bottles with offerings in both surface and sub-surface contexts at the site (bottom). 279

12.7. Handmade dolls with pins and bound with thread, found buried at the site, note the painted round-eye shape on the dolls (bottom); handmade dolls placed at the gravesite after removal of skeletal remains, note the sewn slit-eyes on the dolls (top). 280

12.8. Father Onderwater's reburial procession, led by the Catholic priest and followed by chanting Haitian Catholic community members. 283

12.9. Examples of dental modification and scarification (left) Utopo men from Congo (c.1912) and from Congo (Ota Benga, c.1904); Ota Benga lived in the Bronx Zoo Monkey House 1904–6 (right). 285

12.10. Zoutsteeg skeleton #1 with modified upper incisors and post-mortem loss of lower incisors. 287

12.11. Zoutsteeg skeleton #2 with modified upper and lower incisors. 288

List of Contributors

François Bachellerie completed his doctoral research at the University of Bordeaux. This presented a detailed taphonomic and technological analysis of Châtelperronian assemblages from three open-air sites in the Aquitaine Basin leading to an overall evaluation of the cultural unity of this techno-complex and its role in the so-called 'Middle-to-Upper Palaeolithic transition'. In addition to co-directing new fieldwork at the important Châtelperronian, such as Abri du Loup in the Correze Basin and Saint Césaire in the Charente-Maritime, as well as participating in numerous related field projects, his research interests include lithic technology, taphonomy, and site formation processes. Currently working at Archéologie Alsace and a member of the laboratory De la Préhistoire à l'Actuel: Culture, Environnement et Anthropologie (PACEA) at the University of Bordeaux, his research has been published in such international journals as *Paleo, Bulletin de la Société Préhistorique Française*, and *Quaternary Science Reviews*.

Mary C. Beaudry was Professor of Archaeology and Anthropology at Boston University. Her research interests included: historical and industrial archaeology of the Americas and British Isles; comparative colonialism; culture contact; gender and equity issues in archaeology; and food and foodways. She co-edited numerous books, including: *The Historical Archaeology of Shadow and Intimate Economies* (2019); *Archaeologies of Mobility and Movement* (2013), and *The Oxford Handbook of Material Culture Studies* (2010).

Nicole Boivin is Director of the Department of Archaeology at Max Planck Institute for the Science of Human History. She has undertaken pioneering research in Asia and Africa, exploring a broad range of issues through field, laboratory, and theoretical applications—from human migrations out of Africa in the Late Pleistocene, to cognition, rock art, and material culture. Her ERC-funded Sealinks Project investigated the emergence of long-distance trade and connectivity in the Indian Ocean, and its relationship to processes of biological exchange and translocation.

Marcus Brittain is a Senior Project Officer at the Cambridge Archaeological Unit and a Member of the McDonald Institute for Archaeological Research, University of Cambridge, UK. His research interests primarily relate to the UK, the Antarctic region, and Africa and include pioneer communities of the later prehistoric and later historical periods, the social value of archaeology, and archaeological methods and theory.

Jeb Card is Visiting Assistant Professor in Anthropology at Miami University, Oxford, Ohio. His research interests include indigenous agency and material design in early Spanish Colonial Central America; the nature of statecraft on the southeastern

xiv LIST OF CONTRIBUTORS

boundary of the Maya region; and the history of archaeological practice and public engagement. In addition to articles and chapters on the archaeology of El Salvador, publications include the edited volumes *The Archaeology of Hybrid Material Culture* (2013) and *Lost City, Found Pyramid: Understanding Alternative Archaeologies and Pseudoscientific Practices* (2016).

Gilly Carr is a University Lecturer in Archaeology at the University of Cambridge's Institute of Continuing Education. She is also a Fellow and Director of Studies in Archaeology and Anthropology at St Catharine's College. While her background is in the Roman occupation of Britain, since 2007 she has been pioneering the concept of 'Occupation Archaeology', based on her fieldwork in the Channel Islands. She has completed a number of works on occupation, including: *Victims of Nazism in the Channel Islands* (2019) and *Legacies of Occupation* (2014).

Aline de Carvalho is a specialist in public archaeology based at the Laboratory of Public Archaeology, State University of Campinas, Sao Paulo, Brazil.

Timothy Clack is Chingiz Gutseriev Fellow in Archaeology and Anthropology at the University of Oxford, UK. In addition to cultural contact, his current research concerns heritage and armed conflict, environmental change as a driver of violence, and landscapes and identities. He is Senior Editor for Cultural Heritage of the journal *Cogent—Arts & Humanities.*

Francesco d'Errico is Director of Research of exceptional class with the *Centre National de la Recherche Scientifique*, University of Bordeaux and Professor at the Centre for Early Sapiens Behaviour, University of Bergen. His academic interests focus on the evolution of human cognition and the emergence of symbolic cultural practices in Africa and Eurasia, Neanderthal extinction, and the impact of climate change on cultural evolution. He has published hundreds of articles in high impact academic journals and is the author or editor of several research monographs. Since 2014, he is included by Clarivate Analytics in the list of the world's most cited researchers.

Pedro Funari is Professor of Historical Archaeology based at the History Department, Centre for Advanced Studies, State University of Campinas, Sao Paulo, Brazil. Formerly Secretary of the World Archaeological Congress, he has written and edited books on archaeological theory, historical archaeology, and memory and repression. He is on the editorial board of numerous journals, including *International Journal of Historical Archaeology, Journal of Material Culture*, and *Public Archaeology.*

Brad Gravina completed studies at the Institute of Archaeology, University College London followed by the University of Cambridge, and is currently a member of the laboratory *De la Préhistoire à l'Actuel: Culture, Environnement et Anthropologie* (PACEA) at the University of Bordeaux, where he received his doctorate. His research interests include lithic technology and taphonomy, site formation processes, and investigating the complex question of the disappearance of the Neanderthals with particular emphasis on the final Middle Palaeolithic of Western Europe. Since 2014, he has co-directed excavations at the key Middle Palaeolithic site of Le Moustier (Dordogne, southwestern France). He has co-authored numerous articles in international journals with colleagues from both England and France, including a recent edited monograph (with K. Seetah) entitled *Bones for Tools, Tools for Bones: The Interplay between Objects and Objectives.*

Jay B. Haviser has worked for the Monuments and Archaeology Department of the Government of St Maarten, Dutch Caribbean. He received his doctorate from Leiden University, The Netherlands, in 1987. Since 1999, he has served three terms and is currently President of the International Association for Caribbean Archaeology (IACA). In 2008, he was knighted by Queen Beatrix of The Netherlands for his work in Caribbean archaeology.

Audrey Horning is Professor of Archaeology in the School of Geography, Archaeology, and Palaeoecology, Queen's University Belfast. Her research engages with comparative colonialism and the relationship between archaeology and contemporary identity. Books include *Ireland in the Virginian Sea: Colonialism in the British Atlantic* (2013); *Ireland and Britain in the Atlantic World* (with Nick Brannon, 2009); *Crossing Paths or Sharing Tracks? Future Directions in the Archaeological Study of post-1550 Britain and Ireland* (with Marilyn Palmer, 2009); *The Post-Medieval Archaeology of Ireland* (with Ruairí Ó Baoill, Colm Donnelly, and Paul Logue, 2007), and *In the Shadow of Ragged Mountain* (2005).

Karen Ann Hutchins-Keim holds a PhD in Archaeology from Boston University, USA. In addition to her research interests in African diaspora archaeology in New England, she is currently a principal investigator at EBO Consulting, Inc. She has worked in New England, the mid-Atlantic, and the Caribbean.

Rosemary A. Joyce is Professor of Anthropology at the University of California, Berkeley, where she has been a Professor of Anthropology since 1994. She has directed archaeological fieldwork in Honduras since 1979, in the lower Ulua Valley, in the Department of Yoro, at Los Naranjos, and most recently at the Spanish colonial fort of San Fernando de Omoa. Joyce is the author of six books and co-author of four others, including the path-breaking work on Honduran archaeology *Cerro Palenque: Power and Identity on the Maya Periphery.*

Lara Mallen is affiliated to the Rock Art Research Institute, University of the Witwatersrand, South Africa. She studied for a DPhil from the University of Oxford, UK. Her research interests include hunter-gatherer rock art and multi-cultural interaction in southern Africa.

David G. Pearce is Senior Researcher in the Rock Art Research Institute, University of the Witwatersrand, South Africa. His research interests include Later Stone Age rock art and burial practices in southern Africa, and rock art chronology. Significant publications include *San Spirituality: Roots, Expressions, and Social Consequences* (2004, with David Lewis-Williams) and *Inside the Neolithic Mind: Consciousness, Cosmos and the Realm of the Gods* (2005, with David Lewis-Williams).

xvi   LIST OF CONTRIBUTORS

Andrew Petersen is Professor and Director of Research in Islamic Archaeology at the University of Wales Trinity Saint David. In 2017/18, he held the Alfred Howell Chair of History and Archaeology at the American University of Beirut. He has worked in and carried out research in a number of countries of the Middle East and Africa including, Jordan, Iraq, Palestine, Turkmenistan, the UAE, Oman, Syria, Qatar, Kenya, and Tanzania. His books include The Archaeology of the Syrian Hajj Route in the Medieval and Ottoman Periods (British Academy/ Oxbow) and Dictionary of Islamic Architecture (Routledge).

Mats Roslund is Professor in Historical Archaeology, Department of Archaeology and Ancient History, Lund University, Sweden. His research is directed towards social identity and group dynamics, intersectionality, the social and cultural consequences of exchange, and medieval, Islamic, and Byzantine archaeology. This has directed him towards geographic regions and places where different social identities were negotiated, reproduced, and made discernible in artefacts. Urban centres in Europe and Islamic Sicily are two fields of research. Theoretical and methodological problems connected to objects and their 'meanings' in a wider sense is his area of interest.

Russell N. Sheptak is a Research Associate of the Archaeological Research Facility, University of California, Berkeley. A historical anthropologist, he has conducted research at the Archivo General de Indias (Seville, Spain) and Archivo General de Centroamerica (Guatemala City), microfilmed collections from the Archivo Eclesiastico de Comayagua, and archaeological sites throughout Honduras. He currently directs a project to create a finding aid for the microfilmed Archivo General de Centroamerica. He has authored numerous journal articles and book chapters about the Honduran past.

Archaeologies of Cultural Contact

An Introduction

Marcus Brittain and Timothy Clack

This book is about the diversity of approaches in archaeology that may be employed to examine the material and behavioural attributes of community responses to conditions of cultural contact. Reflecting upon the often unequal terms that bind groups in these circumstances, the book's thirteen chapters refer variously to creolization, ethnogenesis, hybridity, and syncretism, each as theories of social and cultural change—of 'how things come into being' (Liebmann 2013: 27). Such themes provoke critique, particularly with a concern for their analytical value to archaeological discourse; they 'inspire and evoke as much as they refer and denote' (Stewart 2011: 48). And whether regarded as analytical concepts or social processes, or at times as both, they have generated productive debate with a variety of opinions, which are notably expressed in several recent dedicated collections (Stockhammer 2012a; Card 2013; van Pelt 2013; special journal sections in *Historical Archaeology* 2000 and *Journal of Social Archaeology* 2015).

Many of the contributions here identify specific frames of social context within which the individual strengths or weaknesses of these themes may be determined, as well as their applicability to specific research questions. Ultimately, the authors have been encouraged to consider creolization, ethnogenesis, hybridity, and syncretism not necessarily as mutually exclusive models but as contextually specific, diachronic, and interdependent scales of practice within a broader manifestation of cultural change. In building on previous insights through a diverse range of case study contexts, this book serves to further reflect on change in contact encounters across time and space. Expressions of processes of cultural change are thereby demonstrated as both culturally and temporally contingent. Also brought into focus is the active interplay of traditions in resistance to the rhythms of change, that hitherto has received only limited consideration. The chapters collectively chart

Marcus Brittain and Timothy Clack, *Archaeologies of Cultural Contact: An Introduction* In: *Archaeologies of Cultural Contact: At the Interface*. Edited by: Timothy Clack and Marcus Brittain, Oxford University Press.
© Oxford University Press 2022. DOI: 10.1093/oso/9780199693948.003.0001

processes of change through diverse situations of contact and recognize these as cross-directional between mutually active parties.

Across cultural studies more broadly, the dynamics of contact and change are evidently complex and challenging, and have emerged in consideration to globalization, displacement, cultural legitimization and identity politics, both in times of relative peace and upon stages of conflict. In the book's first contributing chapter, Boivin situates such considerations for archaeology, through which it is evident that alternative perspectives may come into focus depending on whether and which elements of creolization, ethnogenesis, hybridity, and syncretism are employed. Each differs in terms of the specificity of their frame of analysis, generally by scale and forms of cultural transformation. Although each approach emerges from, and sometimes refers to, specific historical contexts and pathways, common to these is the production of new cultural forms.

The effervescence of studies into contact and cultural transformation is evident by the temporal and geographic scope of the contributions here: North and South Africa, Indian Ocean, North and South America, Western and Northern Europe, across mainlands and islands, from earliest humans into the twenty-first century; mostly, the setting concerns human cultures, although the applicability of hybridity to non-human cultures also features. Such a scope has not always been collectively represented across approaches to cultural contact, owing largely to the respective contexts of their development as models of cultural change, though their reach and thereby their meaning has with time, like the subjects of their study, taken new forms and associations. To deter uncertainty, definition of these models is a necessity, and it is evident that for different authors, here and elsewhere, subtleties of definition may vary, particularly with regard to creolization and hybridity, and that these may in some instances even be used interchangeably and/or holistically (Weißköppel 2005; Stewart 2011). In any case, as is outlined below, whatever their scale, form, or reference, their meaning is interconnected.

Cultural contact, assimilation, and acculturation

Like the concept of culture and its relationship to archaeological classification, studies of culture contact have a long tradition in archaeology. The term *contact* is broad ranging and may, without due reflection, lack the complexity of relations or the exacting specificity of situations such as in colonialism, for example (Silliman 2005). It has nevertheless long been recognized that culture contact entails messy and dynamic processes expressed differently through individuals, communities, and institutions, understanding of which benefits from a variety of analytical approaches and frames of analysis (Fortes 1936).

Traditionally, in archaeological approaches to cultural contact, notions of acculturation, assimilation, and diffusion have enabled means of explanation for changes in forms of material culture, especially when combined with understanding of their spatial and temporal patterning. During the first half of the twentieth century in particular the adoption of cultural diffusion for general narratives of culture contact were gradually framed with nuances of specificity through readings of acculturation and assimilation. From the 1930s, anthropological studies of acculturation defined this as to comprehend 'phenomena which result when groups of individuals having different cultures come into first-hand contact, with subsequent changes in the original cultural patterns of either or both groups' (Redfield et al. 1936: 149). There is evidently a mould of historical particularity (Cusick 1998) in these early studies of acculturation, connected with political circumstance or orientation (Rowlands 1994). Its use across social sciences centred not just on the dynamism of contact, but also upon its societal consequences, for example during the Great Depression in the United States and British colonial occupation of societies in the southern hemisphere, for where a focus lay upon the search for solutions to practical problems of policy administration (Brandstetter 2006: 23).

Acculturation attends to long-term processes of change in cultural practices and institutions stimulated by strategies of colonial enculturation, often therefore seen as an inevitable stage in forced programmes of assimilation. To advocates of acculturation, changes in artefact types and the ratios between these enable measurement of the degree and pace to which one cultural form transitions to another (Lightfoot 2015). Assimilation is distinguished from acculturation in terms of its relations between differing scales of hierarchy within situations of cultural contact (e.g. dominant and minority groups, colonized and colonizer). Whereas assimilation is generally seen as dependent on the dominant group's acceptance of change, as well as a positive identification towards the dominant group by the minority, acculturation may function irrespective of these.

Those critical of assimilation as a part of acculturation highlight their singular direction illustrated by the necessary internal transformation of the minority group as well as the seeming requirement that it relinquish previous heritage affiliations as a trade-off for joining the dominant group. As Gravina, d'Errico, and Bachellerie argue in this book, acculturation studies often therefore bear the burden of core-periphery that lack consideration of multi-directional dynamics of power and agency. Though, as Silliman (2005) and Beaudoin (2013) show in the context of colonial encounters, even with a core-periphery model the colonized may be shown to engage with their colonizer through their own terms and by their own intentions, as well as taking into account the intentions of the colonizer. By looking at contact as a strategic engagement, therefore, in which the ability of the colonized to engage with, and become accepted by, the colonizer relates to their ability to function and appear assimilated, a two-way exchange or cultural fusion may actually be in operation. But in striving to connect with such phenomena, studies of acculturation and assimilation distinguish from material traces the scalar measurements of degree and duration, a process more of description than interpretation, and one that assumes that in material culture resides an accurate representation of the world and the intentions through which it entered the archaeological record (Lucas 2012: 169–214; Liebmann 2013: 38–9). The authors in this book look to alternative entries to archaeologies of cultural contact, on which the remainder of this chapter will focus.

Themes and challenges: creolization, ethnogenesis, hybridity, syncretism

Throughout this book different models of cultural change and combinations of these are considered either to be complementary or problematic. For example, Roslund considers hybridity and creolization to be mutually interactive, working at different scales within a broadly similar process; in the case of the unfree in eleventh- and twelfth-century Sweden, hybridity may be viewed as an expression of 'observable patterns of material culture which can be the effect of social processes that lead to creolization'. Alternatively, as suggested here by Joyce and Sheptak in reaction to models of creolization that they regard as problematic to an understanding of sixteenth-century Honduras, hybridity may be regarded as a locally emergent material process that, along with new linguistic expressions, may be seen to have been tactically employed within a wider process of ethnogenesis through which new patterns of behaviour and material assemblage become visible. Other contributions (e.g. Beaudry and Hutchins, Haviser, and Petersen) explore similar lines of enquiry whereby, through creolization, local strategies coalesce to form broader new syncretic religious forms.

Studies of ethnogenesis foreground context and sociocultural creativity as central to their focus, and the multidimensional character of identity, both contested and negotiated (Weik 2014: 294–5). Ethnicity is thereby described as a state of belonging or practice underpinned by a consciousness of difference, manifested externally by a negotiation of classificatory distinctions between a 'them' and an 'us' (Voss 2015: 658), and internally by the struggle towards recognition of 'certain cultural practices and historical experiences' by which a community self-identifies (Jones 1997: 91). Voss (2015: 658–9) argues that models of ethnogenesis are most effective in circumstances where complete transformation in structures of identification has occurred and identity practices have been entirely replaced by new forms. The challenge, therefore, is not just to show that social identities have changed over time, but that these changes represent transformations greater than the flux and adaptations of normal 'identity maintenance' (ibid.). As an example, the emergence of Métis as a distinct people around the Labrador Bay peninsular in Canada during the late eighteenth and early nineteenth century may be regarded as the outcome of 'a combination of factors' connected to cultural contact and changing sociopolitical economies resulting from fur trade relations, including intermarriage and colonization (Supernant 2018). Violence, owing to trade restrictions imposed by the two main fur trading companies operating in the region, was a means to recognition of a distinct Métis identity. However, the archaeological evidence for the ethnogenesis of Métis cultural identity has been queried on account of its limited visibility in material assemblages. One explanation for this may be owed to the analytical tools employed in its study, such as inter-site and inter-assemblage comparisons, that may not be sufficient to visualize complexities in the material expression of identity (Silliman 2005). Practising a mobile way of life, a lack of architectural and household materials may be a feature of Métis overwintering assemblages, contrasting against a prevalence of munitions. Moreover, thin-walled pottery seemingly unsuited to Métis mobility may be a distinct characteristic of their material culture, with its curation and repair perhaps also signalling the importance of tea culture as a display of social identification and ethnic integration (Supernant 2018).

As reflected in several of the book's contributions, considerations of ethnogenesis may often also turn to creolization as a related theme. Creolization is defined as a process by which interethnic interactions stimulate cultural transformations through which new forms are created out of a common grammar of shared experience, common institutions of co-production and interlinking social networks (Cohen and Sheringham 2008; Baron and Cara 2011). Creolization therefore is a means by which to conceptualize the emergence of new cultural phenomena out of the necessity to negotiate cultural difference. This involves a creative combination of elements that is not defined by a beginning and an ending, but in degrees of similarity to, and divergence from, what has come before and what is yet to be. Creolization, by its protean nature, is visible by the scale and accent of modifications of cultural, aesthetic, and material forms at the interstices or frontiers of societies (Lightfoot and Martinez 1995). Uttered generally in studies of resistance to dominance, creolization emerges with demand for alternatives to a core-periphery approach in which innovation is unidirectional, transmitted from a dominant centre to a passive periphery. As Hutchins-Keim and Beaudry explore in their contribution, creolization may provide such an alternative with a focus upon creativity, temporal context, and the complexities of internal societal conflicts out of which a string of alliances may be formed.

As also argued here by Petersen, creolization may be read in varying and sometimes divergent ways within a given situation, possibly with negative connotations on the one hand, such as in circumstances of slavery, or otherwise as a positive influence and inclusive by its nature. Turning to Cape Verde on the West African coast as an example, creole identification may be highly selective, either to African slave ancestors or with Eurocentric roots to a Portuguese lineage, each expressed with either positive or negative connotation (Challinor 2008). Within a milieu of diverse attitudes towards identity, this has complex implications for contemporary connections to historical and archaeological remains and their ongoing management (Sørensen et al. 2011; Sørensen and Evans 2011).

As in the Cape Verde example, Gundaker (2000) has noted, any use of creolization is always 'indexical of a political stance'. By this, the relevance of creolization as a creative, internally driven and resistive process of change to many contexts is projected beyond its original meaning stemming from diasporic population studies, notably of languages in colonial situations, in or of the American South and Caribbean. For creolization, such ubiquity is highlighted across cultural studies as one potential weakness that erodes 'its strategic conceptual value' (Hall 2010: 13; cf. Palmié 2006). In this book, Joyce and Sheptak hold misgivings towards models of creolization that are inflexible towards context, which is integral to an understanding of ethnogenesis. Greater diversity of context is therefore fruitfully represented across the book, where creolization is usefully applied as a part of broader syncretic processes in contexts of nineteenth-century New England (Beaudry and Hutchins), Islam in the Middle East, Central Asia and East Africa (Petersen), as well as colonial Brazil (Funari and de Carvalho), and the Caribbean (Haviser), to which the application of creolization is more traditionally assigned.

Creolization and hybridity are generally considered to emphasize or attend to cultural contact in clearly different ways to one another, although significant commonality, especially with regards to dynamics of power, seems often evident by their definition or usage.

The etymological roots of hybrid and hybridity are well rehearsed, and helpfully are recalled in several of the book's contributions. In denoting process, it is the adjective *hybridization* that from eighteenth-century botany and biology designated the enforced cross-fertilization of two species from which a *hybrid* (noun) represented the original, but infertile product. The socio-biological and colonial racial and miscegenous connotations with which hybridity connected in nineteenth-century theories of evolution understandably arouse suspicion or cautionary treatment today (Young 1995: 10). Such criticism attends to the use of hybridity as a metaphor for creativity, effectively extending its Victorian use to designate the creation of new species as a threat to racial purity. Nevertheless, its reinvigoration in postcolonial studies aims to desist from this legacy with new indexical meaning in which hybridity signifies a re-working of pre-existing elements rather than the simple combination of multiple distinct elements. In so doing, hybridity is used to counter ideas of origins and the myth of purity, instead centralizing importance in 'ambivalence, mockery, resistance, and agency' (Liebmann 2013: 43), and looking to 'contested, unsettling, and subversive processes' and forms of appropriation and transference across cultures (Lightfoot 2015: 9221), often of elements thought to be incompatible or conflicting.

Four main critiques of hybridity have been sustained in archaeology. The first concerns the use of hybridity as an analytical scheme that, in principle, may require the existence of a conceptual opposite, which in the case of hybridity is a notion of purity. Moreover, proponents of this view highlight that models of hybridity effectively reify the very concept they aim to critique or resist, thereby potentially compromising the pattern and character of cultural process that hybridity is meant to reveal (Maran 2012). A similar concern of aporia is voiced across cultural studies, where hybridity, used in models of transculturation as an analytical device to counter reified cultural identities, takes the form of a perpetually flexible identity. The counter argument claims that this reduces the world to the sum of its many subjects, embedding hybridity within a circularity of conceptual reification, and thereby exhausting the possibility of hybridity to activate subaltern politics effectively (Syrotinski 2007: 27–39).

Studies of contemporary immigration illustrate the conceptual reification that is risked in the application of hybridity to cultural phenomena. Lisa Lowe (1996: 67), for example, conceives of 'the formation of cultural objects and practices' amongst Asian immigrants in the United States as becoming 'produced by the material trace of the history of Spanish colonialism,

US colonisation, and US neo-colonialism'. Lowe reads this material trace as an historical mixing of race and language that represent not forms of assimilation, but a 'history of survival' by way of hybridized diversity amidst a dominant overbearing power (ibid.). Critique has equated Lowe's view of cultural hybridity as synonymous with, and emblematic of, cultural difference, which is resistance to hegemonic order and an expression of agency under the guise of survival. Cultural difference, if bound as a collective identity, intentionally mobilized to a resistant or subversive end, occurs where tactical countering of one order (hegemony) with another (hybridity) relies on a counterpose—or dialectics—of differences that function within corresponding structures of representation and logic, thereby inadvertently reifying and, importantly, empowering the very system that hybridity is expected to have transformed (Moreiras 1999: 383–4).

Aside to these misgivings, archaeological study of cultural contact may find attraction in the temporal underpinnings of Lowe's approach that is suggestive of things and practices originating from distinct worlds, the histories of which, in coming together, become entangled. Lowe refers to such processes as 'material hybridity' and conceives of the formation of identity as a strategic response to economic and political foundations that, in the case of Asian immigrants to the United States, are deeply racialized and actively opposed to their inclusion as equal but distinct citizens (Lowe 1991, 1996). Material hybridity then combines unequal social relations and imbalances of power within a particular historical context of social relations (material)—this in Lowe's study is a capitalist system—with everyday strategies of innovation and resistance through differing cultural alternatives (hybridity). With a focus on process rather than product, Lowe's blend of power, resistance, creativity and alterity in material hybridity encapsulates the tenor of this book's direction.

In the second critique of hybridity are questions relating to its temporality and where or how in the material record this can be seen to either begin or end. In this view, the process of hybridity leads to the creation of what Silliman (2015) terms 'durable hybrids' that exist in a state of flux and perpetual cultural change. Lacking any visible closure or balance of continuity, hybridity, in this view, is ill suited to any reasonable understanding of long-term social processes. Moreover, according to this argument, the relation of a constant state of hybridity holds little connection to everyday lived experience or to the material reality of archaeological traces.

The third critique is similar to that levied above towards creolization, and in this case is concerned with the location of hybridity and, thereby, its visibility either as an analytical scheme or as an observable analytical subject

(Maran 2012). If, for example, hybridity is used or exists only in specific and often local contexts, then by what measure are hybrids to be differentiated from non-hybrids? Attributing hybridity to particular objects or processes evidently risks projection of present-day preconceptions to an understanding of past societies (Liebmann 2015: 321). Conversely, if hybridity is to be found everywhere then by way of its ubiquity or lack of specificity its explanatory value to intercultural encounters is either compromised or doubtful (Stockhammer 2012b, 2013; Liebmann 2015: 322).

Finally, the fourth main critique has considered that the visibility of hybrids within the material record may be an outcome of overly rigid and representational classificatory schemes rather than bearing any reflection of a lived and appreciated reality (Palmié 2013; Stockhammer 2013; Silliman 2015). And yet, Silliman (2013: 489) again reminds us, for hybridity to have analytical value, it 'requires aspects that we can specify, evaluate, and distinguish'.

Reflection on these issues raises interesting questions for models of cultural change in archaeology. Either creolization or hybridity as a quality or condition of things, peoples, or cultures, or at least as a state of affairs that is gestated and maintained in or as cultural difference, is prone to reducing the world 'merely' to a sum of its subjects. This risks foregoing opportunities for distinguishing durable continuity from perpetual change in the material record.

Such concerns may similarly be directed to observable changes in religious phenomena, generally reserved to studies of syncretism, particularly the combination of religious beliefs, practices, and materials from two or more traditions (Stewart 1994: 128; see also Stewart 2010). Here, the contributions of Petersen and Haviser reflect what Whitehouse (2004) has referred to as the 'Two Modes of Religiosity', doctrinal and imagistic. The doctrinal mode is characterized by a discursive style of codification that relates to the transmission of beliefs by means of ritual, repetition, and routinization, and large 'imagined' communities that control meaning through institutionalized orthodoxy. The imagistic mode relates to a codification style of transmission through intense episodic rituals, and enduring cohesion between localized face-to-face communities of adherents. The doctrinal mode relies upon the cognitive constraints of semantic memory, such as explicit representational recall of a text or generic propositions, by which cultural adaption may be possible through sustained repetition. The imagistic mode relies on episodic or 'autobiographical' memory that is personal, unique, and emotional (Laidlaw 2004: 3), and open to rich idiosyncratic exegesis (Mithen 2004: 19). All religions will have elements of both the doctrinal and imagistic modes but, linked to the mutual interdependence of certain traits characterizing each of the modes of religiosity, there will be a tendency for religions to show more conformity towards one mode rather than the other (Whitehouse 2004). The examples illustrated by Petersen and Haviser in this volume show the different scales and frames of syncretism that may be visible within each of these religious modes.

With origins in Christian theology and frequent pejorative use in the missionary and ethnographic projects during the European colonial period, syncretism undoubtedly retains a challenging heritage, and is viewed either as a concept to be rejected in scholarship, or one that is deserving of rehabilitation (Droge 2001). Syncretism may, for example, be regarded as a productive and positive process in South American postcolonial contexts of 'melting pot' nation-building (see Stewart 1995: 17–20). In other perspectives the connection between syncretistic religion and socio-political power is recognized as a damaging form of religious categorization that is underpinned by an imagined form of authenticity (e.g. Sundkler 1961: 397). Petersen and Haviser look beyond syncretism as a categorization of religious form, and instead approach it as a process directly connected to religious belief encoded under differing contexts of practice by systems of power.

Practice, power, and context may be viewed as core elements in the link between creolization, ethnogenesis, hybridity, and syncretism. Power is emergent through practice and contingent upon context. Our themes of cultural change may be approached as open-ended social expressions that emerge under historically constituted conditions of cultural discourse. Indelibly immersed in a material world, creolization, ethnogenesis, hybridity, and syncretism are most clearly expressed in contexts of colonization often within a frame of tension, translation, and even violence; they are ambiguous and juxtaposed, and latent across most cultural forms.

Practice, power, and context

The focus across this book is the interplay of people and things and their relation to identity under conditions of unequal terms of power. Of more direct concern are new patterns of meaning connected either with existing objects, or with new object forms and behaviours. The relocation and transferral of power is a centralizing theme. Readings of hybridity have, for example, foregrounded its 'ability to shock, transform, and revitalize social life', disrupting the normative order in 'the forcing together of unlike things' (Liebmann 2015: 323; cf. Loren 2013). The works of Bruno Latour and Mikhail Bakhtin have been particularly influential here (see also Van Valkenburgh 2013). In Bruno Latour's (1993) evaluation of hybrids as phenomena not distinct to modernity, one gains a sense of the variety and ubiquity of hybridized forms across cultural practice and, moreover, their purification into distinct ontological entities, often as dual opposites, not just in systems of classification but more broadly as a complex condition of social discourse. Whilst concerns of reification and purification inform critique of cultural processes, there are instances in which these may be drivers of hybridity or creolization, not necessarily in subversion, but 'as a vehicle of dominant political interests' (Van Valkenburgh 2013: 303; see also Apter 1991). In the Latourian view, though seemingly opposites, creativity and internal expression are entangled with domination, hegemony, and enforced conditions of subalternity. As shown also for creolization (Hall 2010: 16), here, in processes leading to new cultural forms, the contradictions of entanglement and power are both at stake.

The second major influence, via Mikhail Bakhtin's (1981) linguistic heteroglossia—that is, the coexistence of distinct varieties within a single 'language'—the ubiquity of hybridity is further acknowledged as an 'organic' form, referring to mixing and blending in all transcultural engagements, unconsciously occurring across and through cultural practice, and determined by social conditions rather than by agents. It is through iterations of this organic hybridity that, Liebmann (2015: 324) has argued, 'may lead archaeologists to theoretical dead ends', whereas more 'intentional' forms of hybridity, in what Bakhtin examines as poetic consciousness, provide through their 'interruptive' capacity an entry to the power dynamics at play in transcultural relations and the ways by which differences are forged, reinforced, or transgressed (see also Maran 2012; Loren 2013). It's an enticing argument, for it highlights the appearance of new cultural forms in contact encounters as emergent from situated transferrals of power, mutually transformative of each cultural entity brought into contact, and defined within an historically contingent context of meaning and comprehension that also undergoes a process of restructuring (Bhabha 1990; 1994; Stewart 2007: 18–20; see also Kraidy 2005).

The visibility of these processes through the archaeological record bears relation to the ways by which archaeological contexts are defined and the systems of typology and classification employed to make sense of these. Contexts relate to a set of relationships between material elements and patterns of association between different contexts: their differences or similarities. Whereas a contextual archaeology sought to register frames of meaning within and between material assemblages, more recent approaches to archaeological context, particularly through Assemblage theory, have drawn attention to the ways by which assemblages themselves contribute to frames of meaning; that is, how in their assembly of things, beliefs, people, and animals, etc. assemblages are active by conditioning the possibility for interpretations of meaning (Jones and Alberti 2013). Assemblages may be thought of as patterns in the world that are made intelligible on account of their practical capacities to coordinate an appropriate response to their material surroundings (Brittain 2013). This applies both to past experiences of assemblages and their formation, and in present engagements with past assemblages, or at least the fragments of these.

Assemblage theory may provoke an alternative entry to cultural change through the archaeological resource by thinking of the relational qualities through which the process of identification of things, places, people, and so on may be unravelled. For example, Sørensen (2015: 89) refers to a 'tyranny of object-form' in which typological distinction between objects is made possible by observing their morphological similarities that emerge from a process of production that is already aware of and referencing other existing objects. Sørensen refers to this as 'inter-object citation' (ibid.). The efficacy of any object is therefore relatable to other objects in time and space, and their forms in this manner are likewise relational and emergent from the interaction between objects. Thinking about types in this way views them as co-emergent, historical by nature of their relationality to other types, and situated within a multidimensional context that together is material, experiential and affective (Fowler 2017). The relational character of assemblages and their component elements may highlight a disjuncture to the connections across and within types, particularly in situations of cultural contact that form the focus of this book.

Other-than-human cultures

For several contributors, hybridity is selected as a model for culture change not exclusively in correspondence with colonial and postcolonial situations. The more extreme proponents of this view draw upon a post-humanist lens that in critique of the relationship of culture to nature examines the viability of hybridity as a model to test consideration of 'other-than-human' culture change (Howard 2013; see also Haraway 2008; Ingold 2008). Here, Clack examines transference of cultural behaviour across differences and changes within communicative gestures and tool use between chimpanzee groups.

Much depends, of course, upon one's definition of culture, a generic reading of which has for some time been deemed applicable in certain parts of the non-human realm (e.g. Wrangham et al. 1994; Boesch and Boesch-Acherman 2000). Nevertheless, resistance to the asserted possibility of forms of cultural adaptation in other-than-human contexts may not be unexpected, though we have chosen to include such perspectives as they disrupt implied boundaries of cultural practices (see Corbey 2005) and their change under conditions of intercultural contact.

The book's chapters

Boivin's opening chapter is primarily focused on the intercultural networks linked by the Silk Road and the Indian Ocean. It highlights the active and dynamic nature of the archaeological record with an examination of ways by which societies internalize hybridized forms over time. Boivin looks to a vigorous moulding of exotica into cultural recognition and familiarization through processes of incorporation and domestication, rarely by unstructured assimilation, but more often seen as a power-driven appropriation through specific sectors of society. With a reminder that hybridization is as much conceptual as it is material, Boivin poses a challenge to models that distinguish clear separation of tradition from innovation.

Through rock art of nineteenth-century Nomansland in the Maloti-Drakensberg region of South Africa Pearce and Mallen explore a material and symbolic response to the arrival of European colonialists, especially their practices of dress and animal husbandry that were frequently the setting for intercultural contact. Pearce and Mallen identify a specific form of rock art as an important 'coping mechanism', an attempt to manipulate, reorder, and control particular areas of social articulation. Important points of social continuity are ensured by enmeshing fine-line images that give reference to the 'old' ways of livestock raiding, with other stylistic depictions of the 'new', thereby serving to align multiple worldviews and language cultures into mutual understanding and collective identity.

Joyce and Sheptak consider colonial encounters at the Honduran city of San Pedro between the sixteenth and eighteenth centuries and argue that a notion of 'cultural contact' lacks the sophistication required to grasp the tone of inequality that flows through contexts of imposition. Drawing upon De Certeau's notion of 'tactics' to occupy and navigate landscapes not under one's control, the experience of colonial survival is approached as a shared project in which identities fluctuate, particularly in contexts of sexual reproduction. Emphasis on local and traceable ancestry as opposed to identity formation through migrant arrival is noted to be manifest in the materiality of everyday practice.

The capacity for species other than human to effect material hybridization is considered by Clack through an examination of what it is to be cultural. Where, for example, chimpanzee communicative gestures and tool use are shown to be specific to groups, though also with aspects transferable to other groups for particular tasks, may such behaviour also evince forms of hybridity? There are no definite answers, though Clack points to areas for research that may take such queries into consideration and argues that looking to such concepts through this angle may benefit their broader application to early human material traces, such as that of the Châtelperronian technologies of Southwest Europe as explored by Gravina, d'Errico, and Bachellerie. Their contribution also highlights methodological challenges for an understanding of acculturation and creolization in early prehistory. This is especially evident, they argue, in situations such as the Châtelperronian where there is little chronological definition. There, the case remains contentious as a possible example of cross-species material hybridity, though nevertheless prompts further consideration that blurs the traditional boundaries concerning humanness, modernity, and advanced behaviour.

Carr's chapter concerns resistance to contact encounters via the repositioning of symbolic content on the Channel Islands throughout World War II. During 1940–5, the islands' locals were subject to occupation by German military forces and were also brought into contact with foreign labourers. An interchange of material signifiers ensued under acts of subjugation, resistance, and defiance, with the potent 'V' sign reproduced in various material forms and registered in competing readings as a prism of multi-sensory communication. Carr however argues that these present a cautionary note to material identifications of hybridity, and instead illustrate direct appropriation of a sign in unique material items that, ultimately, were few in a context of mass production and limited to a short and closed timespan of manufacture. Moreover, understanding of the significance of such objects emerges only within a broader assemblage of relatability, as 'it is only when seen within the range of similar objects that their possible fluid meanings to those who used them becomes clear'.

With a focus on the racial fabric of nineteenth-century New England, Hutchins and Beaudry expose some of the pitfalls and limitations in the manner that archaeologists frame and ask their questions of material culture in contexts of hybridization. They confront the complex and multi-faceted composition of intercultural identities and show that creolization rarely unfolds in a uniform manner but is fractured and situated, with material culture and associated identities often remaining 'differentiated' by the carrying forward of former meanings and associations from one context to another. Whereas in other studies of enslaved persons their social and economic capital may arguably be disentangled from the enterprises of slavery through the production of absence and invisibility (e.g. Andrews and Fenton 2011), Hutchins and Beaudry instead find an 'unblended' configuration whereby the potency of the past is a drag on future coalescence, particularly over short durations.

Horning elaborates on the Ulster plantations in the early modern period and in particular the role of violence in processes of hybridization. Distinguishing between the experiences and displacement strategies of the political elite from those settlers facing the reality of engagement, settlers to the Ulster plantations were overwhelmingly outnumbered and dependent on their Irish neighbours. Horning argues that such reliance was the cause of certain material adaptations, notably relating to hospitality and architecture, and that behavioural and material mimesis was especially employed by settlers to render comfortable familiarity to their situation. Mimesis was however multi-directional; mimetic play was mutually employed through the political elite as a strategy to amplify coercion and to exert their authority.

Through the lens of eleventh- and twelfth-century Sweden, Roslund responds to the challenge of making sense out of multiple, often situationally contingent, identities. This is framed by the stylistic residue of creolization between the free and unfree that involves cultural negotiation through forms of bondage, patronage, and people-raiding. Noting that thralls, or slaves, became central to domestic production, and with a focus on ceramic production rather than product, Roslund refers to previously acquired knowledge used implicitly to manage tasks ('tacit knowledge'), to better register and situate hybrid forms. In ceramic production, therefore, meaning is also in a state of transfer and translation.

Funari and de Carvalho describe some of the long-term work undertaken by the Palmares Archaeological Project. Their focus, syncretism, and creolization at the seventh-century rebel polity of Palmares is demonstrated to have forged a unique identity through resistance to colonial authority. Local wares depict poly-ethnic social interactions and the emergence of a new and cohesive 'maroon identity'. Laden with the flux of past configurations enmeshed with fresh elements, cultures are shown here to be coiled with temporal fluidity, the present resonant with the past, and the past taking form from the present. As a powerful symbol of resistance and subversion within modern Brazilian society, Palmares is a potent example of temporal fluidity. Study of the heritage of rebellious actions of maroons against colonial control was an expression of anti-regime sentiment under the rule of the military junta in Brazil (1964–85) and therefore duly supressed. Funari and de Carvalho show that renewed archaeological study of maroon communities in Brazil remains similarly politically charged.

Petersen outlines the early evidence for Muslim identities in Palestine, East Africa, and Central Asia and in so doing notes in each area the contrasting and complex histories of religious and societal incorporation. The historic gestation of Islam in these areas with multiple underlying confessional groups contrasts with the mono-cultural and monotheist perspectives promulgated by the belief system. Petersen adopts the term 'creole' to describe certain forms of Islamic identities. With this, what is or is not selected for incorporation within specific identifications to Islam, and the meanings associated with these, is contingent to power structures, not only in processes of conversion, such as regulatory texts and the codification of belief, but also in terms of cultural attunement to local orders of practice where relevance may be highly situated. Syncretistic religious formations may therefore not be defined by 'surfaces' or 'cores' but may rather entail 'elements' that are the outcome of local selection.

Haviser focuses on African and European religious syncretism in the Caribbean predominantly from the last two centuries. Covering themes of Obeah voodoo practices and, amongst others, the role of African (and descendent) domestic workers in delivering childcare duties to the households of colonialists, Haviser explains that personal and intimate sympathies held by those raised as European children by African nannies may be linked to the maintenance and re-emergence of prohibited practices and beliefs. This is a useful insight to the wider effects of micro-politics at the household level. Examples drawn from fieldwork at St Maarten confirm the fragmented and rearticulated nature of religious formulations in the absence of an orthodox priesthood within the context of the trans-Atlantic slave trade (cf. Thornton 1998), and that the incorporation of elements born from confrontation with alien ideas and practices was not formulated according to any structured religious orthodoxy. One outcome of this, Haviser argues, may be the local rejection of syncretism, which is supported through a strategic psychological framework of material aesthetics and acts of intimidation.

References

Andrews, S. C. and J. P. Fenton. 2011. 'Archaeology and the invisible man: the role of slavery in the production of wealth and social class in the bluegrass region of Kentucky, 1820–1870'. *World Archaeology* 33: 115–35.

Apter, A. 1991. 'Herskovits's heritage: rethinking syncretism in the African Diaspora'. *Diaspora: Journal of Transnational Studies* 1(3): 235–60.

Bakhtin, M. M. 1981. *The Dialogic Imagination*. Austin: University of Texas Press.

Baron, R. and A. C. Cara. 2011. 'Introduction: creolization as cultural creativity'. In R. Baron and A. C. Cara (eds), *Creolization as Cultural Creativity*. Jackson: University Press of Mississippi, pp. 3–19.

Beaudoin, M. A. 2013. 'A hybrid identity in a pluralistic nineteenth-century colonial context'. *Historical Archaeology* 47(2): 45–63.

Bhabha, H. 1990. 'The third space: interview with Homi Bhabha'. In J. Rutherford (ed.), *Identity, Community, Culture, Difference*. London: Lawrence and Wishart, pp. 207–21.

Bhabha, H. 1994. *The Location of Culture*. London: Routledge.

Boesch, C. and H. Boesch-Acherman. 2000. *The Chimpanzees of the Tai Forest*. Oxford: Oxford University Press.

Brandstetter, A.-M. 2006. 'Anthropological approaches to the study of cultural contact: a short review'. In I. Strecker and J. Lydall (eds), *The Perils of Face: Essays on Cultural Contact, Respect and Self-Esteem in Southern Ethiopia*. Berlin: Lit Verlag, pp. 19–35.

Brittain, M. 2013. 'Assembling bodies, making worlds: an archaeological topology of place'. In B. Alberti, A. M. Jones, and J. Pollard (eds), *Archaeology after Interpretation: Returning Materials to Archaeological Theory*. Walnut Creek: Left Coast Press, pp. 257–76.

Card, J. J., ed. 2013. *The Archaeology of Hybrid Material Culture*. Center for Archaeological Investigations, Occasional Paper No. 39. Carbondale: Southern Illinois University Press.

Challinor, E. 2008. 'Home and overseas: the Janus faces of Cape Verdean identity'. *Diaspora* 17(1): 84–104.

Cohen, R. and O. Sheringham. 2008. 'The salience of islands in the articulation of creolization and diaspora'. *Diaspora* 17(1): 6–17.

Corbey, R. H. 2005. *The Metaphysics of Apes: Negotiating the Animal-Human Boundary*. Cambridge: Cambridge University Press.

Cusick, J. 1998. 'Historiography of acculturation: an evaluation of concepts and their application in archaeology'. In J. Cusick (ed.), *Studies in Culture Contact: Interaction, Culture Change, and Archaeology*. Carbondale: Center for Archaeological Investigations, pp. 126–45.

Droge, A. J. 2001. 'Retrofitting/retiring "syncretism"'. *Historical Reflections/ Réflexions Historiques* 27(3): 375–88.

Fortes, M. 1936. 'Culture contact as a dynamic process: an investigation in the Northern Territories of the Gold Coast'. *Africa* 9: 24–55.

Fowler, C. 2017. 'Relational typologies, assemblage theory and early Bronze Age burials'. *Cambridge Archaeological Journal* 27(1): 95–109.

Gundaker, G. 2000. 'Discussion: creolization, complexity, and time'. *Historical Archaeology* 34: 124–33.

Hall, S. 2010. 'Créolité and the process of creolization'. In R. Cohen and P. Toninato (eds), *The Creolization Reader: Studies in Mixed Identities and Cultures*. London: Routledge, pp. 26–38.

Haraway, D. 2008. *When Species Meet*. Minneapolis: University of Minnesota Press.

Howard, C. 2013 'Posthuman anthropology? Facing up to planetary conviviality in the Anthropocene'. *Impact* 20. https://sites.bu.edu/impact/previous-issues/impact-winter-2017/posthuman-anthropology-facing-up-to-planetary-conviviality-in-the-anthropocene/.

Ingold, T. 2008. 'Binding against boundaries and entanglements of life in an open world'. *Environment and Planning D: Society and Space* 40: 1796–1810.

Jones, S. 1997. *The Archaeology of Ethnicity: Constructing Identities in the Past and Present*. London: Routledge.

Jones, A. M. and B. Alberti. 2013. 'Archaeology after interpretation'. In B. Alberti, A. M. Jones, and J. Pollard (eds), *Archaeology after Interpretation: Returning Materials to Archaeological Theory*. Walnut Creek: Left Coast Press, pp. 15–42.

Kraidy, M. 2005. *Hybridity, or The Cultural Logic of Globalization*. Philadelphia: Temple University Press.

Laidlaw, J. 2004. 'Introduction'. In H. Whitehouse and J. Laidlaw (eds), *Ritual and Memory: Towards a Comparative Anthropology of Religion*. Walnut Creek: AltaMira Press, pp. 1–9.

Latour, B. 1993. *We Have Never Been Modern*. Cambridge, MA: Harvard University Press.

Liebmann, M. 2013. 'Parsing hybridity: archaeologies of amalgamation in seventeenth-century New Mexico'. In J. Card (ed.), *The Archaeology of Hybrid Material Culture*. Center for Archaeological Investigations, Occasional Paper No. 39. Carbondale: Southern Illinois University Press, pp. 25–49.

Liebmann, M. 2015. 'The Mickey Mouse kachina and other "double objects": hybridity in the material culture of colonial encounters'. *Journal of Social Archaeology* 15(3): 319–41.

Lightfood, K. G. 2015. 'Dynamics of change in multiethnic societies: an archaeological perspective from colonial North America'. *Proceedings of the National Academy of Sciences* 112(30): 9216–23.

ARCHAEOLOGIES OF CULTURAL CONTACT 19

Lightfoot, K. G. and A. Martinez. 1995. 'Frontiers and boundaries in archaeological perspective'. *Annual Review of Anthropology* 24: 471–92.

Loren, D. 2013. 'Considering mimicry and hybridity in early colonial New England: health, sin and the body "behung with beades"'. *Archaeological Review from Cambridge* 28(1): 151–68.

Lowe, L. 1991. 'Heterogeneity, hybridity, multiplicity: marking Asian American differences'. *Diaspora: A Journal of Transnational Studies* 1(1): 24–44.

Lowe, L. 1996. *Immigrant Acts. On Asian American Cultural Politics*. Durham: Duke University Press.

Lucas, G. 2012. *Understanding the Archaeological Record*. Cambridge: Cambridge University Press.

Maran, J. 2012. 'One world is not enough: the transformative potential of intercultural exchange in prehistoric societies'. In P. Stockhammer (ed.), *Conceptualizing Cultural Hybridization: A Transdisciplinary Approach*. Berlin Heidelberg: Springer-Verlag, pp. 59–66.

Mithen, S. 2004. 'From Ohalo to Çatalhöyük: the development of religiosity during the early prehistory of Western Asia, 20,000–7,000 BCE'. In H. Whitehouse and L. H. Martin (eds), *Theorizing Religions Past: Archaeology, History and Cognition*. Walnut Creek: AltaMira Press, pp. 17–43.

Moreiras, A. 1999. 'Hybridity and double consciousness'. *Cultural Studies* 13(3): 373–407.

Palmié, S. 2006. 'Creolization and its discontents'. *Annual Review of Anthropology* 35: 433–56.

Palmié, S. 2013. 'Mixed blessings and sorrowful mysteries second thoughts about "hybridity"'. *Current Anthropology* 54(4): 463–82.

Redfield, R., R. Linton, and M. Herskovits. 1936. 'Memorandum for the study of acculturation'. *American Anthropologist* 38: 149–52.

Rowlands, M. 1994. 'Childe and the archaeology of freedom'. In D. Harris (ed.), *The Archaeology of V. Gordon Childe*. London: UCL Press, pp. 35–54.

Silliman, S. W. 2005. 'Culture contact or colonialism? Challenges in the archaeology of native North America'. *American Antiquity* 70(1): 55–74.

Silliman, S. W. 2013. 'What, where, and when is hybridity'. In J. Card (ed.), *The Archaeology of Hybrid Material Culture*. Carbondale: Center for Archaeological Investigations, Occasional Paper No. 39. Southern Illinois University Press, pp. 486–500.

Silliman, S. W. 2015. 'A requiem for hybridity? The problem with Frankensteins, purées, and mules'. *Journal of Social Archaeology* 15(3): 277–98.

Sørensen, M. L. S. 2015. '"Paradigm Lost"—on the state of typology within archaeological theory'. In K. Kristiansen, L. Šmejda, and J. Turek (eds), *Paradigm Found: Archaeological Theory: Present, Past and Future. Essays in Honour of Evžen Neustupný*. Oxford: Oxbow Books, pp. 84–94.

Sørensen, M. L. S. and C. Evans. 2011. 'The challenges and potentials of archaeological heritage in Africa: Cape Verdean Reflections'. *African Archaeological Review* 28: 39–54.

Sørensen, M. L. S., C. Evans, and K. Richter. 2011. 'A place of history: archaeology and heritage at Cidade Velha, Cape Verde'. In P. Lane and K. MacDonald (eds), *Slavery in Africa: Archaeology and Memory*. London: British Academy, pp. 421–42.

Stewart, C. 1994. 'Syncretism as a dimension of nationalist discourse in modern Greece'. In C. Stewart and R. Shaw (eds), *Syncretism/Anti-Syncretism: The Politics of Religious Synthesis*. London: Routledge, pp. 127–44.

Stewart, C. 1995. 'Relocating syncretism in social science discourse'. In G. Aijmer (ed.), *Syncretism and the Commerce of Symbols*. Göteborg: Institute for Advanced Studies in Anthropology, pp. 13–37.

Stewart, C. 2007. *Creolization: History, Ethnography, Theory*. Walnut Creek: Left Coast Press.

Stewart, C. 2010. 'Syncretism and its synonyms: reflections on cultural mixture'. In R. Cohen and P. Toninato (eds), *The Creolization Reader: Studies in Mixed Identities and Cultures*. London: Routledge, pp. 289–305.

Stewart, C. 2011. 'Creolization, hybridity, syncretism, mixture'. *Portuguese Studies* 27(1): 48–55.

Stockhammer, P. W., ed. 2012a. *Conceptualizing Cultural Hybridization: A Transdisciplinary Approach*. Berlin Heidelberg: Springer-Verlag.

Stockhammer, P. W. 2012b. 'Conceptualizing cultural hybridization in archaeology'. In P. Stockhammer (ed.), *Conceptualizing Cultural Hybridization: A Transdisciplinary Approach*. Berlin Heidelberg: Springer-Verlag, pp. 43–58.

Stockhammer, P. W. 2013. 'From hybridity to entanglement, from essentialism to practice'. *Archaeological Review from Cambridge* 28: 11–28.

Sundkler, B. 1961. *Bantu Prophets in South Africa*. 2nd edn. London: Oxford University Press.

Supernant, K. 2018. 'Archaeology of the Métis'. In J. Symonds and V.-P. Herva (eds), *The Oxford Handbook of Historical Archaeology*. London: Oxford University Press. DOI: 10.1093/oxfordhb/9780199935413.013.70.

Syrotinski, M. 2007. *Deconstruction and the Postcolonial*. Liverpool: University of Liverpool Press.

Thornton, J. 1998. *Africa and Africans in the Making of the Atlantic World, 1400–1800*. Cambridge: Cambridge University Press.

van Pelt, W. P., ed. 2013. 'Archaeology and Cultural Mixture'. *Archaeological Review from Cambridge* 28(1).

Van Valkenburgh, P. 2013. 'Hybridity, creolization, mestizaje: a comment'. *Archaeological Review from Cambridge* 28(1): 301–22.

ARCHAEOLOGIES OF CULTURAL CONTACT 21

Voss, B. 2015. 'What's new? Rethinking ethnogenesis in the archaeology of colonialism'. *American Antiquity* 80: 655–70.

Weißköppel, C. 2005. 'Hybridität. Die Ethnografische Annäherung an ein Theoretisches Konzept'. In R. Loimeier, D. Neubert, and C. Weißköppel (eds), *Globalisierung im lokalen Kontext. Konzepte und Perspektiven von Handeln in Afrika*. Münster, Hamburg, New York, and Vienna: LIT Verlag, pp. 311–47.

Weik, T. 2014. 'The archaeology of ethnogenesis'. *Annual Review of Anthropology* 43: 291–305.

Whitehouse, H. 2004. *Modes of Religiosity: A Cognitive Theory of Religious Transmission*. Walnut Creek: AltaMira Press.

Wrangham, R. W., W. C. McGrew, F. B. M. de Waal, and P. G. Heltne, eds. 1994. *Chimpanzee Cultures*. Cambridge, MA: Harvard University Press.

Young, R. 1995. *Colonial Desire: Hybridity in Theory, Culture and Race*. London: Routledge.

PART I
DEALING WITH DIFFERENCE

1

The Domestication of Difference

Globalization, Hybridity, and Material Culture in Archaeological Perspective

Nicole Boivin

In today's globalized world, evidence of cultural mixing is everywhere. Hong Kong crooners sing Mandarin cover versions of Japanese popular ballads that are themselves already a mixture of Japanese and American styles (Nederveen Pieterse 2001). Muslim youths in South London attend classes at their local mosque to learn Brazilian jiu-jitsu, a martial art derived from Japanese Kodokan judo. And middle-class youths in Bombay speak Hindi-peppered English over an 'Asian fusion' meal at a trendy new restaurant that melds South, Southeast, and East Asian elements. Fusion, hybridity, creolization, bricolage, whatever the metaphor one chooses to describe this mixing, the process suggests that the diasporas and migrations, communication technologies and pervasive multi-culturalism of contemporary globalization have led to the erasure, or at least severe disruption, of long-established cultural boundaries and barriers. Fusion feels new, exciting, and cosmopolitan; embraced by youth and eschewed by traditionalists.

But if hybridity is apparent in the galleries, trendy restaurants, and youth haunts of the world's cities, it is no less real in many of the distant towns and villages where crops are grown and internet connections few and far between. A simple, poor farming family sitting on their floor for a traditional Hindu dinner in a rural Indian village, for example, will face a meal that is actually no less hybrid than the one in the new Bombay fusion restaurant. Made from ingredients from their own garden and fields, the meal might nonetheless include okra that derives ultimately from Africa, potato and chilli pepper domesticated in the New World, cabbage from the Mediterranean, and coriander that stems perhaps from Southwest Asia or Armenia (Crosby 2004; Kahlheber and Neumann 2009; Zohary et al. 2012). The *chapatti* that would probably accompany the curried vegetables are made from wheat, originally

Nicole Boivin, *The Domestication of Difference: Globalization, Hybridity, and Material Culture in Archaeological Perspective*
In: *Archaeologies of Cultural Contact: At the Interface*. Edited by: Timothy Clack and Marcus Brittain, Oxford University Press.
© Oxford University Press 2022. DOI: 10.1093/oso/9780199693948.003.0002

26   NICOLE BOIVIN

domesticated in Southwest Asia (Zohary et al. 2012) and transferred in ancient times via routes of communication, migration, and trade to the Indian subcontinent (Fuller 2006). Traditional Indian food is a rich and distinctive cuisine, few components of which can truly be understood as 'Indian'. Instead, it represents the outcome of South Asia's myriad terrestrial and maritime links, from the Neolithic period through to the present day (Kiple and Ornelas 2000; Blench 2003; Fuller 2003; Pilcher 2005; Boivin and Fuller 2009). It is ultimately a hybrid, or creolized, cuisine, numerous elements of which trace back less than a hundred years (though see Lawler's (2012) discussion of some elements that extend back thousands of years; see also Fuller 2006).

The world has always changed, and forces of cultural mixing and creolization have always been part of the story of that change. This is something that has been recognized implicitly in archaeology, but often overlooked theoretically, with concern for the delineation of cultural groups and the boundaries of material culture distribution more often having been the disciplinary norm. While such tendencies were, of course, paramount for culture-historical archaeology; New Archaeology's focus on cultural ecological models, closed systems, and anti-diffusionism was not particularly conducive to the study of intercultural interactions either (Lightfoot and Martinez 1995: 474). The later remedy of trade studies in processual archaeology was only partial, with these tending to focus more on economies and less on processes of cultural mixing. Even postprocessual archaeology has, until recently, devoted little attention to cultural contact and mixing, being concerned more to explore local, historically particular sequences, and the role of the agency of individuals within society in generating change. Explicit disciplinary interest in the processes of hybridization that have also featured in the past has primarily been of recent origin, inspired by work in other disciplines. Furthermore, such research has tended to involve archaeological studies of colonial contact and frontiers, particularly in the Americas (e.g. Loren 2000; Mullins and Paynter 2000; Wilkie 2000), but also in a few more ancient Old World contexts such as Roman Britain (e.g. Webster 2001; Carr 2005).

This recent entry into archaeology of the theories of hybridity, creolization, and syncretism that have been discussed in such fields as linguistics, cultural studies, folklore, cultural anthropology, ethnomusicology, and comparative literature offers fuel to both critics and defenders of these brands of theory. On the one hand, recognition of the historically pervasive and widespread nature of processes of boundary transgression and cultural creolization counterbalances views of hybridity that see it as a limited phenomenon primarily concerned with new and recent cultural expressions that involve a distinctive,

THE DOMESTICATION OF DIFFERENCE   27

usually urban and prosperous, audience—what Pierterse has referred to as the 'world music model of hybridity' (Nederveen Pieterse 2001; see also Thomas 2009). But if hybridity is about more than this, perhaps it is about *too* much more than this; if hybridity is everywhere and in every time, then, its critics ask, how meaningful is it as an idea, an analytical tool, or even a heuristic device (see Friedman 1999 for this critique specifically in regard to creolization; also Palmié 2006)?

In archaeology, it may be argued that processes of hybridization, creolization, and syncretism[1] are important to study because they problematize boundaries (Nederveen Pieterse 2001: 220), and archaeologists have shown perhaps a particular propensity to fetishize boundaries. The extreme, but archaeologically quotidian, challenge of not only creating some sort of sense out of a chronologically and spatial diverse archaeological record, but also linking this material record to the activities of actual people in the past, has encouraged a search for order and the formulation of bounded ancient social entities. Heuristic groupings of data have too frequently become essentialized categories. The shift from 'trait' to 'process' geographies advocated by Appadurai is thus also relevant to archaeology. Appadurai (1999: 232) argues for the need to move beyond 'conceptions of geographical, civilizational and cultural coherence' and to thus see 'significant areas of human organization as precipitates of various kinds of action, interaction and motion—trade, travel, pilgrimage, warfare, proselytization, colonization, exile and the like'. Today, these kinds of issues are perhaps more at the forefront in archaeology than they have ever been in the past, but the theoretical means to do them justice are often lacking.

It is thus relevant, then, that beyond the opportunity to challenge essentialized boundaries and take an interest in the oft-overlooked fuzziness of datasets, models of hybridization offer the opportunity to explore in new ways two areas of current interest within archaeology: transformation and creativity on the one hand, and the construction, negotiation and manipulation of group identities (Lightfoot and Martinez 1995: 474) on the other. What studies of creolization, syncretism, and hybridization in archaeology have tended to focus on are the creative and subversive aspects of cultural mixing, the way that cultural interaction has frequently led to innovation and the development of novel material and cultural formations, and the way that these have

---

[1] There is much overlap between the terms, which all refer to processes of mixing: 'hybridity' draws upon biological parallels, 'syncretism' has generally been used to refer to the melding of religious traditions, and 'creolization' emerges out of studies of cultural and particularly linguistic contact (see Kapchan and Strong 1999).

been drawn upon strategically in the construction and contestation of identities at various levels in cultural contact situations (Lightfoot and Martinez 1995; Loren 2000; Mullins and Paynter 2000; Wilkie 2000; Webster 2001; Carr 2005).

In this chapter, I will begin to explore how these aspects of cultural mixing have played out in certain contexts of long-distance contact and exchange in the ancient Old World, with a focus on the interlinked networks of the Silk Road and what has sometimes been called the Maritime Silk Road of the Indian Ocean. Specifically, I will draw on ideas about 'technological philosophy' and 'domestication' in a cultural sense to examine the ways in which societies have often internalized hybrids; challenging binary oppositions between tradition and innovation. I will focus on a hitherto under-theorized aspect of cultural contact, its material element, and in particular the generation of hybrid material forms. Ultimately, I will aim to explore how archaeology and a *longue durée* perspective may begin to shed light on contemporary processes of globalization and the factors that render them historically distinctive.

Technological philosophies

Ancient trade networks in the Old World brought vastly different societies into contact with each other over the course of several millennia, leading to the creation of hybrids of varying kinds. From a biological point of view, contact led to the transfer of both wild and domestic plants and animals, as well as commensals, often accompanied by genetic hybridization of different varieties, or genetic changes due to adaptation to new ecological and cultural niches. In the Indian Ocean and also along the Silk Road (and earlier the Steppe Road; Christian 2000; Mei 2003; Rawson 2010), an enormous range of crops and domesticated animals flowed by maritime and terrestrial routes, sometimes leading to dramatic changes in agricultural practice and local cuisine, as well as the generation of hybrid varieties of, for example, cattle, coconut, and rice (Boivin and Fuller 2009; Fuller and Boivin 2009; Mather et al. 2010; Gunn et al. 2011; Boivin et al. 2013). Creolized societies were also created, an archetypal example being the Swahili communities of East Africa (Bryceson 2010), who strategically employed exotic trade goods, hybrid forms of cuisine and architecture, and new contact-inspired social and religious practices to create a distinctive identity and mediating role between the African interior and Indian Ocean worlds (Horton and Middleton 2000; Mitchell 2005; LaViolette 2008). Religions spread, particularly along the Silk Road,

THE DOMESTICATION OF DIFFERENCE   29

generating new syncretic forms and art styles. Qualities of hybridity even extended to individual items of material culture. Along the Silk Road, for example, styles, technologies, and materials from different societies transgressed cultural boundaries (e.g. Bentley 1993; Linduff and Mei 2009; Rawson 2010), creating new types of hybrid goods that themselves flowed across contextual and cultural boundaries. Even the most minute and basic item of material culture might, upon further examination, prove to be a hybrid. The tiny glass 'trade-wind' beads of the Indian Ocean, for example, might be made of raw materials that came from one continent, were processed into glass in another, and formed into beads in yet a third location (Wood 2000; Francis 2002). Colourants added to the glass could add a further dimension to the beads' hybridity, as could their tendency to be reworked, recycled into new beads, combined with other beads and objects in new ways, and used in an extraordinary range of contexts around the Indian Ocean (Francis 2002; Lankton and Dussubieux 2006; Dussubieux et al. 2008; Robertshaw et al. 2010).

The creation of hybrids is probably not terribly surprising in the context of the dramatic new forms of long-distance cultural contact that emerged in association with the myriad trade routes of the ancient world. What is, however, perhaps something of a puzzle is the way that hybrids were often subsumed within everyday material and social networks; their hybrid origins eventually forgotten. While some creolized forms were celebrated for their exoticness, many others became 'invented traditions', upstart arrivals that assumed established pedigrees. The process by which the exotic became part of the everyday is one that I wish to address in this chapter. As outlined earlier, my focus is on the materiality of cultural contact, and both the creative and subversive roles of hybrids within society.

A window into the process of hybrid formation and adoption can be acquired by considering more closely the nature of the hybrid, which can be created through the acquisition of new materials, technologies, and/or styles. One way in which hybrid material forms were created in the ancient world was through the combination of new materials with existing technologies. In many cases, exotic materials that entered into society nonetheless appear to have been processed using traditional technologies; sometimes borrowed across conceptual realms. Sillar (1996) has written about one aspect of this process in the Andes and described the impact of what he calls 'technological philosophy', a kind of cultural propensity to process different things in the same or similar ways. Traditional Andean processing, for example, often involves technologies of grinding and crushing. These are applied across multiple areas of practical activity, including food production, as well as the processing of clay for ceramics and warfare. Pre-Hispanic warfare thus involved the use of crushing blows and projectiles, instead of the use of blades. Grinding is used in Andean society as a cultural metaphor for enculturation and re-creation; after grinding them down, both flour and defeated people become productive resources (ibid. 267). In Europe, by contrast, technologies of production were often blade-oriented—blade technology was borrowed across very different activities, being used to peel a potato, shave, sharpen a pencil, or scrape the subcutaneous fat off of a hide. Sillar (ibid. 260) describes a 'European fascination with metal and blade technology that has been central to much of the region's social and technological development'. Not only did this fascination shape the techniques applied to vegetable processing, carpentry, and tailoring, it also provided cultural and linguistic metaphors: the notion of 'sharp' ideas and 'cutting edge' innovations, for example. Lechtman (1984: 9) has also recognized the role of cultural perceptions in shaping technologies across activity realms; she points out that metal never had the impact in the New World that in had in the Old, where it was employed in warfare, transport, and agriculture. In the New World, metal instead 'performed primarily in the realm of the symbolic'.

The notion of technological philosophy provides insights into the formation of hybrids. Exotic materials may enter society, but the action of powerful cultural perceptions about the 'right' way to do things ensures that they are 'brought under control' and processed according to standard cultural conventions. Thus wheat, when it moves eastwards into East Asia in ancient times, is made not into bread but is rather boiled or steamed, and by Han times is processed into noodles, in accordance with a set of cultural norms that favour the application of boiling technologies to the processing of food (Fuller and Rowlands 2009; Boivin et al. 2013; Boivin and Fuller n.d.). An eastern technological philosophy of boiling is linked to the early Palaeolithic development of ceramic technology (Kuzmin 2006; Wu et al. 2012), and a cultural preference for soft and cohesive foods that even leads to the emergence of 'sticky' mutations in a variety of crops. In contrast, the West—from India to Africa and Europe—has traditionally tended to favour technologies of grinding and roasting, and these culinary preferences again demonstrate Palaeolithic origins, and lead eventually to the emergence of bread-based cultures, where bread features as a central religious metaphor, and the preference is for dry and textured food. Rice in southern India, for example, is not traditionally boiled, but rather ground into a flour and made into steamed and fried breads. Technological philosophies thus become creative forces, generating novel hybrid cuisines, which then themselves flow across social and cultural boundaries. Chinese noodles eventually travel around the fifteenth century westwards to Italy to become pasta, a staple, along with tomatoes from the New World, of 'traditional' Italian cuisine (Goody 1982).

If cuisine provides a powerful illustration of the acculturation of exotic things through technological philosophies, metallurgy provides another. While increasing evidence suggests a diffusion of early metallurgy across the Old World, rather than separate independent inventions (Roberts et al. 2009; Thornton and Roberts 2009), metallurgical traditions have nonetheless been strongly shaped regionally by cultural practices. Thus, metallurgy spread in the Bronze Age across the Steppe Road to China (Linduff and Mei 2009; Rawson 2010) but was transformed there into a distinctive Chinese tradition heavily influenced by a pre-existing long-term technological orientation. In China, the technological focus on ceramics for processing that led to their early emergence in the East, and was linked to a culinary emphasis on boiling, became the basis not only for a highly sophisticated ceramic technology that emerged directly from the Neolithic tradition, but also for a distinctive approach to bronze casting (Wood 1989; Wagner 2008). For whereas conventional bronze casting employed the 'lost wax' method, early Chinese bronze vessels were created through the distinctive use of ceramic piece moulds. As Wood (1989: 50) notes, 'ceramic processes and materials are at the heart of early Chinese bronze casting'.

This unique, ceramic-oriented approach to bronze casting enabled the development of a highly sophisticated technology in China by the time of the Shang dynasty, when some of the most complex and original vessels ever created by bronze founding were manufactured in the service of ritual expressions of ancestor worship (Wood 1989: 50). While other objects, like weapons and bells, were also created out of bronze, it is in the bronze vessels that we see the greatest celebration and elaboration of casting technology, a fact that probably underscores the importance of ceramics in Chinese culture. The earliest Chinese bronzes closely copied some contemporary ceramic shapes, though by 1300 BCE the range of forms created was vast, and the original ceramic models had been left far behind (Wood 1989: 51). We can see then that China adopted a foreign technology—metallurgy—but made it distinctly Chinese by shaping it according to its own technological and cultural traditions (also Rawson 2010). Chinese metallurgical technology was a hybrid material culture, but one that became increasingly invisible, to the point that a significant school of thought posits an independent invention of bronze metallurgy in China (e.g. Barnard 1993).

32 NICOLE BOIVIN

The kind of technological transfer across conceptual realms that saw ceramics used for such a wide variety of purposes and over such a long time period in China can also be seen in Southeast Asia. Here, various researchers have noted a cultural emphasis on fermentation as a processing technology. Fermentation in Southeast Asia is used not only to process and preserve foods, but also to decorate cloth, make hemp, and even ritually treat the dead (Adams 1977; Metcalf and Huntington 1991). The process is essentially one of decomposition, involving rotting, fermentation, and extraction. Cloth, for example, is commonly coloured blue-black using dye that has been prepared by soaking and rotting the roots and stems of the indigo plant. The liquid that forms during the rotting process is extracted and fermented with lime to produce the dye. Fermentation is also widely used to render toxic foods edible or to preserve perishable foods. It produces a characteristic astringent flavour in foods that is culturally distinctive and preferred and has, accordingly, led fermentation to be employed even when not strictly necessary. Perhaps the most culturally unique use of fermentation, however, is in mortuary rituals. The Berawan of Borneo, for example, decompose corpses in large jars, draining off the liquids using a bamboo tube and preserving the bones. While the origins of the methods of soaking and rotting, so widely employed in the processing of materials in Southeast Asia, remain unknown, it is possible that they initially emerged in the context of the processing of root crops such as taro and yam that contain toxins that must be removed prior to eating through soaking or fermentation. There is evidence for the very long-term use and domestication of these crops in the region (Denham et al. 2003), suggesting the possibility that the Southeast Asian technological orientation towards fermentation may have very ancient roots. Subsequently, introduced crops like rice from East Asia and hemp from Central Asia, which arrived in Southeast Asia through vectors of migration and trade, both terrestrial and maritime, were then processed using parallel techniques; leading to the creation of 'hybrid' dishes and materials.

Domesticating things

What all these various examples demonstrate is not only the fascinating, and probably cognitively important, propensity that humans have for drawing upon solutions derived for one area of practical activity to deal with challenges in another, but also the way that societies tend to incorporate and acculturate foreign materials and technologies. This ability, to take what is

THE DOMESTICATION OF DIFFERENCE   33

foreign and different, and render it culturally useful and appropriate, may be referred to as a process of 'domestication'. Prestholdt (2008) uses this term to refer to the processes through which Swahili societies in East Africa received a wide range of globally circulating goods in the nineteenth century, but, at the same time, localized or domesticated them to render them appropriate to Swahili and inland societies. He notes the connotations of domestication as 'the process of making familiar or usable, controlling, and bringing into intimate spaces' (ibid. 8). His emphasis is on the agency inherent in processes of domestication, which helps to shift understanding away from passive notions of African involvement in global trade. This recognition of agency is also, I believe, important in the context of understanding processes of hybridization more widely. Hybrids often involve taking what is foreign and putting the clear stamp of the local on it. They involve internalizing and transforming the foreign to such a degree that it is often no longer recognized as foreign at all. Processes of hybridization can enable cultures to be transformed and altered by flows of trade, exchange, migration, and colonization, and yet at the same time to resist homogenization and the loss of identity.

Prestholdt's book *Domesticating the World* (2008) offers examples of ways other than the application of technological philosophies that goods can be transformed and hybrids created. His emphasis is on African aesthetics and styles, and the way that they shaped both production abroad and the subsequent alteration of imported goods in Africa itself. His examples include numerous material hybrids—*kisutu*, for example, a cloth popular across East Africa in the nineteenth century, was a plain English cotton that had been dyed in Bombay according to African tastes (ibid. 66–7). African aesthetic tastes, far from leading, as myth proclaimed, to the acceptance of any 'old baubles' from colonial visitors, were varied, fickle, and highly demanding. The inability to recognize this could lead to the return of entire cargoes to their land of origin, or the failure of inland trade expeditions. Goods were not only shaped abroad, but also within Africa itself. Caravan leaders, for example, purchased the kinds of cloth or beads they thought to be in demand in a particular locale, and then, just outside the area where they intended to trade, they stopped and redesigned goods in ways that would increase their appeal to local consumers (ibid. 68). One of only two types of cloth the Maasai would accept in the late 1800s, for example, was called *naibere*, and it was produced in Africa by sewing colourful Indian dyed cloth onto unbleached cloth, and subsequently fraying the edges of the cloth and binding this with a strip of red or dark purple fabric. The task of making the hybrid *naibere* cloth might occupy one hundred members of a trade expedition for several days.

Prestholdt's argument is that these kinds of hybrid goods, which were extremely common, force us to rethink traditional core-periphery models that see Africa as the exporter of raw materials, and the passive recipient of finished products. As elsewhere, material hybrids not only involved a creative element, but also a subversive one, reflecting the agency of African traders and consumers in the face of asymmetrical global trade networks.

While such examples focus on the material hybridity of goods—the physical reworking of foreign items as an outcome of the application of local technological or aesthetic processes—hybridity is in other examples less material than conceptual. Goods might enter a society and remain completely unaltered physically yet be utterly transformed in terms of meaning by local cosmological or political systems. Thus, simple brass lacetags from Europe were transformed into ritual and grave goods in post-contact Cuba (Martinòn-Torres et al. 2007; Cooper et al. 2008). This was in keeping with local cosmological systems, which ascribed different values to metals based on qualities like colour and smell. Within this system, gold was the least valued, and brass the highest. A gold-copper-silver alloy known as *guanín* was valued for its peculiar colour, iridescence, and smell, all of which made it especially appealing to local elites, who wore ornaments made of *guanín* to display and reinforce their sacred status, and role as mediators between the natural and the supernatural. When brass arrived from the Old World, it was held in even higher esteem; it was called *turey* because the sky was *turey* and it was seen as a thing from the heavens. Thus, simple, disposable brass lacetags from Europe assumed a particular sacred significance in post-contact Cuba, emerging as kinds of hybrid items that were at once foreign, but at the same time intimately embraced within Cuban cosmological belief systems that ascribed them with entirely new meanings. Contradictory value systems formed the basis for a system of trade in which each side received what it saw as highly valuable in exchange for that which was low value and easily parted with. Similar complementary value systems existed for several centuries after 1500 CE in China and the West, which valued silver differently, leading to a global system of arbitrage that saw silver and gold move back and forth between the two regions, creating wealth through what has been termed a 'global silver recycling process' (Hobson 2004: 172).

Hybrids might also emerge in the context of social and political arenas of status negotiation and display. Prestholdt (2008) has highlighted the fact that both umbrellas and clocks were imported to Zanzibar in the nineteenth century but served primarily a social display rather than practical function. Zanzibaris incorporated European and American clocks into their cityscape

THE DOMESTICATION OF DIFFERENCE   35

but did not regulate their day by the clock. As he notes, clocks were domesticated, becoming symbols rather than functional objects in Zanzibar. Even when clocks were used, the 'domestication of the clock was not a conspicuous Europeanization of time' (2008: 107); instead, clocks were set to Zanzibari time, with the day beginning with sunrise at one o'clock, and with clocks being adjusted every ten days to account for the changing length of the day. The European timepiece was adapted to Zanzibari perceptions of time (ibid. 108). Again, we can see how hybridization is allied not with homogenization, but rather with the subversion of tendencies toward homogenized globalization. Hybrids often play such a role; as Kapchan and Strong (1999: 241) note, creole phenomenon often have, 'at their root, the encounter with difference and with power differentials'. Frontier contexts, where hybrids often proliferate, present important arenas for the negotiation of status, the creation of identities, and the contestation of power (Lightfoot and Martinez 1995). Hybrid forms of material culture play an active role in these processes, and do not simply passively reflect the impacts of colonization or globalization.

From domesticating to domesticated?

These various historical and archaeological examples lend weight to the notion that hybrids are not new phenomena in human societies; indeed, it would appear that they have proliferated in cultural contact situations through the ages. Material hybrids, with which archaeologists, in particular, may be concerned, have often been generated through processes of 'domestication' according to which that which is foreign and external is tamed, internalized and brought into the cultural fold, through material, technological, cosmological, and/or social processes. And yet looking at some of the examples that have been presented, it is clear that, at least in recent times, processes of hybridization have ultimately lost out to more powerful forces of homogenization. Gold, for example, is without a doubt the global currency today, its value comparable from Cuba to Zanzibar to China. The same twenty-four-hour clocks, meanwhile, are used everywhere to schedule activities in an increasingly capitalist world. Hybrids themselves are often dismissed as superficial (Thomas 2009), trivial (Friedman 1999), inauthentic and elitist (ibid.), and their identification by social scientists is argued by some to reflect a misunderstanding of culture and history (Thomas 2009) or a dissolution of difference that contributes to rather than challenges cultural homogenization (Kapchan and Turner Strong 1999; Palmié 2006).

If the effects of globalization are so much more apparent today than in the past, then perhaps there are significant differences in the way that networks of trade, interaction, and hybridization unfolded in the ancient world compared to the way they proceed today. Indeed, this view is at the heart of much contemporary research into globalization, and it has often led to a tendency to downplay early global interaction. The latter is accordingly characterized as relatively small in scale, infrequent, and focused on luxury goods, for example. Others, however, argue that this is a very problematic way of understanding early global interaction, and see such interaction as having been, in fact, of genuine economic, as well as cultural and biological, significance (Bentley 1993, 1996, 1998). And yet, at the same time, it would be disingenuous to argue that there are not differences between the processes of globalization that operate today and the kinds of global interactions and translocations that occurred in the past. These differences, I would argue, have shaped both patterns of domestication as well as the ways in which hybrids are created and employed in the contemporary world.

In comparing past and contemporary globalization, it is perhaps useful to ask two key questions: what (or who) is being domesticated, and whose interests do hybrids serve? While I outlined above a wide range of examples from the past illustrating the role of societies in domesticating and encompassing both difference and the exotic, there appears to be a pattern today in which societies themselves are becoming increasingly domesticated. Notions of 'technology transfer' are often, for example, about the wholesale export of foreign technologies, without consideration of local social and cultural contexts. The marketing of goods, meanwhile, increasingly involves globally salient images, symbols, and methods. These draw upon a capitalist desire to domesticate societies in order to create a new kind of homogeneous, cross-cultural consumer, and a genuinely global consumer base. Theodore Levitt outlines, tellingly, in the 'globalization of markets' the difference between old-fashioned multinational corporate marketing strategies and those of the new global corporation:

> The *multinational* corporation operates in a number of countries, and adjusts its products and practices to each—at high relative costs. The *global* corporation operates with resolute constancy—at low relative cost—as if the entire world ... were a single entity; it sells the same things in the same way everywhere ... Ancient differences in national tastes or modes of doing business disappear.   (Levitt 1983, cited in Klein 2001; emphasis added)

THE DOMESTICATION OF DIFFERENCE   37

While societies have often seen other societies as consumers, even in ancient times, there has always been a tendency for the parties involved in trade and cultural contact to both accept and deliberately create difference. In the contemporary world, the rise of the truly global corporation and the attendant creation of globally pervasive forms of communication, interaction, and engagement have led to new possibilities of boundary erasure, at least where it matters: in consumer markets. Other boundaries, meanwhile, have often remained as pervasive as ever.

This is perhaps part of the reason why contemporary hybrids are often seen as superficial and inauthentic. On the one hand, many of them float on a consumer surface that masks deeper seated social inequalities, wealth differentials, and stark cultural differences. Critics have accordingly argued that the optimistic view of hybrids that is sometimes taken in the academic literature is problematic. On the other hand, hybrids are today, in addition, increasingly the creations of corporations, which recognize that 'diversity sells' (Robertson 1995: 29). As Grossberg (1995: 184–5) reflects, 'it is no longer a matter of capitalism having to work with and across differences . . . today . . . it is difference which is now in the service of capital'. Klein (2001: 117) describes the selling of diversity in the 1990s in her book *No Logo*:

> Today the buzzword in global marketing isn't selling America to the world, but bringing a kind of market masala to everyone in the world. In the late nineties, the pitch is less Marlboro Man, more Ricky Martin: a bilingual mix of North and South, some Latin, some R&B, all couched in global party lyrics. This ethnic-food-court approach creates a One World placelessness, a global mall in which corporations are able to sell a single product in numerous countries without triggering the old cries of Coca-Colonization.

Cook and Crang (1996: 132) describe Klein's 'ethnic food court' in some detail in a paper that addresses the contemporary marketing of global cuisine. They note that diversity and geographical displacement serve to 're-enchant food commodities', with processes of 'global miniaturization' (ibid. 136) helping consumers to 'gaze upon and collect the signs and images of many cultures' (ibid. 135).

These various examples highlight the emergence of new kinds of hybrids in the framework of contemporary globalization. The global marketing of hybridity, while drawing upon more authentic processes of hybridization, has at the same time helped to re-shape both hybrids and their meanings.

As hybridity today finds itself more and more in the service of a capitalist machine that is increasingly domesticating rather than domesticated, the way hybrids are used to create, maintain, and subvert identities has been radically altered. While we need to be wary of creating new essentialisms and of drawing overly stark differences between domesticating societies of the past and domesticated societies of the present, we need to be cautious nonetheless about equating the hybrids of ancient and past societies with those of the present. The material culture goods of the past, while they also participated in global flows and networks, and entered processes that led to the creation of hybrids, were nonetheless different from the commodities of today, and study of material hybridity needs accordingly to be contextualized appropriately.

Conclusions

If this review has strayed into territory—the contemporary world and globalization—normally distant to the concerns of archaeology, it has done so primarily to highlight the fact that the creation of hybrid or creole cultures, material or otherwise, occurs in different ways in the contexts of trade, colonization, migration, globalization, and other processes of miscegenation. Terms like 'hybrid' and 'creole', while useful and productive theoretical constructs in many contexts, can also mask important differences between the phenomena in these different contexts. It is only by exploring in greater detail the nature and meaning of processes of hybridization in culturally specific contexts, both past and present, that scholars will come to better understand the nature and implications of globalization, hybridization, tradition, and change.

The study of processes of hybridization in the past helps us to understand that there is little that is culturally 'pure'—societies have mixed and transgressed boundaries, formed and reformed, for countless millennia. The notion that hybrids, then, involve a process of pollution, a transgression and a coming together of otherwise pure, essentialized categories is very much problematized by a study of the past. These, and other caveats regarding the notion of hybridity do not, however, discount its utility as a heuristic term and area of analysis in archaeology (or indeed elsewhere). The study of creolization and hybridity is an under-theorized realm that deserves greater interest from archaeologists, especially given the continued limitations of our understanding of how and why change occurs in society—and indeed how and why things sometimes stay the same over long periods of time or despite continued intercultural contact. Studies of hybridity also help to highlight the

THE DOMESTICATION OF DIFFERENCE   39

obvious limitations of an approach to the past that favours the study of boundaries over the fuzziness that occurs between our categories of data. Mixing, and the processes of hybridization, domestication, subversion, and creation that attended it in the past, constitute key and exciting areas for future research and theorization in archaeology, and mark this volume of papers as an important contribution to the field.

Acknowledgements

This chapter developed out of a paper I presented at the workshop on 'Contact and Creativity in the Ancient World', jointly organized by Chris Gosden and me, and held at Keble College, Oxford, on 13 November 2010. I am grateful to the participants of the workshop for useful feedback and suggestions. I am also very grateful to Dorian Fuller and Jessica Rawson for many interesting and enlightening discussions, which have contributed to the ideas presented here. This paper reflects output of the Sealinks Project, funded through the European Research Council as part of Grant Agreement No. 206148.

References

Adams, M. J. 1977. 'Style in Southeast Asian materials processing: some implications for ritual and art'. In H. Lechtman and R. Merrill (eds), *Material Culture: Studies, Organization and Dynamics of Technology*. St. Paul: West Publishing Company, pp. 21–52.

Appadurai, A. 1999. 'Globalization and the research imagination'. *International Social Science Journal* 51(160): 229–38.

Barnard, N. 1993. 'Thoughts on the emergence of metallurgy in pre-Shang and early Shang China, and a technical appraisal of relevant bronze artifacts of the time'. *Bulletin of the Metals Museum* 19: 3–48.

Bentley, J. H. 1993. *Old World Encounters: Cross-Cultural Contacts and Exchanges in Pre-Modern Times*. Oxford: Oxford University Press.

Bentley, J. H. 1996. 'Cross-cultural interaction and periodization in world history'. *The American Historical Review* 101(3): 749–70.

Bentley, J. H. 1998. 'Hemispheric integration, 500–1500 CE'. *Journal of World History* 9(2): 237–54.

Blench, R. 2003. 'The movement of cultivated plants between Africa and India in prehistory'. In K. Neumann, A. Butler and S. Kahlheber (eds), *Food, Fuel and Fields: Progress in African Archaeobotany*. Cologne: Heinrich Barth Institute, pp. 273–92.

Boivin, N., A. Crowther, R. Helm and D. Q. Fuller. 2013. 'East Africa and Madagascar in the Indian Ocean world'. *Journal of World Prehistory* 26(3): 213–81.

Boivin, N. and D. Q. Fuller. n.d. 'Niche construction and cultural practice: Bridging evolutionary and cultural perspectives on human society'.

Boivin, N. L. and D. Q. Fuller. 2009. 'Shell middens, ships and seeds: exploring coastal subsistence, maritime trade and the dispersal of domesticates in and around the ancient Arabian peninsula'. *Journal of World Prehistory* 22: 113–80.

Bryceson, D. F. 2010. 'Swahili creolization'. In R. Cohen and P. Toninato (eds), *The Creolization Reader: Studies in Mixed Identities and Cultures*. London, Routledge, pp. 364–75.

Carr, G. 2005. 'Woad, tattooing and identity in Later Iron Age and Early Roman Britain'. *Oxford Journal of Archaeology* 24(3): 273–92.

Christian, D. 2000. 'Silk Road or Steppe Roads? The Silk Roads in world history'. *Journal of World History* 11(1): 1–26.

Cook, I. and P. Crang. 1996. 'The world on a plate: culinary culture, displacement and geographical knowledges'. *Journal of Material Culture* 1(2): 131–53.

Cooper, J., M. Martinòn-Torres, and Valcárcel Rojas.2008. 'American gold and European brass: metal objects and indigenous values in the cemetery of El Chorro de Maìta, Cuba'. In C. L. Hofman, M. L. P. Hoogland, and A. Van Gijn (eds), *Crossing the Borders: New Methods and Techniques in the Study of Material Culture in the Caribbean*. Tuscaloosa: University of Alabama Press, pp. 34–42.

Crosby, A. W. 2004. *Ecological Imperialism: The Biological Expansion of Europe, 900–1900*. Cambridge: Cambridge University Press.

Denham, T., S. G. Haberle, C. Lentfer, R. Fullagar, J. Field, M. Therin, N. Porch and B. Winsborough. 2003. 'Origins of agriculture at Kuk Swamp in the Highlands of New Guinea'. *Science* 189: 189–93.

Dussubieux, L., C. M. Kusimba, V. Gogte, S. B. Kusimba, B. Gratuze, and R. Oka. 2008. 'The trading of ancient glass beads: new analytical data from South Asia and East African soda-aluminium glass beads'. *Archaeometry* 50(5): 797–821.

Francis, P. 2002. *Asia's Maritime Bead Trade: 300 B.C. to the Present*. Honolulu: University of Hawai'i Press.

Friedman, J. 1999. 'The hybridization of roots and the abhorrence of the bush'. In M. Featherstone and S. Lash (eds), *Spaces of Culture: City-Nation-World*. London: Sage, pp. 230–55.

Fuller, D. Q. 2003. 'African crops in prehistoric South Asia: a critical review'. In K. Neumann, A. Butler, and S. Kahlheber (eds), *Food, Fuel and Fields. Progress in African Archaeobotany*. Cologne: Heinrich-Barth Institute, pp. 239–71.

Fuller, D. Q. 2006. 'Agricultural origins and frontiers in South Asia: a working synthesis'. *Journal of World Prehistory* 20: 1–86.

THE DOMESTICATION OF DIFFERENCE 41

Fuller, D. Q. and N. Boivin. 2009. 'Crops, cattle and commensals across the Indian Ocean: Current and potential archaeobiological evidence'. *Plantes et Sociétés: Etudes Ocean Indien* 42–3: 3–46.

Fuller, D. Q. and M. Rowlands. 2009. 'Towards a long-term macro geography of cultural substances: food and sacrifice tradition in East, West and South Asia'. *Chinese Review of Anthropology* 12: 1–37.

Goody, J. 1982. *Cooking, Cuisine and Class: A Study in Comparative Sociology.* Cambridge: Cambridge University Press.

Grossberg, L. 1995. 'The space of culture, the power of space'. In I. Chambers and L. Curti (eds), *The Post-Colonial Question: Common Skies, Divided Horizons.* London: Routledge, pp. 169–88.

Gunn, B., L. Baudouin, and K. M. Olsen. 2011. 'Independent origins of cultivated coconut (*Cocos nucifera* L.) in the Old World Tropics'. *PLoS One* 6(6): 1–8.

Hobson, J. 2004. *The Eastern Origins of Western Civilisation.* Cambridge: Cambridge University Press.

Horton, M. C. and J. Middleton. 2000. *The Swahili: The Social Landscape of a Mercantile Society.* Cambridge: Blackwell.

Kahlheber, S. and K. Neumann. 2009. 'The development of plant cultivation in semi-arid West Africa'. In T. P. Denham, J. Iriarte, and L. Vrydaghs (eds), *Rethinking Agriculture: Archaeological and Ethnoarchaeological Perspectives.* Walnut Creek: Left Coast Press, pp. 318–44.

Kapchan, D. A. and P. Turner Strong. 1999. 'Theorizing the hybrid'. *Journal of American Folklore* 112(445): 239–53.

Kiple, K. F. and K. C. Ornelas. 2000. *Cambridge World History of Food.* Cambridge: Cambridge University Press.

Klein, N. 2001. *No Logo.* London: Harper.

Kuzmin, Y. V. 2006. 'Chronology of the earliest pottery in East Asia: progress and pitfalls'. *Antiquity* 80(308): 362–71.

Lankton, J. and L. Dussubieux. 2006. 'Early glass in Asian maritime trade: a review and interpretation of compositional analysis'. *Journal of Glass Studies* 48: 121–44.

LaViolette, A. 2008. 'Swahili cosmopolitanism in Africa and the Indian Ocean world, AD 600–1500'. *Archaeologies* 4: 24–49.

Lawler, A. 2012. 'The ingredients for a 4000-year-old proto-curry'. *Science* 337: 288.

Lechtman, H. (1984). 'Andean value systems and the development of prehistoric metallurgy'. *Technology and Culture* 15(1): 1–36.

Levitt, T. 1983. 'The globalization of markets'. *Harvard Business Review* 61(3): 92–102.

Lightfoot, K. G. and A. Martinez. 1995. 'Frontiers and boundaries in archaeological perspective'. *Annual Review of Anthropology* 24: 471–92.

Linduff, K. M. and J. Mei. 2009. 'Metallurgy in ancient Eastern Asia: retrospect and prospects'. *Journal of World Prehistory* 22: 265–81.

Loren, D. D. 2000. 'The intersections of colonial policy and colonial practice: creolization on the eighteenth-century Louisiana/Texas border'. *Historical Archaeology* 34(3): 85–98.

Martinòn-Torres, M., R. Valcàrcel Rojas, J. Cooper, and T. Rehren. 2007. 'Metals, microanalysis and meaning: a study of metal objects excavated from the indigenous cemetery of El Chorro de Maìta, Cuba'. *Journal of Archaeological Science* 34(2): 194–204.

Mather, K. A., J. Molina, J. M. Flowers, S. Rubinstein, B. L. Rauh, A. M. Y. Lawton-Rauh, A. L. Caidedo, and M. D. Purugganan. 2010. 'Migration, isolation and hybridization in island crop populations: the case of Madagascar rice'. *Molecular Ecology* 19(22): 4892–905.

Mei, J. 2003. 'Cultural interaction between China and Central Asia during the Bronze Age'. *Proceedings of the British Academy* 121: 1–39.

Metcalf, P. and R. Huntington. 1991. *Celebrations of Death: The Anthropology of Mortuary Rituals.* Cambridge: Cambridge University Press.

Mitchell, P. 2005. *African Connections: Archaeological Perspectives on Africa and the Wider World.* Walnut Creek: AltaMira Press.

Mullins, P. R. and R. Paynter. 2000. 'Representing colonizers: an archaeology of creolization, ethnogenesis, and indigenous material culture among the Haida'. *Historical Archaeology* 34(3): 73–84.

Nederveen Pieterse, J. 2001. 'Hybridity, so what? The anti-hybridity backlash and the riddles of recognition'. *Theory, Culture & Society* 18(2–3): 219–45.

Palmié, S. 2006. 'Creolization and its discontents'. *Annual Review of Anthropology* 35: 433–56.

Pilcher, J. M. 2005. *Food in World History.* London: Routledge.

Prestholdt, J. 2008. *Domesticating the World: African Consumerism and the Genealogies of Globalization.* Berkeley: University of California Press.

Rawson, J. 2010. 'Carnelian beads, animal figures and exotic vessels: traces of contact between the Chinese states and Inner Asia, ca. 1000–650 BC'. *Archäologie in China* 1 Bridging Eurasia: 1–42.

Rawson, J. 2010. 'From Steppe Road to Silk Road: Inner Asia's interaction with and impact on China, 2000 BC–AD 1000'. Lecture, 21 October. University of Oxford.

Roberts, B., C. Thornton, and V. Pigott. 2009. 'Development of metallurgy in Eurasia'. *Antiquity* 83: 1012–22.

Robertshaw, P., M. Wood, E. Melchiorre, R. S. Popelka-Filcoff, and M. D. Glascock. 2010. 'Southern African glass beads: chemistry, glass sources and patterns of trade'. *Journal of Archaeological Science* 37: 1898–1912.

Robertson, R. 1995. 'Globalization: time-space and homogeneity-heterogeneity'. In M. Featherstone, S. Lash, and R. Robertson (eds), *Global Modernities*. London: Sage, pp. 25–44.

Sillar, B. 1996. 'The dead and the drying: techniques for transforming people and things in the Andes'. *Journal of Material Culture* 1(3): 259–89.

Thomas, N. 2009. 'Cold fusion'. *American Anthropologist* 98(1): 9–25.

Thornton, C. and B. Roberts. 2009. 'Introduction: the beginning of metallurgy in global perspective'. *Journal of World History* 22: 181–4.

Wagner, D. 2008. *Science and Civilisation in China*. Vol. 5: *Chemistry and Chemical Technology*, Part 11: *Ferrous Metallurgy*. Cambridge: Cambridge University Press.

Webster, J. 2001. 'Creolizing the Roman provinces'. *American Journal of Archaeology* 105(2): 209–25.

Wilkie, L. 2000. 'Culture brought: evidence of creolization in the consumer goods of an enslaved Bahamian family'. *Historical Archaeology* 34(3): 10–26.

Wood, M. 2000. 'Making connections: relationships between international trade and glass beads from Sashe-Limpopo area'. Goodwin Series 8 *African Naissance: the Limpopo Valley 1000 Years Ago*: 78–90.

Wood, N. 1989. 'Ceramic puzzles from China's Bronze Age'. *New Scientist* 1652: 50–3.

Wu, X., C. Zhang, P. Goldberg, D. Cohen, Y. Pan, T. Arpin, and O. Bar-Yosef. 2012. 'Early pottery at 20,000 years ago in Xianrendong Cave, China'. *Science* 336(6089): 1696–1700.

Zohary, D., M. Hopf, and E. Weiss. 2012. *Domestication of Plants in the Old World: The Origin and Spread of Domesticated Plants in South-West Asia, Europe, and the Mediterranean Basin*. 4th edn. Oxford: Oxford University Press.

2

Nodes of Interaction

Changing Rock Paintings in the Eastern Cape Mountains of South Africa

Lara Mallen and David G. Pearce

Syncretism, the union, or attempted fusion of different worldviews, although involved in a full spectrum of social constructs, is often exemplified in dictionary definitions in relation to religion. This is, perhaps, because some of the most powerful examples of the process of syncretism are found within the realm of belief. The *Oxford English Dictionary*, for instance, provides an example of Roman conquerors assimilating local gods into their pantheon. This point is echoed in the role syncretism plays in relation to southern African hunter-gatherer rock art. It has been cogently argued to be shamanistic in nature, that is, it is meaningfully associated with the fundamental religious beliefs and diverse rituals of the San cosmos (Lewis-Williams and Dowson 1989; Lewis-Williams and Pearce 2004a).

Overlaps in the ritual systems of past hunter-gatherers and agro-pastoralists in several parts of southern Africa have been suggested as loci of interaction amongst these economically disparate groups (e.g. Hall 1994; Loubser and Laurens 1994; Jolly 1996; Hall and Mazel 2005; van Doornum 2006; Schoeman 2007; Challis 2008). This paper examines an archaeological case study from the Drakensberg Mountains in the Eastern Cape Province of South Africa (Fig. 2.1). In this region, once known as Nomansland, autochthonous hunter-gatherers met various incoming groups of Khoekhoen herders and Nguni and Sotho agro-pastoralists. Indeed, the overall region of the Maloti-Drakensberg Mountains is 'among the best possible regions in the world for studying the interactions between communities practising different forms of subsistence, and organised at varying levels of social and political complexity' (Mitchell 2009: 15).

Lara Mallen and David G. Pearce, *Nodes of Interaction: Changing Rock Paintings in the Eastern Cape Mountains of South Africa* In: *Archaeologies of Cultural Contact: At the Interface.* Edited by: Timothy Clack and Marcus Brittain, Oxford University Press. © Oxford University Press 2022. DOI: 10.1093/oso/9780199693948.003.0003

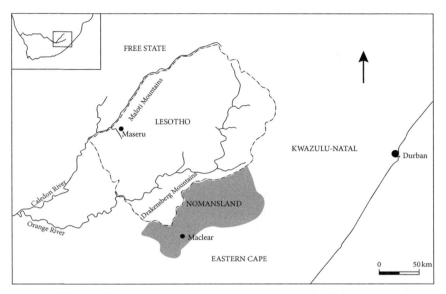

Fig. 2.1. The area historically known as Nomansland, in which the paintings we describe are found, lies below the Drakensberg escarpment in the eastern part of South Africa.

Autochthonous hunter-gatherers

Taking into account that only relatively little research into this period has been carried out, the earliest evidence for hunter-gatherer occupation in Nomansland dates to about 29,000 years ago (Opperman 1996). People seemingly descended from hunter-gatherers remained in the area until the early twentieth century (Jolly 1986; 2000; Lewis-Williams 1986; Blundell 2004). The most prolific sign of these hunter-gatherers is the rock art that is painted in many hundreds of rock shelters throughout the region (e.g. Fig. 2.2). There is little direct dating available for these sites, but paintings at one site were recently directly dated by AMS radiocarbon to between 2,120 and 1,890 cal. BP (Bonneau et al. 2011).

Based on considerable research, mostly using analogies drawn from San ethnographies, much is understood about the meaning of this rock art. It is, fundamentally, religious in nature, concerned with accessing and manipulating a notional spirit world (Lewis-Williams and Dowson 1989; Lewis-Williams and

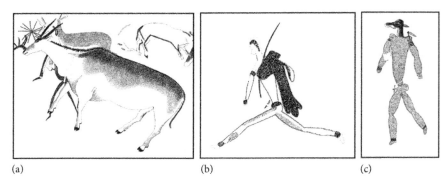

Fig. 2.2. Examples of hunter-gatherer paintings from the case study area, showing the attention to detail and artistic skill characteristic of this tradition: (a) eland antelope, (b) running human figure, (c) therianthrope that conflates human and antelope features.

Pearce 2004a). The cosmos is conceived in three tiers: a human world, with a spirit world above and below. Religious specialists, usually referred to as shamans, traverse levels of the cosmos to undertake various tasks, most notably curing the sick, controlling the movements of game, controlling the rain, and visiting far-off places (Lewis-Williams and Pearce 2004a). This is accomplished through a ritual known as the trance dance, in which shamans enter altered states of consciousness (Marshall 1969). The art depicts parts of the dance as well as creatures, activities, and experiences of the spirit world.

There is also evidence that both the production and subsequent consumption of the art was ritualized (Lewis-Williams 1995). Given the intrinsic power of paintings, it is not surprising that they became involved in other social processes. Thomas Dowson (1994; 1998; 2000), for instance, has argued that as societies changed, the role and importance of shamans within society also changed and, importantly, these changes were not only depicted in paintings but were also facilitated and legitimized by the 'supernatural sanction' given by the paintings. This was later expanded by Geoffrey Blundell (2004) in his identification of further examples in Nomansland. In other cases, it seems that paintings of rain animals were used by rain shamans to negotiate, and entrench, their positions of prestige within society (Lewis-Williams and Pearce 2004b).

The following brief overview provides insight into the conditions encountered by other groups of people as they moved into areas previously occupied solely by hunter-gatherers.

Incoming groups

From about 1,700 years ago, various Khoekhoen herding groups occupied large areas of what is now the Eastern Cape Province (Derricourt 1977). Although there are historical mentions of some of these groups, there has not been any archaeological work undertaken across inland areas (some research has been done on coastal sites). How these groups may have interacted with hunter-gatherers is unclear at this stage. It does, however, seem that Nguni agro-pastoralists living in the Transkei were involved in a long process of interaction with Khoekhoen herders as is demonstrated by linguistics, genetics, religion, and names of numerous features in the landscape (Harinck 1969; Peires 1981; Hodgson 1982; Nurse et al. 1985; Feely and Bell-Cross 2011).

From about the same time, various groups of Bantu-speaking farmers moved into the area. As with the Koekhoen, only little archaeological work has been carried out on these earlier groups, and not a great deal is known about them prior to the seventeenth century (but see Feely 1987; Prins and Granger 1993; Binneman 1996; Feely and Bell-Cross 2011). Although excavated evidence from the Maloti-Drakensberg more generally emphasizes early (from 400 CE) overlaps in modes of subsistence and material culture (Mazel 1997; Hobart 2003; Mitchell and Whitelaw 2005; Mitchell et al. 2008; Mitchell 2009), the details for Nomansland are as yet under-researched. Agropastoralists in this area do, however, seem to have been in contact with hunter-gatherers, and this contact seems to relate to a series of paintings of cattle and elephants at a number of sites within the area. These paintings were made in the typical fine-line hunter-gatherer manner. Such depictions may at first glance suggest economic changes or interaction in economic activities between groups, and this may indeed have been so; however, the inclusion of these subjects in rock paintings suggests very strongly that they had taken on some sort of religious role, or that religion was recruited to the service of those activities. There is little else to go on with these earlier 'contact' paintings, and they are currently being actively researched. We mention them so as not to leave a temporal gap in our discussion. It is unfortunate that we currently know so little about these paintings because the relationships that developed around paintings at this stage undoubtedly influenced what came afterwards.

A great deal more is known about more recent Bantu-speaking groups, both historically and anthropologically. It seems likely that from 1593 CE, an Nguni language was being spoken in the Eastern Cape (Hair 1980), and that this original population was enlarged by successive Nguni-speaking agro-pastoralists, who migrated into the area, moving initially into the coastal areas of the Eastern Cape Province, and then gradually occupying more and more of the arable land up into the foothills of the Drakensberg Mountains (Hammond-Tooke 1962; Derricourt 1974; Feely 1987; Wright and Mazel 2007; Feely and Bell-Cross 2011). The Mpondo currently occupy an area of the Eastern Cape Province in which they have lived since at least 1686, when they were observed there by the survivors of the shipwreck *Stavenisse* (Soga 1930: 302). The Mpondomise are said to be descended from the same ancestral group as the Mpondo and are thus closely related to them (ibid.: 334). The Mpondomise moved from the sources of the Umzimvubu River to parts of the Transkei, adjacent to Nomansland, where they still reside today (ibid.: 335). The Thembu settled in the coastal belt of the north Eastern Cape Province some time before the Mfecane forced the other groups mentioned above to migrate into the area. The earliest date of their occupation appears to have been sometime after 1620 (ibid.: 466).

Another agro-pastoralist group, the Phuthi (a Sotho-speaking group), made forays from the north over the Maloti-Drakensberg escarpment and established transitory settlements on the edges of Nomansland in the early eighteenth century (Ellenberger 1912: 24; King 2014). Further Sotho influences took the form of Nehemiah Moshoeshoe, King Moshoeshoe's junior son, and Joel, a Sotho petty chief, entering Nomansland in 1858 and 1881 respectively (Macquarrie 1958: 164; Van Calker 2004: 69). The Griquas, a large and organized group, that recognized certain Khoekhoen origins (Ross 1974, 1976) moved through Nomansland in the late 1850s and early 1860s, finally settling further east in what is now KwaZulu-Natal Province (Ross 1976). European settlers (traders, farmers, and missionaries) began arriving in the area in the 1820s. There is thus a long period in which interaction among numerous incoming groups and the original hunter-gatherer inhabitants occurred. It is the nature of this interaction that we now consider.

Cross-cultural interaction

The way in which interaction occurred in the broader Maloti-Drakensberg region, and in the north Eastern Cape specifically, has been the subject of debate for more than two decades. Initial research argued strongly for the cultural encapsulation of hunter-gatherer communities by the more politically powerful agro-pastoralists (Jolly 1996). It is now accepted that there is no a priori reason for this argument; indeed, sharing in the opposite direction demonstrably occurred. In particular, Cape Nguni groups incorporated a number of linguistic and ritual elements from hunter-gatherer society (Hammond-Tooke 1997, 1998, 1999). A great deal of linguistic and genetic evidence suggests a strong hunter-gatherer influence on Bantu-speakers (Richards et al. 2004), particularly Nguni-speakers. Other traits probably flowed in the other direction, but no extant groups remain in which to identify these. Rather than a focus on the directionality of cultural borrowing, we suggest an approach in which research is directed towards details of the ways in which cultural syncretism occurred in this area.

Although phrases such as 'border area' and 'frontier zone' (Crais 1992: 14) are often used to describe areas such as Nomansland, these words fail to evoke the complexity of the situation in the north Eastern Cape in the eighteenth and nineteenth centuries. Social relations over the last five hundred years in that area were complex and constantly shifting. Nomansland was populated by a multiplicity of both groups and individuals, who interacted across numerous constantly shifting boundaries, both geographical and social. As a result of these changing boundaries, relationships between different groups and different individuals were contingent and often volatile. A combination of Bantu-speakers, San, Khoe, Griqua, people described as 'coloureds', and a scattering of European magistrates, traders, and missionaries created what is often described as a 'melting pot' of people in this area. The inhabitants of Nomansland were involved in trading, raiding, intermarriage, co-operation, and conflict.

Fredrik Barth (1969: 15) has argued that situations of interaction involve recognition on the part of those involved that there are 'limitations on shared understandings', and that as a result interaction will be largely restricted to 'sectors of assured common understanding and mutual interest'. That being said, interaction also results in a reduction of differences, because it requires what Barth (ibid. 16) described as a 'congruence of codes and values'. Barth (ibid. 16) also suggested that there are a variety of sectors of articulation and separation that structure interaction, and that these will change depending on the interaction. This concept of sectors of articulation is significant for an understanding of syncretism in Nomansland. The available records suggest interaction between the former hunter-gatherers and farmers in two main areas of society: stock raiding and ritual (e.g. Wright 1971; Vinnicombe 1976; Hammond-Tooke 1997, 1998, 2002; Jolly 2000; Mitchell and Whitelaw 2005). We suggest that stock raiding represents what Barth refers to as a sector of articulation. This activity would have been a sphere in which people had mutual understanding and interest, despite their different backgrounds and cultural affinities.

The situation with ritual seems to have been more complicated. Nguni-speaking groups took on aspects of hunter-gather ritual whereas Sotho-speakers seem not to have done so, although they had as much contact with the hunter-gatherers. David Hammond-Tooke (2002) examined this question and concluded that Nguni social structure made them predisposed towards taking on aspects of hunter-gatherer ritual. Specifically, he identified heavily patriarchal unilinear descent, an impersonal concept of the ancestors, and a disempowered position held by women, as social circumstances allowing for the incorporation of aspects of hunter-gatherer trance dancing into Nguni mediumistic divination. An additional important point he makes is that only a part of the original ritual was adopted and that it was not used in the same way in its new context: rather than the core of the ritual as for hunter-gatherers, it became a part of the training of novice diviners.

As mentioned above, we know from historical evidence that stock raiding and ritual services were two areas of interaction between former hunter-gatherers and farmers during later periods. Although apparently disparate—one economic and one religious—we suggest that these activities were brought together in 'nodes' of intense interaction.

Stock raiding

In the 1800s, hunting and gathering as an exclusive way of life was no longer in evidence. These former hunter-gatherers were now known as 'Bushmen' or 'San'. From about 1837 we have more detailed historical information on the San of Nomansland through the diaries of Henry Francis Fynn (Fynn 1950), a colonial agent for the Mpondo, and later from his successor, Walter Harding (Blundell 2004: 36). It seems that three major San groups operated in the wider Nomansland area during this period: the Thola under chief MBelekwana, a group united under a San man called Mdwebo, and a group under a San man named Nqabayo (Wright 1971; Wright and Mazel 2007: 89–91). Drawing on historical information about these three San leaders in the area, Blundell (2004) points out that by the nineteenth century, the 'San groups' in the Nomansland area were no longer composed of only San people. Rather, they consisted of a nucleus of San, orbited by people with other cultural identities, whose membership of these groups was often transitory and probably expedient. All groups seem to have been involved in stock raiding and trading (Wright 1971; Shephard 1976; Vinnicombe 1976; Moths 2004; Van Calker 2004).

By the late 1850s and early 1860s the San had begun to lose their autonomy in the area, and all the previously San-led groups sought the protection of larger Bantu-speaking polities (Wright and Mazel 2007: 92–3). In particular, the remnants of Nqabayo's group who went to live with the Mpondomise, and another group of San who lived under the protection of the Phuthi. Although many of the followers of the powerful San leaders were scattered, various multi-cultural groups continued to operate in Nomansland even after San-led groups had been crushed. These groups seem also to have been united around stock raiding. Some are recorded historically (Brownlee 1873 in Orpen 1964: 185; Macquarrie 1958; Ross 1974: 131; Shephard 1976: 68–9; Vinnicombe 1976: 60), but there are almost certainly other groups that formed in this area that were not recorded.

All these groups were actively involved in the raiding of livestock. This was not small-scale raiding for subsistence purposes, but the raiding of often large herds that were subsequently traded on to other groups in distant areas.

Raiders' art

Besides the more numerous fine-line hunter-gatherer art, another tradition of painting is found in the Nomansland area. It is characterized by a limited range of subject matter that encompasses finger-painted and rough brush-painted monochrome human beings, felines, and quadrupedal images (e.g. Fig. 2.3; Mallen 2008). The paintings are predominantly made with a distinctive coarse pinkish red paint that is applied thickly to the rock surface (although a variety of other colours are known from lower-lying areas [Henry 2010]). The stylistic cohesiveness, as well as the repetitive occurrence of a restricted range of subjects within the corpus of this art suggests that it is

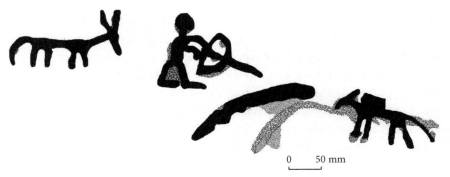

Fig. 2.3. Type 3 paintings are typically finger painted and include human figures, often carrying bows and arrows, and quadrupeds, most of which seem to be horses. Black represents red, stipple represents faded red.

distinct from the fine-line art clearly associated with hunter-gatherers. We refer to this tradition as Type 3.

Although Type 3 art is significantly different from typical fine-line rock art, it also draws on certain distinctive aspects of fine-line painting and hunter-gatherer material culture. It is sometimes brush-painted, a technique otherwise exclusively characteristic of fine-line imagery in southern Africa; it interacts with the topography of the rock surface, a distinctive characteristic of fine-line art in the southeastern mountains. Although figures are depicted with a broad range of material culture, including knobkierries (clubs with a knobbed end, traditionally used as weapons by Bantu-speakers) and spears, some carry bows with arrows, which are otherwise known to be associated with hunter-gatherers in this area.

Although we have emphasized the extent to which Type 3 art draws on fine-line rock art, it also displays certain independent traits. One of these is the use of pigment. A distinctive aspect of Type 3 rock art is the use of monochrome red paint, which often appears slightly powdery. The raw material used to make Type 3 rock art can be seen around the valleys of Nomansland, often located near to the rock art sites in which Type 3 paintings are made. It is soft and therefore easily procured and may have been used for reasons of expedience. This is in direct contrast to what we know about the making of paint used to produce fine-line rock art images: it was a complicated process involving much ritual (see Lewis-Williams 1995). Given that almost all Type 3 rock art images are monochrome, and that the pigment did not require much effort to procure, it seems that the artists either did not know about the details and rituals involved in the production of pigment for fine-line rock art, or they were not concerned with that aspect of the production of rock art. The same ritual processes associated with the making of pigment were not necessary for the purpose that Type 3 rock art served. Another sphere in which we see this gulf of difference is in the restricted subject matter of Type 3 rock art and the lack of detail. While fine-line rock art is known for its broad range of subject matter, and intricate attention to detail, these aspects of making images do not seem to have been important to Type 3 artists. Similarly, the technique differs. Although some of the Type 3 images are brush-painted, many of them are finger-painted. With the exception of dots made with finger-tips that have been argued to be part of the corpus of San rock art (e.g. Lewis-Williams and Blundell 1997), finger-painting is not something that is found in fine-line rock art.

Two significant issues arise out of the relationship between fine-line art and Type 3 art. The first is insight into how the Type 3 tradition came into being, and the second is that the differences between these two rock art traditions imply a social disjuncture. We suggest that something quite significant changed in Nomansland society when Type 3 rock art began to be made, and that it is a product of a syncretic process of cultural fusion. This tradition is found at only a small number of sites in a restricted geographical area, suggesting that it emerges, changes, and disappears within a short space of time. Indeed, it is possible to assign a tentative date range to the Type 3 rock art, partly because of its relationship to the fine-line rock art, and partly because of its subject matter. Where a super-positioning relationship exists between the two traditions, Type 3 rock art is always superimposed on fine-line rock art, and there are no known instances in which the converse occurs. This means that Type 3 rock art was made after the fine-line rock art and suggests that Type 3 imagery is relatively more recent.

In addition, figures are depicted as wearing European-style dresses at two of the sites in the region: RSA BUX1 (Fig. 2.4) and RSA LAB1. There is an emphasis on depicting the dress with a 'protrusion' at the rear. This is almost certainly a reference to the wearing of a bustle pad, which was common practice at various times between the seventeenth and twentieth centuries in Europe (Bradfield 1981). Bustles were worn by some of the earliest European colonists in South Africa. Jan van Riebeeck's wife and daughters are depicted in dresses with bustles (Strutt 1975: 2), suggesting that they were in use in the mid-seventeenth century in the Cape Colony. By the early 1800s, European women's dress in South Africa had become simpler, with slim-line skirts and no bustles (Strutt 1975: 183). In the early 1860s, however, bustles seem to reappear in colonial South African fashions (Strutt 1975: 202), and by the 1890s, they are no longer worn by colonial South African women.

Another chronological indicator is horses. They were first introduced into South Africa in the mid-seventeenth century by the Dutch East India Company (Child 1967) but were only present in the southeastern mountain range relatively late—probably sometime around the 1830s. The point at which dresses with bustles and horses overlap occurs during the latter half of the nineteenth century. Type 3 imagery is thus a very recent addition to the Nomansland landscape.

Fig. 2.4. Several of the Type 3 human figures wear European-style dresses with bustle pads. Black represents white, stipple represents yellow.

A node of interaction

The presence of Type 3 rock art in Nomansland provides us with a rare archaeological insight into the invention of tradition, as articulated by Eric Hobsbawm (1983: 1):

> Invented tradition is taken to mean a set of practices, normally governed by overtly or tacitly accepted rules and of a ritual or symbolic nature, which seek to inculcate certain values and norms of behaviour by repetition, which automatically implies continuity with the past. In fact, where possible, they normally attempt to establish continuity with a suitable historic past.

Hobsbawm drew a distinction between 'tradition' and 'custom'. Using the example of judges in a court, he suggested that 'custom' is what judges *do*, whilst 'tradition', or invented 'tradition', is the 'wig, robe and other formal paraphernalia and ritualised practices surrounding their substantial action' (1983: 3). The decline of custom will change the tradition with which it is enmeshed. This distinction between 'tradition' and 'custom' is important. It seems almost certain that various customs that had previously been part of the social order in Nomansland would have declined. We know from historical information that this would have occurred through interaction, contestation of identity, new and different economic practices, changing relationships with one's neighbours, shifting power relations and group allegiance, and the disappearance of certain groups from the landscape. This decline or change in custom seems to have led to a change in the traditions with which it was enmeshed, hence the end of the classic fine-line painting tradition and the inception of 'other' painted imagery, such as Type 3 rock art.

Type 3 art exemplifies the invention of tradition. It seems to have been a response to a 'novel situation', which arose as a result of nineteenth-century Nomansland being a heterogeneous society in flux. Type 3, however, also references the 'old situation', the 'historic past', through the act of making rock art itself, and through the links that may be made between this rock art and the more traditional fine-line rock art. It seems likely that the references to fine-line rock art that are evident in Type 3 images may be a means of establishing the credentials of the tradition, by drawing on what had gone before it and implying continuity with that past. Although it references the past, it is also an active response to or manipulation of a society in flux. In Nomansland, this novel situation is most likely the economic shift towards stock raiding, and probably occurred in tandem with the breakdown of hunter-gatherer communities.

In the nineteenth century in this area, small multi-cultural groups coalesced around the economic activity of stock raiding (Wright 1971; Shephard 1976; Vinnicombe 1976; Van Calker 2004; Moths 2004). As we note, until the late 1850s, the majority of these groups were led by powerful San individuals. After this, however, new groups would have formed around new and different leaders. It is the processes involved in the changing power relations and the formation of a new collective identity that we probe in order to better understand these composite raiding groups and ultimately the production and consumption of Type 3 art. Blundell (2004: 153) suggests, for example, that these processes entailed prolonged periods of creolization and hybridization and the emergence of new identities. The legacy of the culture-historical approach means that quite often group identities are represented archaeologically as unified, monolithic wholes, with linear and continuous histories. Historical information shows that this is clearly not the case in Nomansland, and Blundell (2004) is right to emphasize the potential for change and flux and the development of new identities. However, the concept of hybridization put forward by Blundell (2004) must be considered in more detail.

One of the problems with the word 'hybrid' is that it conflates two processes into one. That of genetic 'mixing', and that of cultural 'mixing'. Importantly, these two things do not necessarily go together. Does the existence of composite groups, for which we have ample historical evidence, automatically mean that these people would also have had 'hybrid identities'? Interaction and even intermarriage do not necessarily create a hybrid culture, although they may, and in some instances, clearly do (see Challis 2008 for an example of this in the KwaZulu-Natal Drakensberg). This is where Barth's concept of sectors of articulation is useful. Rather than talking broadly about 'hybridity of culture' as a result of interaction, we are able to consider specific sectors of society in which new identities were forged, while being aware that this would not necessarily have occurred in all sectors of society. We argue that although new collective identities would have formed around the practice of stock raiding in Nomansland, the individuals involved in these groups may well have retained other aspects of their original identities, such as cultural affiliation. This is strongly suggested by the evidence from the multi-cultural group under Nqabayo's leadership. Once their leader was deposed, this group scattered, and those with Khoekhoen affiliation sought shelter with the Griqua, and Silayi, a Thembu man, went back to live with the Thembu (Stanford 1910;

Macquarrie 1962: 32). A useful definition of creolisation is 'a difference which refuses to fall back into its binary elements' (Hall 2010). Rather than a hybrid or creole identity in these raiding groups, we see a proliferation of multiple cultural identities that may be used and discarded at will. This situation is more in line with the concept of syncretism, with the lack of permanence of fusion of worldviews that this term implies—it is a negotiated situation that is open to change.

It seems likely that various features of this new social milieu made those involved in it predisposed to take on certain aspects of hunter-gatherer ritual and belief, as with the Cape Nguni and the trance dance (Hammond-Tooke 2002). We argue that the use of rock art in this way is an example of partial borrowing in a similar way to that demonstrated by Hammond-Tooke with the trance dance: only certain aspects of the original painting tradition were taken up, and they were applied in a different way in their new context.

The making of Type 3 imagery was probably related to existing members of Nomansland society, as well as to the memory of past inhabitants of the area. Although we cannot know for sure, we suggest below two main reasons (which are not mutually exclusive) why rock art was a useful symbolic tool.

The super-positioning of Type 3 art may have been related to the political nature of the underlying fine-line images themselves. Type 3 art may thus have been used to make a similar statement about leadership and control of the space in which the imagery is made as has been argued for fine-line art in the area (e.g. Dowson 2000; Blundell 2004).

Type 3 art may have been produced as an emphasis on the presence of a new raiding group in the area, who had physically replaced the by now politically disempowered San-led groups and were emphasizing their power and control over the space, in relation to the memory of the San-led groups that had controlled the area before them.

Type 3 rock art would thus have been implicated in the formation, maintenance, and probably contestation of a relational collective identity centred on stock raiding. Identity is, of course, subject to change, and as Clifton Crais suggests (1992: 101): 'the issue is not which is the "correct" representation, but rather when and why one representation attains a certain, and frequently fragile, hegemony.' In late nineteenth-century Nomansland, a fragile sector of articulation, in which economics and ritual were united, was expressed in the invention of a new rock art tradition: one that referenced the past, even as it was involved in the negotiation of new and syncretic social processes.

Acknowledgements

We are grateful to Peter Mitchell and Timothy Clack for many valuable discussions. The research was funded by the Clarendon Fund and the South African National Research Foundation under the African Origins Platform.

References

Barth, F. 1969. 'Introduction'. In F. Barth (ed.), *Ethnic Groups and Boundaries*. Oslo: Universitetsforlaget, pp. 9–38.

Binneman, J. 1996. 'Preliminary results from investigations at Kulubele, an Early Iron Age farming settlement in the Great Kei River valley, Eastern Cape'. *Southern African Field Archaeology* 5: 28–35.

Blundell, G. 2004. *Nqabayo's Nomansland: San Rock Art and the Somatic Past*. Uppsala: Uppsala University Press.

Bonneau, A., F. Brock, T. Higham, D. G. Pearce and A. M. Pollard. 2011. 'An improved pre-treatment protocol for radiocarbon dating black pigments in San rock art'. *Radiocarbon* 53(3): 419–28.

Bradfield, N. 1981. *Costume in Detail: Women's Dress 1730–1930*. London: Harrap.

Challis, W. 2008. *The Impact of the Horse on the AmaTola 'Bushmen': New Identities in the Maloti-Drakensberg Mountains of Southern Africa*. Unpublished DPhil thesis, University of Oxford, Oxford.

Child, D. 1967. *Saga of the South African Horse*. Cape Town: Timmins.

Crais, C. 1992. *The Making of the Colonial Order: White Supremacy and Black Resistance in the Eastern Cape, 1770–1865*. Cambridge: Cambridge University Press.

Derricourt, R. M. 1974. 'Settlement in the Transkei and Ciskei before the Mfecane'. In R. Derricourt and C. Saunders (eds), *Beyond the Cape Frontier: Studies in the History of the Transkei and Ciskei*. London: Longman Group Ltd, pp. 39–82.

Derricourt, R. 1977. *Prehistoric Man in the Ciskei and Transkei*. Cape Town: Struik.

Dowson, T. A. 1994. 'Reading art, writing history: rock art and social change in southern Africa'. *World Archaeology* 25(3): 332–45.

Dowson, T. A. 1998. 'Like people in prehistory'. *World Archaeology* 29(3): 333–43.

Dowson, T. A. 2000. 'Painting as politics: exposing historical processes in hunter-gatherer rock art'. In P. P. Schweitzer, M. Biesele, and R. Hitchcock (eds), *Hunters and Gatherers in the Modern World: Conflict, Resistance and Self-Determination*. New York: Berghahn Books, pp. 413–26.

Ellenberger, D. F. 1912. *History of the Basuto: Ancient and Modern*. London: Caxton Publishing Company.

58 LARA MALLEN AND DAVID G. PEARCE

Feely, J. M. 1987. *The Early Farmers of Transkei, Southern Africa before A.D.1870*. Oxford: B.A.R.

Feely, J. M. and S. M. Bell-Cross. 2011. 'The distribution of Early Iron Age settlement in the Eastern Cape: some historical and ecological implications'. *South African Archaeological Bulletin* 66: 105–12.

Fynn, H. F. 1950. *The Diary of Henry Francis Fynn*. Pietermaritzburg: Shuter and Shooter.

Hair, P. E. H. 1980. 'Portuguese contacts with the Bantu languages of the Transkei, Natal and southern Mozambique 1497–1650'. *African Studies* 39(1): 3–46.

Hall, S. 1994. 'Images of interaction: rock art and sequence in the Eastern Cape'. In T. A. Dowson and J. D. Lewis-Williams (eds), *Contested Images: Diversity in Southern African Rock Art Research*. Johannesburg: Witwatersrand University Press, pp. 61–82.

Hall, S. 2010. 'Créolité and the Process of Creolization'. In R. Cohen (ed.), *The Creolization Reader: Studies in Mixed Identities and Cultures*. New York: Routledge, pp. 26–32.

Hall, S. and A. Mazel. 2005. 'The private performance of events: colonial period rock art from the Swartruggens'. *Kronos* 31: 124–51.

Hammond-Tooke, W. D. 1962. *Bhaca Society: A People of the Transkeian Uplands, South Africa*. Cape Town: Oxford University Press.

Hammond-Tooke, W. D. 1997. 'Whatever happened to/Kaggen? A note on Cape Nguni/Khoisan borrowing'. *South African Archaeological Bulletin* 55: 22–4.

Hammond-Tooke, W. D. 1998. 'Selective borrowing? The possibility of San shamanistic influence on Southern Bantu divination and healing practices'. *South African Archaeological Bulletin* 53: 9–15.

Hammond-Tooke, W. D. 1999. 'Divinatory animals: further evidence of San–Nguni borrowing'. *South African Archaeological Bulletin* 54: 128–32.

Hammond-Tooke, W. D. 2002. 'The uniqueness of Nguni mediumistic divination in southern Africa'. *Africa* 72: 277–92.

Harinck, G. 1969. 'Interaction between Xhosa and Khoi: emphasis on the period between 1620–1750'. In L. Thompson (ed.), *African Societies in Southern Africa*. London: Heinemann, pp. 145–70.

Henry, L. 2010. *Rock Art and the Contested Landscape of the North Eastern Cape, South Africa*. Unpublished MA dissertation, University of the Witwatersrand, Johannesburg.

Hobart, J. H. 2003. *Forager-Farmer Relations in Southeastern Southern Africa: A Critical Reassessment*. Unpublished DPhil dissertation, University of Oxford, Oxford.

Hobsbawm, E. 1983. 'Introduction: inventing traditions'. In E. Hobsbawm and T. Ranger (eds), *The Invention of Tradition*. Cambridge: Cambridge University Press, pp. 1–14.

Hodgson, J. 1982. *The God of the Xhosa*. Cape Town: Oxford University Press.

Jolly, P. 1986. 'A first generation descendant of the Transkei San'. *South African Archaeological Bulletin* 41: 6–9.

Jolly, P. 1996. 'Interaction between south-eastern San and Southern Nguni and Sotho Communities c. 1400 to c. 1800'. *South African Historical Journal* 35: 30–61.

Jolly, P. 2000. 'Nguni diviners and the south-eastern San: some issues relating to their mutual cultural influence'. *Natal Museum Journal of Humanities* 12: 79–95.

King, R. 2014. *Voluntary Barbarians of the Maloti—Drakensberg: The BaPhuthi Chiefdom, Cattle Raiding, and Colonial Rule in Nineteenth-Century Southern Africa*. Unpublished DPhil thesis, University of Oxford, Oxford.

Lewis-Williams, J. D. 1986. 'The last testament of the southern San'. *South African Archaeological Bulletin* 41: 10–11.

Lewis-Williams, J. D. 1995. 'Modelling the production and consumption of rock art'. *South African Archaeological Bulletin* 50: 143–54.

Lewis-Williams, J. D. and G. Blundell. 1997. 'New light on finger-dots in southern African rock art: synesthesia, transformation and technique'. *South African Journal of Science* 93: 51–4.

Lewis-Williams, J. D. and T. A. Dowson. 1989. *Images of Power: Understanding Bushman Rock Art*. Johannesburg: Southern Book Publishers.

Lewis-Williams, J. D. and D. G. Pearce. 2004a. *San Spirituality: Roots, Expressions, and Social Consequences*. Walnut Creek: AltaMira Press.

Lewis-Williams, J. D. and D. G. Pearce. 2004b. 'Southern African San rock painting as social intervention: a study of rain-control images'. *African Archaeological Review* 21(4): 199–228.

Loubser, J. and G. Laurens. 1994. 'Depictions of domestic ungulates and shields: hunter/gatherers and agro-pastoralists in the Caledon River Valley area'. In T. A. Dowson and J. D. Lewis-Williams (eds), *Contested Images: Diversity in Southern African Rock Art Research*. Johannesburg: Witwatersrand University Press, pp. 83–118.

Macquarrie, J. W. 1958. *The Reminiscences of Sir Walter Stanford*, vol. 1. Cape Town: Van Riebeeck Society.

Macquarrie, J. W. 1962. *The Reminiscences of Sir Walter Stanford*, vol. 2. Cape Town: Van Riebeeck Society.

Mallen, L. R. 2008. *Rock Art and Identity in the North Eastern Cape Province*. Unpublished MA dissertation, University of the Witwatersrand, Johannesburg.

Marshall, L, 1969. 'The medicine dance of the !Kung Bushmen'. *Africa* 39: 347–81.

Mazel, A. D. 1997. 'Hunter-gatherers in the Thukela Basin during the last 1500 years, with special reference to hunter-gatherer/agriculturalist relations'. In A. Bank (ed.), *The Proceedings of the Khoisan Identities and Cultural Heritage Conference*. Cape Town: Arts and Culture Trust, pp. 94–101.

Mitchell, P. J. 2009. 'Hunter-gatherers and farmers: some implications of 1800 years of interaction in the Maloti-Drakensberg region of southern Africa'. In K. Ikeya, H. Ogawa, and P. Mitchell (eds), *Interactions between Hunter-gatherers and Farmers: From Prehistory to Present*. Osaka: National Museum of Ethnology, pp. 15–46.

Mitchell, P. J. and G. Whitelaw. 2005. 'The archaeology of southernmost Africa *c.* 2000 BP to the early 1800s: a review of recent research'. *Journal of African History* 46: 209–41.

Mitchell, P. J., I. Plug, N. Bailey, and S. Woodborne. 2008. 'Bringing the Kalahari debate to the mountains: late first millennium AD hunter-gatherer/farmer interaction in highland Lesotho'. *Before Farming* 2008/2: 1–22.

Moths, P. 2004. 'Heinrich Meyer: a stalwart of the mission field'. In T. Keegan (ed.), *Moravians in the Eastern Cape, 1828–1928: Four Accounts of Moravian Mission Work on the Eastern Cape Frontier*. Cape Town: Van Riebeeck Society, pp. 144–201.

Nurse, G. T., J. S. Weiner, and T. Jenkins. 1985. *The Peoples of Southern Africa and Their Affinities*. Oxford: Oxford University Press.

Opperman, H. 1996. 'Excavation of a Later Stone Age deposit in Strathalan Cave A, Maclear District, northeastern Cape, South Africa'. In G. Pwiti and R. Soper (eds), *Aspects of African Archaeology*. Harare: University of Zimbabwe Press, pp. 335–42.

Orpen, J. M. 1964. *Reminiscences of Life in South Africa from 1846 to the Present Day*. Cape Town: Struik.

Peires, J. B. 1981. *The House of Phalo*. Johannesburg: Ravan Press.

Prins, F. E. and J. E. Granger. 1993. 'Early farming communities in northern Transkei: the evidence from Ntsitsana and adjacent areas'. *South African Journal of Humanities* 5: 153–74.

Richards, M., V. Macaulay, A. Carracedo, and A. Salas. 2004. 'The archaeogenetics of the Bantu dispersals'. In M. Jones (ed.), *Traces of Ancestry: Studies in Honour of Colin Renfrew*. Cambridge: McDonald Institute Monographs, pp. 75–88.

Ross, R. 1974. 'The Griqua in the politics of the eastern Transkei'. In R. Derricourt and C. Saunders (eds), *Beyond the Cape Frontier: Studies in the History of the Transkei and Ciskei*. London: Longman Group Ltd, pp. 127–44.

Ross, R. 1976. *Adam Kok's Griquas: A Study in the Development of Stratification in South Africa*. Cambridge: Cambridge University Press.

Schoeman, M. H. 2007. *Clouding Power? Rain-Control, Space, Landscapes and Ideology in Shashe-Limpopo State Formation*. Unpublished PhD thesis, University of the Witwatersrand, Johannesburg.

Shephard, J. 1976. *In the Shadow of the Drakensberg: The Story of East Griqualand and Its People*. Durban: T.W. Griggs & Co.

Soga, J. H. 1930. *The South-Eastern Bantu*. Johannesburg: Witwatersrand University Press.

Stanford, W. E. 1910. 'Statement of Silayi, with reference to his life among the Bushmen'. *Transactions of the Royal Society of South Africa* 1: 435–40.

Strutt, D. H. 1975. *Fashion in South Africa, 1652–1900*. Cape Town: A. A. Balkema.

Van Calker, E. 2004. 'A century of Moravian mission work in the Eastern Cape Colony and Transkei'. In T. Keegan (ed.), *Moravians in the Eastern Cape, 1828–1928: Four Accounts of Moravian Mission Work on the Eastern Cape Frontier*. Cape Town: Van Riebeeck Society, pp. 1–44.

Van Doornum, B. L. 2006. *Changing Places, Spaces and Identity in the Shashe Limpopo Region of Limpopo Province, South Africa*. Unpublished PhD thesis, University of the Witwatersrand, Johannesburg.

Vinnicombe, P. 1976. *People of the Eland: Rock Paintings of the Drakensberg Bushmen as a Reflection of their Life and Thought*. Pietermaritzburg: Natal University Press.

Wright, J. B. 1971. *Bushman Raiders of the Drakensberg 1840–1870*. Pietermaritzburg: University of Natal Press.

Wright, J. B. and A. Mazel. 2007. *Tracks in a Mountain Range: Exploring the History of the Ukhahlamba-Drakensberg*. Johannesburg: Wits University Press.

3

Becoming One or Many

Material Mediation of Difference in Honduras

Rosemary A. Joyce and Russell N. Sheptak

Archaeology in the Americas over the past two decades has supported development of new understandings of colonial situations originally conceived of as 'culture contact' (Lightfoot 1995; Lightfoot et al. 1998). Colonization by Europeans, who introduced diverse populations of African origin alongside surviving indigenous populations of equally diverse origins, resulted in a colonial situation of great complexity. Critiques of the idea of contact accompanied the development of detailed investigations of specific historical engagements that blurred the lines between what could be considered original or novel, 'authentic' or hybrid (Silliman 2005, 2010).

The framework of ethnogenesis was developed in the Americas as an alternative to what critics saw as problematic models of creolization (Weik 2004; Palka 2005; Voss 2008). Weik specifically advocated use of ethnogenesis in situations in Latin America where 'Africans and Amerindians were intimately associated within and beyond colonial settlements' (Weik 2004: 32). He defined ethnogenesis as 'the formation of *new or different* sociocultural groups from the interactions, intermixtures, and antagonisms among people who took part in global processes of colonialism and slavery' (Weik 2004: 36). The landscape we examine in Honduras, where Spanish colonialism brought together a diversity of indigenous, European, and African populations starting in the sixteenth century, witnesses this kind of emergence of new social formations that exceeds the vocabulary of creolization, calling for the adoption of new analyses of hybridity and ethnogenesis (Sheptak and Joyce 2019).

Rosemary A. Joyce and Russell N. Sheptak, *Becoming One or Many: Material Mediation of Difference in Honduras*
In: *Archaeologies of Cultural Contact: At the Interface.* Edited by: Timothy Clack and Marcus Brittain, Oxford University Press. © Oxford University Press 2022. DOI: 10.1093/oso/9780199693948.003.0004

Entangled landscapes: the province of the Rio Ulua in colonial Honduras

Our work takes place in the region around the modern city of San Pedro Sula, part of the Honduran province of the Captaincy General of Guatemala. San Pedro was founded in 1536 CE as a Spanish *villa* (incorporated town). It flourished as the centre for transmission of products of local gold mines toward Caribbean ports, until the early 1580s. At that point, gold founding was moved inland to the colonial capital city, Comayagua. This was followed by a steady decline of the numbers of Spanish *vecinos* (citizens) of San Pedro, reaching a low point around 1610.

Even before the founding of San Pedro, indigenous towns in northern Honduras had experienced impacts of disease, forced labour in the mines, military conflicts between Spanish factions, and a well-developed indigenous military resistance that succeeded for a decade in warding off incorporation of the 'province of the Río Ulúa' into the Spanish colony. Our analysis shows that between 1536 and 1582 population declined by at least 80 percent, and up to 90 percent, in the indigenous towns that persisted (Sheptak and Joyce 2019). Thereafter, the populations of the remaining towns began to recover. By the beginning of the nineteenth century, two *pueblos de indios* (Indian towns), Ticamaya and Candelaría, existed in the San Pedro district, each of which could be traced back to sixteenth-century roots.

By the end of the sixteenth century, the majority population in the region, although much reduced in size, was still officially recognized as indigenous. The minuscule number of *vecinos* listed as living in San Pedro in the beginning of the sixteenth century by no means should be considered the entire city or regional European population, whose size remains uncertain. This small number of citizens with full legal rights would have been complemented by a population of Europeans lacking *vecindad* (civil rights in the city), including the offspring or descendants of couples of mixed European and indigenous background.

An as-yet undetermined number of persons of African descent also formed part of the city and regional population. Centres for the importation of enslaved Africans had been established at the Caribbean port of Puerto Caballos (today Puerto Cortes) before 1550 in response to the demand for labour for mining (Sherman 1979; Newson 1986). Additional flows of African descendant populations into the region in the eighteenth century came from multiple sources (Cáceres 2003).

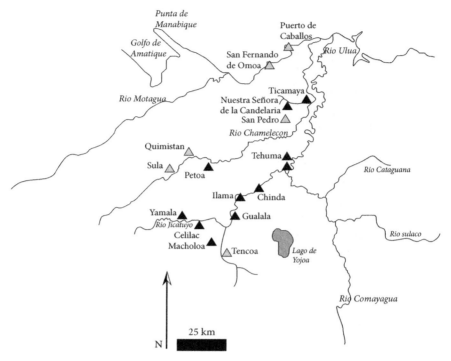

Fig. 3.1. Map showing *pueblos de indios* (grey) and Spanish towns in the San Pedro district of northern Honduras c.1780.

By the late eighteenth century (Fig. 3.1), the district of San Pedro was occupied by a large population of partial African descent, variously described as *negro*, *pardo*, and *mulato*. The residents of late colonial *pueblos de indios* in the district were accounted as indigenous by definition, spoke Spanish as a primary language, and in some cases lived in households with individuals marked as of other backgrounds. A small number of families claimed Spanish identity, usually not marked but sometimes indicated by the designation *español* (Spanish) or (very rarely) *blanco* (white).

Our investigations of this complicated social landscape draw on both a discursive and a material register. We cite unpublished documents from civil and ecclesiastical archives that we have personally transcribed and analysed. We also discuss materials recovered through archaeological excavations at Ticamaya (Blaisdell-Sloan 2006; Sheptak et al. 2011a; Sheptak et al. 2011b). Ticamaya was occupied from before the first Spanish entry into the region through to the early nineteenth century. We compare these archaeological materials to those we excavated at the site of the eighteenth-century Spanish town and Fort of Omoa (Joyce et al. 2008). Around 1750, construction began on the first fort at Omoa (Hasemann 1986). Our excavations identified colonial occupation of the second fort at Omoa from *c.*1760 to 1810; and detected residences in the town dating from before 1780 to around 1800.

The archaeological sites are each documented in the archives. Men from Ticamaya and the neighbouring *pueblo de indios* Candelaria worked in rotation at the fort as a continuing labour force. Hand-built earthenware and Spanish-tradition mayolica pottery excavated at Omoa are indistinguishable from late eighteenth-century material excavated at Ticamaya. Fired clay net weights, of distinctive form and local manufacture, were found in both sites. These overlapping materials are evidence of a regional society in which the people of Omoa and those of Ticamaya and Candelaria formed a single network. Precisely how this network played out is partly structured by Spanish policy, and partly by pragmatic needs of this Caribbean outpost. In this interplay of external policies and local actions we see a case offering an opportunity to examine how creolization, hybridity, ethnogenesis, and other related concepts serve our analyses.

Spanish colonial policies and Honduran colonial practices

In the initial colonization efforts of the sixteenth century, the Spanish administration had extended to the Americas concerns born in the peninsula about legitimacy of descent, in part shaped by policing of religious ancestry. Tamar Herzog (2003) describes colonial Spanish American society as based on the city or town, governed by its own officials, and populated by *vecinos. Vecinos* were 'bearers of rights' (such as access to common land) and 'burdened with duties' (including taxes, service in militia, and service to the municipality). *Vecindad* was determined locally, not centrally. Criteria included being married into an existing *vecino* family, living in the community (for ten years), being Catholic, and owning a house. *Vecindad*, or these citizenship rights in a city or town, depended on legitimacy of birth, which required proof (Twinam 1999). Transmission of property rights could be contested by casting doubt on the line of descent, on the purity of religion, or on the religious sanction of marriage of one's ancestors.

The outcome of these concerns was a more-or-less well-defined structure of three recognized groups in the Spanish colonial world, forming what Jorge

Cañizares-Esguerra (2007) argued was a quasi-racial hierarchy. Descendants of Europeans, constituting an unmarked category in most of the documents, had the potential for *vecindad* in Spanish cities and towns. They had power over communities of *indios*, who were required to serve communally either individual *vecinos* of the colonial towns, or work collectively on colonial governmental projects. The degree of hierarchy can be exaggerated: *indios* had legally inscribed rights as corporate communities, and in Honduras, many petitioned successfully for protection of their rights (Sheptak 2013). Throughout the eighteenth century, residents of *pueblos de indios* were able to accumulate considerable capital through such institutions as *cofradias*, collective religious aid associations.

Cañizares-Esguerra (2007) situates Africans as a third group, at the bottom of his proposed colonial hierarchy. For Honduras, as for much of colonial Central America, this is a problematic formulation. African descendant peoples did not form a single category. The jural status of being free or enslaved was a critical distinction among African descendant populations. Free African descendant people appear in many roles in Honduran colonial history, and it is hard to impute categorical position even to free African descendants. In studies of African descendant enlistment into militias in the eighteenth century, Paul Lokken (2004) cites evidence that in Central America, *pardo* militias were considered more trustworthy than *indios*, rather than remaining suspect at the bottom of local social hierarchies.

By the eighteenth century, Iberian administrators attempted to impose a grid of racialized identities on what had been a somewhat fluid network of formal and informal sexual relations in the colonies. The new categories, collectively called *casta*, were never effectively imposed uniformly across Spanish America (Katzew 2004). In Honduras, population documents from the early eighteenth-century use what would later be *casta* terms, such as *mestizo* and *mulato*, to identify individuals living in *pueblos de indios*, but there is no uniform practice of accounting of identities then or even later in the eighteenth century.

Caribbean coastal Honduras consequently provides a useful case for understanding how new mixtures emerged through a long-term process of colonization. We first consider the domain of language. We follow up our exploration of hybridization of language with an examination of the evidence for emerging categorical identities within the heterogeneous population of the district of San Pedro, evident starting around 1700. The resulting populations might be called 'creole' (encompassing both the meaning of Spanish-identified population born in the colonies, and offspring of different racial-ethnic groups), but in Honduras the Spanish analogue of this term is never used this way. In the final section of the paper, we turn from domains that are primarily evident in documents—language and population identity—to everyday practices, including religious practice. Here, we can juxtapose documentary and artefact data to explore how regimes of use of things were adjusted throughout the colonial period by the diverse population that was learning to be Honduran.

Talking with each other

Pueblos de indios in the district of San Pedro required translation from their own languages, referred to consistently as *lengua materna* (mother tongue), until the early eighteenth century. While unidentified in modern terms, the languages these speakers probably used from birth were likely in the Lenca language family (Sheptak 2007). These towns already included individuals capable of complex communication in the language of governance, Spanish, in the seventeenth century. These speakers promoted the creation of a new Honduran Spanish, produced through the dialogic process of conversation evident in historic documents.

Words that we might treat as simply Spanish had distinctive implications as a result of their histories of use. This is not unlike the argument Hanks (2010) makes for Yucatan, although there, the new emergent language was colonial Yucatec, with grammar and vocabulary that appears at first to be authentically rooted in pre-Hispanic communities. Hanks argues nonetheless that colonial Yucatec is distinct from both precolonial Yucatec and Spanish, the two languages from which it was formed. He shows how what people needed to say in the early colonial process of conversion led to new ways of talking that cannot be separated into authentic pre-Hispanic Yucatec and inauthentic Spanish-influenced neologisms.

After the Spanish invasion of northern Honduras in the 1520s and 1530s succeeded in establishing new settlements and new institutions of labour and governance, it became necessary for the different populations that occupied the now-shared territory to communicate different understandings of their situation. We use the concept of dialogics, a framework for thinking about language as communication developed by Mikhail Bakhtin, to guide our own understanding of how these necessary exchanges worked. This is not simply a consideration of translation or language change, since the dialogic perspective we use applies both when the speakers were divided by differences in

68   ROSEMARY A. JOYCE AND RUSSELL N. SHEPTAK

original language, and when they are theoretically using a single shared language. The core concept of dialogics is that every utterance is formed in anticipation of a response from another (Bakhtin 1984). Bakhtin wrote that, 'each sphere in which language is used develops its own, relatively stable types of utterances... [which] we may call speech genres' (Bakhtin 1986: 60). For Bakhtin, genres consequently had a historical character. As Hanks (1987: 668) notes genres 'are the historically specific elements of social practice'. Dialogues are thus more than mere exchanges of words; values are affirmed, contested, revised, and reborn through the patterns of responses. Dialogics is, from this perspective, a way to move from an analysis of speech to an understanding of action and its meanings to different speakers: 'speaking and discourse production are ways of taking up positions in social fields' (Hanks 2005: 73).

We can explore Honduran colonial dialogics through petitions created by or on behalf of residents of the seventeenth-century *pueblo de indios* called Masca, that, renamed Candelaria, provided continuing labour to the eighteenth-century fortress of Omoa (Sheptak 2013). In 1675, a petition in the name of Blás Cuculí on behalf of Masca was launched in the main court in Santiago de Guatemala. The original petition is short; just two brief pages. Written out in Spanish by a scribe who describes it as being 'as spoken', it makes no reference to the use of a translator, although not long before, in 1662, a formal Spanish ceremony enacted at Masca used the services of such a linguistic interlocutor. The only non-Spanish words in the petition, *tequio* and *tesine*, are actually terms introduced by the Spanish administration to describe particular forms of individual labour, borrowings from Mexican languages (Sherman 1979).

Blás Cuculí, identified concisely at the beginning of the petition as *indio vecino y natural del pueblo de San Pedro Masca* ('Indian, resident with legal rights, and born in the town of Masca'), indicates ambivalence through his choice of words. He describes himself as having come before the *corte* ('court') previously on behalf of the justices of *his* town (*mi pueblo*) on business that concerned *their* community (*su comunidad*). At one and the same time he identifies with the town and differentiates himself from the community governed by its officials, all entirely in Spanish.

Officials from the families governing towns like Masca continued to use indigenous names as surnames (Sheptak 2013). In later petitions, they referred to themselves as *tlatoques chicos*. The first word is recognizable as a term borrowed from the Mexican Nahuatl language. Combined with the Spanish word *chico* ('small'), it meant something like 'petty lords'. The phrase persisted in self-referential use into the eighteenth century, after the use of translators was no longer needed in the *pueblos de indios*.

There is every reason to think that *tlatoque* had been borrowed in pre-Hispanic Honduras through multilingual networks of exchange controlled by wealthy families that extended into Yucatan and through indirect links reached the eastern edge of the Mexica (Aztec) tribute state, where *tlatoque* would have had local linguistic significance. Its use in written petitions recorded by scribes working exclusively in Spanish suggests that in the seventeenth century, it had become a part of the vocabulary of Honduran Spanish, serving as nothing from Iberian Spanish could, to elevate a social group that had theoretically no existence in these Honduran *pueblos de indios*, a native nobility.

Blás Cuculí provides a description of Masca in 1675 and its social relations, a network of duties and rights, which relies on the colonial institution of *encomienda* ('tributary service') for much of its force. In response to demands for added personal service by *vecinos* of the city of San Pedro, Masca claims the right to be exempt because it is part of an *encomienda*, responsible to a *vecino* of the more distant Honduran provincial capital, Comayagua.

Our argument is that by this point, the Spanish used in the Honduran colony was a new language, one in which words of Spanish origin (such as *encomienda*) had been historically shaped by a shared experience of colonial survival to reflect circumstances on the ground rather than the formalisms of Spanish or the unrecorded sentiments that might have been expressed in the original *lengua materna* of Masca's residents. The most 'indigenous' language in the 1675 petition, repeated in later petitions by Masca, is in fact entirely Spanish: a claim of exemption from service as *tequios* and *tesines* due to giving service as *vigias*—vigils, in a coastal watch system that, while recognized widely in the district of San Pedro, had no standing as part of Spanish governance.

Living with others

A history of cohabitation and sexual reproduction between the Spanish colonists and indigenous population in the district of San Pedro can be teased out from even the earliest documents (Sheptak et al. 2011a). During more than a decade of military resistance against Spanish domination from the mid-1520s to the mid-1530s, both men and women of Spanish origin entered indigenous communities, some as captives and some as 'renegade' allies.

A letter from 1536 describes a 'Christian Spanish woman...from Sevilla', originally married to a Spanish soldier who died in an assault on an outpost destroyed in the 1520s, said to be held by the main leader of resistance against the Spanish as his 'woman'.

The Spanish terms used differentiate the civil status of being married (recognized between the woman and the dead Spanish soldier) from that of being someone's 'woman', part of a pattern of denying recognition of liaisons that were happening on both sides of the conflict. In a study of similar situations in the Spanish colonial Southwest, James Brooks (2002: 17–18) suggests that, 'the capture of "enemy" women and children was...one extreme expression along a continuum of exchange...they could serve as agents and objects of the full range of exchanges, from the peaceful to the violent'. He sees these cross-cultural, cross-religion sexual liaisons as rooted in tactics adopted during the slow war to recover control of the Iberian Peninsula from Moorish kingdoms that reached its end in the 1490s (Brooks 2002: 19–26).

The 'woman from Sevilla' was incorporated into the household of the man who led the town of Ticamaya in resistance against Spanish rule. In areas where the reception of the colonists was more positive, Spanish men moved into native households. In the same letter from 1536 describing the captivity of the woman of Sevilla, the governor complained about mutinous men of the colony who 'took pleasure in an establishment outside the town'. The word used, *estancia*, implies a farming household or community that contrasted with the official town under the governor's authority. His complaint reiterated one he had made a year earlier, when he was more direct: the rebellious elements in his party were engaged in sexual liaisons outside the Spanish population: 'they go to their women and houses'. Like the later *estancia*, the 'houses' where these Spanish rebels went were located outside the official colonial town. Again, the governor used the term 'women' to differentiate these sexual relationships taking place between Spanish men and indigenous women in indigenous settlements from the Christian marriages he recognized.

Sexual relations across group boundaries in the early colony were likely critical to its survival. The initial population of San Pedro at its establishment in 1536 was fifty *vecinos*. By the end of the sixteenth century the count of *vecinos* dwindled to eight, yet San Pedro remained a viable city. Its population may well have included offspring of the kinds of liaisons reported in earlier colonial records, who would have lacked necessary credentials for vecindad. While not yet subject to classification in racialized *casta* terms, the offspring of Spanish-indigenous liaisons was in fact 'creolized'. Yet the term *criollo* was used in sixteenth-century documents, as elsewhere in the Americas, to

BECOMING ONE OR MANY   71

describe a person raised in the colonial city where he continued to live. The most relevant fact for identity seems to have been distinguishing those with local roots from those who came into the town from elsewhere (cf. Palmié 2007: 69).

A distinction between local and non-local was also relevant in *pueblos de indios*. Censuses dating to the late seventeenth and early eighteenth centuries provide examples of many terms that would later be enlisted in the classificatory logic of *casta*, particularly *mestizo* and *mulato*. However, the most consistently noted departure from the taken-for-granted identity of *indio* in these surveys is the use of the term *forastero*, meaning non-local person. These censuses record instances of movement of individuals to other *pueblos de indios* for marriage. In the home community they are listed by name and described as *ausente* ('absent'). In the town of residence, the same person is listed and labelled *forastero* or *forastera*. *Criollo*, seen only in documents about Spanish *vecinos* living in cities, and *forastero*, employed only in descriptions of the population of *pueblos de indios*, are both intelligible as terms related, not to ancestry, but to stable identification with place.

In the late eighteenth century, terms like *forastero* singled out people who were not local in origin. A few individuals were distinguished from others in a town by the use of *casta* terms, but these were not mobilized consistently, even in the late eighteenth century. Cross-cutting these two frameworks, the administrator registering population might single out some residents as different from the main population using a novel term, *ladino*. The sense of *ladino* and of the *casta* terms employed emerges most clearly in practice when we can examine how the same population is registered over time.

In 1780 the residents of the *pueblos de indios* Ticamaya and Candelaria were listed as part of a comprehensive summary of payments of a special assessment collected by the commander of Fort Omoa. In the case of all the Spanish towns, *ranchos* ('ranches'), and the fort itself, individuals paying this assessment were listed with no *casta* terms. Some individuals, given the honorific title 'Don', were assessed double what was charged to all others. The lack of *casta* terms is notable even in the town of Omoa itself, where census records a few years earlier employed the *casta* terms *negro* and *pardo*, as well as the otherwise rare term *blanco*.

In the case of the two *pueblos de indios*, each town listing was headed with an introduction citing a contrast *within* the town: at Ticamaya, the list is of '*indios* as well as *ladinos*', while at Candelaria, the description reads '*indios naturales*... and the other *ladinos*'. The Ticamaya document is divided into two groups, one headed *indios*, the other *ladinos*. The Candeleria document has only one heading, *indios*, but towards the end of the page, a group of names are linked with a parenthesis and the word *mulatos* is added in the margin. In the Ticamaya document, the first person listed under the heading *ladino* is described as 'Don Ignacio Nicolas de Yzarraga, Español'. The word *forasteros* precedes the last pair of names. To confuse matters further, eight of the men listed in the Candeleria document under the heading *indios* also appear in the accounting from Omoa itself (where they were temporarily living). In the Omoa summary, they are not explicitly described with the *casta* term *indios*; instead, they are listed under the heading 'Candeleria', the name of their town.

While there were clearly people recognized as of different statuses and kinds in the two small *pueblos de indios*, the way that terminology was used simply cannot be reduced to any logic of racial or ethnic identity. The main contrast, as indicated by the superscriptions on both documents, was between *indios* and others (*demas*) collectively called *ladinos*. *Ladino* has generally been understood as a term applied in Central America to people of indigenous descent recognized as hispanicized, either through language, dress, everyday practices, or a combination.

In the Ticamaya listing, the term covers a heterogeneous group, including residents of non-local origin, a person marked explicitly as high in status and 'Spanish' in affiliation, and others of less certain status. While these others are not explicitly marked in *casta* terms, the listing from Candelaria, which lacks a clear separation of *ladinos* like that employed at Ticamaya, does have a small group labelled with the racialized *casta* term *mulato*, in the ideal *casta* system meaning a person whose parents were of different groups (i.e. African and indigenous).

The 1780 lists can be compared with a census for the same places from 1809, an ecclesiastical document for the curate of San Pedro Sula. According to its heading, it is a combined listing of *indios* of Ticamaya and Candelaria. The names of most residents have no *casta* descriptions. The two exceptions are families composed of a woman identified as *mulata*, a child explicitly identified as *indio* or *india*, and the child's father, in one case deceased, also explicitly labelled *indio*.

One of these women, Eugenia Gertrudis, was already resident in Ticamaya in 1780. At the time, she was not distinguished in *casta* status, but was described as the wife of Santiago Ferrera. By 1809, Ferrera, still described as a tribute-paying *indio* of Ticamaya, had died. His widow, named Gertrudis Andara in this document, was now labelled *mulata*, contrasting with her deceased husband and living son, Juan Lazaro Ferrera, enumerated as *indio*.

Between 1780 and 1809 the assessment of the *casta* status of Eugenia Gertrudis Andara, wife of Santiago Ferrera, changed; she went from being an unmarked *india* to a marked *mulata*, a person of *indio* and African descent. At the same time, her civil marital status changed: in 1780 the wife of a living *indio*, in 1809 she was the widow of the same man. Why did the Spanish census taker in 1809, Jose Manuel Troncoso, see her as *mulata* when Juan Galindo, the official recording payments of tribute in 1780, had not? Eugenia Gertudis herself might have offered this identification, since it would have changed her status with respect to tribute expectations. We have recorded late eighteenth-century petitions from individuals asking to be reclassified as *mulato*, apparently to be exempt from certain payments. That this change (or clarification) was ambiguous either to authorities, to her own community, or both, is suggested by the insistence that her son—then twenty-four years old and single—was an *indio*, in violation of *casta* norms under which he would have been otherwise demarcated.

The two women described as *mulatas* must have stood out quite specifically in Ticamaya to be the only individuals with a *casta* classification. It would be easy to conclude that they were singled out through physical characteristics, since that is the logic both of race and racialized *casta*. Nonetheless, the patterns of discrimination of persons in late eighteenth-century Honduras do not support this. Locality of origin is most consistently marked, whether by the term *ausente* (still in use in 1809), *forastero*, or *criollo*. The labelling of some residents of Ticamaya and Candelaria in 1780 as *ladino* seems best understood as an overarching way to recognize otherness. The people grouped as *ladinos* could include higher-ranking Spanish, people of recognized mixed race, and others simply from somewhere else, all understood in contrast to the unity of the *pueblo de indios*.

Making other things: the materiality of everyday practice

We can compare the diversity in descriptions of civil and *casta* status at Ticamaya from 1780 to 1809 to the archaeological materials for the same period (Blaisdell-Sloan 2006; Sheptak et al. 2011a; Sheptak et al. 2011b; Sheptak 2013). One household there used and discarded a variety of colonial Spanish tradition materials, trash that was produced when the summary of population singled out some people living at Ticamaya as *ladino*. This household yielded the only examples of European tradition ceramics recovered from the site, fragments from at least seven majolica vessels. Blown glass fragments show that commodities contained in glass bottles were consumed by the residents of this household. Bones from pig and cow in the same area are the only examples of European domesticated animals recovered from the site. Warning us not to simply see this as a household of 'Spanish' identity, the same area yielded three very small quartzite flakes, evidence of the practice of indigenous stone-working techniques. It is likely that the people who used this unusual assemblage would have been accounted as *ladinos* under the logic employed in 1780. They served food in distinctive, non-local tableware, and the food they served was itself unusual, incorporating pork and beef, and whatever was originally contained in the bottles (possibly wine or vinegar). They were other in practice, not simply in an abstract classification.

The residents of this household were not the only people of late eighteenth-century Ticamaya who showed signs of hybrid practices. Bottle glass and local chipped stone formed part of the household trash of a second household. Foodways attested here were different, with bone from turtles and caimans, edible snail shells, and a net-weight, an indication of fishing. The residents of this household hunted both large and small wild animals. It would be tempting here to see this as the location of an indigenous family, using long-established practices to provision themselves, whilst enjoying limited access to some bottled commodities. Yet this also would be too simple a story. The profile of this household in terms of hunting and fishing departs from previous generations at Ticamaya as much as the household using beef and pork does. Like the more European-appearing household, this second family was also living a hybrid life.

Hand-modelled earthenwares from this household, in the form of bowls and small jars, were either unslipped or slipped red and fired at low temperatures (see Figs 3.2 and 3.3). In form and surface colour they appear similar to those from earlier households at the site. Yet they were manufactured using slightly different techniques, as if the goal was to make the same kinds of vessels, but the makers lacked knowledge of the steps of production employed by others living at Ticamaya before them. The assemblage of hand-built, low fired earthenware pottery from contemporary Omoa shows the same subtle traces of different techniques. Facets on the body suggest the use of paddle and anvil, a technique unknown in pre-Hispanic pottery from the region. Some fragments show evidence of the use of sharp-edged punches, probably pieces of metal (such as nails) to apply modest decorative devices.

Pottery like this was a product of a hybrid industry, combining indigenous techniques of forming, finishing, and firing vessels with novel ways of producing the same, or very similar, vessels. We believe it is no accident that

Fig. 3.2. Brushed, red slipped jar rim from Omoa, c.1770–1800.

Fig. 3.3. Unslipped bowl rim from Omoa, c.1770–1800. (a) Exterior showing groove and punched marks made using punch. (b) Interior showing facet from forming with paddle.

these innovations become visible at the same time that documents tell us that groups of men from the *pueblos de indios* were living and working at Omoa, and some men from *pueblos de indios* married women, eventually identified in censuses as of African descent, who relocated to their towns, including from Omoa.

A recent analysis of handmade earthenwares in Caribbean sites describes them as a pragmatic innovation in response to 'conditions of slavery and the failure of the markets to meet demands of colonial populations' (Hauser 2011: 437). Hauser (ibid. 437–42) argues that between 1760 and 1810 in Jamaica, such new ceramics were a product of household production by women. Jamaica was a major port in the traffic in African slaves that ultimately reached Honduras (Cáceres 2003). We suggest that at least some of the production of hand-built earthenware pottery in Omoa and Ticamaya reflected the participation in ceramic production of women of African descent, not inculcated in local ways of making pottery.

Rina Cáceres has studied the routes through which enslaved Africans came to Omoa (Cáceres Gomez 2003). She identified the surname 'Andara' among lists of *pardo* families in Omoa, just prior to the 1780 record showing Eugenia Andara living at Ticamaya. Around the same time, we see new foodways in one household at Ticamaya, with emphasis on collecting riverine resources and hunting a wider range of wild animals than was previously attested. We suggest that just as the *ladino* families in Ticamaya were marked by distinct practices of everyday life, so also the households of women like Eugenia Gertrudis, and possibly others composed of couples that also crossed *casta* lines but were never singled out, engaged in hybrid domestic practices that are visible in the material register.

By 1809, the distinctive position of a few women at Ticamaya was flagged using *casta* terms. Rather than serving as a classificatory categorization of blood purity, which would have required their children to be labelled differently than they are, the description *mulata* for two women may have been recognition of a heritage distinctive enough to be recognized, which these women reproduced in observable daily practices.

The kind of hybridity we are suggesting is evident in pottery from late eighteenth-century Omoa and Ticamaya is, of course, well recognized in the archaeological literature on what has been called 'colonoware': pottery produced in the Americas using hand-building techniques and earthenware firing, where scholars debate whether we can see the distinct contributions of African-descendant and indigenous producers. We agree with others who have suggested that such new pottery be treated not as divisible between two distinct pre-existing cultural traditions but as products of emergence of novel practices in changing communities (Card 2007; Silliman 2010; Hauser 2011). Rather than tracing stable identities and their mixtures in ceramic form or manufacture, archaeological materials are media for the production of the new colonial order.

In the late eighteenth-century district of San Pedro Sula, labour was extracted primarily from indigenous and African-descendant people, and marriage alliances between people of these different ancestries led to cohabitation in what have usually been seen as homogeneous Indian villages. Yet we would not want to leave our account at this, suggesting a kind of stratification of European-derived elites over a group of labourers that could be subsumed as 'non-European'. The hybridity of cultural production in colonial Honduras also provides us with evidence of the articulation of practices, and their specific materialities, linking Spanish traditions and *pueblos de indios*, in what has been called, we think inadequately, religious syncretism.

Writing about the Maya conversion in Yucatan, Hanks (2010: 8) notes that syncretism describes Christian practices as a thin layer on a 'deep indigenous core'. We follow him in seeing conversion as something more extensive, that cannot be sorted out into a simple mixture of two pre-existing things. Churches have often been treated as unambiguous markers of European institutions that penetrated passive indigenous communities. Yet we have noted that churches were a major focus of indigenous community practices throughout the colonial period (Sheptak et al. 2011a). Conversion to Roman Catholicism was key to the persistence of *pueblos de indios*.

In theory, every *pueblo de indios* required its own church. Archaeological surveys of the district of Santa Barbara, upriver from the San Pedro district, identified seven possible churches (Weeks and Black 1991; Weeks 1997). These buildings yielded all the European materials recovered by this project (glazed ceramics, roof tiles, iron nails, and glass beads). In consequence, they might be viewed as European intrusions into the *pueblos de indios* where they were found. Yet the documentary record produced by the people of one of these towns, Yamala, tells us something quite different about the place of the church in community life.

By the eighteenth century, the *pueblo de indios* of Yamala was investing substantially to replace an original church made of perishable materials. In 1778, the community petitioned for relief from taxation so they would have the resources to complete rebuilding of the church. The original church is described as small and rustic, with a thatched roof. In its place, the *pueblo de indios* had begun construction of a wood, brick, and partly stone church. In 1796, the *pueblo de indios* initiated a new request to fund the final expenses for completing the church roof. Their petition was opposed by Honduran authorities, who would have lost income, and ultimately, they were told to use assets in land and cattle owned by local *cofradias* to cover the costs.

Cofradias were voluntary aid associations that patronized masses on saints' days. In 1742, Yamala's *cura* identified one *cofradia* there, dedicated to the Annunciation. In 1768, another document identified two land parcels held by the *cofradias* of San Juan (the town's patron saint) and Nuestra Señora de la Encarnación. Thus, by the time of the rebuilding of the church, there were at least two, and possibly three, *cofradias*, controlling property in land and cattle, and also holding custody of sacred images and regalia used in masses and processions. The 1768 document also referenced the participation of Yamala's saints' images in inter-village visitation of patron saints, a practice known in the Lenca language as *guancasco*. In both *cofradia* and *guancasco* celebrations, churches—seen as the epitome of the architecture of European institutions of colonization—were sites for practices directed by residents of colonial *pueblos de indios*.

Catholic religious observances were a focus of community identity in colonial *pueblos de indios*. The significance of saints' images to indigenous communities, and of the churches where they were housed, is made clear in petitions in 1679 by the people of Jetegua, and twenty years later by the people of Masca (later Candelaria), both in the district of San Pedro (Sheptak 2013). Each asked permission to relocate to gain security from raiding pirates. Each cited the sacking of their churches and the removal of the images and sacred vessels as losses motivating the desire to move. When Masca described its move in later years, it listed the reestablishment of the church along with houses and agricultural fields as defining its refounding (Sheptak 2013, 2019).

Discussion: mediating difference

Honduras is an excellent case study for what has been covered by the term 'creolization': the creation of a new population with heterogeneous racial or ethnic roots. The Honduran case demonstrates the need for concepts that are more flexible, and that are able to link across different domains—daily practice, religion, marriage, and speech—that have been subjects of distinct theoretical debates about creolization, syncretism, and the like.

Historian Rina Cáceres (Cáceres Gomez 2003: 133) noted that in Honduras, Spanish colonial structures provided opportunities for African descendants to find power, citing the use of the honorific title 'Don' as an example. Writing about what might be seen from the outside as a single group to be treated as one party in a model of creolization or syncretism, she notes that along the Caribbean coast, people called *negros* (blacks), *mulattos*, and *pardos* did not form a homogeneous social order. To the contrary, identities were constructed around social roles in the framework of complex geopolitical relations, which explains the diversity of paths followed by different groups of Africans and their descendants in the region. Their identities were not fixed in time but rather were the products of the ever-changing relationships between these groups and the elites in power, and of the tactics those of African descent used to overcome exclusion. We would extend her insights to include the *pueblos de indios* as well. Far from occupying a single, simply defined place in a hierarchical order, people from *pueblos de indios* used tactics to find places where they could persist and thrive in a colonial society designed to exploit them.

Drawing on the work of Michel de Certeau (1984), we have suggested that a concept of 'tactics' is particularly useful in understanding and representing the Honduran colonial case (Sheptak 2019). Tactics are 'ways that human subjects occupy social landscapes that they do not entirely control...exceeding the intentions of those who seek control, seizing the moment for one's own pragmatic ends' (Sheptak et al. 2011a: 149–50). Some of the tactics people of African descent and residents of *pueblos de indios* used were innovative, taking advantage of the materials and opportunities at hand, regardless of their origins. So, for example, in making petitions to resist new labour demands, the people of Masca used Spanish discursive forms to advance claims based on community roles in a multi-community network, basically re-envisioning the hierarchy of the Spanish colony in a flatter form. The residents of small eighteenth-century *pueblos de indios* like Ticamaya and Candelaria ensured their demographic survival through marriages that incorporated new people, including African descendants, who quite likely brought with them innovative foodways and whose approaches to producing craft products may have introduced slightly different techniques to the local earthenware tradition. Marriage across presumed racial or *casta* boundaries already had a long history in Honduras—at least as long as the first violent and peaceful entanglements between Spanish colonists and *pueblos de indios* in the sixteenth century. It is actually difficult to say whose strategies or tactics we are talking about, because these practices were taken up on the spot by those engaged in the task of survival without concern for group identification.

We suggest that the concept of ethnogenesis works better to aid understanding this situation. Ethnogenesis, in contrast with creolization, emphasizes what emerges from the situation, not what preceded it. Barbara Voss (2008), in her study of a new 'Californio' identity at the eighteenth-century Spanish Presidio of San Francisco, demonstrated that what emerged cannot be separated into component parts. In Honduras, the emergent identity may best be understood as Honduran, or even (in the area we study) more locally as *sampedrano*. Attempts to disarticulate the new identities into discrete pieces and trace their origins inevitably end up privileging some participants in the project of persistence over others. Was Eugenia Gertrudis Andara an

80   ROSEMARY A. JOYCE AND RUSSELL N. SHEPTAK

india, as she was recorded in 1780, or *mulata*, as in 1809? Do we need to credit her contributions to the survival of Ticamaya as a viable community to one *casta* group or the other?

Our conclusion is closest to the argument made by Stephan Palmié (2007: 71), who sees *casta* as hybridity: 'an impossibly complicated taxonomy of degrees of racial mixtures within a culturally rapidly homogenizing social sector.' Where Palmié stresses the place of *casta* in the social sector distinct from enslaved Africans and the corporate *pueblos de indios*, we see in Honduras a more pervasive presence of 'culturally rapidly homogenizing' social situations in which *vecinos* of Spanish towns, residents of *pueblos de indios*, and free and enslaved African descendants were often enlisted together in new social formations. Like Palmié, we see these processes taking place through novel quotidian practices in the shadow of the Spanish colonial state—new ways of eating, pairing up sexually, comporting themselves, and interacting with one another—that completely evaded legal categories and ethnic labels. While the literature on creolization is useful in focusing our attention on language, population, and practices, in the end, the continued emphasis on defining boundaries is problematic. Like William Hanks (2010: 93–4), who sees the attempt 'to divide an indigenous inside from a Hispanicized exterior' as 'sundering the person into two parts', possible only if each belongs to a distinct social field, we argue for the emergence of new forms through tactical engagement in linguistic and material practices. In the Honduran colony, despite the surface appearance of spatial segregation of distinct groups, what we see is actors taking up positions in social fields that link those different spaces, and gave rise to the historically attested shared project of colonial survival from which emerged a Honduran identity.

References

Bakhtin, M. 1984. *Problems of Dostoevsky's Poetics*. C. Emerson (trans.). Minneapolis: University of Minnesota Press.

Bakhtin, M. 1986. *Speech Genres and Other Late Essays*. C. Emerson and M. Holquist (eds). V. McGee (trans.). Austin: University of Texas Press.

Blaisdell-Sloan, K. 2006. *An Archaeology of Place and Self: The Pueblo de Indios of Ticamaya, Honduras (1300–1800 AD)*. Ann Arbor: UMI.

Brooks, J. F. 2002. *Captives and Cousins: Slavery, Kinship, and Community in the Southwest Borderlands*. Chapel Hill: University of North Carolina Press.

Cáceres Gómez, R. 2003. 'On the frontiers of the African Diaspora in Central America: the African origins of San Fernando de Omoa'. In P. Lovejoy and D. Trotman (eds), *Trans-Atlantic Dimensions of Ethnicity in the African Diaspora*. London: Continuum, pp. 115–37.

Cañizares-Esguerra, J. 2007. 'Creole Colonial Spanish America'. In C. Stewart (ed.), *Creolization: History, Ethnography, Theory*. Walnut Creek: Left Coast Press, pp. 26–45.

Card, J. 2007. *The Ceramics of Colonial Ciudad Vieja, El Salvador: Culture Contact and Social Change in Mesoamerica*. Ann Arbor: UMI.

de Certeau, M. 1984. 'Making Do: Uses and Tactics'. In *The Practice of Everyday Life*, S. Rendail (trans.). Berkeley: University of California Press, pp. 29–42.

Hanks, W. F. 1987. 'Discourse genres in a theory of practice'. *American Ethnologist* 14: 668–92.

Hanks, W. F. 2005. 'Pierre Bourdieu and the practice of language'. *Annual Review of Anthropology* 34: 67–83.

Hanks, W. F. 2010. *Converting Words: Maya in the Age of the Cross*. Berkeley: University of California Press.

Hasemann, G. 1986. *Investigaciones Arqueológicas en la Fortaleza de San Fernando y el Asentamiento Colonial de Omoa*. Tegucigalpa: Instituto Hondureño de Antropología e Historia.

Hauser, M. 2011. 'Routes and roots of empire: pots, power, and slavery in the 18th-century British Caribbean'. *American Anthropologist* 113: 431–47.

Herzog, T. 2003. *Defining Nations: Immigrants and Citizens in Early Modern Spain and Spanish America*. New Haven: Yale University Press.

Joyce, R. A., R. N. Sheptak, and L. A. Wilkie. 2008. 'Arqueología y la comunidad y la Fortaleza de Omoa: un informe sobre la marcha de los trabajos. Simposio Internacional *Esclavitud, Ciudadania y Memoria: Puertos Menores en el Caribe y el Atlantico'*. Del 13 al 16 de noviembre 2008, Museo de Antropología e Historia de San Pedro Sula, y Fortaleza San Fernando de Omoa, Honduras.

Katzew, I. 2004. *Casta Painting: Images of Race in Eighteenth-Century Mexico*. New Haven: Yale University Press.

Lightfoot, K. G. 1995. 'Culture contact studies: redefining the relationship between prehistoric and historical archaeology'. *American Antiquity* 60: 199–217.

Lightfoot, K. G., A. Martinez, and A. M. Schiff. 1998. 'Daily practice and material culture in pluralistic social settings: an archaeological study of culture change and Ppersistence from Fort Ross, California'. *American Antiquity* 63: 199–222.

Lokken, P. 2004. 'Useful enemies: seventeenth-century piracy and the rise of pardo militias in Spanish Central America'. *Journal of Colonialism and Colonial History* 5(2): 1–18.

Newson, L. 1986. *The Cost of Conquest: Indian Decline in Honduras Under Spanish Rule*. Boulder: Westview Press.

Palka, J. 2005. *Unconquered Lacandon Maya: Ethnohistory and Archaeology of Indigenous Culture Change*. Gainesville: University Press of Florida.

Palmié, S. 2007. 'The "c-word" again: from colonial to postcolonial semantics'. In C. Stewart (ed.), *Creolization: History, Ethnography, Theory*. Walnut Creek: Left Coast Press, pp. 63–83.

Sheptak, R. N. 2007. 'Los Toqueguas de la costa Norte de Honduras en la época colonial'. *Yaxkin* 13: 140–57.

Sheptak, R. N. 2013. *Colonial Masca in Motion: Tactics of Persistence of a Honduran Indigenous Community*. Unpublished PhD dissertation, Faculty of Archaeology, Leiden University. http://hdl.handle.net/1887/20999.

Sheptak, R. N. 2019. 'Moving Masca: persistent indigenous communities in Spanish colonial Honduras'. In H. Law Pezzarossi and R. Sheptak (eds), *Indigenous Persistence in the Colonized Americas*. Albuquerque: University of New Mexico Press, pp. 19–38.

Sheptak, R., K. Blaisdell-Sloan, and R. A. Joyce. 2011a. 'In-between people in colonial Honduras: reworking sexualities at Ticamaya'. In B. L. Voss and E. Casella (eds), *The Archaeology of Colonialism: Intimate Encounters and Sexual Effects*. Cambridge: Cambridge University Press, pp. 156–72.

Sheptak, R. N. and R. A. Joyce. 2019. 'Hybrid cultures: the visibility of the European invasion of Caribbean Honduras in the sixteenth century'. In C. L. Hofman and F. W. M. Keehnen (eds), *Material Encounters and Indigenous Transformations in the Early Colonial Americas: Archaeological Case Studies*. Leiden: Brill, pp. 219–35.

Sheptak, R., R. A. Joyce, and K. Blaisdell-Sloan. 2011b. 'Pragmatic choices, colonial lives: resistance, ambivalence, and appropriation in northern Honduras'. In M. Liebmann and M. Murphy (eds), *Enduring Conquests*. Santa Fe: School for Advanced Research, pp. 149–72.

Sherman, W. L. 1979. *Forced Native Labor in Sixteenth-Century Central America*. Lincoln: University of Nebraska Press.

Silliman, S. 2005. 'Culture contact or colonialism? Challenges in the archaeology of native North America'. *American Antiquity* 70: 55–74.

Silliman, S. 2010. 'Indigenous traces in colonial spaces: archaeologies of ambiguity, origins, and practice'. *Journal of Social Archaeology* 10: 28–58.

Twinam, A. 1999. *Public Lives, Private Secrets: Gender, Honor, Sexuality and Illegitimacy in Colonial Spanish America*. Stanford: Stanford University Press.

Voss, B. 2008. *The Archaeology of Ethnogenesis: Race and Sexuality in Colonial San Francisco*. Berkeley: University of California Press.

Weeks, J. 1997. 'The Mercedarian mission system in Santa Bárbara de Tencoa, Honduras'. In J. Gasco, G. Smith, and P. Fournier-Garcia (eds), *Approaches to the Historical Archaeology of Mexico, Central and South America.* Los Angeles: The Institute of Archaeology, UCLA, pp. 91–100.

Weeks, J. and N. Black. 1991. 'Mercedarian missionaries and the transformation of Lenca society in Western Honduras, 1550–1700'. In D. H. Thomas (ed.), *Columbian Consequences,* Vol. 3: *The Spanish Borderlands in Pan American Perspective.* Washington, DC: Smithsonian Institution Press, pp. 245–61.

Weik, T. 2004. 'Archaeology of the African Diaspora in Latin America'. *Historical Archaeology* 38: 32–49.

4

Other Than Human Hybridity?

Timothy Clack

But why disappoint them? If he were to stumble and fall, cut himself open, knock himself out, then be set upon by wolvogs or pigoons, what difference would it make to anyone but himself? The Crakers are doing fine, they don't need him anymore. For a while they'll wonder where he's gone, but he's already provided an answer to that: he's gone to be with Crake. He'll become a secondary player in their mythology, such as it is—a sort of backup demiurge. He'll be falsely remembered. He won't be mourned.

Margaret Atwood (2003), *Oryx and Crake*

Introduction

Atwood's searing post-apocalyptic vision in *Oryx and Crake* is one where the concept of hybridity, both biological and cultural, is examined through the interaction of human, non-human, and 'in-between' entities. A world is presented where unintended and unexpected consequences shape the future of humanity.

The history of humanity is one of evolution, migration, and creativity. As such, it would be logical to assume that the archaeology of the deep past might hold significant evidence of hybridity. Not only between groups from the same species but also perhaps from separate but contemporaneous species. After all, recent findings have suggested that the present phenomenon of a solitary human species on earth was more the exception than the rule (Spoor 2015; Haile-Salassie et al. 2016; Detroit et al. 2019; Haile-Salassie et al. 2019). Moreover, the implication is that migratory waves, such as the 'Out of Africa' dispersals and Eurasian expansions and refluxes, were highly likely to have put species into long-term contact in multiple locations. Despite being the primary focus of this book, modern humans (*Homo sapiens*) may not

Timothy Clack, *Other than Human Hybridity?* In: *Archaeologies of Cultural Contact: At the Interface.* Edited by: Timothy Clack and Marcus Brittain, Oxford University Press. © Oxford University Press 2022.
DOI: 10.1093/oso/9780199693948.003.0005

have been the only species to exhibit the capacity for hybridity. Indeed, this chapter raises some potential evidence of cultural hybridity in other species, in particular Neanderthals (*Homo neanderthalensis*) and chimpanzees. It also articulates the potential for hybridity as an avenue of research in these contexts.

The question of non-human culture has received considerable multi-disciplinary scrutiny (see Laland and Galef 2009). A number of species have received attention, particularly the great apes and cetaceans. As might be expected, the strongest cases for non-human culture are found amongst those species that live in extended social groups and demonstrate complex intelligence. Accordingly, the concept of culture is applied routinely to chimpanzee communities (e.g. Wrangham et al. 1994; Boesch and Boesch-Acherman 2000; Reynolds 2005). Indeed, the discipline of cultural *pan*thropology (Whiten et al. 2003) and reclassification of the *Homo* genus to include chimpanzees (Wildman et al. 2003) have both been proposed. These two proposals being underpinned by the observed similarities between chimpanzees, including both common (*Pan troglodytes*) and bonobo (*Pan paniscus*) species, and humans in terms of culture and biology respectively. Nonetheless, there is substantial opposition, in particular from anthropologists who assert the incomparability of animal traditions to human cognition, language, knowledge accumulation, and rituality (see Hill 2009). The same argument is found in objections to the idea of Neanderthal culture. For the purposes of this chapter the question should be asked: if chimpanzees and Neanderthals are/were cultural animals, is hybridity observed or possible?

The theme of power is recognized as significant in this discussion and explored. In alignment with human interactions, interspecies forms of contact and entanglement are not devoid of power, with dominance and subservience being key elements to the expression of social organization in certain species. At this point, it is important to consider the bio-evolutionary definition and use of the concept of hybridity. This tends to be used separately from the forms of cultural hybridity explored elsewhere in this book. However, this chapter posits that there are some useful conceptual and lexical associations between the biological and cultural and, at times, it may be appropriate to use the biological in conjunction with the cultural and material. Finally, rather than asking 'when' hybridity—or the capacity for it—emerged, this chapter asks instead what cognitive and material conditions might be illustrative of such capacity.

Biology to and from culture

Hybridity is 'a slippery, ambiguous term, at once literal and metaphorical, descriptive and explanatory' (Burke 2009: 54–5). The etymology of the word 'hybrid' is from the Latin *hibrida*, which referred to the offspring of a domesticated sow and a wild boar but was also applied, for example, to the child of a freeman and a slave. From the outset, the word has at once held both biology and culture in frame. In recent discourse, the biological notions of variation and cross-fertilization have proven useful and translated into the cultural domain. For example, taken out of the biological arena, hybrid vigour, the additional growth observed in hybrid organisms, might also apply to cultures, languages, and discourse genres (Stross 1999; see below).

As this chapter draws from ethological and human evolutionary studies, it is important to distinguish between biological and cultural understandings of hybridity. Although we must accept that biological models are socially constructed and, as such, biological and cultural hybridity may not be as different as first supposed, for instance in lexical and metaphorical allusion, there are clear differences in areas of application, meaning, and history.

There are three biological applications of the category of hybridity. The first is the admixture of populations from within a single species. The reproductive results from different domesticated canine breeds being a familiar example. The second concerns reproduction across two different species or genera. For example, the mule, the offspring of a male donkey and female horse. Both of these types of hybridity happen naturally but the latter is less common and often associated with human intervention, especially if relating to species whose natural territories do not overlap. The third is a chimera, a single organism that is composed of cells from two or more individuals, i.e. at least two sets of DNA are present. These occur naturally in a number of circumstances (e.g. when a foetus absorbs its twin) but modern surgical (e.g. bone marrow transplantation) and reproductive technologies (e.g. genetic modification of cells to produce different embryonic origins) have opened further prospects. The possibility of generating human organs inside of human-pig chimeras via a process called interspecies blastocyst complementation, for example, has stimulated considerable ethical concern (Koplin and Wilkinson 2019; see also Capps 2017).

The strict biological definition of a species states that it is reproductively isolated. However, as indicated above, many clearly defined species regularly hybridize often to the point that new species emerge. This has posed problems in taxonomically classifying hybrids and their conservation status.

Pacheco-Sierra et al. (2018) have, for example, explored genetic admixture in the context of the American (*Crocodylus acutus*) and Morelet's (*Crocodylus moreletii*) species of crocodile. They identified two evolutionary distinct hybrid lineages, which are genetically discernible from the parental species. These species have been hybridizing biologically for millions of years, though purer and more isolated populations of each exist in different areas. Of most relevance to the discussion here, is their point that, to conserve only 'non-hybridized populations' is to exclude a range of long-term natural and adaptive diversity. Whilst the notion of a 'non-hybridized' population is more viable in biological terms than cultural ones, due to genetic levels of consistency exhibited inside the group, it still implies an inappropriate primordial essence. Given heterozygosity, complete genetic purity and uniformity is an impossibility (see below). That noted, the crocodilian case illustrates the hybridity cycle, whereby a 'hybrid form' becomes a 'purebred' and then parent of another hybrid (Stross 1999). Applying to both the biological and cultural domains, the hybridity cycle captures the tension between dynamism and stasis and the staging of periods of both, driven potentially by geographical segregation. In reference to the hybridity cycle, we need to recognize that although there is a requirement to envision 'pre-hybrid states', there is no such thing as an anterior purity.

When taken out of the organic context, the descriptive lexicon associated with biological hybridity tends to be used pejoratively. Despite the objectiveness of the categories and naturalness of the processes, terms such as 'mongrel', 'impurity', and even 'chimera' convey a sense of aberration, dilution, pollution, and/or enfeeblement. Associated negative meanings have transitioned from the biological to the cultural. The early biological approach to hybridity, for example, was to inform nineteenth-century European imperialist ideas associated with cultural origins and identity. Instead of two species mixing physically, hybridity in this sense referenced the mixture of two or more categories of culture or identity. In the colonial scheme, race was hierarchical, with 'whiteness' linked with intellectual and moral superiority. Hybridity was thus dangerous, politically charged, and reproductive of impure entities that upset the conventional social order.

From the late twentieth century, the concept of hybridity was rehabilitated. In postcolonial theory and other areas, hybridity was recognized as embodying positive and resistive forms of cultural translation (Burke 2009; Stockhammer 2012). The significance of power in the choreography of hybrid contexts has also been reappraised fruitfully (Bhabha 2007; Silliman 2009). It is interesting that a corresponding reinterpretation of hybridity might be also

88 TIMOTHY CLACK

proposed in biological terms on the basis of variability and fitness. Variability holds the potential for environmental adaptation and, as such, underpins natural and sexual selection. Heterogeneity and heterozygosity are in essence variability. Heterogeneity, is the condition of embodying non-uniform genetic and phenotypic composition and properties. This often refers to heterozygosity, where different variants of genes occupy the same location on corresponding chromosomes.

In relation to adaptation, the phenomenon of hybrid vigour, which is also referred to as heterosis or outbreeding enhancement, is relevant. Essentially, this relates to the increased growth rate, size, and fecundity often observed in a hybrid organism over its parents (Baker 1965: 83–8; Birchler et al. 2003). Oft-cited examples of hybrid vigour include the strength and endurance of the mule and enhanced yields realized from crossbred maize (Thrupp 2000). However, as humans demonstrate high levels of relatedness and comparatively limited genetic diversity (Hawks 2013), hybrid vigour precipitated by global migration has been suggested in explanation of the so-called Flynn effect, the increase in intelligence around the world over at least the past two centuries (Mackintosh 2011: 291). Migration and genetic exchange in the deep past are also likely to have resulted in forms of hybrid vigour which, in turn, might have manifested in power relations. To be stronger, more intelligent and creative, and/or additionally reproductively viable would offer opportunities for inter- and intra-group forms of social dominance.

There is not scope in this short chapter to make more than some provisional comments on the potential for hybridity research amongst human evolutionary and non-human subjects. Therefore, attention will focus on two particular cases: Neanderthals and chimpanzees. Preceding the discussion of these examples, it is worth reflecting on hominin cognitive evolution.

Neurological, cognitive, and material evolution

Hominin brain evolution involved periods of growth, reorganization, and lateralization. Despite physical evidence, however, it has proven difficult for researchers to relate neurobiological changes to cognitive and behavioural ones. It is certainly the case that neurological reorganization occurred relatively early in hominin evolution (Holloway et al. 2004) but that these changes did not result at the same time in traits considered to be part of the modern behavioural repertoire.

In modern humans, symbolism is associated with the left hemisphere and visuospatial skills with the right. Whilst there can be no gradual amplification of symbolic resonance (Gamble 1994), it is interesting to register that the related pattern of hemispheric lateralization is evidenced in australopithecine fossil data (Holloway 1997). Indeed, brain lateralization of different degrees is apparent in many hominin species (see Fig. 4.1). Sociality and communication—and later language—shaped the hominin brain and, in doing so, likely facilitated the development of the capacity for cultural hybridity.

The Neanderthal brain differs from that of modern humans in a number of ways (Bruner et al. 2003). The size of the two species' brains overlap but those of adult Neanderthals tend to be larger—endocranial volume of 1520 cc in Neanderthals and 1340 cc in modern humans on average—but this is correlated with their larger bulk (Klein 2009: 377–8). Among humans, moreover, it is known that the internal organization of the brain is more relevant to cognition than absolute size. Thus, differences in patterns of brain development contribute to contrasting cognitive capabilities. Gunz et al. (2010), for example, have shown that Neanderthals demonstrated unique patterns of brain development after birth, especially during the first year. The connections between brain regions are established during this period of neurological plasticity and in humans are important for higher-order social and

Fig. 4.1. Photograph of four hominin endocasts: (from left to right) Neanderthal, AMH, *Homo erectus* and *Australopithecus africanus* (photo: T. Clack and Natural History Museum London).

communicative functions. The expression of different cognition in material remains should also be considered.

The issue of whether cultural hybridity may only be presupposed by a robust notion of 'culture' and the advent of symbolism is complex. On the one hand, if culture is present then hybridity is unlikely to be absent. On the other hand, what if there are only episodic or contested indications of cultural or symbolic behaviour? The attribution of culture to hominins is notoriously difficult, especially on the basis of limited archaeological evidence. A range of evidence is often proposed as indicating culture, including: manufacture of meta-technologies; adaptation of fire; complex social organization; environmental inhabitation, e.g. home-basing; symbolic markers, e.g. parietal and portable art; and mortuary routine. The point is that this evidence is highly selective, intermittent, and open to misinterpretation. Moreover, absence of evidence is not evidence of absence, and complex behaviour does not have to be mirrored in complex material culture. Although these advanced behaviours may not in themselves indicate culture, the more of them that are present in the same context the greater likelihood that culture is present. The rationale being that such characteristics are likely underpinned by creativity, pedagogy, and symbolic and grammatical communication.

Archaeological evidence suggests that the onset of cognitive modernity and with it the clear potential for linguistic and cultural hybridity, seems to have occurred long *after* the emergence of anatomically modern humans. Mithen (2000), for example, argues that modern cognition originated with the onset of some fashion of neurological fluidity, whereby different psychological domains or intelligences became integrated. In this sense, modern humans might be considered the first to be possessed of uniquely hybrid minds, underpinned by the cognitive capacity to superimpose symbolic, natural history and other intelligences. Symbolism and language are, of course, inherently about mixture, albeit the latter underpinned by syntactic rules (Chomsky 1988; Deacon 1997).

The 'symbolic explosion' manifested in the material assemblages of the Upper Palaeolithic has been proposed as evidence for the emergence of cognitive fluidity and the related origins of art, religion, and language (Mithen 1996). It is worth mentioning that a range of evidence of symbolism has been proposed prior to the European Upper Palaeolithic (see e.g. Bednarik 1995; d'Errico et al. 2005) and may indicate either an earlier date for cognitive fluidity or, less likely, a more gradual and spasmodic emergence of higher cognitive functions. The Upper Palaeolithic exhibits a proliferation of advanced behaviours and symbolic artefacts (Mellars 1991; Lewis-Williams 2002;

Hayden 2003). Certain artefactual evidence from this period, for example therianthropic depictions and figurines, are themselves striking hybrid constructs the outcome of cultural, psychological, and environmental stimuli, with indisputably elaborate albeit largely contestable, if unknowable, meanings.

Dated to approx. 40,000 years ago, the mammoth ivory löwenmensch ('lion-man') figurine from Stadel Cave, Baden-Württemberg (see Fig. 4.2), is often asserted as the earliest indisputably symbolic art. It is also often interpreted as religious and associated with anthropomorphic supernatural beings

Fig. 4.2. The löwenmensch ('lion-man') figurine photographed from two angles. The statuette is carved mammoth ivory (height 311 mm, width 73 mm) from Hohlenstein-Stadel Cave, Asselfingen, Baden-Württemberg, Germany (photo: Y. Mühleis © Stuttgart State Office for Historic Preservation).

92 TIMOTHY CLACK

(Marshack 1990). The figure and associated artefacts, including arctic fox teeth and a cache of reindeer antlers, were excavated in an inner chamber of the cave. Wear on the figure suggests it was handled and passed around. In light of this, it has been proposed that the cave was a ritual location, 'where people would come together...to share a particular understanding of the world articulated through beliefs, symbolised in sculpture and acted out in rituals' (Cook 2007). More importantly for present purposes, and linked to contemporaneous evidence from nearby caves, including a smaller lion-headed human sculpture and other carved figures and flutes, it has been suggested that the löwenmensch indicates that, 'Aurignacian people may have practiced shamanism [and]...that it should be considered strong evidence for fully symbolic communication and cultural modernity' (Coolidge and Wynn 2011: 174).

The löwenmensch figure should be considered not only as an artefact but the hybrid outcome of cultural, cognitive, and environmental factors. The mixture of these different elements—reproduced through ritual articulation—informed a mythological worldview. The löwenmensch figure has been interpreted as a ritual object used in shamanic contexts (Cook 2007). With its lion head and human body, the figure may represent a shaman in flight and transformed into a cave lion. The ability to transpose knowledge and symbols from different cognitive domains indicates the capacity for abstract thought, culture, and hybrid acts.

Shamanism is, of course, a hybrid ritual act. It is a feature of contemporary societies (Walter and Fridman 2005) but has also played a prominent role in the past (Staller and Currie 2001; Aldhouse-Green 2005; Whitley 2009).[1] Experienced as ecstasy and 'magical flight' (also referred to 'soul flight' and, by psychologists, as altered states of consciousness), and induced by repetitive stimulation, purging, austerities, and sometimes psychoactive substances, the shaman is able to enter the spirit world (Eliade 1951). The shamanic flight takes many forms but includes frequently a separation from the physical body, translocation to the spirit world, and interaction with spirit entities. This flight might be experienced in corporeal form or in the transformed guise of animals or spirit allies (Winkelman 2012). On this basis, the Upper Palaeolithic parietal and portable art interpreted as shamanistic

---

[1] Interestingly, there persists some concern as to the validity and existence of the shaman except as an invention of the Western imagination (Winkelman 2012: 47). Although this is not the view of this author, the shaman, in this sense, could be proposed as the hybrid outcome of ethnographic practice and scientific categorization and interpretation.

(see e.g. Lewis-Williams 2002), is representative of a potential cognitive capacity for hybridization, especially if other markers of culture are present.

Humans and Neanderthals: bridging the species divide

The cognitive capabilities of the Neanderthals are also relevant for discussion of hybridity. Albeit with increasing opposition, it has been suggested that Neanderthals lacked the intellectual prowess to develop modern behaviours and technologies. Thus, sites which are associated with advanced technologies, in particular personal ornamentation, are interpreted as examples of imitation without understanding. The lack of clarity on Neanderthal language abilities further complicates discussion. The evidence implying language includes anatomical markers (e.g. hyoid bone and enlarged hypoglossal canal) and behavioural markers (e.g. burial and possible instances of symbolic imagery and material culture). From the confluence of anatomical, archaeological, and genetic evidence, it seems likely that Neanderthals did exhibit some language abilities, if not necessarily fully modern syntactic language. Nonetheless, the level of symbolic and linguistic skill exhibited remains highly contentious (Mithen 2007; Martinez et al. 2008; Dediu and Levinson 2018). In light of the evident contact and if Neanderthals were living in symbolic worlds, the case for interspecies hybridity could be a strong one.

A consequence of Neanderthals and anatomically modern humans being closely related, is that at certain times and places they interbred and produced fertile offspring. Owing to chronological overlap and co-existence between Neanderthals and modern humans, identification of 'hybrid specimens' possessing physical features from both species has been claimed (Duarte et al. 1999; Trinkaus et al. 2003; Soficaru et al. 2006; Rougier et al. 2007). Ancient DNA evidence from archaic hominins has also revealed a rich tapestry of genetic admixture between early modern humans, Neanderthals, and Denisovans (Slatkin and Racimo 2016). The genetic evidence for interbreeding is indisputable. Although it has proved difficult to disentangle, the Neanderthal genomic contribution to modern Eurasians varies but is up to 4 percent in certain places (Sankararaman et al. 2014; Vernot and Akey 2014). It has been suggested that 'many centuries of [biological] hybridization led to mosaic fossils with human cranial and dental features mixed with Neanderthal proportions' (Mason and Short 2011: 1). Clearly, if archaic hominins were in such proximity that they were in a position to transfer genetic material, it follows that cultural and material elements were also plausibly exchanged and

94 TIMOTHY CLACK

mixed. Unsurprisingly, the paucity of archaeological and fossil evidence from the deep past curtails investigations. Nonetheless, certain locations offer tantalizing albeit fragmentary potential glimpses of interspecies cultural admixture.

Southwest Europe during the Upper/Middle Palaeolithic transition offers perhaps the greatest available spatio-temporal conditions to explore the material dimensions of admixture between anatomically modern humans and Neanderthals. Is the material culture of the Châtelperronian evidence of an allochthonous development derived from contact between these two species? Whilst, in general, Aurignacian layers sit atop Châtelperronian ones and thus indicate a more recent date and discontinuity, at certain sites, such as Grotte du Reune and Arcy-sur-Cure, where the two industries are interstratified, this is not the case. In terms of artefacts, the Châtelperronian indicates continuity with Mousterian (Acheulean Type B), e.g. backed and retouched blades, but also some distinctive Upper Palaeolithic traits, e.g. scrapers and burins. Moreover, there is consistent evidence for bone manufacture and personal ornamentation.

The Châtelperronian has been recommended by some as offering clear indications of acculturation between late Middle Palaeolithic or pre-Aurignacian modern humans and Europe's final Neanderthal populations (Davies 2007; see also Mellars and Gravina 2008). Explanations that have been proposed linked to Neanderthal agency include imitation by Neanderthals (White 1993, 1995) and the collection and transportation of abandoned objects (Mellars 1996; d'Errico et al. 1998). Others reject acculturation models entirely and instead propose independent development (e.g. d'Errico et al. 1999). Given that there is no unequivocal evidence that interspecies cultural contact even occurred in southwest France, Tolmie (2013) also proposes an autochthonous development for the Châtelperronian. Put simply, she posits that it is unsurprising that two populations exposed to similar socioenvironmental pressures and sharing similar lithic industries would respond independently in the same manner (2013: 287–8). Thus, Tolmie suggests that archaeologists should focus less on acculturation to explain the assemblages of the Châtelperronian and more on the increasing need for communities to express cultural identity and group membership in response to ecological and climatic shifts. That noted, contact with another hominin species and concomitant social stresses, would likely precipitate greater concern for the expression of group identity.

The conclusions that Gravina et al. (this volume) present are understandably cautious, noting the importance of chronology, taphonomy, and disciplinary frameworks as drivers of various competing interpretations of the evidence. It is only with amplified understandings of sites and their stratification and temporal horizons that the potential to critically employ hybridity as an analytical concept for these timeframes can be assessed. The concept of acculturation, the term often used to describe what may be happening in the Châtelperronian, tends to imply short-term encounters rather than long-term entanglements. As Silliman (2009: 16) notes, 'this tends to downplay the severity of interaction and radically different levels of political power, and to privilege predefined cultural traits over creative or new cultural products'. With acculturation in archaeology often taken to indicate the reaction of subject groups to dominant ones, the complexities of bilateral and bicultural interaction are overlooked.

Thus, a related issue even in evolutionary contexts is that of power. Given the available evidence, which can only be interpreted in terms of greater technological and behavioural sophistication being demonstrated by modern humans, it is highly likely that in the late Middle Palaeolithic timeframe, contact, if and where it occurred, was far from neutral and Neanderthals lived a subordinate existence. This is characteristic of other hybrid contexts. For as Bhabha (2007) makes clear, hybridity is political and symbolic of the strategies the subaltern develops in order to adapt to their situations. Thus, in line with Tolmie's (2013) attempts to foreground environmental adaptation, it remains conceivable that the Châtelperronian was an adaptive response to changing socio-political circumstances resulting from some fashion of contact with modern humans. In such a scenario, those new behaviours and technologies brought into contact were mediated by existing social structures and meanings.

Given the current difficulties in recognizing the proximity through which Neanderthals and modern humans lived their lives, it is impossible to explore the types of entangled existences that may have been present in certain contexts. But if we accept the possibility of contact, interaction and entanglement between modern human and Neanderthals in the contexts of Southwest Europe but also perhaps areas of Asia, then interpretive value may be found in other inter-species considerations. Haraway's (2008) work, for example, has been particularly impactful in raising awareness of companion species and is relevant not least as power and dominance shape interactions between species. As Haraway (2008: 4) notes, 'to be one is always *to become* with many'. For example, Brives (2019: 124) recognizes how an approach formulated on reciprocity has, through what they term 'entanglement' and 'inclusive communities', the advantage of restoring respective agencies to different human and non-human entities (Stepanoff and Vigne 2019: 11, 14).

96 TIMOTHY CLACK

The biological concept of unconscious selection may also have some relevance in this discussion of inter-species cultural hybridity. Unconscious selection has played an enormous role in the evolution of certain species. The house mouse (*Mus musculus*), for example, has undergone morphological change whilst adapting to anthropized environments (Stepanoff and Vigne 2019: 9–10). Neanderthal communities would have adapted their behaviour to what they encountered in their environments, and it is tempting to acknowledge the possibility that this included modern humans. In this regard, it must be noted that behavioural transference has been observed to take place between humans and free-ranging populations of chimpanzees (Lestel 2004; Persson et al. 2008). There are other reasons for considering in more detail the case of chimpanzees and these will be explored below.

Relations of hybridity: the chimpanzee

For many decades it has been recognized that long-term studies of great ape communities offer analogical prospects for the interpretation of the evolutionary past. Indeed, the so-called 'Trimates', Dian Fossey, Jane Goodall, and Birutė Galdikas, were recruited by the archaeologist Louis Leakey in the 1960s to study gorillas, chimpanzees, and orangutans respectively in order to generate data for this and other purposes (Morell 1993).

Over the past two decades, there has been considerable research exploring culture in great apes. Whiten et al. (1999) conducted the first systematic large-scale investigation. Synthesizing over 150 years of observation, the group compared behaviours across populations to explore variability. Explained in terms of social innovation and learning, the study registered that thirty-nine of sixty-five behaviours were customary at one or more sites, but not all. Indeed, they were able to note a combined repertoire of highly distinctive behavioural patterns in each community. Incorporating long-term studies of populations in Borneo and Sumatra, Schaik et al. (2003) put the spotlight on orangutan cultural behaviour, which the authors defined as socially transmitted, geographically variable but not underpinned by ecological differences. On the basis of behaviours, such as social signals and specialized feeding techniques, the authors asserted boldly that 'great ape cultures exist, and may have done so for at least 14 million years'.

In the debate on non-human culture, a shift in focus from content to mechanism of transmission has proved helpful in shaping understanding. This has focused on vertical (intergenerational) and horizontal (peer-to-peer)

OTHER THAN HUMAN HYBRIDITY? 97

transmission, the tension between tradition and innovation, and the 'ratchet effect' underpinning complexity of form. Although the level of homogeneity of behaviour within a community has been proposed as providing a potential metric to explore social influence on learning, including the statistical signatures of rates, pathways, and patterns of spread (Laland et al. 2009: 189–96), there are no known examples in the literature of diffusion resulting in anything described as hybridity or similar. However, Sterelny (2009) notes that social education is not an individual trait but derived from interaction and, as such, niche construction, developmental plasticity, and hybrid learning. This fits with other research that claims certain learning is born out of a desire to conform, and can be independent of external reinforcement. This might relate to neurobiology, for example mirror neurons, that seem to facilitate in certain species of social animal, the 'tuning' of individuals to the actions and intentions of other group members (de Waal and Bonnie 2009).

Chimpanzees show flexibility of action that is pertinent for an apparently infinite range of contexts (McGrew 1992: 2) and some of this is likely attributed to social as well as environmental factors (McGrew 1983). For example, nut-cracking is exclusive to West African chimpanzees and leaf-grooming to East African ones (Reynolds 2005: 80–5). Whilst oil palm is present in the territorial ranges of the East African communities of Kasoje, Gombe, and Lope, Kasoje communities eschew its nutritional value (McGrew 1992: 10–14). Particular gestural patterns in the styles of grooming hand-clasps have been shown to distinguish chimpanzees into diverse behavioural groups (McGrew 1992: 68; 2004: 26). The practice in which participants clasp palm to palm with arms fully extended overhead, either or both then grasping the other's wrist or hand, is the description for so-called K-group behaviour. Alternative to this, the M-group behaviour, is where two participants make minimal contact, touching only through crossed wrists. The grooming hand-clasp of chimpanzees is a well-studied candidate for a non-subsistence form of cultural behaviour, and diffusion of cultural behaviour between groups can also be evinced from long-term studies. Two individuals at Kasoje from K-group emigrated to M-group, for example, and took with them the ability to produce and use bark tools for termite fishing.[2] The related behaviours subsequently spread throughout M-group (McGrew 1992: 81). It is unclear if

---

[2] Chimpanzee tool use has been documented since the 1960s, when Goodall first observed chimpanzees manufacturing twigs into crude tools for 'ant dipping'. Until that time scientists had thought that tool-making was an activity unique to humans. When Goodall sent a telegram to the archaeologist Louis Leakey detailing her observations, he made his now famous response, 'now we must redefine tool, redefine man, or accept chimpanzees as human' (Goodall pers. comm.).

the outcome of this inter-group transmission in the new context is in any way novel and, of course, any associated meanings are likely unknowable.

Chimpanzee behaviour often also becomes modified as a result of human influence. The process of habituation, whereby free-ranging chimpanzees are familiarized to the presence of human observers, often through food provisioning, changes natural patterns of feeding and ranging, including propensity for meat-eating, daily activities, and inter- and intra-group relationships (see Reynolds 1975). Chimpanzees have also been observed to imitate and emulate human behaviours that they have observed. Amongst free-ranging chimpanzees, individuals have learnt behaviours from their observers and modified them, including the use of levers to open provisioning boxes (Goodall 1986: 207) and making percussive noises on kerosene cans (Goodall 1988: 109–15). There are also countless relevant examples from captive and laboratory contexts: for example, the use of lexicon keyboards and other tools (Savage-Rumbaugh et al. 1998).

Chimpanzees engage routinely with human material culture in the contexts described but what is happening when they do? Are these behaviours in any way indicative of hybridity? Without a greater understanding of the proto-symbolic and cognitive worlds of chimpanzees, it is impossible to use the known examples as evidence of appropriation, objectivization, incorporation, or transformation. These are categories, which usually occur simultaneously, devised by Stockhammer (2012) in order to distinguish different elements of material entanglement:

- *Appropriation*. The process whereby personal possessions are created, including through making changes to objects;
- *Objectivization*. The ascription of an object to an existing category of objects, including the attribution of meaning;
- *Incorporation*. The competence to deal with the object in the 'right way'; and
- *Transformation*. The attribution of new meanings to objects dependent on local context.

According to this framework, chimpanzees may be engaged minimally in practices of appropriation in their manufacture of tools, for instance the short wooden spears produced by Fongoli chimpanzees to hunt bush babies in tree hollows (Pruetz et al. 2015). Moreover, the adoption and use of proximal human material culture as a tool could indicate objectivization. But to recognize whether the material results of such behaviours are appropriation requires greater understanding of chimpanzee cognitive worlds. There are meanings associated with the state of 'personal possession', not least an implied state of personhood, which complicate the analysis. Nonetheless, if it is uncontentious to recognize that chimpanzee and human cognition is different and that chimpanzees exist in at least a proto-cultural if not fully cultural world, then it is possible to anticipate the attribution of new meanings to objects in such instances (see Stockhammer 2012: 48). This holds the possibility for a transformative form of hybridity but one that at the most can only be recognized as meaningful without perhaps any real possibility of understandings of the meanings in question. It can also be recognized that if the cognitive conditions are materially evident for Neanderthal/modern human exchange—not only for biological attributes but also of cultural phenomena that illustrate the capacity for cross-species practices of hybridization—then this should also extend to other non-human species for whom behavioural diversity and exchange is observed.

At present, primatological observation does not indicate cultural hybridity but it remains possible that stronger evidence may emerge, especially as a result of long-term studies. As an exercise, the question could be asked: what evidence/conditions would be indicative? Hypothetically, if a non-ecological behaviour was transmitted socially between two chimpanzee groups, ideally ones that had come into contact but were previously isolated, and as a result of that contact a new practice emerged that was predicated on behavioural elements previously exhibited by both communities, the case would be strong. An innovated grooming hand-clasp between the M-group and K-group, perhaps interdigitating or touching the back of the hand, would also be of interest to the hybridity researcher, in particular if it then spread throughout the group at the expense of anterior practices. Given the hierarchical social organization of chimpanzee communities, power relationships are likely to also be evident and relevant. The contagion of behavioural innovations is likely to be amplified when associated with dominant individuals. The difficulty would be the ascription of meaning to such hypothetical observations.

Chimpanzee social hierarchy is well documented with instances of individual dominancy, group fission, and inter-group conflict, including the so-called 'Gombe Chimpanzee War', which lasted four years and saw eight adult males from the Kasakela group kill all six males of the Kahama group (Goodall 1986; also see Morris 2014: 284; Wilson et al. 2014). Feldblum et al. (2018) have concluded that the war was likely the consequence of a power struggle between three high-ranking males, exacerbated by an unusual scarcity of fertile females. Chimpanzees also possess Theory of Mind and exhibit

100 TIMOTHY CLACK

what is labelled 'Machiavellian intelligence' in that they will, for example, pretend not to notice resources or hide them in order to access at a later time. Moreover, they will also engage in covert sexual liaisons outside of the social hierarchy (Goodall 1986). Whilst adaptive in terms of maximizing access to resources and navigating the social environment, these behaviours may also be considered a form of resistance. Resistance to certain behaviours linked to social dominance can thus be proposed and, if recognized, would also be informative in the present discussion. Would hybrid behaviours relate to the dominant and subordinate alike?

Creativity

Observational learning is exhibited by chimpanzees and indicated for Neanderthals. It is known that both behavioural and cognitive modelling have a potent effect on creativity (Bandura 1986; Kaufman et al. 2011). Hybridity is inseparably connected to creativity. Drawing on animal behaviour, behavioural neuroscience, and creativity theories, a three-level framework for non-human creativity has been proposed (Kaufman et al. 2011). The first level involves the capacity to recognize and seek out novelty; the second is observational learning, which ranges in complexity from imitation to cultural transmission of creative behaviour; and the third is innovative behaviour, which involves generating a thing or behaviour with the understanding that it is original and different. Neurobiologically, the levels are associated with hippocampal function and dopamine reward, cerebellum and cortical regions, and prefrontal cortex and hemispheric function, respectively. Thus, brain evolution and complexity impinge upon the level of creativity possible. Innovation, the highest level of creativity in the framework, is only possible in those species, like modern humans, with prefrontal cortex and lateralized brains, implicated in the higher executive functions, including language, complex planning, decision-making, social behaviour, and decision-making (Dietrich 2004). Though to a lesser degree than in modern humans, lateralization and prefrontal cortices are apparent in endocast evidence from chimpanzees and Neanderthals (Holloway et al. 2004).

Kochiyama et al. (2018) present a detailed virtual reconstruction of the Neanderthal brain using computational anatomy and described a relatively smaller cerebellar hemisphere, particularly on the right side. A larger cerebellum is associated with the higher cognitive functions, including executive and language functions. Thus, Neanderthals were likely constrained in their capacities in these areas. Moreover, Neanderthals also had a smaller faculty for working memory (Wynn and Coolidge). This could have had far-reaching implications. Indeed, the lack of ability to innovate adaptations to changing environment has been proposed as a possible reason for the demise of the Neanderthals. For present purposes, though, it is important to recognize these factors as likely limiting in terms of cognitive capacity, including in terms of creativity, but that they do not make implausible at least some level of cultural hybridity.

Conclusion

This chapter has attempted to posit the question as to whether certain behaviours, practices, and material culture associated with non-human species might be addressed under the theme of hybridity. Although the question remains some way from being answered, various pertinent aspects and threads of future work have been registered. For both Neanderthals and chimpanzees, the potential for expressions of cultural hybridity has been advanced albeit cautiously. Whilst the Châtelperronian offers perhaps the finest available circumstances to explore hybridity between Neanderthal and modern human societies, a more granular understanding of chronology and stratification is required to enhance clarity. Similarly, the prospects of hybridity taking place amidst chimpanzee societies are apparent, but recognition relates primarily to a greater understanding of their cognitive worlds. In both cases neurobiological evolution underpinned necessary cognitive capabilities. Neanderthal cognition surpassed that of chimpanzees, not least in the areas of memory, language, and innovation. Nonetheless, in the brains of both species there existed the potential for some level of 'culture' and, consequently, hybridity.

The definition and conceptualization of culture which is being deployed becomes central to the exploration of hybridity in other species. If we accept that culture equates to human based on the recognition that language is a higher-level aspect of cognition, unique to humans, then even the potential for hybridity becomes difficult to discern. However, if we dispense with the circularity inherent in such a definitional approach, and instead adopt a broad definition of culture that encompasses complex behaviours, pedagogy, tool use, and levels of proto-language and self-awareness, then potential indicators of cultural hybridity may be apparent. After all, Miles et al. (1996: 289) described a process of 'enculturation' in laboratory apes whereby subjects become 'immersed in a system of meaningful human relations that include language, behaviour, beliefs and material culture'.

This discussion also forces the realization that biological and cultural hybridization should not be considered processes of pollution nor the transgression of boundaries. Indeed, integrity and purity are illusory and underpinned by, for example, the culturally defined dichotomies between human and nature, and indigene and alien (Latour 1993; Descola 2013; Lescureux 2019). From this platform, it can also be recognized that the exploration of hybridity in non-humans and between species favours approaches that draw on the complementarity of biological and social approaches. Thus, research into non-human hybridity is a worthwhile avenue for the future, principally amongst archaeologists, physical anthropologists, and primatologists.

This discussion of non-human hybridity urges us to think about hybridity more generally. Hybridity is a dynamic practice but it is often only the product of the process that gets measured. This presents a problem for both archaeologists and behaviouralists. The archaeological record offers only a static and fragmentary manifestation of past dynamism. For behaviouralists, techniques for assessing processes are rudimentary and require a high level of communication with those involved (Kaufman et al. 2011: 262).

The applicability of hybridity to archaeological analyses is being newly critiqued, with greater attention to the power imbalances inherent in cultural exchange. Future implications of hybrid studies rest largely on how to address these imbalances, an exploration that can be inspired by practices of material culture (Stockhammer 2012). However, the issue of power will prove especially challenging to those exploring non-human forms of hybridity. Although chimpanzees live in hierarchical societies, and Neanderthals undoubtedly inhabited environments under conditions of internal and external group power relations, the possibilities of fully discerning these through behavioural and material practices are low.

Let us return to *Oryx and Crake*. For as Atwood articulates astutely through her 'unique' protagonist, Snowman, the prospect of future acknowledgement and understanding is predicated on a common vernacular. This vernacular requires a temporal 'shelf-life' that can span the epochs between transmission and receipt. Through disparate research endeavours in the 'culture sciences' we are collectively piecing together the means to understand elements of material culture and behavioural repertoire. Aptly, our (inadvertent) joint enterprise simultaneously embodies, utilizes, and creates the hybridity we examine. In this cycle of discovery, new answers generate new questions;

bringing us perhaps closer to the creation of a meaningful cipher. For now, the cultural characteristics of our hominin ancestors and primate relations remain tantalizingly both close and castaway.

> He too is a castaway of sorts. He could make lists. It could give his life some structure....But even a castaway assumes a future reader, someone who'll come along later and find his bones and his ledger, and learn his fate. Snowman can make no such assumptions: he'll have no future reader, because the Crakers can't read. Any reader he can possibly imagine is in the past.

References

Aldhouse-Green, M. 2005. *The Quest for the Shaman*. London: Thames & Hudson.

Atwood, M. 2003. *Oryx and Crake*. London: Bloomsbury.

Baker, H. 1965. *Plants and Civilisation*. Belmont: Wadsworth.

Bandura, A. 1986. *Social Foundations of Thought and Action*. Englewood Cliffs: Prentice Hall.

Bednarik, R. 1995. 'Concept-mediated marking in the Lower Paleolithic'. *Current Anthropology* 36(4): 605–34.

Bhabha, H. 2007. *The Location of Culture*. London: Routledge.

Bircher, J., D. Auger, and N. Riddle. 2003. 'In search of the molecular basis of heterosis'. *The Plant Cell* 15(10): 2236–9.

Boesch, C. and H. Boesch-Acherman. 2000. *The Chimpanzees of the Tai Forest*. Oxford: Oxford University Press.

Brives, C. 2019. 'From fighting against to becoming with: viruses as companion species'. In C. Stepanoff and J.-D. Vigne (eds), *Hybrid Communities: Biosocial Approaches to Domestication and Other Trans-Species Relationships*. London: Routledge, pp. 115–26.

Bruner, E., G. Manzi, and J. Arsuaga. 2003. 'Encephalization and allometric trajectories in the genus *Homo*: evidence from the Neandertal and modern lineages'. *Proceedings of the National Academy of Science* 100: 15335–40.

Burke, P. 2009. *Cultural Hybridity*. Cambridge: Polity Press.

Capps, B. 2017. 'Do chimeras have minds? The ethics of clinical research on a human-animal brain model'. *Cambridge Quarterly of Healthcare Ethics* 26: 577–91.

Chomsky, N. 1988. *Syntactic Structures*. The Hague: Mouton and Co.

Cook, J. 2007. 'The lion-man. An Ice Age masterpiece'. British Museum Blog. https://blog.britishmuseum.org/the-lion-man-an-ice-age-masterpiece/ (accessed 11 September 2019).

Coolidge, F. and T. Wynn. 2011. *The Rise of Homo Sapiens: The Evolution of Modern Thinking*. London: John Wiley & Sons.

Davies, W. 2007. 'Re-evaluating the Aurignacian as an expression of modern human mobility and dispersal'. In P. Mellars, K. Boyle, O. Bar-Yosef, and C. Stringer (eds), *Rethinking the Human Revolution*. Cambridge: McDonald Institute for Archaeological Research monographs, 263–274.

Deacon, T. 1997. *The Symbolic Species: The Co-evolution of Language and the Brain*. New York: W. W. Norton and Co.

Dediu, D. and C. Levinson. 2018. 'Neanderthal language revisited: not only us'. *Current Opinion in Behavioral Sciences* 21: 49–55.

Descola, P. 2013. *Beyond Nature and Culture*. Chicago: University of Chicago Press.

Dietrich, A. 2004. 'The cognitive neuroscience of creativity'. *Psychonomic Bulletin & Review* 11: 1011–26.

Duarte, C., J. Mauricio, P. Pettitt, P. Souto, E. Trinkaus, H. van der Plicht, and J. Zilhao. 1999. 'The early Upper Paleolithic human skeleton from the Abrigo do Lagar Velho (Portugal) and modern human emergence in Iberia'. *Proceedings of the National Academy of Sciences USA* 96: 7604–9.

d'Errico, F., J. Zilhao, M. Julien, D. Baffier, and J. Pelegrin. 1998. 'Neanderthal acculturation in Western Europe: a critical review of the evidence and its interpretation'. *Current Anthropology* 39: S1-44.

d'Errico, F., C. Henshilwood, M. Vanhaeren, and K. van Niekerk. 2005. 'Nassarius kraussianus shell beads from Blombos Cave: evidence for symbolic behaviour in the Middle Stone Age'. *Journal of Human Evolution* 48: 3–24.

Detroit, F., A. Mijares, J. Corny, G. Daver, C. Zanolli, E. Dizon, E. Robles, R. Grun, and P. Piper. 2019. 'A new species of *Homo* from the Late Pleistocene of the Philippines'. *Nature* 568: 181–6.

de Waal, F. and K. E. Bonnie. 2009. 'In tune with others: the social side of primate culture'. In K. Laland and B. Galef (eds), *The Question of Animal Culture*. Cambridge, MA: Harvard University Press, 19–39.

Eliade, M. 1951. *Shamanism: Archaic Techniques of Ecstasy*. New York: Pantheon Books.

Feldblum, J., S. Manfredi, I. Gilby, and A. Pusey 2018. 'The timing and causes of a unique chimpanzee community fission preceding Gombe's 'four-year war''. *American Journal of Physical Anthropology* 166(3): 730–744.

Gamble, C. 1994. 'Human evolution'. In T. Ingold (ed.), *Companion Encyclopaedia of Anthropology*. London: Routledge.

Goodall, J. 1986. *The Chimpanzees of the Gombe: Patterns of Behavior*. Cambridge, MA: Harvard University Press.

Goodall, J. 1988. *In the Shadow of Man*. London: Houghton Miffin.

Gunz, P., S. Neubauer, B. Maureille, and J. Hublin. 2010. 'Brain development after birth differs between Neanderthals and modern humans'. *Current Biology* 20: R921–2.

Haile-Salassie, Y., S. Melillo, and D. Su. 2016. 'The Pliocene hominin diversity conundrum: do more fossils mean less clarity?'. *Proceedings of the National Academy of Sciences USA* 113: 6364–71.

Haile-Selassie, Y., S. Melillo, A. Vazzana, S. Benazzi, and T. Ryan. 2019. 'A 3.8 million-year-old cranium from Woranso-Mille, Ethiopia'. *Nature* DOI: 10.1038/s41586-019-1513-8.

Haraway, D. 2008. *When Species Meet*. Minneapolis: University of Minneapolis Press.

Hawks, J. 2013. 'Significance of Neandertal and Denisovan genomes in human evolution'. *Annual Review of Anthropology* 42: 433–49.

Hayden, B. 2003. *A Prehistory of Religion: Shamans, Sorcerers and Saints*. Washington, DC: Smithsonian Institution Press.

Hill, K. 2009. 'Animal "culture"?'. In K. Laland and B. Galef (eds), *The Question of Animal Culture*. Cambridge, MA: Harvard University Press, 269–80.

Holloway, R. 1997. 'Brain evolution'. In R. Dulbecco (ed.), *Encyclopedia of Human Biology*. New York: Academic Press, pp. 189–200.

Holloway, R., D. Broadfield, M. Yuan, J. Schwartz, and I. Tattersall, eds. 2004. *The Human Fossil Record: Brain Endocasts*. London: John Wiley & Sons.

Kaufman, A., A. Butt, J. Kaufman, and E. Colbert-White. 2011. 'Towards a neurobiology of creativity in nonhuman animals'. *Journal of Comparative Psychology* 124(3): 255–72.

Klein, R. 2009. *The Human Career: Human Biological and Cultural Origins*. Chicago: University of Chicago Press.

Kochiyama, T., N. Ogihara, H. Tanabe, O. Kondo, H. Amano, K. Hasegawa, H. Suzuki, M. de Leon, C. Zollikofer, M. Bastir, C. Stringer, N. Sadato, and T. Akazawa. 2018. 'Reconstructing the Neanderthal brain using computational anatomy'. *Scientific Reports* 8: 6296.

Koplin, J. and D. Wilkinson. 2019. 'Moral uncertainty and the farming of human-pig chimeras'. *Journal of Medical Ethics* 45: 440–6.

Laland, K. and B. Galef, eds. 2009. *The Question of Animal Culture*. Cambridge, MA: Harvard University Press.

Laland, K., J. Kendal, and R. Kendal. 2009. 'Animal culture: problems and solutions'. In K. Laland and B. Galef (eds), *The Question of Animal Culture*. Cambridge, MA: Harvard University Press, 174–97.

106 TIMOTHY CLACK

Latour, B. 1993. *We Have Never Been Modern*. Cambridge, MA: Harvard University Press.

Lescureux, N. 2019. 'Beyond wild and domestic: human complex relationships with dogs, wolves, and wolf-dog hybrids'. In C. Stepanoff and J.-D. Vigne (eds), *Hybrid Communities: Biosocial Approaches to Domestication and Other Transspecies Relationships*. London: Routledge, pp. 65–79.

Lestel, D. 2004. *L'animal singulier*. Paris: Seuil.

Lewis-Williams, J. 2002. *The Mind in the Cave*. London: Thames & Hudson.

Mackintosh, N. 2011. *IQ and Human Intelligence*. Oxford: Oxford University Press.

Marshack, A. 1990. 'Early hominid symbolism and the evolution of human capacity'. In P. Mellars (ed.), *The Emergence of Modern Humans*. Edinburgh: Edinburgh University Press, pp. 457–98.

Martinez, I., J. Arsuaga, R. Quam, J. Carretero, A. Garcia, and L. Rodriguez 2008. 'Human hyoid bones from the middle Pleistocene site of the Sima de los Huesos (Sierra de Atapuerca, Spain)'. *Journal of Human Evolution* 54: 118–24.

Mason, P. H. and R. V. Short 2011. 'Neanderthal-human hybrids'. *Hypothesis* 9(1): 1–5.

McGrew, W. 1983. 'Animal foods in the diets of wild chimpanzees: why cross-cultural variation?'. *Journal of Ethology* 1: 46–61.

McGrew, W. 1992. *Chimpanzee Material Culture: Implications for Human Evolution*. Cambridge: Cambridge University Press.

McGrew, W. 2004. *The Cultured Chimpanzee: Reflections on Cultural Primatology*. Cambridge: Cambridge University Press.

Mellars, P. 1991. 'Cognitive changes and the emergence of modern humans'. *Cambridge Archaeological Journal* 1: 63–76.

Mellars, P. 1996. 'Symbolism, language and the Neanderthal mind'. In P. Mellars and K. Gibson (eds), *Modelling the Early Human Mind*. Cambridge: McDonald Institute, pp. 15–32.

Mellars, P. and B. Gravina 2008. 'Châtelperron: theoretical agendas, archaeological facts, and diversionary smoke-screens'. *PaleoAnthropology* 2008: 43–64.

Miles, H., R. Mitchell, and S. Harper. 1996. 'Simon says: the development of imitation in an enculturated orangutan'. In A. Russon, K. Bard, and S. Parker (eds), *Reaching into Thought: The Minds of Great Apes*. Cambridge: Cambridge University Press, pp. 278–99.

Mithen, S. 1996. *The Prehistory of the Mind: A Search for the Origins of Art, Religion and Science*. London: Thames & Hudson.

Mithen, S. 2000. 'Mind, brain and material culture'. In P. Carruthers and A. Chamberlain (eds), *Evolution and the Human Mind: Modularity, Language and Meta-Cognition*. Cambridge: Cambridge University Press, pp. 207–17.

Mithen, S. 2007. *The Singing Neanderthal: The Origins of Music, Language, Mind and Body*. Cambridge, MA: Harvard University Press.

Morrell, V. 1993. 'Called "Trimates", three bold women shaped their field'. *Science* 260: 420–5.

Morris, I. 2014. *War! What Is It Good For?* London: Profile.

Pacheco-Sierra, G., E. Vazquez-Dominguez, J. Perez-Alquicira, M. Suarez-Atilano, and J. Dominguez-Laso. 2018. 'Ancestral hybridization yields evolutionary distinct hybrids, lineages and species boundaries in crocodiles, posing unique conservation conundrums'. *Frontiers in Ecology and Evolution* 6(138). DOI: 10.3389/fevo.2018.00138.

Persson, T., G. Sauciuc, and E. Madsen 2008. 'Spontaneous cross-species imitation in interactions between chimpanzees and zoo visitors'. *Primates* 59(1): 19–29.

Preutz, J., B. Bertolani, K. Ontl, S. Lindshield, M. Shelley, and E. Wessling. 2015. 'New evidence on the tool-assisted hunting exhibited by chimpanzees (*Pan troglodytes verus*) in a savannah habitat at Fongoli, Senegal'. *Royal Society Open Source* 2(4). DOI: 10.1098/rsos.140507.

Reynolds, V. 1975. 'How wild are the Gombe chimpanzees?'. *Man* 10: 123–5.

Reynolds, V. 2005. *The Chimpanzees of the Budongo Forest: Ecology, Behaviour, and Conservation*. Oxford: Oxford University Press.

Rougier, H., S. Milota, R. Rodrigo, M. Gherase, L. Sarcina, O. Moldovan. 2007. 'Pestera cu Oase 2 and the cranial morphology of early modern Europeans'. *Proceedings of the National Academy of Sciences USA* 104: 1165–70.

Sankararaman, S., S. Mallick, M. Dannemann, K. Prufer, J. Kelso. S. Pääbo, N. Patterson, and D. Reich. 2014. 'The genomic landscape of Neanderthal ancestry in present-day humans'. *Nature* 507: 354–7.

Savage-Rumbaugh, S., S. Shanker, and T. Talbot. 1998. *Apes, Language, and the Human Mind*. Oxford: Oxford University Press.

Schaik, C., M. Ancrenaz, G. Borgen, B. Galdikas, C. Knott, I. Singleton, A. Suzuki, S. Utami, and M. Merrill. 2003. 'Orangutan cultures and the evolution of material culture'. *Science* 299: 102–5.

Silliman, S. 2009. 'Blurring for clarity: archaeology as hybrid practice'. In P. Bikoulis, D. Lacroix, and M. Peuramaki-Brown (eds), *Postcolonial Perspectives in Archaeology: Proceedings of the 39th Annual Chacmool Archaeological Conference, University of Calgary, Alberta, Canada*. Calgary: University of Calgary.

Slatkin, M. and F. Racimo. 2016. 'Ancient DNA and human history'. *Proceedings of the National Academy of Sciences USA* 113: 6380–7.

Soficaru, A., A. Dobos, and E. Trinkhaus. 2006. 'Early modern humans from the Pestera Muierii, Baia de Fier, Romania'. *Proceedings of the National Academy of Sciences USA* 103: 17196–201.

108   TIMOTHY CLACK

Spoor, F. 2015. 'The middle Pliocene gets crowded'. *Nature* 521: 432–3.

Staller, J. and E. Currie, eds. 2001. *Mortuary Practices and Ritual Associations.* Oxford: Archaeopress.

Stepanoff, C. and J.-D. Vigne. 2019. 'Introduction'. In C. Stepanoff and J.-D. Vigne (eds), *Hybrid Communities: Biosocial Approaches to Domestication and Other Trans-Species Relationships.* London: Routledge, pp. 1–20.

Sterelny, K. 2009. 'Peacekeeping in the culture wars'. In K. Laland and B. Galef (eds), *The Question of Animal Culture.* Cambridge, MA: Harvard University Press, pp. 288–304.

Stockhammer, P. 2012. 'Conceptualizing cultural hybridization in archaeology'. In P. Stockhammer (ed.), *Conceptualizing Cultural Hybridization: A Transdisciplinary Approach.* Berlin: Springer, pp. 43–58.

Stross, B. 1999. 'The hybrid metaphor: from biology to culture'. *Journal of American Folklore* 112(445): 254–67.

Thrupp, L. 2000. 'Linking agricultural biodiversity and food security'. *International Affairs* 76(2): 265–81.

Tolmie, C. 2013. 'The Châtelperronian: hybrid culture or independent innovation'. In J. Card (ed.), *The Archaeology of Hybrid Material Culture.* Carbondale: Southern Illinois University, pp. 279–94.

Trinkaus, E., O. Moldovan, S. Milota, A. Bilgar, L. Sarcina, and S. Athreya. 2003. 'An early modern human from the Pestera cu Oase, Romania'. *Proceedings of the National Academy of Sciences USA* 100: 11231–6.

Vernot, B. and J. Akey. 2014. 'Resurrecting surviving Neandertal lineages from modern human genomes'. *Science* 343 (6174): 1017–21.

Walter, M. and E. Fridman, eds. 2005. *Shamanism: An Encyclopedia of World Beliefs, Practices and Culture.* Santa Barbara: ABC Clio.

White, R. 1993. 'A social and technological view of the Aurignacian and Castelperronian personal ornaments in France'. In V. Cabrera Valde (ed.), *El Origen del Hombre Moderno en el Suroeste de Europa.* Madrid: Universidad Nacional de Educacion a Distancia, pp. 327–57.

White, R. 1995. 'Ivory personal ornaments of Aurignacian age: technological, social and symbolic perspectives'. In J. Hahn, M. Menu, Y. Taborin, P. Walter, and F. Widemann (eds), *Le Travail et L'Usage de l'Ivoire au Paleolithique Superieur.* Ravello: Instituto Poligrafico Zecca dello Stato, pp. 29–62.

Whiten, A., J. Goodall, W. McGrew, T. Nishida, V. Reynolds, Y. Sugiyama, C. Tutin, R. Wrangham, and C. Boesch. 1999. 'Culture in chimpanzees'. *Nature* 399: 682–5.

Whiten, A., V. Horner, and S. Marshall-Pescini. 2003. 'Cultural panthropology'. *Evolutionary Anthropology* 12(2): 92–105.

Whitley, D. 2009. *Cave Paintings and the Human Spirit. The Origin of Creativity and Belief.* Amherst: Prometheus Books.

Wildman, D., M. Uddin, G. Liu, L. Grossman, and M. Goodman. 2003. 'Implications of natural selection in shaping 99.4% nonsynonymous DNA identity between humans and chimpanzees: enlarging genus *Homo*'. *PNAS* 100(12): 7181–8.

Wilson, M., C. Boesch, B. Fruth, T. Furuichi, I. Gilby, C. Hashimoto, C. Hobaiter, G. Hohmann, N. Itoh, K. Koops, J. Lloyd, T. Matsuzawa, J. Mitani, D. Mjungu, D. Morgan, M. Muller, R. Mundry, M. Nakamura, J. Pruetz, A. Pusey, J. Riedel, C. Sanz, A. Schel, N. Simmons, M. Waller, D. Watts, F. White, R. Wittig, K. Zuberbühler, and R. Wrangham. 2014. 'Lethal aggression in *Pan* is better explained by adaptive strategies than human impacts'. *Nature* 513: 414–17.

Winkelman, M. 2012. 'Shamanism in cross-cultural perspective'. *International Journal of Transpersonal Studies* 31(2): 47–62.

Wrangham, R., W. McGrew, F. de Waal, and P. Heltne, eds. 1994. *Chimpanzee Cultures*. Cambridge, MA: Harvard University Press.

Wynn, T. and F. Coolidge. 2004. 'The expert Neanderthal mind'. *Journal of Human Evolution* 46: 467–87.

5

Disentangling Neanderthal-Modern Human Interactions in Western Europe

A Heuristic Odyssey

Brad Gravina, Francesco d'Errico, and François Bachellerie

Introduction

Prehistory is, in no small way, a chronicle of movement. Populations expand and contract, certain disperse irreversibly; profoundly recasting the cultural landscape in their wake, whereas others may be momentary expressions of short-lived pioneering groups or simply unlucky colonizers. Certain episodes are punctuated by local extinctions or continuities, while others likely signal demographic replacements and complex processes of bio-cultural admixture and exchange. Palaeolithic archaeology and palaeoanthropology have increasingly documented traces of many such episodes during the Pleistocene using an array of different interlocking proxies (genetics, stable isotopes, palaeontological evidence, material culture) coupled with, and influenced by geoclimatic parameters such as vegetation or annual rainfall (see d'Errico et al. 2012; Henn et al. 2012 for a review of the factors underlying human expansions).

Several, but certainly not all of these hominin expansions likely imply some degree of contact with local populations, including the pan-African and eventual European expansion of the Acheulean, the complex palaeoanthropological record of Southeast Asia (e.g. Dennell 2009; Bae et al. 2012), the initial but unsuccessful expansion of early modern human populations into the Neanderthal-occupied Levant by at least some 190 kya (Grün et al. 2005; Hershkovitz et al. 2018) or the ultimate, irrevocable dispersal of modern human groups across the globe beginning at the latest some 50 kya (Mellars 2004b; Hublin et al. 2020) and possibly as early as 55 kya (Hershkovitz et al. 2015). While seemingly straightforward on the surface, the precise chronology, duration, and 'fossil species' associated with such processes remain contentious, with at least some of the material culture proxies used to

Brad Gravina, Francesco d'Errico, and François Bachellerie, *Disentangling Neanderthal-Modern Human Interactions in Western Europe: A Heuristic Odyssey* In: *Archaeologies of Cultural Contact: At the Interface*. Edited by: Timothy Clack and Marcus Brittain, Oxford University Press. © Oxford University Press 2022. DOI: 10.1093/oso/9780199693948.003.0006

trace and model them being equally a matter of debate (e.g. Bar-Yosef and Belfer-Cohen 2013). Unsurprisingly, the further we venture back into deep prehistory, the sparser and more ambiguous the archaeological record becomes. The obvious corollary being whether traces of such expansions are sufficiently visible archaeologically, which itself evokes questions regarding the possibility of untangling a 'species range expansion', as defined from an ecological perspective, from the bona fide demographic history of a specific population.

For the period between approximately 50,000 and 40,000 BP in Western Europe, such discussions have mainly focused on the Châtelperronian, Lincombien-Ranisian-Jerzmanowician, and Ulluzian industries of the so-called Middle to Upper Palaeolithic 'transition', with the complex and protean question of the expansion/dispersal of anatomically modern humans and possible cultural interactions with local Neanderthal groups having fascinated generations of researchers (Fig. 5.1). However, does the Western European

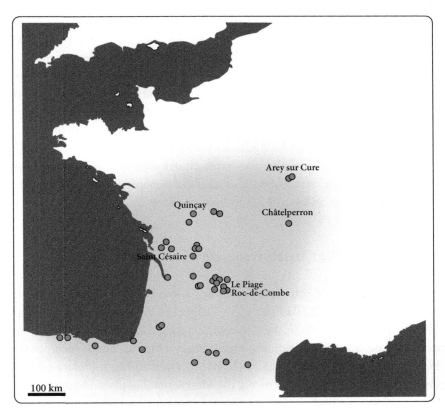

Fig. 5.1. Distribution of the Châtelperronian including main sites mentioned in the text.

archaeological record actually present the requisite resolution for addressing such a possibility? If so, what factors intervene in the different ways archaeologists theorize and interpret the widely different data they themselves deem relevant for investigating this issue? What types of material culture expressions are the most reliable proxies of population interactions? And finally, how, in this specific context, is archaeological praxis influenced by national research traditions?

These questions are further complicated by the fact that the large majority of well-documented historical cases of 'culture-contact' occurred within clearly asymmetrical contexts involving a technologically dominant culture with little secure evidence for *softer*, more nuanced encounters between concurrent hunter-gatherer groups on which an interpretive framework for this period could be developed. Our interest here is to use the Châtelperronian as a balanced case study to investigate how the nature and form of available data, coupled with the specific choices of appropriate cultural traits and material proxies, informs heuristic mechanisms held to explain so-called 'transitional' techno-complexes and whether related processes may or may not be relatable to something resembling cultural 'hybridization'. In the present context, it appears most apt to view such a potential 'process' as the emergence of new material culture traditions and ethno-cultural identities from direct or indirect interaction of variable intensity between hitherto unrelated groups. This would imply the restructuring or reinterpretation of particular techno-cultural elements via an array of possible transfer mechanisms (Stewart 2007). Finally, such a discussion also inevitably contributes to overarching issues concerning to what extent traces of specific human dispersals and their consequences are detectable in the archaeological record.

The Châtelperronian: a brief history

First identified at the Grottes des Fées near Châtelperron in the Allier department of central France (Bailleau 1869; Delporte 1957), the Châtelperronian did not assume its place in the Palaeolithic sequence until Breuil (1911) re-evaluated de Mortillet's unilinear evolutionary cultural 'progression' of the Western European archaeological record. By overturning the placement of the Solutrean immediately following the Mousterian based on the presence of bifacial pieces in both industries, Breuil's prescient revision of numerous archaeological sequences not only correctly placed the Aurignacian between the Solutrean and Mousterian but also sub-divided the former into at least three periods, one of which he referred to as the *Aurignacien type-Châtelperron*. The sense of a chrono-culturally mixed industry with the persistence of certain ancestral traits is already evident in Breuil's definition, which he portrayed as having a 'substantial flake component, often retouched into ovoid endscrapers, a high frequency of persistent Mousterian forms, and above all, the form of certain retouched blades or Châtelperronian points'. Furthermore, Breuil considered the appearance of the Aurignacian in Western Europe to reflect the colonization of the region by allochthonous anatomically modern humans.

Some twenty years later, Denis Peyrony (1933) introduced a new organization of Breuil's Aurignacian based on his reading of the archaeological sequence in southwestern France. Not only did he partition the Aurignacian into five successive stages, he also extracted a parallel phyla from Breuil's Middle Aurignacian, the Perigordian, of which the Châtelperronian or Perigordian I occupied its first chronological phase. His conflation of certain layers that clearly contained artificially associated Mousterian and Upper Palaeolithic components further reinforced the supposed 'mixed' character of the Châtelperronian. Furthermore, Peyrony's dual phyla model infused a demographic contingency that saw the temporary replacement (or displacement) of members of the Combe-Cappelle 'race', the presumed authors of the Perigordian, by 'Cro-Magnon man' associated with the Aurignacian. Both Breuil's and Peyrony's models emphasized the mixed and intrusive nature of this industry. Unaware of the taphonomic and geological considerations now fundamental to modern Palaeolithic archaeology, they followed the overriding epistemological tenor of a period dominated by the naturalistic fallacy that led them to accept *what is, as what ought to be* or, in this case, *have been*.

Subsequent developments in Palaeolithic systematics only slightly loosened the typological straightjacket that bound interpretations of the Palaeolithic record, and, as we note below, this continued emphasis on typological similarities between tool types would have significant ramifications for the postulated origins of the Châtelperronian. François Bordes, contradicting Breuil's unilineal trajectory, was a partisan of Peyrony's dual phyla model for the initial Upper Palaeolithic, proposing that the Perigordian and Aurignacian developed simultaneously in Southwest Europe. In demographic terms, Bordes saw the Aurignacian as having an eastern origin, while the fully 'Upper Palaeolithic' Perigordian had its roots in a local cultural substrate, namely the Mousterian of Acheulean Tradition (MTA) with its supposed increased Upper Palaeolithic tool-type component alongside 'backed knives' and 'Audi points' superficially resembling Châtelperronian points (Bordes 1972). This typological 'legacy', combined with the then understood stratigraphic position of the MTA as occurring towards the end of the Mousterian sequence garnered further support for an ancestral link—a pattern and interpretation developed further (e.g. Mellars 1996, 2004a; Pelegrin and Soressi 2007). However, Bordes (1958), like Breuil, considered the MTA, and hence the Perigordian, to be the product of emergent local anatomically modern human populations.

Laplace (1966) would put a different spin on the industry's seemingly 'mixed' character. His analytical approach led him to believe that the Châtelperronian represented the 'undifferentiated synthetotype' combining existent elements wherefrom both Peyrony's Perigordian and Aurignacian phyla would have emerged. Laplace once again reaffirmed the Châtelperronian's apparent hybrid character, although his use of 'codes' for describing artefact characteristics rather than 'types', and the general lack of acceptance of his method by contemporary prehistorians have largely marginalized his contributions. Laplace, however, advanced no clear hypothesis regarding the authorship of the various industries.

It is now widely accepted that the Aurignacian is not a monolithic cultural phenomenon across Western Europe and the Levant. It entails an initial phase first identified by Laplace (1966) as the Proto-Aurignacian, subsequently referred to as the Aurignacian 0 (Delporte 1984) or Aurignacian 1a (Demars 1992), but now generally accepted in Laplace's original formulation, followed by the Early or Archaic Aurignacian (Bon 2002; Bordes 2006; Banks et al. 2013). While diagnostically modern human remains are associated with the latter (Bailey and Hublin 2005; Verna et al. 2012), the biological affiliation of the makers of the Proto-Aurignacian is still matter of debate in some anthropological circles.

While questions lingered regarding the authorship of the Châtelperronian, the 1979 discovery of a partial Neanderthal skeleton within a level attributed to the Châtelperronian at La-Roche-à-Pierrot, Saint Césaire in southwest France seemingly resolved the conflict (Lévêque and Vandermeersch 1980). F. Bordes (1981), exposing his continued conviction that the Châtelperronian was the handiwork of anatomically modern humans, described the Saint Césaire discovery as *encombrant* (troublesome). Interestingly, he suggested that the remains were that of a woman insomuch as, in his eyes, Palaeolithic human groups preferred to 'exchange genes rather than customs' (Bordes 1981: 644). Nonetheless, this find lent further support to the isolated teeth recovered some twenty-five years earlier from a Châtelperronian level at the Grotte du Renne, Arcy-sur-Cure, originally suspected to be Neanderthal by the excavator (Leroi-Gourhan 1958). Such an association lent succour to the 'Multi-Regional Model' proposed by Milford Wolpoff (1989), which posited the local bio-cultural evolution of Neanderthals into modern humans across their known range.

During the 1990s, the idea that the Neanderthals were indeed the authors of the Châtelperronian gained ground, in step with renewed interest in the subject driven by technological studies of material derived from modern excavations. Pelegrin (1990, 1995) demonstrated that Châtelperronian technology, despite being essentially laminar in character, differed from that of the Early Aurignacian. On the other hand, this very same analysis suggested a typological link between the MTA type B and the Châtelperronian—based on the occasional presence in the former of flake tools with sometimes curved retouched edges reminiscent of the backed pieces—the Châtelperronian points—typically associated with the latter. This industry therefore appeared as an 'epi-Mousterian' distinct from the Classic or Early Aurignacian associated with anatomically modern humans. The subsequent publication of a Neanderthal temporal bone and isolated teeth from Arcy-sur-Cure (Hublin et al. 1996; Spoor et al. 2003: Bailey and Hublin 2006) further buttressed the idea that the Châtelperronian was made by Neanderthals.

The emergence of competing models

By the mid- to late '90s, the interpretive backdrop of the Châtelperronian had substantially evolved; modern excavations, the publication of a new corpus of radiometric ages combined with technological and taphonomic re-evaluations of several important sites, and revision of previously excavated collections, culminated, paradoxically but not unsurprisingly, in the emergence of two predominant models explaining the appearance and composition of this industry—acculturation versus innovation. Following a brief review of the essential interpretive elements of these two competing models, we investigate how such diametrically opposed positions can be based on the differential employment of basically the same set of data.

Acculturation

The acculturation hypothesis was first expressed in its modern form by Richard Klein (1973) and subsequently elaborated (Otte 1990; Hublin et al. 1996, 2012; Mellars 1996, 2005; Hublin 1998, 2000). The hypothesis essentially posits that the innovative components of the Châtelperronian to be the ineluctable product of cultural contact or stimulus diffusion (Kroeber 1940) of new ideas from dispersing and expanding modern human populations that ultimately 'replaced' autochthonous Neanderthal populations. This is based primarily on the hypothesis that the emergence of the presumed Neanderthal-made Châtelperronian is effectively contemporaneous with the spread of anatomically modern humans associated with the Proto-Aurignacian and Aurignacian techno-complexes. Tacitly implied in some, but by no means all conceptions of what is perceived to be a somewhat asymmetrical cultural exchange is the inferior cognitive capacities of the Neanderthals (although see Speth 2004 for a thought-provoking parody of some of the extreme elements of this model) or, at the very least, superior technological abilities possessed by modern human groups replete with symbolic expressions, personal ornaments, pigment use, bone tools, and, perhaps most importantly, a tacitly assumed but not demonstrated more expansive network of information exchange. The emergence of new technologies and symbolic innovations coincident with the appearance of modern human populations in the same region as the Châtelperronian after tens of thousands of years of perceived cultural stasis amongst local Neanderthal populations has been described as an 'impossible coincidence' (Mellars 2005) or a 'strange synchronism' (Demars 1998). In other words, the arrival of modern humans or the 'bow-wave' diffusion (Mellars 2005) of ideas proper to these groups irrevocably altered the behavioural trajectory of culturally inert Mousterian populations (Fig. 5.2).

Independent/indigenous innovation

The end of the 1990s saw the development of a new perspective on the origins of the Châtelperronian and the intellectual capacities of the Neanderthals (d'Errico et al. 1998; Zilhão and d'Errico 1999; d'Errico 2003; Zilhão 2006a, 2011). Building on the initial observations of Rigaud (1996), this alternative scenario maintains that everywhere across its known geographic range, the Châtelperronian chronologically precedes and stratigraphically underlies the initial Aurignacian industries. Although the Neanderthal authorship of the Châtelperronian remained unquestioned, this major revision of the taphonomy and chronology of a large portion of the corpus of sites dated to the 'transition' across Western Europe did question the underlying mechanisms responsible for the observed techno-cultural transformations. While not denying that certain innovations in the two 'groups' did develop, in some part as a consequence of mutual influence or contact, the germ of these new

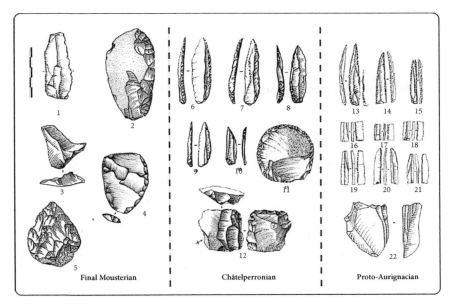

Fig. 5.2. Diagnostic stone tools of the final Mousterian (1–5), Châtelperronian (6–12), and Proto-Aurignacia (13–22) industries of southwestern France; (1) MTA backed knife, (2) large sidescraper, (3) pseudo Levallois point, (4) scraper on a Levallois flake, (5) biface, (6–9) Châtelperronian point, (10) oblique truncation, (11) circular endscraper, (12) blade core on a flake, (13–15) bladelets with a point created by direct bilateral retouch, (16–21) Dufour bladelets, (22) nucleiform burin (modified after Bachellerie 2011; Bordes 1972; Bordes 2002; Thiébaut 2005; Mazière 1978; Primault 2003).

material culture forms is seen to predate the arrival of anatomical modern humans in the region in question (d'Errico et al. 1998). In these terms, the acculturation model is seen to inadequately explain the observed stability in respect to the Châtelperronian's lithic technology and personal ornamentation. In other words, in a situation where one of two contiguous populations exerted more influence, why does the Châtelperronian not portray rapid changes perceptible in associated cultural adaptations (Zilhão et al. 2006)? Furthermore, in deemphasizing the biological determinism inherent in the acculturation model, this perspective places little heuristic value in demonstrating whether innovations were acquired through contact, as it would shed scant light on the cognitive capacities of the Neanderthals and even less on their biological ability to innovate. Finally, in decoupling biology from cultural development, this perspective presents a model that gives priority to historical contingencies and cultural exchange (common in the ethnographic

118 GRAVINA, D'ERRICO AND BACHELLERIE

record), including reciprocal transfer and ecological convergence, as the most parsimonious explanations for the character of the Châtelperronian.

Different interpretations, same data: who, when and how?

These two dominant but clearly conflicting perspectives are based essentially on the same dataset, inevitably evoking certain interpretive conundrums implicit in the manner in which they are coalesced by proponents of either inferential model. The fundamental tenets of both positions turn around three basic questions: who, when, and how? In this final section, we investigate what forms of data are available to address these questions and how they are articulated in these two discordant positions. Although some of the following may appear as minor technicalities in an ostensibly 'either/or' scenario, the manner in which they are employed by different researchers has substantive repercussions for our ability to detect processes akin to cultural hybridization, as well as our ability to elaborate and test hypotheses related to such processes.

Who?

One of the major tenets of both models is the Neanderthal authorship of the Châtelperronian, which has increasingly become a topic of debate (Bar-Yosef 2007; Bar-Yosef and Bordes 2010), echoing F. Bordes's (1981) initial challenge of the St. Césaire find. The Neanderthal-Châtelperronian association is predicated upon the recovery of Neanderthal skeletal material in reported direct association with Châtelperronian cultural material at only two sites: St. Césaire and Arcy-sur-Cure.

La Roche-à-Pierrot, Saint-Césaire. The primary critique of the reported St. Césaire 'burial' was that, 'without detailed stratigraphic information concerning the components of the Châtelperronian layer, its spatial relationships with the layer below, it will be difficult to ascertain the attribution of the burial to the Châtelperronian' (Bar-Yosef and Bordes 2010: 591). The difficulty in assessing the reliability of the Neanderthal-Châtelperronian association at this key site was due in no small part to the limited amount of archaeological material, especially the lithic component, which had been studied and published (Lévêque 1993; Morin 2008; Soressi 2010). This was exacerbated by confusion surrounding the nature and context of the skeletal material; in particular how many individuals are present in what may or may not be a secondary burial. However, a recent detailed techno-typological, taphonomic, and spatial analysis, which included a systematic refitting programme and vertical projections of piece-plotted lithic objects, focused on a much larger sample of lithic material from Saint-Césaire. This study conclusively demonstrated that (a) the level containing the Neanderthal remains to be almost entirely Mousterian in composition, containing only a smattering of diagnostic Châtelperronian material (less than 4 percent) and (b) that it is impossible to reliably associate the Neanderthal remains with *either* the Châtelperronian or the Mousterian at the site (Gravina et al. 2018). With a reliable Neanderthal-Châtelperronian association at St. Césaire now excluded (although see discussion of radiocarbon dates below), only the Grotte du Renne at Arcy-sur-Cure remains as a potential example of such a direct connection.

La Grotte-du-Renne, Arcy-sur-Cure. The Neanderthal skeletal material from the Arcy-sur-Cure Châtelperronian levels (X–VII) comprises isolated teeth recovered by the original excavator (Leroi-Gourhan 1958), together with a fragmentary temporal bone of a child (Hublin et al. 1996; Spoor et al. 2003). A combination of taphonomic and chronological arguments for and against this association neatly illustrates diverging interpretations concerning archaeological data of effectively the same nature. The integrity of the site's stratigraphy, already questioned by White's (2001) analysis of the ornaments and associated by-products, has been further questioned by Bar-Yosef and Bordes (2010: 589), whose reading of the published material evinces for them clear indications of stratigraphic intrusions into the Châtelperronian deposits. These would result from the 'digging and levelling' of the underlying Mousterian layer by the Châtelperronian inhabitants, leading them to suggest that the Neanderthal teeth found in the lowermost Châtelperronian levels derive from the underlying Mousterian deposits. They cite stratigraphic discrepancies in the original radiocarbon ages as further evidence for the post-depositional mixing of archaeological material. This observation had already been made (Leroi-Gourhan and Leroi-Gourhan 1964) and acknowledged in a later synthesis (d'Errico et al. 1998). The argument of mixed layers has also recently received some support from Higham et al. (2010), who produced a Bayesian age model based on new radiocarbon ages. Here, ^{14}C ages identified as 'outliers' by the Bayesian age model are interpreted as proxies for taphonomic admixture or post-depositional disturbance. The relative abundance of incongruent radiocarbon ages suggested to the authors that the site's stratigraphic integrity is questionable. This position has been refuted by a recent statistical analysis of the stratigraphic distribution of culturally diagnostic tool

120 GRAVINA, D'ERRICO AND BACHELLERIE

types (i.e. Châtelperronian points, blades, and bladelets, Levallois products) and innovative items of material culture (pigments, personal ornaments, bone tools, etc.) (Caron et al. 2011). This analysis suggested the horizontal and vertical distribution of artefacts to be congruent with minimal stratigraphic disturbance. Embedded in this conclusion is the idea that the anomalous radiometric determinations are most likely the result of contaminated samples (Zilhão et al. 2011), a hypothesis strongly rejected by the researchers responsible for the dating (Higham et al. 2011a). However, a recent analysis of the underlying Discoid-Denticulate Mousterian level IX produced evidence for some (around 7 percent) admixture of what were reported as Châtelperronian and Aurignacian lithic artefacts in the site's final Mousterian level, directly underlying the lowermost Châtelperronian one (Rocca et al. 2017). Additionally, this layer being essentially discoidal in technology questions the previous use of Levallois products as a proxy (see above, Caron et al. 2011) for evaluating the potential movement of objects between the final Mousterian level and earliest Châtelperronian at the site. The discoidal nature of the uppermost Mousterian layer at Arcy is also intriguing in that the 'Mousterian' component of the Arcy-sur-Cure Châtelperronian levels appears best described as 'discoidal' (Connet 2002). This description is echoed by Leroi-Gourhan's (1968) initial publication of the site's *petit racloir châtelperronien* (small Châtelperronian scraper), which, based on his illustrations, appear to be made on pseudo-Levallois points, an artefact type typical of discoidal reduction. It is also interesting to note the co-occurrence of Middle Palaeolithic typo-technological elements in Châtelperronian assemblages has repeatedly proved to be the result of post-depositional processes (Rigaud 1996; Bordes 2002; Bachellerie 2011; Gravina et al. 2018). Moreover, unlike Saint-Césaire, there is currently no means of evaluating differences in the preservation of the two chrono-cultural components of the Arcy lithic assemblages, their distribution, and hence the overall integrity of the site's Châtelperronian levels.

Taken together, this would seem to add additional support to Bar-Yosef and Bordes's (2010) contention of admixture between the final Mousterian and lowermost Châtelperronian. Additionally, a recent review of available contextual information concerning the provenance of the radiocarbon dated material from the site also noted that nearly half of the samples from the lowermost Châtelperronian occupation come from problematic squares (see Discamps et al. 2015 for more details concerning sample provenance and the site's Bayesian modelling). Further complicating the situation is the recent publication of the faunal lists for the Arcy Châtelperronian (David and

Tolmie 2019). The presence of significant numbers of cave bear remains throughout the sequence, especially in the uppermost Châtelperronian level VII, where this species represents over 60 percent of identified remains (n = 932) and comprises at least fifty individuals, including twenty-four cubs, poses real questions as to the impact of bear digging activities during denning and hibernation on the spatial and stratigraphic integrity of the underlying deposits.

Different forms of data available in the recently published Grotte du Renne monograph (Julien et al. 2019) would argue against the idea of any substantial mixture between the final Mousterian and lowermost Châtelperronian layers. The study of the rich and varied bone industry from the Grotte du Renne Châtelperronian layers, particularly layers IX and X, marks a stark contrast between this assemblage and the much less numerous bone industry from the site's Aurignacian. These differences are reflected not only in the raw materials used for tool manufacture, antler being absent in the Châtelperronian layers and accounting for 40 percent of all bone tools in the Aurignacian layers, but also in tool types and the techniques used to produce bone tool preforms. These recent analyses have, for example, highlighted the production of several types of ivory points with spherical cross-sections, some of which are particularly large and likely reflect a novel hafting method. Apart from a single bone awl, attributed during excavations to the underlying Mousterian layer XI, but similar to the numerous awls found in the Châtelperronian layers, no other tool made from osseous materials were recovered from the site's Mousterian layers. Similar conclusions were reached by researchers who recently completed the first comprehensive analysis of personal ornaments from the site's Châtelperronian layers and compared them to those found in the overlying Aurignacian and Gravettian layers (Vanhaeren et al. 2019).

Like the bone tools, the ornaments from the Châtelperronian layers are significantly more numerous than those found in the Gravettian and Aurignacian layers, with the most important assemblage coming from the lowermost Châtelperronian layer. No personal ornaments can be definitively attributed to the underlying Mousterian layer. Moreover, there are clear differences between the personal ornaments found in the site's Gravettian layer, composed exclusively of fossil gastropods, the limited number of comparable objects from the Aurignacian layer, consisting almost exclusively of fragments of ivory pendants, and the high quality and variety of objects from Châtelperronian layers IX and X. The personal ornaments from these layers also clearly differ in terms of exploited raw materials. Many of these objects were suspended on a cord via a groove around the root of the tooth, a suspension technique absent from the other layers. The only possible indication of

122   GRAVINA, D'ERRICO AND BACHELLERIE

admixture of personal ornaments between layers is the presence of an ivory pendant from layer VIII, already recognized by Leroi-Gourhan as an archaeologically poor layer and subject to possible disturbance. The spatial distribution of the piece-plotted (X and Y coordinates only) ornaments appears to confirm the absence of admixture: on several occasions, identical objects, probably originally forming part of the same composite personal ornament or coming from the same animal (e.g. talons of the same raptor) were discovered in close proximity during excavations. The most recent studies of pigments from the Arcy Châtelperronian layers (Salomon 2019) and associated Neanderthal human remains reached the same conclusion, i.e. the lack of evidence of stratigraphic reworking.

A series of radiocarbon ages produced by Hublin et al. (2012) were equally used to argue that not only is the site's stratigraphy intact but that Neanderthals are indeed responsible for the Arcy Châtelperronian deposits, a conclusion seemingly corroborated by the direct albeit slightly younger age obtained on the St. Césaire skeletal material. As readily admitted by the authors, the low collagen yield (0.8 percent) of the *single* age obtained from the St. Césaire Neandertal warrants some caution (Hublin et al. 2012).

The chronology of the site has also been addressed via the production of multiple new Bayesian models of all the available radiocarbon dates from Arcy (Banks and d'Errico 2019). The results of this study indicate that the discrepancies between ages, attributed by Higham et al. to the reworking of layers and by Hublin et al. to the fact that the former dated bones with a low collagen content are, in fact, better explained by the excessive number of layers taken into account by Higham et al., who included each sub-level of the Châtelperronian occupation (Xa, Xb, Xc), considered by Leroi-Gourhan more as *décapages* (spits) rather than genuine archaeological layers. As a consequence, this distribution of radiocarbon ages artificially increased the number of outliers, and thus the impression of inter-level admixture. Based on the Bayesian models produced by Banks and d'Errico (2019, there is no reason to consider the Châtelperronian layers of the Grotte du Renne underwent any significant reworking.

Additionally, a recent innovative use of zooarchaeology by mass spectrometry (ZooMS) to determine the biological affinity of small bone fragments produced additional evidence of Neanderthal bones within the lowermost Châtelperronian levels of the Grotte du Renne (Welker et al. 2016); however, this does not in any way alleviate continuing questions concerning potential inter-level migration of artefacts and hence the reliability of a Neanderthal-Châtelperronian association at this site.

This discussion, beyond specific issues tied to radiocarbon chronologies and associated methodologies (see below), is an illustrative example of how using one form of data, in this case chronological, to interpret another (taphonomic), and vice versa, can be influenced by the epistemic weight researchers assign to particular types of data. The importance assigned to each of these two contrasting data forms, chronological and stratigraphic, each with somewhat independent means for testing their consistency (geochemistry and Bayesian modelling for the former; horizontal and vertical artefact distributions and refitting for the later) clearly influences vying interpretations. In other words, Higham et al.'s (2010) position privileges the radiocarbon chronology with outliers and inconsistencies effectively interpreted as the product of stratigraphic disturbances, while others (e.g. d'Errico et al. 1998; Bordes 2002, 2003; Zilhaõ et al. 2011) invest more weight in what can be understood from a site's stratigraphy, spatial distribution of artefacts and post-depositional history.

Interestingly, both perspectives implicitly or overtly accept that the systematic search for inter- and intra-level refits at the Grotte du Renne remains the most tried and tested means for untangling stratigraphic admixture (Hublin et al. 2012 do provide limited refitting data), thereby potentially suggesting that arguments relying solely on chronology are somewhat precarious. Forebodingly perhaps, a recent, more detailed publication of additional lithic refits from the site's lowermost Châtelperronian level X produced evidence of connections across the level's three sub-levels, a, b, and c (Connet 2019). This would also be consistent with the original excavator's view of these 'sub-levels' reflecting an artefact of excavation rather than multiple archaeological layers (see above).

Until recently, the question of who made the Châtelperronian seemed, for all intents and purposes to be resolved, leaving only issues surrounding its chronology and the transformative mechanisms responsible for its emergence and unique character. The Neanderthal-Châtelperronian association now seems far less absolute, a development further complicated by a recent publication reporting dental remains (two deciduous molars) from the Grotta del Cavallo's Ulluzian deposits (Benazzi et al. 2011) to be anatomically modern human. This anti-paradigmatic proposition has, however, also become the subject of a heated debate. Zilhão et al. (2015) have questioned the Cavallo evidence, arguing that the mixed nature of the layer containing the teeth, problems of provenience, the post-excavation re-assignment of material to different levels, and post-depositional reworking of the deposits undermines the reliability of the modern human-Ulluzian association at the site. Finally, this

124 GRAVINA, D'ERRICO AND BACHELLERIE

uncertainty has recently been extended to the Aurignacian (Ramirez-Rozzi et al. 2009), traditionally associated with modern humans, with a juvenile mandible purportedly showing both anatomically modern and Neanderthal features being recovered from an Aurignacian context at the site of Les Rois in southwestern France. Although both cases undoubtedly warrant further scrutiny, they possibly provide interesting contextual information with regards to emergent palaeogenetic and palaeogenomic perspectives.

Neanderthal and modern human palaeogenetics and palaeogenomics

While archaeological evidence better characterizing the Châtelperronian and the Middle to Upper Palaeolithic 'transition' in general continued to accumulate, the 1997 publication of the complete Neanderthal genome (Krings et al. 1997) heralded a new era for palaeogenetics, with subsequent genetic analyses providing clear evidence not only for genetic admixture between Neanderthals and multiple Pleistocene modern human populations but where and when this these interactions potentially occurred. The weak signal of Neanderthal genes present in all non-African populations, while providing evidence of genetic admixture and hence contact between modern human and Neanderthal groups (Krause et al. 2007), does not provide clear indications of when and where such contact occurred or eliminate the possibility that most of the admixture took place well before the arrival of modern humans in Europe. With that said, Fu et al's (2015) analysis of the Oase 2 (Romania) skeletal material indicated gene flow between the two populations to have occurred sometime around 40 kya, with a similar study of a 45 kya modern human individual from Ust-Ishim in western Siberia by the same research group suggesting an introgression event around 60,000 years ago (Fu et al. 2014).

The recent reporting of a partial anatomically modern human calvaria from Manot Cave (Israel), dated by uranium-thorium to approximately 55 kya (Herskovitz et al. 2015), dental remains from Bacho Kiro in Bulgaria (Hublin et al. 2020) and a modern human skull from Czechia (Prüfer et al. 2021) would appear to support this proposed interbreeding chronology. Although the subject of continuous modelling efforts, the exact degree of genetic introgression (~ 1–4 percent) and, as a corollary, the intensity of contact and interbreeding between the two populations, remains heavily debated (e.g. Currat and Excoffier 2004; Serre et al. 2004; Ghirotto et al. 2011). However, the possibility that the sub-structures of archaic African population were responsible for the observed genetic signature seems to have already been ruled out (Yang et al. 2012). Furthermore, the recent DNA sequencing of remains (albeit a single phalanx) recovered from Denisova Cave in the Russian Altai provided evidence of a previously unknown hominin, the Denisovans, whose genetic signature is present in modern Papua New Guinean and East Asian populations. Evidence for genetic exchanges between Neanderthals and the Denisovans has also recently emerged (Prüfer et al. 2013; Slon et al. 2018). Recent analysis and sequencing of the Altai Neandertal genome equally provided evidence of an anatomically modern human genetic input to the ancestors of this population sometime around 100 kya (Kuhlwilm et al. 2016), pushing back the potential introgression chronology some 40,000 years. Overall, these analyses, and those likely to emerge in the coming years, present a much more complex bio-cultural scenario than previously anticipated (e.g. Alves et al. 2012; Prüfer et al. 2013; Bergström et al. 2020) and that when these groups met, which was likely to be rather frequently, admixture followed.

Comparisons of genetic data from North African populations have also shown traces of genetic admixture with Neanderthals (Sanchez-Quinto et al. 2012), thus shedding new light and raising further questions regarding the geography of these encounters. Interestingly, the fact that pre-Neolithic populations bear significantly augmented traces of Neanderthal ancestry, compared to living European populations, suggest that the substantial demic diffusion of Neolithic populations around 7 kya likely diluted evidence of what may have been a greater degree of admixture between Neanderthals and the initial anatomically modern human groups in Eurasia (Hawkes 2012). This input would have further swamped an already attenuated Neanderthal genetic contribution tied to an inferred population bottleneck during the Late Glacial Maximum (Semino et al. 2000; Reich et al. 2001; Posth et al. 2016) and again at the Pleistocene-Holocene transition (Fernández-López de Pablo et al. 2019). It therefore remains possible that the degree of contact between the two populations was more substantial than is currently detectable in the genetic diversity of modern European populations.

While this short section presents only the most basic developments relevant to the questions at hand, in a matter of only few short years the intense and continued scrutiny of the genetic record not only realigned our paradigms concerning Pleistocene demographics and populations expansions but also provided evidence that material culture is at pains to elucidate, and effectively nullified the model of Neanderthals being completely replaced by modern human populations. As previously and succinctly formulated by Zilhão (2006: 183) and now clearly substantiated by genetic evidence,

'Neanderthals and Moderns Mixed and It Matters', the question remains as to the timeframe and scale of interaction, and whether the possible consequences are, in fact, detectable in the archaeological record and, in either case, how this should be interpreted.

When?

The advent of radiocarbon dating irreversibly changed the landscape of Palaeolithic archaeology, and the continued development and refinement of associated methodologies combined with more sophisticated and taphonomically informed sampling strategies have made considerable advances in improving the chronological resolution of the Middle to Upper Palaeolithic 'transition'. This growing emphasis on radiometric dating has emerged with the development of ultrafiltration techniques (Bronk-Ramsey et al. 2004; Higham et al. 2006) that help to eliminate contamination and, when combined with a new calibration curve that now reaches to nearly 50 kya (Reimer et al. 2011; Bronk-Ramsey et al. 2012) as well as increasingly sophisticated Bayesian modelling techniques, have improved the chronological resolution of the timespan during which the discussed cultural phenomena unfolded. The Châtelperronian now appears to date roughly to between 45,000 BP and 42,000 BP, and the few dates available for the Proto-Aurignacian fall between 40,000 BP and 42,000 BP (Banks et al. 2013).

Despite these advances, the debate continues to centre around two diametrically opposed readings of the same corpus of radiometric ages associated with the Late Mousterian, Châtelperronian, and Proto- and Early Aurignacian. Partisans of the 'acculturation' model see an overlap or contemporaneity of the Châtelperronian and earliest manifestations of the Aurignacian, while those who support an 'indigenist' perspective see a strict anteriority of the Châtelperronian and hence its emergence as being unconnected to the appearance of modern human populations in the region. The issue is further complicated by the possibility of penecontemporaneous dates for populations living in different regions of Europe, for example in the Swabian Alps, northern Italy, or the Balkans having no direct contact but who could, nonetheless, have, one way or another, exerted mutual influence (see below). In the absence of diagnostic artefacts of the purported 'influencing' population identified in the material culture of 'recipient' groups in which emergent innovations are of different nature and form, how can the archaeological signature of 'acculturation' be discerned?

Biases in dated sites

The current chronology of the Châtelperronian is built from some 109 dates from a small sample of around fifteen of ninety-two (~ 16 percent) sites known to have or once had Châtelperronian material (based on data available in Bachellerie 2011). Furthermore, at the time of writing, roughly 65 percent of these dates come from three levels of a single site, the Grotte du Renne at Arcy-sur-Cure. The situation is even more disheartening in view of the paucity of available ages for the succeeding Proto-Aurignacian, which includes roughly thirty dates from twelve sites (Banks et al. 2013). Methodological issues aside (see below), it is immediately clear that both models are based on what remains a somewhat limited radiometric dataset wherefrom either could reasonably garner support given calibration imprecisions coupled with the use of at least three different radiometric dating techniques (AMS, conventional radiocarbon, thermoluminescence). Although a slow consensus seems to be building for which the *earliest* dates for the Châtelperronian generally precede the appearance of the Aurignacian, a series of new dates from Les Cottés, Grotte du Renne, and St. Césaire have nonetheless led Hublin et al. (2012:18747) to conclude that the Châtelperronian occupations at these sites, 'clearly postdate the earliest likely modern human remains documented in western Europe and largely overlap in time with the early Aurignacian in the Swabian area and in southwestern France'. Logically, both positions cannot be correct and appear self-contradictory insomuch as they are only as *true* as the data they contain.

Put another way, the present chronological resolution and attendant contextual issues (for example, the debate between Higham et al. 2014; Higham and Heep 2019; and Discamps et al. 2015, 2017; as well as Banks and d'Errico 2019 on Grotte du Renne) for the period in question is such that it allows a significant amount of heuristic flexibility that is largely dependent on the choices of what data particular researchers deem acceptable or relevant to the question and the reliability of the contexts from which they come.

What's dated and what to date?

Unlike the Early Aurignacian, for example, which is associated with split-based bone points, neither the Châtelperronian nor the Proto-Aurignacian contain a securely *diagnostic* organic tool component that can be sampled for dating. This absence, combined with the extreme rarity of preserved charcoal, has resulted in a radiocarbon chronology built almost entirely on dates procured from faunal remains, which has its own suite of problems. Foremost amongst which is whether certain dated artefacts can be confidently attributed to human rather than carnivore action; a problem compounded by the fact that this period likely witnessed interspecific competition and some niche overlap between large predators, most notably hyenas, and hominin groups (Discamps 2011; Discamps et al. 2011). Attempts to compensate and circumvent issues related to reliability have produced new methodological debates independent of improvements in sample preparation, calibration, or instrumentation. The case of the Grotte du Renne at Arcy-sur-Cure is again instructive. Recent dates produced by Higham et al. (2010: 20235) relied upon a series of fifty-nine artefacts (eventually producing thirty-one dates) including, 'cut-marked bones, horse teeth presumably smashed by humans, bone points or awls, ornaments made of animal teeth [no ages however were produced from ornaments] and mammoth ivory tusks interpreted as elements of structures', which they deemed most likely to be the product of human agency. In contrast, it has been noted that researchers, 'targeted those areas that yielded Châtelperronian body ornaments or diagnostic Neanderthal remains', thus avoiding worked bones that might bear traces of contaminants and selecting unmodified bones with good collagen preservation' (Hublin et al. 2012: 18744). Unsurprisingly, the two assays produced discordant results, which Hublin et al. consider to be the result of insufficient collagen preservation in some of the samples dated by Higham et al. (see Fig. 5.3). On the other hand, Hublin's team conclude (contra Higham et al.) that the site's stratigraphy is largely undisturbed, attributing the high number of outliers found by the opposing camp to insufficient collagen preservation in some of the samples dated by Higham et al.

Higham et al. (2012) reject these charges and consider the lack of coherence between the two series of dates to be due to the different way in which Hublin et al. set the priors for their Bayesian model. While Higham et al.'s ages are presented stratigraphically in five layers, a Proto-Aurignacian occupation at the top of the sequence (layer VII), followed by three Châtelperronian (VIII to X) levels, and an underlying Mousterian (XI) layer, Hublin et al. separated the ^{14}C determinations for the Châtelperronian into two, rather than three, chrono-stratigraphic units based on what, for the moment, appears to be a sole refit between layers X and IX. Whether such a combination is taphonomically justifiable will undoubtedly be the subject of further discussion, although this is consistent with the refitting data for the layer X sub-levels (see above) and would seemingly collaborate Hublin et al.'s contention that ^{14}C dating

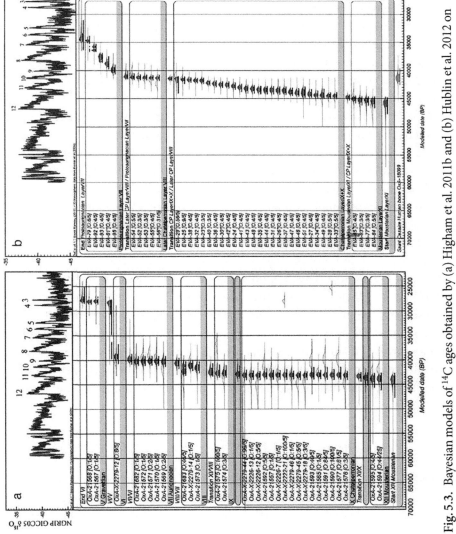

Fig. 5.3. Bayesian models of ^{14}C ages obtained by (a) Higham et al. 2011b and (b) Hublin et al. 2012 on bone samples from the Châtelperronian levels of the Grotte du Renne, Arcy-sur-Cure. Note the absence of 'outliers' and the merging of levels IX and X into a single stratigraphic unit in the Hublin et al. model.

alone, when appropriately conducted, can potentially demonstrate the stratigraphic coherence of the site.

It is clear from Leroi-Gourhan and Leroi-Gourhan's (1964) report on the site's stratigraphy, and from discussing the issue with the team in charge of the recently published analysis of the Châtelperronian layers (Julien et al. 2019) and archaeological material found therein, that the original excavators placed little emphasis on the stratigraphic limit between layer X and IX, and that these two layers represent a continuum in terms of their sedimentology and archaeological content. In such a situation, imposing a boundary between layer X and IX in the Bayesian model will, unsurprisingly, produce a large number of outliers.

In plainer terms, the more an archaeological sequence is sub-divided or consolidated, either during excavations or afterwards, inherently increases or decreases the chances that certain dates will appear as outliers. While such a conclusion seems relatively obvious on the surface, it nevertheless reveals that the fundamental difference between these two visions of the site is less connected to issues of sample contamination or provenience, but to how the 'outlier machine' (i.e. the Bayesian model) is *greased*.

The above shows that despite Bayesian modelling being a powerful tool for calculating the more probable age and timespan of past natural and cultural phenomena, as well as detecting potential inconsistencies in a chronological dataset, it nevertheless remains heavily dependent on the quality of the data analysed and the perceived precision of the stratigraphic provenience of the dated samples. Dates today considered as idiosyncratic 'outliers' can easily fall into tomorrow's main corpus of data once the stratigraphy of a site has been critically reassessed or methodological refinements and new ^{14}C determinations significantly shift the age range of a given event or cultural phase.

How?

Issues tied to the chronology and authorship of the Châtelperronian, while arguably more 'archaeological' in nature, somewhat pale in comparison to the catalogue of inherent conceptual difficulties and discordances between researchers when discussing 'how' or 'why' technological innovations and symbolically charged artefacts appeared in the material culture of the late Neanderthals. For some time, one of the core arguments of the 'acculturation' position has been based on the reported interstratifications of Châtelperronian and Aurignacian levels at Le Piage, Roc de Combe, and possibly the Grotte des Fées in France, and El Pendo in Northern Spain. Such interstratifications were interpreted as direct evidence that Châtelperronian Neanderthals and Aurignacian moderns alternately frequented the same sites, thus facilitating extensive and sustained cultural contact and the incorporation of 'modern' behaviours into cultural adaptations of late Neanderthals. A thorough taphonomic analysis, including a substantial systematic refitting programme, demonstrated interstratifications at Le Piage, Roc de Combe, and El Pendo to be artefacts of post-depositional processes (d'Errico et al. 1998; Montes and Sanguino 2001; Bordes 2002, 2003; Montes et al. 2005). The reassessment of the Grotte des Fées sequence (Châtelperron, Allier, France)—the type-site of the Châtelperronian—stimulated a long controversy that is to a large extent emblematic of difficulties addressing cultural contact during this crucial period. The publication of a series of ^{14}C ages, initially used by Gravina et al. (2005) to support the existence of an interstratification at this site, was strongly criticized by Zilhão et al. (2006, 2008). The latter combined unpublished excavation data with reassessment of lithic and faunal remains from the site to challenge the interpretation of the poorly recorded stratigraphy proposed in the 1950s by the excavator of the site. By showing that alternative explanations for the interstratification were equally, if not more, effective in accounting for the evidence, Zilhão et al. (2006, 2008) clearly highlighted the risk of basing definite scenarios of Neanderthal-modern interactions on single ill-documented archaeological sequences, even when the more advanced dating methods are applied to them.

The rejection of the interstratification/acculturation equation has apparently eliminated the only direct archaeological evidence documenting the putative long-term, local contemporaneity of the two populations, thus substantially reducing the possibility of formulating interaction models directly supported by empirical evidence. To remedy this shortcoming, one could consider turning to the ethnographic record to develop sound models that may be tested against empirical evidence. However, technological asymmetries between European colonial populations and indigenous populations in, for example, the Americas or the Western Pacific were of such a magnitude that they provide little help in untangling the subtleties of cultural contact between two Pleistocene hunter-gatherer populations whose lifeways were for all intents and purposes ostensibly identical or, at the very least, empirically and archaeologically indistinguishable.

Seemingly, the product of an archaeological record composed essentially of stone tools and a very limited number of bone tools and ornaments, whose chronology is still somewhat equivocal, these conceptual obstacles are not unique to the archaeological record of the final Neanderthals and initial anatomically modern humans. Some 35,000 years later, the Mesolithic/Neolithic 'transition', which benefits from a chronology whose precision is on the order of centuries rather than millennia, coupled with an infinitely more complete and diverse material record documented from hundreds rather than dozens of sites, nonetheless struggles with similar issues. These include not only theorizing cultural change and teasing apart developments provoked by demographic expansions, the diffusion of innovations and processes comparable to 'acculturation' (Robb and Miracle 2007), but also accurately identifying the loci of such changes and their material proxies.

Problems of similitude: difference and rupture, similarity and continuity

Lithic technology

In the case of the Châtelperronian, numerous scholars posit or tacitly accept that changes in a group's cultural traditions, purportedly brought about by contact, will be automatically reflected in aspects of their lithic technology. Notwithstanding the assumption that lithic industries are the best proxy to educe such cultural 'contact', the question remains as to which aspects of stone tools most effectively evince the transmission of *savoir-faire* between hunter-gatherer groups and how best to interpret their impact.

Concerning the case at hand, the typologically superficial resemblance of 'backed knives', from a very limited number of so-called 'MTA type B' assemblages, some excavated over a hundred years ago, to Châtelperronian points is meant to evince an evolutionary link between the two industries. However, the Mousterian-Châtelperronian 'typological' resemblance and possible technological connection (e.g. Pelegrin and Soressi 2007, Reubens et al. 2015) appears beset by several archaeological and conceptual complications, amongst which is the assumption that lithic industries are the best proxy to educe cultural 'contact'. This is further compounded by increasing evidence that the supposed *direct* ancestor of the Châtelperronian, the MTA, is not the final manifestation of the Mousterian and that the continued use of the moniker actually masks a substantial degree of techno-typological evidence in late Middle Palaeolithic assemblages and, therefore, should be abandoned (Gravina et al. 2015; Faivre et al. 2017; Gravina 2017). In fact, what was once described as a straightforward chronological, read *cultural*, succession of late Mousterian assemblage types eventually giving way to the 'transitional' Châtelperronian (e.g. Mellars 1996) now seems anything but. Recent revisions of several key archaeological sequences in southwestern France have clearly demonstrated that at least two techno-complexes, one discoidal (Thiébaut 2005), the other Levallois-based (Asselin 2005), chronologically and, at a number of sites, stratigraphically overlie assemblages assigned to the so-called 'MTA' and conclude the Middle Palaeolithic sequence (Jaubert 2010, 2012; Discamps et al. 2011; Jaubert et al. 2011; Gravina et al. 2012; Gravina and Discamps 2015). The quintessentially Mousterian character (Discoid or Levallois reduction methods combined with the absence of genuinely laminar products) of these late Neanderthal industries highlights a clear cultural and technological discontinuity with the ensuing Châtelperronian. This rupture is further borne out by recent techno-economic analyses that not only demonstrate the Châtelperronian's reportedly 'mixed' character to be largely an artefact of stratigraphic intrusions or mixing (Rigaud 1996; Gravina et al. 2018) but that its laminar component is fully 'Upper Palaeolithic' in conception (Bachellerie et al. 2007; Bachellerie 2011; Bordes and Teyssandier 2011; Roussel et al. 2016; Fig. 5.4). One of the fundamental differences between Mousterian and Châtelperronian 'backed' artefacts resides in the teleology of two technological projects. Blade blanks selected for 'backing' in the Châtelperronian fulfilled strict, preconceived morpho-metric criteria (Bachellerie 2011; Baillet 2017), whereas ostensibly

Fig. 5.4. Refitting of Châtelperronian blades onto their core (after Bachellerie et al. 2007).

similar Mousterian tool forms were made on a multitude of blanks types of widely different morphologies and dimensions, and issuing from different technologies (Gravina and Discamps 2015; Ruebens et al. 2015; Gravina 2016; Thomas and Gravina, 2019).

While further distanced technologically from the Mousterian, the continued documentation of the Proto-Aurignacian, especially its lithic component, has begun to attenuate any stark technological contrasts with the Châtelperronian (Bordes 2006), suggesting that the very idea of a 'transition' may itself be a misnomer in this context (Bordes and Teyssandier 2011). It has recently been suggested that interactions between presumed Châtelperronian Neanderthal and Proto-Aurignacian modern humans may have entailed a certain degree of idea exchange and diffusion materialized as independent bladelet production associated with Dufour bladelets (Roussel et al. 2016) in what once again takes the form of a *from/to* scenario; in other words, a unidirectional flow of innovation. This blade-bladelet component of Châtelperronian lithic assemblages has been interpreted as Neanderthal groups 'imitating' incoming modern human populations (Demars and Hublin 1989), a hypothesis seemingly reinforced by the recent discovery of inversely retouched bladelets (i.e. Dufour types), one of the type fossils of the Early Aurignacian, from several Châtelperronian contexts (see Roussel 2011; Roussel et al. 2016).

Privileging stone tool technology as the *singular* proxy of inter-group cultural transmission therefore flounders somewhat when confronted by recent re-evaluations of its technological composition and affinities, which is further frustrated by a reliance on a similitude of form divorced from content and context (see below). In light of the above, should the Châtelperronian be seen as marking the arrival of new (modern human or Neanderthal?) groups into southwestern France that led to the rapid adoption of new technical innovations (the hafting of Châtelperronian points, for example) that quickly realigned the technical repertoire of local groups (Pelegrin 1990), or the evidence a genetic/cultural admixture between Neanderthal and incoming modern populations? For the moment, the Grotte du Renne record, however, appears to be inconsistent with the view of the Châtelperronian industry being made by modern humans but is this the case for the entire Châtelperronian?

Personal ornaments, bone tools, and pigment use

While agentive perspectives have increasingly emphasized the role of lithic and organic technologies in social praxis, particularly in later Palaeolithic contexts (e.g. Dobres 2000; Sinclair 2000), there is general agreement that personal adornment in the form of ornaments or body painting play numerous, often simultaneous, social roles and functions, including being implicated in courtship, ethnic and social identification, communication and information exchange, amongst others (see Vanhaeren 2002). In this respect, these artefact types may provide interesting contextual information concerning possible Neanderthal-modern human interactions. Known from a small number of sites, the production and use of personal ornaments in the Châtelperronian is attested to by perforated and grooved pendants fashioned from animal teeth and fossils alongside decorated bone tools (d'Errico et al. 1998; Fig. 5.5). While production methods appear to differ between Proto- and Early Aurignacian examples (White 2001), these artefacts have nonetheless been interpreted to be the result of 'imitation without understanding' (Hublin et al. 1996) within a contact scenario characterized by substantial unidirectional 'acculturation'.

With regards to pigment use and bone tools, two interesting and telling patterns can be observed. In behavioural terms, the documentation of significant quantities of black colorants from Mousterian contexts, such as Pech de

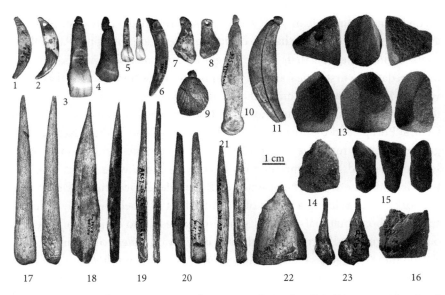

Fig. 5.5. Bone tools, ornaments, and pigments from the Châtelperronian levels of Grotte du Renne, Arcy-sur-Cure (after Caron et al. 2011). Personal ornaments made of perforated and grooved teeth (1–6, 11), bones (7–8, 10), and a fossil (9); red (12–14) and black (15–16) colorants bearing facets produced by grinding; bone awls (17–23).

L'Aze I and IV, Le Moustier, or Combe Grenal, and the presence of colorants and bone tools at sites that clearly predate the arrival of modern humans into Europe (Zilhão et al. 2010; Roebroeks et al. 2012; Soressi et al. 2013; Dayet et al. 2019; Martí et al. 2019) effectively rules out any cognitive or 'acculturationist' arguments for Neanderthal innovations in this domain. Furthermore, while still only documented from a handful of sites, the consistent co-occurrence of black and red colorants in Châtelperronian contexts could be seen as reaffirming the cultural unity already apparent in the Châtelperronian's lithic component (Bachellerie 2011; Dayet-Bouillot et al. 2014). Not unexpectedly, these interpretations reflect the interpretive and methodological issues surrounding the chronology of the Châtelperronian and the earliest manifestations of the Aurignacian outlined above. For a model in which the former is seen to predate the latter, the imitation hypothesis becomes seemingly impossible to support.

Several studies (e.g. Hublin 2013; Ruebens et al. 2015) have recently attempted to circumvent these inconsistencies by proposing what could be described as a 'deep acculturation' model, wherein innovations evident in the late Mousterian also stem from long-distance stimuli 'emitted' from distant modern human populations. In doing so, however, chronological and interpretive inconsistencies implicit in such a hypothesis are left unaddressed. First, all available evidence suggests that the earliest manifestations of Upper Palaeolithic traits amongst Neanderthals (e.g. pigment use, personal ornaments, etc.) not only predate the first appearance of techno-complexes traditionally associated with AMH, such as the Ahmarian, but most likely the so-called transitional techno-complexes of still unknown authorship, such as the Bohunician in Central Europe and the Kozarnikian in Bulgaria. Second, if these Neanderthal groups were so receptive and predisposed to integrate innovations from a source thousands of kilometres away from where they were living, wouldn't this demonstrate the very existence of highly developed cultural exchange networks, contradicting a vision of Neanderthals as a behaviourally different species, whose material cultures were impermeable to innovations due to built-in cognitive differences? And, even if this was proved to be correct, why should these exchanges be uniquely *unidirectional*, and not *bidirectional*, with elements of Neanderthal culture passing to AMH, including, for example, the use of black pigments themselves? This recent proposition is paradigmatic of interpretive biases typical of the debate surrounding Neanderthal behavioural adaptations. A traditional hypothesis-testing approach would entail documenting early occurrences of systematic black pigment use in the various techno-complexes of the Middle to Upper Palaeolithic transition, dating them, and proposing tentative scenarios for both the origin of this practice and its eventual spread. In the above case, the argument appears driven by the assumption that no symbolic or technological innovation could possibly have independently arisen in the Neanderthal world.

Implicit presumptions regarding Neanderthal cognitive or symbolic capacities aside (and bearing in mind the multitude of uses and functions of personal ornaments evident in the ethnographic record), any number of equally valid alternative explanations for this development could be advanced. Foremost amongst these is the likelihood that the complex bio-cultural mosaic in Western Europe during this period provoked both innovations and mutually influenced reconfigurations in a heterogeneous bio-cultural landscape where distinguishing between Neanderthal and modern human groups appears increasingly delicate (Trinkaus and Zilhão 2012). Moreover, viewed in more complex and theoretically informed terms, 'acculturation' processes have been shown to intervene on multiple scales, often involving elements of integration, assimilation, rejection, and marginalization that rarely operate in one direction (Berry 2005, 2009). While the chronological and taphonomic issues addressed above appear inseparable from the data sets solicited, interpretations of these symbolically charged artefacts and behaviours appear overtly subjective, conditioned by the theoretical penchant of individual researchers. Regardless of the manifold diversity of social scenarios in which personal ornamentation plays a fundamental role, the intensity and continuity of demographic interactions were likely instrumental to their importance.

Demography, cultural transfer, and hybridization

The handful of models advanced for explaining not only innovations evident in the Châtelperronian but the eventual extinction of the Neanderthals and the modern human colonization of Western Europe hinge on related issues of demography, population structure, and climatic change. While such scenarios are not new (Leroyer and Leroi-Gourhan 1983), a revolution in the available palaeoclimatic data available for this period (Sánchez-Gõni et al. 2008; Fletcher et al. 2010) and a continued refinement of modelling efforts based on this new data linked to substantial enhancements in calibrating radiocarbon chronologies (Bronk-Ramsey et al. 2012) have led to new debates and uncertainties surrounding the exact role played by sometimes rapid climatic oscillations, such as the Dansgaard-Oeschger events (Dansgaard et al. 1993) and European-wide ecological reconfigurations in Late Pleistocene population dynamics. In particular, the question as to what extent climatic factors, possibly coupled with competition with intrusive anatomically modern human groups, may have been implicated in the ultimate disappearance of the Neanderthals (e.g. Mellars 1996, 2004a, 2004b; d'Errico and Sánchez-Gõni 2003; Finlayson 2004; Zilhão 2006b; Finlayson and Carrion 2007; Sepulchre et al. 2007; Banks et al. 2008).

Banks et al.'s (2008) employment of eco-cultural niche modelling for tracking and comparing potential variances in territories exploited by anatomically modern humans and Neanderthals across three successive climatic phases not only seems to provide further support for the late survival of Neanderthal groups in the southern Iberian Peninsula, but suggests that some form of inter-group competition effectively reduced the size of the latter's eco-cultural niche. In addition to questioning climate as being the overriding factor governing the extinction of the Neanderthals, eco-cultural niche modelling provides an interesting perspective on demographic shifts tied to the adaptive systems of these Pleistocene hunter-gatherer groups and hence possible cultural interactions between the two. However, demonstrating 'competition' or the contraction of an ecological niche is not the same as elucidating the multiple interrelated causes (mutual avoidance, genetic assimilation, violent replacement, etc.) potentially implicated in such processes.

The relevance of these results to the present discussion is hopefully self-evident—while plainly true that ideas inevitably diffuse more quickly than people do, innovations are necessarily maintained and transferred between individuals. Estimates exist for the composition of Neanderthal 'bands', e.g. twelve to twenty-four individuals (Hayden 2012). But in the absence of any robust evidence for Neanderthal or anatomically modern human social structure or kinship systems, both being aspects significantly implicated in the transmission and maintenance of cultural traits including innovations, the clarification of large-scale demographic patterns is the essential first step to modelling the cultural landscape of the period. Unfortunately, herein perhaps lies the 'Achilles heel' of the hybridization paradigm or similar ideas concerning the diffusion or transfer of cultural elements during this period. Beyond sweeping and difficult to substantiate transfer mechanisms, such as stimulus or 'bow-wave' diffusion, we currently lack the requisite demographic and geospatial resolution for teasing apart and genuinely untangling the intricacies of Neanderthal-modern human interactions.

Conclusion

There seems little doubt that processes and historical contingencies akin to 'hybridity' or 'creolization' inevitably formed part of the complex and changeable cultural mosaic throughout prehistory, acting to variable degrees and effective at different spatio-temporal scales. Proponents of both models discussed above would, by perforce of their argumentation, have to accept that some degree of cultural exchange and or transmission intervened at some time between 45,000 and 40,000 BP, if not earlier. Although the ultimate and lasting effects of such interactions will likely remain a matter of substantial debate for the foreseeable future, what emerges from the preceding discussion is simply that the weight different researchers, formed by different research traditions, give to the constituent elements of the debate irrevocably intercedes in the interpretation of the archaeological record of the Late Mousterian and Châtelperronian.

This conclusion should not come as a shockingly new revelation, being one of the central tenets of the post-processual project. However, with that being the case, it is nonetheless remarkable how such a relatively restricted spectrum of evidence (stone tool typology and technology, a smattering of bone tools, ornaments, and elements of chronology) proves to be so incredibly agile, producing such outwardly conflicting and occasionally paradoxical models. Certain positions are explicit, whilst others seemingly rely upon an impossible conflation of process and the idea of a 5,000-year-long 'event'. In either case, mobilising essentially archaeological and stratigraphic data to transform a millennial scale phenomenon into a historical event, interpretable by recourse to models of culture change developed in other social sciences is confounded on at least two fronts. Firstly, concepts such as 'hybridization', 'creolization', or 'acculturation' flounder when confronted with the period's current temporal resolution.

Furthermore, any theory of culture change inherently involves individual or group level interactions (e.g. mutual avoidance, violent acculturation) and mechanisms of cultural exchange (e.g. indirect borrowing, direct transfer, mutual exchange) whose various possible forms and degree of influence essentially remain undetectable in the archaeological record of this period. Perhaps the most judicious avenue for addressing the possibility of culture exchange during this period inherently involves perceptions of scale and resolution. Different amplitudes of cultural reticulation and exchange across Western Europe and Eurasia, including those between different anatomically modern human populations and intermittently implicating contemporaneous

Neanderthal groups, of technological and related cultural elements during the period 45,000–35,000 years BP, inevitably wove different patterns of cultural expression involving both independent innovations and influences. A similar conception has recently been advanced for the Aurignacian itself, whereby the different elements of its cultural 'identity' appeared at different rhythms, resulting from socio-cultural interactions of various intensities amongst members of the same biological population (Bon et al. 2010).

However, distilling causal relationships underlying culture exchange phenomena that leave little or no tangible traces or signatures in the archaeological record remains difficult, if not impossible, and disagreements surrounding the exact locus of change continue. While a majority of archaeologists consider changes during this crucial period in human evolution to be connected to internal cultural evolution acting at the group level, including environmental adaptations and technological innovations associated with new hunting strategies, the formative mechanisms and archaeological signatures of such probabilities remain under-theorized. A notable exception is, perhaps, Tostevin's (2000, 2007) considered effort to operationalize Pleistocene 'culture exchange'.

In the present context, the satisfactory resolution of debates surrounding the Châtelperronian relies, first and foremost, upon a thorough archaeological and taphonomic analysis addressing not only the Arcy-sur-Cure record but also a large proportion of Late Mousterian and Early Upper Palaeolithic sites mobilized in current models of cultural change during this critical period. Moreover, this should be combined with the critical employment of more anthropologically informed and theoretically developed models of culture change adapted to the particular artefactual circumstances of the Middle/ Upper Palaeolithic 'transition'. Moreover, the fact that the Châtelperronian is now rightly considered the first industry of the European Upper Palaeolithic (Bachellerie 2011; Bordes and Teyssandier 2011; Roussel et al. 2016) rather than a 'transitional' facies adds further difficultly to a 'hybridization' perspective. The body of critical theory subsumed under the rubric of 'hybridity' or 'creolization' may indeed prove profitable for Palaeolithic archaeology in the future, provided that the continued refinement of this period's chronological record is coupled with new taphonomic analyses testing the reliability and integrity of relevant archaeological contexts. As a final thought, studies of cross-cultural contact, exchange, and influence in later prehistoric, historic, colonial, or postcolonial contexts are increasingly emphasizing both the inherent complexity in the emergence of new cultures, and perhaps more importantly, the understanding that to some extent all cultures are in a certain sense 'hybridized' (Card 2013). In other words, with the sparse archaeological record at our disposal, how sure can we accurately pinpoint the locus and vector of change from the pool of demonstrably complex mechanisms conditioning the spread, adoption, and even rejection of new culture traits?

Acknowledgements

The authors are grateful to the editors for their kind invitation to participate in this volume and for their patience. We would also like to thank William Banks, Jean-Guillaume Bordes, and João Zilhão for their constructive comments. Francesco d'Errico's work was supported by the Programme Talents (grant number: 191022_001), and the *Grand Programme de Recherche* 'Human Past' of the Initiative d'Excellence (IdEx) of the Bordeaux University as well as the Research Council of Norway through its Centre's of Excellence funding scheme, SFF Centre for Early Sapiens Behaviour (SapienCE) (project number: 262618), Brad Gravina benefited from support by the *Projet Némo—Neandertal face à la mort* directed by J.-Ph. Faivre, C. Lahaye, and B. Maureille (financed by the *Agence Nationale de la Recherche: Investissements d'avenir* ANR-10-LABX-52).

References

Alves, I., A. Šrámková Hanulová, M. Foll, and L. Excoffier. 2012. 'Genomic data reveal a complex making of humans'. *PLoS Genet* 8(7): e1002837.

Asselin, G. 2005. *Étude techno-typologique et spatiale du material lithique de niveau J du site moustérien de Rochers de Villeneuve, Lussac-les-Châteaux, Vienne (86)*. Mémoire de Master 2, Université de Bordeaux 1.

Bachellerie, F. 2011. *Quelle unité pour le Châtelperronien? Apport de l'analyse taphonomique et techno-économique des industries lithiques de trois gisements aquitains de plein air: le Basté, Bidart (Pyrénées-Atlantiques) et Canaule II (Dordogne)*. Unpublished PhD thesis, University of Bordeaux I, Bordeaux.

Bachellerie, F., J.-G. Bordes, A. Morala, and J. Pelegrin. 2007. 'Étude typo-technologique et spatiale de remontages lithiques de Canaule II, site Châtelperronien de plein-air en Bergeracois (Creysse, Dordogne)'. *Paléo* 19: 259–80.

Bae, C., K. Bae, and W. Wang. 2012. 'Current multi-disciplinary approaches to deciphering the East and Southeast Asian paleoanthropological record'. *Quaternary International* 281: 1–4.

Bailey, S. E., and J.-J. Hublin. 2005. 'Who made the Early Aurignacian? A reconsideration of the Brassempouy dental remains'. *Bulletins et Mémoires de la Société d'Anthropologie de Paris* 17(1–2): 115–21.

Bailey, S. E. and J.-J. Hublin. 2006. 'Dental remains from the Grotte du Renne at Arcy-sur-Cure (Yonne)'. *Journal of Human Evolution* 50(5): 485–508.

Bailleau, J.-G. 1869. *Grotte des Fées de Châtelperron*. Moulins: Desrosiers.

Baillet, M. 2017. *Eclairage de la tracéologie lithique sur le système nomade châtelperronien*. Unpublished Doctoral Dissertation, University of Bordeaux.

Banks, W. and F. d'Errico. 2019. 'La chronologie des couches Châtelperroniennes de la Grotte du Renne'. In M. Julien (ed.), *Le Châtelperronien de la Grotte du Renne (Arcy-Sur-Cure)*. Supplément à *Paléo*, pp. 83–99.

Banks, W. E., F. d'Errico, T. Peterson, M. Kageyama, A. Sima, and M.-F. Sánchez-Goñi. 2008. 'Neanderthal extinction by competitive exclusion'. *PloSOne* 3(12): e3972.

Banks, W., F. d'Errico, and J. Zilhão. 2013. 'Human–climate interaction during the Early Upper Paleolithic: testing the hypothesis of an adaptive shift between the Proto-Aurignacian and the Early Aurignacian'. *Journal of Human Evolution* 64: 39–55.

Bar-Yosef, O. 2007. 'The dispersal of modern humans in Eurasia: a cultural interpretation'. In P. Mellars, K. Boyle, O. Bar-Yosef, and C. B. Stringer (eds), *Rethinking the Human Revolution*. Cambridge: McDonald Institute for Archaeological Research, pp. 207–18.

Bar-Yosef, O. and A. Belfer-Cohen. 2013. 'Following Pleistocene road signs of human dispersals across Eurasia'. *Quaternary International* 285: 30–43.

Bar-Yosef, O. and J.-G. Bordes. 2010. 'Who were the makers of the Chatelperronian culture?' *Journal of Human Evolution* 59(5): 586–93.

Benazzi S., K. Douka, C. Fornai, C. Bauer, O. Kullmer, J. Svoboda, I. Pap, F. Mallegni, P. Bayle, M. Coquerelle, S. Condemi, A. Ronchitelli, K. Harvati, and G. W. Weber. 2011. 'Early dispersal of modern humans in Europe and implications for Neanderthal behaviour'. *Nature* 479(7374): 525–8.

Bergström, A., S. A. McCarthy, R. Hui, M. A. Almarri, Q. Ayub, P. Danecek, Y. Chen, S. Felkel, P. Hallast, J. Kamm, H. Blanché, J. F. Deleuze, H. Cann, S. Mallick, D. Reich, M. S. Sandhu, P. Skoglund, A. Scally, Y. Xue, R. Durbin, C. Tyler-Smith. 2020. Insights into human genetic variation and population history from 929 diverse genomes. Science 367(6484): eaay5012.

Berry, J. 2005. 'Acculturation: living successfully in two cultures'. *International Journal of Intercultural Relations* 29(6): 697–712.

Berry, J. 2009. 'A critique of critical acculturation'. *International Journal of Intercultural Relations* 33(5): 361–71.

Bon, F. 2002. *L'Aurignacien entre mer et Océan. Réflexion sur l'unité des phases anciennes de l'Aurignacien dans le Sud de la France*. Paris: Mémoire de la Société Préhistorique Française, t.XXIX.

Bon, F., N. Teyssandier, and J.-G. Bordes. 2010. 'La significance culturelle des équipement lithique'. In M. Otte (ed.), *Les Aurignaciens*. Paris: Éditions errance, pp. 49–72.

Bordes, F. 1958. 'Le Passage du Paléolithique moyen au Paléolithique supérieur'. In *Hundert Jahre Neanderthaler: Neanderthal Centenary, 1856–1956*. New York: Wenner-Gren Foundation for Anthropological Research, pp. 175–81.

Bordes, F. 1972. 'Du Paléolithique moyen au Paléolithique supérieur, continuité ou discontinuité?'. In *Origine de l'Homme moderne*, Actes du colloque de l'UNESCO, Paris, pp. 211–18.

Bordes, F. 1981. 'Un néandertalien encombrant'. *La Recherche* 122: 644–5.

Bordes, J.-G. 2002. *Les interstratifications Châtelperronien/Aurignacien du Roc de Combe et du Piage (Lot, France): analyse taphonomique des industries lithiques, implications archéologiques*. Unpublished PhD thesis, University of Bordeaux I, Bordeaux.

Bordes, J.-G. 2003. 'Lithic taphonomy of the Châtelperronian/Aurignacian interstratifications in Roc de Combe and Le Piage (Lot, France)'. In J. Zilhão and F. d'Errico (eds), *The Chronology of the Aurignacian and of the Transitional Technocomplexes: Dating, Stratigraphies, Cultural Implications*. Lisbon: Instituto Português de Arqueologia, pp. 223–44.

Bordes, J.-G. 2006. 'News from the West: a reevaluation of the classical Aurignacian sequence of the Perigord'. In O. Bar-Yosef and J. Zilhão (eds), *Towards a Definition of the Aurignacian*. Lisbon: Instituto Português de Arqueologia, pp. 147–71.

Bordes, J.-G. and N. Teyssandier. 2011. 'The Upper Paleolithic nature of the Châtelperronian in South-Western France: Archeostratigraphic and lithic evidence'. *Quaternary International* 246(1–2): 382–8.

Breuil, H. 1911. 'Études de morphologie II. L'industrie de la grotte de Châtelperron (Allier) et autres gisements similaires'. *Revue de l'École d'Anthropologie* 21: 320–40.

Bronk-Ramsey, C., T. Higham, A. Bowles, and R. Hedges. 2004. 'Improvements to the pretreatment of bone at Oxford'. *Radiocarbon* 46(1): 155–163.

Bronk-Ramsey, C., R. Staff, C. L. Bryant, F. Brock, H. Kitagawa, J. Van der Plicht, G. Schlolaut. 2012. 'A complete terrestrial radiocarbon record for 11.2 to 52.8 kyr BP'. *Science* 338(6105): 370–4.

Card, J. J. 2013. 'Introduction'. In J. J. Card (ed.), *The Archaeology of Hybrid Material Culture*. Center for Archaeological Investigations, Occasional Paper No. 39. Carbondale: Southern Illinois University Press, pp. 1–22.

Caron, F., F. d'Errico, P. Del Moral, F. Santos, and J. Zilhão. 2011. 'The reality of Neandertal symbolic behavior at the Grotte du Renne, Arcy-sur-Cure, France'. *PLoS ONE* 6(6): e21545.

Connet, N. 2002. 'Le Châtelperronien: réflexions sur l'unité et l'identité techno-économique de l'industrie lithique: l'apport de l'analyse diachronique des industries lithiques des couches châtelperroniennes de la grotte du Renne à Arcy-sur-Cure (Yonne)'. Unpublished PhD Thesis, University of Lille I.

Connet, N. 2019. 'Approche taphonomique, les limites de l'exercice 50 ans après les fouilles'. In M. Julien (ed.), *Le Châtelperronien de la Grotte du Renne (Arcy-Sur-Cure)*. *Paléo* supplement Annexe 2. pp. 505–25.

Currat, M. and L. Excoffier. 2004. 'Modern humans did not admix with Neanderthals during their range expansion into Europe'. *PLoS Biology* 2(12): 2264–74.

d'Errico, F. 2003. 'The invisible frontier: a multiple species model for the origin of behavioural modernity'. *Evolutionary Anthropology* 12(4): 188–202.

d'Errico, F., W. Banks, and J. Clobert. 2012. 'Human expansion: research tools, evidence, mechanisms'. In J. Clobert, M. Baguette, and T. Benton (eds), *Dispersal Ecology and Evolution*. Oxford: Oxford University Press, pp. 433–47.

d'Errico, F. and M. Sánchez-Goñi. 2003. 'Neanderthal extinction and millenial scale climatic variability of OIS 3'. *Quaternary Science Reviews* 22(8–9): 769–88.

d'Errico, F., J. Zilhão, D. Baffier, M. Julien, and J. Pelegrin. 1998. 'Neanderthal acculturation in Western Europe. A critical review of the evidence and its interpretation'. *Current Anthropology* 39(S1): S1-S44.

Dansgaard, W., S. J. Johnsen, H. B. Clausen, D. Dahl-Jensen, N. S. Gundestrup, C. U. Hammer, and C. S. Hvidberg. 1993. 'Evidence for general instability of past climate from a 250-kyr ice-core record'. *Nature* 364(6434): 218–20.

David, F. and C. Tolmie. 2019. 'L'exploitation de la faune terrestre'. In M. Julien, M. Girard, A. Roblie-Jouve (eds), *Le Châtelperronien de la grotte du Renne (Arcy-sur-Cure, Yonne, France). Les fouilles d'André Leroi-Gourhan (1949–1963)*. *Paléo*, Numéro spéciale, pp. 103–29.

Dayet, L., J-Ph. Faivre, F-X. Le Bourdonnec, E. Discamps, A. Royer, É. Claud, C. Lahaye, N. Cantin, E. Tartar, A. Queffelec, B. Gravina, A. Turq, and F. d'Errico. 2019. Manganese and iron oxide use at Combe-Grenal (Dordogne, France): A proxy for cultural change in Neanderthal communities. *Journal of Archaeological Science Reports*, 25: 239–256.

Dayet-Bouillot, L., F. d'Errico, R. Garcia Moreno Mazel. 2014. 'Searching for consistencies in Châtelperronian pigment use'. *Journal of Archaeological Science* 44: 180–93.

Delporte, H. 1957. 'La grotte des Fées de Châtelperron (Allier)'. *Congrès Préhistorique de France* (Poitiers-Angoulême), 15–27 juillet 1957, pp. 452–77.

Delporte, H. 1984. 'L'Aurignacien de La Ferrassie'. Paris: *Études Quaternaires* 7: 145–234.

Demars, P.-Y. 1992. 'L'Aurignacien ancien en Périgord. Le problème du Protoaurignacien'. *Paléo* 4: 101–22.

Demars, P.-Y. 1998. 'Comments on d'Errico, Zilhão, Baffier, Julien, and Pelegrin (1998): "Neanderthal acculturation in Western Europe. A critical review of the evidence and its interpretation"'. *Current Anthropology* 39(S1): S1-S44.

Demars, P.-Y. and J.-J. Hublin. 1989. 'La transition néandertaliens/Hommes de type moderne en Europe occidentale: aspects paléontologiques et culturels'. In B. Vandermeersch (ed.), *L'Homme de Néandertal*, Vol. 7: *L'extinction*. Actes du Colloque International de Liège, pp. 23-37.

Dennell, R. 2009. *The Paleolithic Settlement of Asia*. Cambridge: Cambridge University Press.

Discamps, E. 2011. *Hommes et hyènes face aux recompositions des communautés d'Ongulés (MIS 5-3): éléments pour un cadre paléoécologique des sociétés du Paléolithique moyen et supérieur ancien d'Europe de l'Ouest*. Unpublished PhD thesis, University of Bordeaux I, Bordeaux.

Discamps, E., B. Gravina, and N. Teyssandier. 2015. 'In the eyes of the beholder: contextual issues for Bayesian modelling at the Middle-to-Upper Palaeolithic transition'. *World Archaeology* 47(4): 601-21.

Discamps, E., B. Gravina, and N. Teyssandier. 2017. 'Comments on Higham and Heep (2018): 'Reply to: "In the eye of the beholder: contextual issues for Bayesian modelling at the middle-to-upper Palaeolithic transition", by Discamps, Gravina and Teyssandier (2015)'. *World Archaeology* 51(1): 1-6.

Discamps, E., J. Jaubert, and F. Bachellerie. 2011. 'Human choices and environmental constraints: deciphering the variability in large game procurement from Mousterian to Aurignacian times (MIS 5-3) in southwestern France'. *Quaternary Science Reviews* 30: 2755-75.

Dobres, M.-A. 2000. *Technology and Social Agency*. Oxford: Blackwell Publishers.

Fernández-López de Pablo, J., M. Gutiérrez-Roig, M. Gómez-Puche, R. McLaughlin, F. Parracho Silva, and S. Lozano. 2019. Palaeodemographic modelling supports a population bottleneck during the Pleistocene-Holocene transition in Iberia. *Nature Communications*, 10, 1872.

Faivre, J-P., B. Gravina, L. Bourguignon, E. Discamps, and A. Turq. 2017. Late Middle Palaeolithic lithic technocomplexes (MIS 5-3) in the northeastern Aquitaine Basin: Advances and challenges. *Quaternary International*, 433, 116-131.

Finlayson, C. 2004. *Neanderthals and Modern Humans: An Ecological and Evolutionary Perspective*. Cambridge: Cambridge University Press.

Finlayson, C. and J. Carrion. 2007. 'Rapid ecological turnover and its impact on Neanderthal and other human populations'. *Trends in Ecology and Evolution* 22(4): 213-22.

Fletcher, W. J., M. F. Sanchez-Goñi, J. R. Allen, R. Cheddadi, N. Combourieu Nebout, B. Huntley, I. Lawson, L. Londeix, D. Magri, V. Margari, U. Müller,

F. Naughton, E. Novenko, K. Roucoux, and P. C. Tzedakis. 2010. 'Millennial-scale variability during the last glacial in vegetation records from Europe'. *Quaternary Science Reviews* 29: 2839–64.

Fu, Q., M. Hajdinjak, O. T. Moldovan, S. Constantin, S. Mallick, P. Skoglund, N. Patterson, N. Rohland, I. Lazaridis, B. Nickel, B. Viola, K. Prufer, M. Meyer, J. Kelso, D. Reich, and S. Paabo. 2015. 'An early modern human from Romania with a recent Neanderthal ancestor'. *Nature* 524, 216–19.

Fu, Q., H. Li, P. Moorjani, F. Jay, S. M. Slepchenko, A. A. Bondarev, P. L. F. Johnson, A. Aximu-Petri, K. Prüfer, C. de Filippo, M. Meyer, N. Zwyns, D. C. Salazar-García, Y. V. Kuzmin, S. G. Keates, P. A. Kosintsev, D. I. Razhev, M. P. Richards, N. V. Peristov, M. Lachmann, K. Douka, T. F. G. Higham, M. Slatkin, J.-J. Hublin, D. Reich, J. Kelso, T. B. Viola, and S. Pääbo. 2014. 'Genome sequence of a 45,000-year-old modern human from western Siberia'. *Nature* 514, 445–9.

Ghirotto, S., F. Tassi, A. Benazzo, and G. Barbujani. 2011. 'No evidence of Neandertal admixture in the mitochondrial genomes of early European modern humans and contemporary Europeans'. *American Journal of Physical Anthropology* 146(2): 242–52.

Gravina, B. 2016. 'La fin du Paléolithique moyen en Poitou-Charentes et Périgord: considérations à partir de l'étude taphonomique et techno-économique des sites du Moustier (niveaux G à K) et La Roche-à- Pierrot, Saint Césaire (niveau EJOP supérieur)'. Unpublished PhD Thesis, University of Bordeaux.

Gravina, B. 2017. 'Intra-level technological change and its implications for Mousterian assemblage variability. The example of Le Moustier, layer G'. *Quaternary International* 433: 132–9.

Gravina, B., F. Bachellerie, S. Caux, et al. 2018. 'No reliable evidence for a Neanderthal-Châtelperronian association at La Roche-à-Pierrot, Saint-Césaire'. *Scientific Reports* 8: 15134.

Gravina, B., F. Bachellerie, M. Discamps, J.-G. Bordes, and J. Jaubert. 2012. 'A new ending for the Mousterian in south-western France? A revision of the Final Middle Palaeolithic record in south-western France and its implications'. *Proceedings of the European Society for the Study of Human Evolution* 1: 89.

Gravina, B. and E. Discamps. 2015. 'MTA-B or not to be? Recycled bifaces and shifting hunting strategies at Le Moustier and their implication for the late Middle Palaeolithic in southwestern France'. *Journal of Human Evolution* 84: 83–98.

Gravina, B., P. Mellars, and C. Bronk-Ramsey. 2005. 'Radiocarbon dating of inter-stratified Neanderthal and early modern human occupations at the Chatelperronian type-site'. *Nature* 438(7064): 51–6.

Grün, R., C. Stringer, F. McDermot, R. Nathan, N. Porat, S. Robertson, L. Taylor, G. Mortimer, S. Eggins, and M. McCulloch. 2005. 'U-Series and ESR analyses of bones and teeth relating to the human burials from Skhul'. *Journal of Human Evolution* 49(3): 316–34.

Hawkes, J. 2012. 'Evaluating recent evolution, migration and Neanderthal ancestry in the Tyrolian Iceman'. *Proceedings of the European Society for the Study of Human Evolution* 1: 97.

Hayden, B. 2012. 'Neanderthal social structure?'. *Oxford Journal of Archaeology* 31(1): 1–26.

Henn, B. M., L. L. Cavalli-Sforza, and M. W. Feldman. 2012. 'The great human expansion'. *Proceedings of the National Academy of Sciences* 109(44): 17758–64.

Hershkovitz, I., O. Marder, A. Ayalon, M. Bar-Matthews, G. Yasur, E. Boaretto, V. Caracuta, B. Alex, A. Frumkin, M. Goder-Goldberger, P. Gunz, R. L. Holloway, B. Latimer, R. Lavi, A. Matthews, V. Slon, D. B. Mayer, F. Berna, G. Bar-Oz, R. Yeshurun, H. May, M. G. Hans, G. W. Weber, O. Barzilai. 2015. 'Levantine cranium from Manot Cave (Israel) foreshadows the first European modern humans'. *Nature, advance online publication*. Retrieved from DOI: 10.1038/nature14134.

Hershkovitz, I., G. W. Weber, R. Quam, M. Duval, R. Grün, L. Kinsley, A. Ayalon, M. Bar-Matthews, H. Valladas, N. Mercier, J. L. Arsuaga, M. Martinón-Torres, J. M. Bermúdez de Castro, C. Fornai, L. Martín-Francés, R. Sarig, H. May, V. A. Krenn, V. Slon, L. Rodríguez, R. García, C. Lorenzo, J. M. Carretero, A. Frumkin, R. Shahack-Gross, D. E. Bar-Yosef Mayer, Y. Cui, X. Wu, N. Peled, I. Groman-Yaroslavski, L. Weissbrod, R. Yeshurun, A. Tsatskin, Y. Zaidner, M. Weinstein-Evron. (2018). 'The earliest modern humans outside Africa'. *Science* 359(6374): 456–9.

Higham, T., C. B. Ramsey, I. Karavanić, F. H. Smith, and E. Trinkaus. 2006. Revised direct radiocarbon dating of the Vindija G1 Upper Paleolithic Neandertals. *Proceedings of the National Academy of Sciences of the United States of America*, 103(3), 553–557.

Higham, T., F. Brock, C. Bronk-Ramsey, R. Wood, and L. Basell. 2011a. 'Chronology of the site of Grotte du Renne, Arcy-sur-Cure, France: implications for Neanderthal symbolic behaviour'. *Before Farming* 2011(2): 1–9.

Higham, T., T. Compton, C. Stringer, R. Jacobi, B. Shapiro, E. Trinkaus, B. Chandler, F. Groning, C. Collins, S. Hillson, P. O'Higgins, C. FitzGerald, and M. Fagan. 2011b. 'The earliest evidence for anatomically modern humans in northwestern Europe'. *Nature* 479 (7374): 521–4.

Higham, T., F. Brock, C. Bronk-Ramsey, R. Wood, W. Davies, and L. Basell. 2012. 'Radiocarbon dating & Bayesian modelling from the Grotte du Renne & a Neanderthal origin for the Châtelperronian'. *Before Farming* 2012 (3): 1–6.

Higham, T., K. Douka, R. Wood, C. B. Ramsey, F. Brock, L. Basell, M. Camps, A. Arrizabalaga, J. Baena, C. Barroso-Ruíz, C. Bergman, C. Boitard, P. Boscato, M. Caparrós, N. J. Conard, C. Draily, A. Froment, B. Galván, P. Gambassini, A. Garcia-Moreno, S. Grimaldi, P. Haesaerts, B. Holt, M. J. Iriarte-Chiapusso, A. Jelinek, J. F. Jordá Pardo, J. M. Maíllo-Fernández, A. Marom, J. Maroto, M. Menéndez, L. Metz, E. Morin, A. Moroni, F. Negrino, E. Panagopoulou,

M. Peresani, S. Pirson, M. de la Rasilla, J. Riel-Salvatore, A. Ronchitelli, D. Santamaria, P. Semal, L. Slimak, J. Soler, N. Soler, A. Villaluenga, R. Pinhasi, R. Jacobi. 2014. The timing and spatiotemporal patterning of Neanderthal disappearance. *Nature* 512(7514): 306–9.

Higham, T. and G. Heep. 2019. 'Reply to: "In the eye of the beholder: contextual issues for Bayesian modelling at the Middle-to-Upper Palaeolithic transition", by Discamps, Gravina and Teyssandier (2015)', *World Archaeology* 51(1), 126–33.

Higham, T., R. Jacobi, and C. Bronk-Ramsey. 2006. 'AMS radiocarbon dating of ancient bone using ultrafiltration'. *Radiocarbon* 48(2): 179–95.

Higham, T., R. Jacobi, M. Julien, F. David, L. Basell, R. Wood, W. Davies, and C. Bronk-Ramsey. 2010. 'Chronology of the Grotte du Renne (France) and implications for the context of ornaments and human remains within the Châtelperronian'. *Proceedings of the National Academy of Sciences* 107(47): 20234–9.

Hublin, J.-J. 1998. 'Comments in d'Errico, Zilhão, Baffier, Julien, and Pelegrin (1998): "Neanderthal acculturation in Western Europe. A critical review of the evidence and its interpretation"'. *Current Anthropology* 39 (S1): S1–S44.

Hublin, J.-J. 2000. 'Modern-non-modern hominid interactions: a Mediterranean perspective'. In O. Bar-Yosef and D. Pilbeam (eds), *The Geography of Neanderthals and Modern Humans in Europe and the Greater Mediterranean.* Cambridge: Peabody Museum Bulletin vol. 8, Harvard University, pp. 157–82.

Hublin, J.-J. 2013. 'The makers of the Early Upper Paleolithic in western Eurasia'. In F. H. Smith and J. C. M. Ahern (eds), *The Origins of Modern Humans: Biology Reconsidered.* Hoboken: John Wiley & Sons, pp. 223–52.

Hublin, J. J., N. Sirakov, V. Aldeias, et al. 2020. 'Initial Upper Palaeolithic *Homo sapiens* from Bacho Kiro Cave, Bulgaria'. *Nature* 581: 299–302.

Hublin, J.-J., F. Spoor, M. Braun, F. Zonneveld, and S. Condemi. 1996. 'A late Neanderthal associated with Upper Paleolithic artefacts'. *Nature* 38(381): 224–6.

Hublin, J.-J., S. Talamo, M. Julien, F. David, N. Connet, P. Bodu, B. Vandermeersch, and M. P. Richards. 2012. 'Radiocarbon dates from the Grotte du Renne and Saint-Césaire support a Neandertal origin for the Châtelperronian'. *Proceedings of the National Academy of Sciences* 109(46): 18743–8.

Jaubert, J. 2010. 'Les archéoséquences du Paléolithique moyen en Poitou-Charentes'. In J. Buisson-Catil and J. Primault (eds), *Préhistoire entre Vienne et Charente, hommes et sociétés du paléolithique.* Mémoire 38, Association des publications chauvinoises: Chauvigny, pp. 51–5.

Jaubert, J. 2012. 'Archéoséquences du Paléolithique moyen du Sud-Ouest de la France: quel bilan un quart de siècle après François Bordes?'. In F. Delpech and J. Jaubert (eds), *François Bordes et la préhistoire.* 134e Congrès national des sociétés historiques et scientifiques, Bordeaux, 2009. Paris: CTHS, pp. 235–56.

Jaubert, J., J. G. Bordes, E. Discamps, and B. Gravina. 2011. 'A new look at the end of the middle Palaeolithic sequence in southwestern France'. In A. P. Derevianko and M. V. Shunkov (eds), *Characteristic Features of the Middle to Upper Paleolithic Transition in Eurasia*. Novosibirsk: Asian Palaeolithic Association, pp. 102–15.

Julien, M., M. Vanhaeren, and F. d'Errico. 2019. 'L'industrie osseuse châtelperronienne de la Grotte du Renne, (Arcy-sur-Cure)'. In M. Julien (ed.), *Le Châtelperronien de la Grotte du Renne (Arcy-Sur-Cure)*. Supplément à *Paléo*, pp. 139–90.

Klein, R. G. 1973. *Ice-Age Hunters of the Ukraine*. Chicago: University of Chicago Press.

Krause, J., L. Orlando, D. Serre, B. Viola, K. Prufer, M. Richards, J.-J. Hublin, C. Hanni, A. Derevianlko, and S. Pääbo. 2007. 'Neanderthals in Central Asia and Siberia'. *Nature* 449(7164): 902–4.

Krings, M., A. Stone, R. W. Schmitz, H. Krainitzki, M. Stoneking, and S. Pääbo. 1997. 'Neandertal DNA sequences and the origin of modern humans'. *Cell* 90(19): 9–30.

Kroeber, A. L. 1940. 'Stimulus diffusion'. *American Anthropologist* 42(1): 1–20.

Kuhlwilm, M., I. Gronau, M. J. Hubisz, C. de Filippo, J. Prado-Martinez, M. Kircher, Q. Fu, H. A. Burbano, C. Lalueza-Fox, M. de la Rasilla, A. Rosas, P. Rudan, D. Brajkovic, Ž Kucan, I. Gušic, T. Marques-Bonet, A. M. Andrés, B. Viola, S. Pääbo, M. Meyer, A. Siepel, S. Castellano, 2016. 'Ancient gene flow from early modern humans into Eastern Neanderthals'. *Nature* 530: 429–33.

Laplace, G. 1966. *Recherches sur l'origine et l'évolution des complexes leptolithiques*. Mélanges d'Archéologie et d'Histoire, Ecole française de Rome, Editions de Boccard.

Leroi-Gourhan, A. 1958. 'Étude des vestiges humains fossiles provenant des grottes d'Arcy-sur-Cure'. *Annales de Paléontologie* 64: 87–147.

Leroi-Gourhan A. 1968. 'Le petit racloir châtelperronien'. In M. Mazières (ed.), *La Préhistoire, Problèmes et Tendances*. Paris: CNRS éditions; pp. 275–82.

Leroi-Gourhan, A. and A. Leroi-Gourhan. 1964. 'Chronologie des grottes d'Arcy-sur-Cure (Yonne). I: Climats du quaternaire récent. II: Industries du Paléolithique supérieur'. *Gallia Préhistoire* 7(1): 36–64.

Leroyer, X. and A. Leroi-Gourhan. 1983. 'Problèmes et chronologie: le castelperronien et l'aurignacien'. *Bulletin de la Société Préhistorique Française* 80(2): 41–4.

Lévêque, F., ed. 1993. *Context of a Late Neandertal: Implications of Multidiciplinarity Research for the Transition to Upper Paleolithique Adaptations at Saint-césaire, Charente-maritime, France*. Madison: Monographs in World Archaeology 16.

Lévêque, F. and B. Vandermeersch. 1980. 'Les découvertes de restes humains dans un horizon castelperronien de Saint-Césaire (Charente-Maritime)'. *Bulletin de la Société Préhistorique Française* 77(2): 35.

Martí, A. P., F. d'Errico, A. Turq, E. Lebraud, E. Discamps, and B. Gravina. 2019. Provenance, modification and use of manganese-rich rocks at Le Moustier (Dordogne, France). *PLoS ONE* 14(7): e0218568.

Mazière, G. 1978. *Le Paléolithique en Corrèze*. Mémoire de doc torat de l'Université de Paris X.

Mellars, P. 1996. *The Neanderthal Legacy: An Archaeological Perspective from Western Europe*. Princeton: Princeton University Press.

Mellars, P. 2004a. 'Stage 3 climate and the Upper Palaeolithic revolution in Europe: evolutionary perspectives'. In J. Cherry, C. Scarre, and S. Shennen (eds), *Explaining Social Change: Studies in Honour of Colin Renfrew*. Cambridge: McDonald Institute for Archaeological Research Monographs, pp. 27–43.

Mellars, P. 2004b. 'Neanderthals and the modern human colonization of Europe'. *Nature* 432(7016): 461–5.

Mellars, P. 2005. 'The impossible coincidence. A single-species model for the origins of modern human behaviour in Europe'. *Evolutionary Anthropology* 14(1): 12–27.

Montes, R. and J. Sanguino, eds. 2001. *La Cueva del Pendo. Actuaciones Arqueológicas 1994–2000*. Ayuntamiento de Camargo/Gobierno de Cantabria/Parlamento de Cantabria, Santander.

Montes, R., J. Sanguino, P. Martín, A. J. Gómez, and C. Morcillo. 2005. 'La secuencia estratigráfica de la cueva de El Pendo (Escobedo de Camargo, Cantabria): problemas geoarqueológicos de un referente cronocultural'. In M. Santonja, A. Pérez-González, M. Machado (eds), *Geoarqueología y patrimonio en la Península Ibérica y el entorno mediterráneo*. ADEMA, Almazán (Soria), pp. 127–38.

Morin, E. 2008. 'Evidence for declines in human population densities during the early Upper Paleolithic in Western Europe'. *Proceedings of the National Academy of Sciences* 105(1): 48–53.

Otte, M. 1990. 'From the Middle to the Upper Palaeolithic: the nature of the transition'. In P. Mellars (ed.), *The Emergence of Modern Humans: An Archaeological Perspective,* Edinburgh: Edinburgh University Press, pp. 438–56.

Pelegrin, J. 1990. 'Observations technologiques sur quelques séries du Châtelperronien et du MTA B du sud-ouest de la France. Une hypothèse d'évolution'. In C. Farizy (ed.), *Paléolithique moyen récent et Paléolithique supérieur ancien en Europe*. Actes du colloque international de Nemours, Mémoire du Musée de Préhistoire d'Ile-de-France 3, pp. 195–201.

Pelegrin, J. 1995. *Technologie lithique: le Châtelperronien de Roc-de-Combe (Lot) et de la Côte (Dordogne)*. Cahiers du Quaternaire 20, Paris, CNRS editions.

Pelegrin, J. and M. Soressi. 2007. 'Le Châtelperronien et ses rapports avec le Moustérien'. In B. Vandermeersch and B. Maureille (eds), *Les Néandertaliens. Biologie et cultures*. CTHS, Paris, pp. 284–96.

HUMAN INTERACTIONS IN WESTERN EUROPE 151

Peyrony, D. 1933. 'Les industries "aurignaciennes" dans le bassin de la Vézère'. *Bulletin de la Société Préhistorique Française* 30(10): 543–59.

Posth, C., G. Renaud, A. Mittnik, D. G. Drucker, H. Rougier, C. Cupillard, F. Valentin, C. Thevenet, A. Furtwängler, C. Wißing, M. Francken, M. Malina, M. Bolus, M. Lari, E. Gigli, G. Capecchi, I. Crevecoeur, C. Beauval, D. Flas, M. Germonpré, J. van der Plicht, R. Cottiaux, B. Gély, A. Ronchitelli, K. Wehrberger, D. Grigorescu, J. Svoboda, P. Semal, D. Caramelli, H. Bocherens, K. Harvati, N. J. Conard, W. Haak, A. Powell, J. Krause. 2016. 'Pleistocene Mitochondrial genomes suggest a single major dispersal of non-Africans and a Late Glacial population turnover in Europe'. *Current Biology* 26, 827–33.

Primault, J. 2003. *Exploitation et diffusion des silex de la région du Grand-Pressigny au Paléolithique*. Thèse, Université Paris X–Nanterre.

Prüfer, K., C. Posth, H. Yu, A. Stoessel, A. Spyrou, T. Deviese, M. Mattonai, E. Ribechini, T. Higham, P. Veleminsky, J. Bruzek, J. Krause. 2021. 'A genome sequence from a modern human skull over 45,000 years old from Zlatý kůň in Czechia'. *Nature Ecology and Evolution* 5: 820–5.

Prüfer, K., F. Racimo, N. Patterson, F. Jay, S. Sankararaman, S. Sawyer, A. Heinze, G. Renaud, P. H. Sudmant, C. de Filippo, H. Li, S. Mallick, M. Dannemann, Q. Fu, M. Kircher, M. Kuhlwilm, M. Lachmann, M. Meyer, M. Ongyerth, M. Siebauer, C. Theunert, A. Tandon, P. Moorjani, J. Pickrell, J. C. Mullikin, S. H. Vohr, R. E. Green, L. I. Hellmann, P. L. F. Johnson, H. H. Blanche, H. Cann, J. O. Kitzman, J. Shendure, E. E. Eichler, E. S. Lein, T. E. Bakken, L. V. Golovanova, V. B. Doronichev, M. V. Shunkov, A. P. Derevianko, B. Viola, M. Slatkin, D. Reich, J. Kelso, S. Paabo, K. Prüfer, S. Pääbo. 2013. 'The complete genome sequence of a Neanderthal from the Altai Mountains'. *Nature* 505: 43–9.

Ramirez Rozzi, F. V., F. d'Errico, M. Vanhaeren, P. M. Grootes, B. Kerautret, V. Dujardin. 2009. 'Modern and cutmarked human remains bearing Neandertal features associated with the Aurignacian at Les Rois'. *Journal of Anthropological Science* 87: 153–85.

Reich, D. E., M. Cargill, S. Bolk, J. Ireland, P. C. Sabeti, D. J. Richter, T. Lavery. 2001. 'Linkage disequilibrium in the human genome'. *Nature* 411(6834): 199–204.

Reimer, P. J., M. G. Baillie, and E. Bard. 2011. 'IntCal09 and Marine09 radiocarbon age calibration curves, 0–50,000 years cal BP'. *Radiocarbon* 51(4): 1111–50.

Rigaud, J.-P. 1996. 'L'émergence du Paléolitique supérieur en Europe occidentale. Le rôle du Castelperronien'. In O. Bar-Yosef, L. Cavallo-Sforza, R. March, and M. Piperno (eds), *The Lower and Middle Palaeolithic*. Actes des colloques IX et X de l'U.I.S.P.P., pp. 219–23.

Robb, J. and P. Miracle. 2007. 'Beyond "migration" versus "acculturation": new models for the spread of agriculture'. In A. Whittle and V. Cummings (eds), *Going Over: The Mesolithic-Neolithic Transition in North-West Europe*. Oxford: Oxford University Press, pp. 99–115.

Rocca, R., N. Connet, and V. Lhomme. 2017. 'Before the transition? The final middle Palaeolithic lithic industry from the Grotte du Renne (layer XI) at Arcy-sur-Cure (Burgundy, France)'. *Comptes Rendus Palevol*:16. 878–93.

Roebroeks, W., M. J. Sier, T. K. Nielsen, D. De Loecker, J. M. Parés, C. E. Arps, and H. J. Mücher. 2012. 'Use of red ochre by early Neandertals'. *Proceedings of the National Academy of Sciences* 109(6): 1889–94.

Roussel, M. 2011. *Normes et variations de la production lithique durant le Châtelperronien. La séquence de la Grande- Roche-de-la-Plématrie à Quinçay (Vienne).* Unpublished PhD thesis: Université Paris Ouest Nanterre-La Défense, Paris.

Roussel, M., M. Soressi, J.-J. Hublin. 2016. 'The Châtelperronian conundrum: blade and bladelet lithic technologies from Quinçay, France'. *Journal of Human Evolution* 95: 13–32.

Ruebens, K., S. J. P. McPherron, J.-J.Hublin. 2015. 'On the local Mousterian origin of the Châtelperronian: integrating typo-technological, chronostratigraphic and contextual data'. *Journal of Human Evolution* 86, 55–91.

Salomon, H. 2019. 'Les matières colorantes'. In M. Julien (ed.), *Le Châtelperronien de la Grotte du Renne (Arcy-Sur-Cure).* Supplément à *Paléo*, pp. 213–58.

Sánchez-Gõni M. F., A. Landais, W. J. Fletcher, F. Naughton, S. Desprat, and J. Duprat. 2008. 'Contrasting impacts of Dansgaard-Oeschger events over a Western European latitudinal transect modulated by orbital parameters'. *Quaternary Science Reviews* 27: 1136–51.

Sánchez-Quinto, F., L. R. Botigué, S. Civit, C. Arenas, M. C. Ávila-Arcos, C. D. Bustamante, and D. Comas 2012. 'North African populations carry the signature of admixture with Neandertals'. *PLoS ONE* 7(10): e47765.

Semino, O., G. Passarino, P. J. Oefner, A. A. Lin, S. Arbuzova, L. E. Beckman, G. Benedictis, and G. De. 2000. 'The genetic legacy of Paleolithic Homo sapiens sapiens in extant Europeans: a Y-chromosome perspective'. *Science* 290(5494): 1155–9.

Sepulchre, P., G. Ramstein, M. Kageyama, M. Vanhaeren, G. Krinner, M.-F. Sánchez-Goñi, and F. d'Errico. 2007. 'H4 abrupt event and late Neanderthal presence in Iberia'. *Earth and Planetary Science Letters* 258(1–2): 283–92.

Serre, D., A. Langaney, M. Chech, M. Teschler-Nicola, M. Paunovic, P. Mennecier, M. Hofreiter, G. Possnert, and S. Pääbo. 2004. 'No evidence of Neandertal mtDNA contribution to early modern humans'. *PLoS Biology* 2(3): 313–17.

Sinclair, A. 2000. 'Constellations of knowledge: human agency and material affordance in lithic technology'. In M.-A. Dobres and J. Robbs (eds), *Agency in Archaeology.* London: Routledge, pp. 196–212.

Slon, V., F. Mafessoni, B. Vernot, C. de Filippo, S. Grote, B. Viola, M. Hajdinjak, S. Peyrégne, S. Nagel, S. Brown, K. Douka, T. Higham, M. B. Kozlikin, M. V. Shunkov, A. P. Derevianko, J. Kelso, M. Meyer, K. Prüfer, S. Pääbo. 2018.

The genome of the offspring of a Neanderthal mother and a Denisovan father. *Nature* 561(7721): 113–116.

Soressi, M. 2010. 'La Roche à Pierrot à Saint Césaire (Charente-Maritime), nouvelles données sur l'industrie lithique du Châtelperronien'. In J. Buisson-Catil and J. Primault (eds), *Préhistoire entre Vienne et Charente, hommes et sociétés du paléolithique*. Mémoire 38, Association des publications chauvinoises: Chauvigny, pp. 191–202.

Soressi, M., S. P. McPherron, M. Lenoir, T. Dogandzic, P. Goldberg, Z. Jacobs, Y. Maigrot, N. L. Martisius, C. E. Miller, W. Rendu, M. Richards, M. M. Skinner, T. E. Steele, S. Talamo, and J. P. Texier. 2013. 'Neandertals made the first specialized bone tools in Europe'. *Proceedings of the National Academy of Sciences of the United States of America*. 110(35): 14186–90.

Speth, J. 2004. 'News flash: negative evidence convicts Neanderthals of gross mental incompetence'. *World Archaeology* 36(4): 519–26.

Spoor, F., J.-J. Hublin, M. Braun, and F. W. Zonneveld. 2003. 'The bony labyrinth of Neanderthals'. *Journal of Human Evolution* 44(2): 141–65.

Stewart, C., ed. 2007. *Creolization: History, Ethnography, Theory*. Walnut Creek: Left Coast Press.

Thiébaut, C. 2005. *Le Moustérien à denticulés: Variabilité ou diversité techno-économique?* Unpublished PhD thesis, Aix-Marseille I Université de Provence, Marseille.

Thomas, M. and B. Gravina. 2019. 'Analyse techno-économique d'un assemblage Discoïde du Moustérien récent de l'abri inférieur du Moustier (Dordogne, France)'. *PALEO* 30–1: 300–17.

Tostevin, G. B. 2000. 'The Middle to Upper Paleolithic transition from the Levant to Central Europe: *in situ* development or diffusion?'. In J. Orschiedt and C. Weninger (eds), *Neanderthals and Modern Humans: Discussing the Transition: Central and Eastern Europe from 50.000–30.000 BP*. Mettmann: Neanderthal Museum, pp. 92–111.

Tostevin, G. B. 2007. 'Social intimacy, artefact visibility and acculturation models of Neanderthal-Modern Human interaction'. In P. Mellars, K. Boyle, O. Bar-Yosef, and C. Stringer (eds), *Rethinking the Human Revolution: New Behavioural and Biological Perspectives on the Origin and Dispersal of Modern Humans*. Cambridge: McDonald Institute for Archaeological Research, pp. 341–57.

Trinkaus, E. and J. Zilhão. 2012. 'Paleoanthropological implications of the Peştera cu Oase and its contents'. In E. Trinkaus, S. Constantin, and J. Zilhão (eds), *Life and Death at the Peştera cu Oase: A Setting for Modern Human Emergence in Europe*. Oxford: Oxford University Press, pp. 389–400.

Vanhaeren, M. 2002. *Les fonctions de la parure au Paléolithique supérieur; de l'individu à l'unité culturelle*. Unpublished PhD thesis, University of Bordeaux I, Bordeaux.

Vanhaeren, M., M. Julien, F. d'Errico, C. Mourer-Chauviré, and P. Lozouet. 2019. 'Les objets de parure'. In M. Julien (ed.), *Le Châtelperronien de la Grotte du Renne (Arcy-Sur-Cure)*. Supplément à *Paléo*, pp. 259–85.

Verna, C., V. Dujardin, and E. Trinkaus. 2012. 'The Early Aurignacian human remains from La Quina-Aval (France)'. *Journal of Human Evolution* 62(5): 605–17.

Welker, F., M. Hajdinjak, S. Talamo, K. Jaouen, M. Dannemann, F. David, M. Julien, M. Meyer, J. Kelso, I. Barnes, S. Brace, P. Kamminga, R. Fischer, B. M. Kessler, J. R. Stewart, S. Pääbo, M. J. Collins and J-J. Hublin. 2016. 'Palaeoproteomic evidence identifies archaic hominins associated with the Châtelperronian at the Grotte du Renne'. *PNAS* 113(40): 11162–11167.

White, R. 2001. 'Personal ornaments from the Grotte du Renne at Arcy-sur-Cure'. *Athena Review* 2(4): 41–6.

Wolpoff, M. H. 1989. 'Multiregional evolution: the fossil alternative to Eden'. In P. Mellars and C. Stringer (eds), *The Human Revolution: Behavioural and Biological Perspective on the Origins of Modern Humans*. Princeton: Princeton University Press, pp. 62–108.

Yang, M. A., A.-S. Malaspinas, E. Y. Durand, and M. Slatkin. 2012. 'Ancient structure in Africa unlikely to explain Neanderthal and non-African genetic similarity'. *Molecular Biology and Evolution* 29(10): 2987–95.

Zilhão, J. 2006a. 'Neandertals and moderns mixed, and it matters'. *Evolutionary Anthropology* 15(5): 183–95.

Zilhão, J. 2006b. 'Chronostratigraphy of the Middle-to-Upper Paleolithic transition in the Iberian Peninsula'. *Pyrenae* 1: 7–84.

Zilhão, J. 2011. 'Aliens from outer time? Why the "human revolution" is wrong, and where do we go from here?' In S. Condemi and G.-C. Weniger (eds), *Continuity and Discontinuity in the Peopling of Europe: One Hundred Fifty Years of Neanderthal Study*. New York: Springer Science, pp. 331–66.

Zilhão, J. and F. d'Errico 1999. 'The chronology and taphonomy of the Earliest Aurignacian and its implications for the understanding of Neandertal extinction'. *Journal of World Prehistory* 13(1): 1–68.

Zilhão J., F. d'Errico, J.-G. Bordes, A. Lenoble, J.-P. Texier, and J.-P. Rigaud. 2006. 'Analysis of Aurignacian interstratification at the Châtelperronian-type site and implications for the behavioral modernity of Neandertals'. *Proceedings of the National Academy of Sciences* 103(33): 12643–8.

Zilhão J., F. d'Errico, J.-G. Bordes, A. Lenoble, J.-P. Texier, and J.-P. Rigaud. 2008. 'Grotte des Fées (Châtelperron): history of research, stratigraphy, dating'. *Paleoanthropology* 2008: 1–42.

Zilhão, J., D. E. Angelucci, E. Badal-García, F. d'Errico, F. Daniel, L. Dayet, and K. Douka. 2010. 'Symbolic use of marine shells and mineral pigments by Iberian Neandertals'. *Proceedings of the National Academy of Sciences* 107(3): 1023–8.

Zilhão, J., W. E. Banks, F. d'Errico, P. Gioia. 2015. 'Analysis of site formation and assemblage integrity does not support attribution of the Uluzzian to modern humans at Grotta del Cavallo'. *PLoS ONE* 10: e0131181.

Zilhão, J., F. d'Errico, M. Julien, and F. David. 2011. 'Chronology of the site of Grotte du Renne, Arcy-sur-Cure, France: implications for radiocarbon dating'. *Before Farming* 2011(3): 1–14.

PART II
CONFLICT, POWER, AND BELIEF

6

The Biographies of Resistant Material Culture in Occupied Landscapes

The Channel Islands and World War II

Gilly Carr

Introduction: a memory landscape of resistance

During the German occupation of the Channel Islands (1940–5) a wide range of resistant activities were undertaken by members of the population of Guernsey, Jersey, and Sark (Carr et al. 2014). These people were among the 25,000 in Guernsey and 43,000 in Jersey who had not evacuated in advance of the occupation. They and the German army each produced a distinctive material culture during this time (Carr 2009), although many of those made by the Germans incorporated island symbols, appearing to be what unwary archaeologists might pronounce as 'hybrid objects'. It is the items which pertained to resistant activities by islanders—and the response by the occupiers in the creation of potentially 'hybrid' objects—that will be considered here.

This chapter focuses on fast-moving and escalating symbolic, non-verbal conversations, arguments, and battles within the realm of material culture—specifically those made using coins and their symbols—that took place from the early summer of 1941 onwards. This unspoken tussle, which left its trace only in diaries and in museum objects now removed from their biographies, is unpacked here. I focus on the minutiae, which enables us to see swift change over time in response to external events and communications, and repressive responses by the occupiers. It also allows us to see how rapid changes in, and trajectories of, material culture were made for reasons of appropriation—and evasion of appropriation—rather than being driven primarily by any true hybridity.

Unsurprisingly, given the short period of time for which the islands were occupied, no true hybrid objects exist from this period—by which I mean, no object which fused (equally or unequally) the symbols of the occupier and the

Gilly Carr, *The Biographies of Resistant Material Culture in Occupied Landscapes: The Channel Islands and World War II*
In: *Archaeologies of Cultural Contact: At the Interface*. Edited by: Timothy Clack and Marcus Brittain, Oxford University Press.
© Oxford University Press 2022. DOI: 10.1093/oso/9780199693948.003.0007

occupied *and which was willingly made by islanders*—*no* material culture of collaboration in this sense, for this is what we imply when we talk about hybridity in the context of a military occupation. With regards to objects made by the occupiers, however, we see such an apparent fusion. This paper discusses why attempts to label such objects as 'fusions' or 'hybrids' are superficial at best and—at worst—simply wrong. The analysis presented here, made with respect to objects made within living memory, allows us to see that something quite different was happening; something better illuminated with reference to object biographies.

The disciple of hybridity might draw attention to Stephen Silliman's work, for whom hybridity was defined at a basic level as an 'accommodation of difference, whether by individuals balancing old and new worlds or by communities adjusting to familiar and unfamiliar people', or even more generally as 'a quality of multicultural interactions' (2013: 488, 492). Such a general definition may hold true, but I suggest that such 'accommodation of difference' is in the eye of the beholder. The people whose eyes I consider here were doing nothing of the sort.

What is more clearly apparent—at least in this WWII context—is a theft, followed by a battle (or exploitation), of symbols between occupiers and occupied who silently waged war over certain images, symbols, and letters, and their meanings. The material culture of resistance was not confined to symbols and images; it also comprised disguised crystal radio sets, underground news-sheets, fake identity cards, and defiant artwork made in the islands' prisons. But even these made up just one small part of the repertoire of resistance carried out in the occupied Channel Islands.

Resistance in the Channel Islands was different to other parts of German-occupied Europe in that it was almost entirely unarmed and was carried out by individuals or small groups acting alone rather than by any unified underground organisation. Such examples of defiance against the Germans and their orders included escaping from the islands with espionage information; giving humanitarian assistance to Jews and forced and slave labourers; resistance by public servants such as teachers, police, doctors, and government officials; illicitly listening to the BBC and printing underground newspapers; defying deportation orders; economic resistance; demonstrations and protests; and quasi-military resistance by teenage boys and young men (Carr et al. 2014).

Despite the low profile both of resistance and those who committed acts of defiance and protest during the occupation, and despite the marginalization of much of its heritage (Carr 2014a, 2019), the dataset is a rich one. The symbolic nature of some of the seemingly lowest-risk acts of defiance (which still

THE BIOGRAPHIES OF RESISTANT MATERIAL CULTURE   161

led to deportation of those who were caught) means that, for the material culture specialist, there is still a wealth of information available.

Material culture, biographies, and resistance

Diaries and memoirs can be a great boon to the historical archaeologist, and many of them describe how patriotic symbols were worn or used during the occupation. These help to give a context to the objects that survive, mostly divorced from their biographies, in museums in the islands today. We can divide the artefacts that come under the banner of 'symbolic resistance' into four (sometimes overlapping) groups, and most of these can be considered trench art as defined by Saunders (2003: 11). The four groups are: those which incorporated the letter V for victory; those which used the islands' crests; those which featured a patriotic image such as the King; and those which incorporated the patriotic colours of red, white, and blue. The first three of these, incorporating symbols rather than symbolic colours, will be discussed in this chapter. Each share their origin in coins, which were prime bearers of symbols and patriotic images.

The German order of 28 August 1940, published on 8 November of that year, relating to 'associations, meetings, distinctive emblems and beflagging', is central to our understanding of the dangers of using such symbols. This order forbade the wearing of 'distinctive apparel and uniform emblems' and carried a punishment of 'imprisonment not exceeding one year and with a fine'. Whether or not this included the wearing of symbols, it was always wise to exercise caution when interpreting German orders. But there were always those who were prepared to take risks, driven by a patriotic determination to 'do something anti-German every day', as Colonel Britton encouraged them to do. Colonel Britton (otherwise known as Douglas Ritchie) was a BBC broadcaster who was part of a wider team who transmitted the 'V-for victory' propaganda campaign to occupied Europe during the first half of 1941. In the early summer of 1941, Ritchie broadcast to the English-speakers of Europe, and it was at this point that Channel Islanders became aware of the campaign. Although I have explored the biography of the V-sign campaign and its arte-factual correlates in the Channel Islands in more detail elsewhere (Carr and Heaume 2004; Carr 2010, 2012), it will be relevant to give some further details of the case study here.

Understanding the biography of the objects under investigation here is one of the keys to understanding their change over time. In Kopytoff's (1986) original conceptualization, the biography of an object, at its simplest, examined its social life, change in value and meaning over time, and change in context from its creation onwards. For Gosden and Marshall (1999: 169), 'as people and objects gather time, movement and change, they are constantly transformed, and these transformations of person and object are tied up with each other'. Such biographical approaches encourage us to have an understanding of objects at more than a single point in their existence.

Unlike other classes of objects studied by anthropologists, the artefacts discussed in this chapter did not gain their meaning during the occupation through ownership or manufacture by certain people, even if this informs their meaning today. Meaning was instead created through use, wearing, or performance, the mode of which was likely to have varied depending on gender and age. Jody Joy's (2009: 544) call for a 'reinvigorated' object biography examined the interplay between people and objects, focusing on how biographies can consist of 'connected jumps as the object becomes alive within certain clusters of social relationships and is inactive at other points in time and space'. Joy was particularly interested in the 'drama' in the performance of the object, and how such moments invested the object with meaning. This strongly resonates with the resistant material culture discussed here, which 'became alive' and invested with meaning at moments of 'drama' as it was performed to certain audiences, as we shall see.

More recently, Hahn and Weiss (2013: 7–8) have critiqued the concept of the biography; they observed that pinpointing the moment of 'birth' and 'death' are difficult, especially for objects that enter an extended period of stasis (such as decades spent in a museum cabinet, during which time those who could have explained their meaning have passed away). Instead, they propose the idea of the non-linear object 'itinerary', which allows for periods of inertness, moments of rapid transformation, and a mobile existence. Such an approach also finds resonance with the case study presented here, which witnessed periods of rapid change in form of highly mobile objects whilst coupled with stability of meaning. During their 'itinerary', these objects attempted to evade appropriation. They changed form in the face of attempts to shut them down and end their manufacture and performance. We will return to this later. First let us examine the rapid change in form—but continuity of meaning—of this resistant material culture.

At the start of the V-sign campaign, islanders chalked or painted the letter V on walls, doors, streets, and signs (Cruikshank 2004: 168; Sanders 2005: 101). Although the Germans were quick to punish such actions, islanders soon took up the as-yet unprohibited 'V-sound', introduced on 27 June 1941

THE BIOGRAPHIES OF RESISTANT MATERIAL CULTURE   163

(Rolo 1943: 139). This was the rhythm of the Morse letter V (three dots and a dash), and the European service broadcast this played on an African kettle-drum by percussionist James Blades, followed by the 'da-da-da-dum' opening theme of Beethoven's Fifth Symphony, which preceded the news (Blades 1977: 179). Islanders were soon knocking on each other's doors in Morse code (e.g. Falla 1981: 57–9) or playing Beethoven's Fifth Symphony full blast on their radios. It gave a great deal of satisfaction to be (briefly) legally defiant. While such open displays of defiance may not have changed the course of the war in military terms, it was an excellent way for islanders to signal to each other their anti-German feelings and to vent their anger.

The campaign reached its height on 20 July 1941; this was the date that the BBC had chosen for the mobilization of the 'V-Army' all over Europe. Although the campaign was not aimed at Channel Islanders because of the unfeasibility of organized resistance in the islands and the dangers that it would bring (Sanders 2005: 100), islanders certainly heard the broadcasts, which many recorded in their diaries (e.g. Sinel 1945: 48; Harvey 1995: 83; Le Ruez 2003: 33; Evans 2009: 52–3). In this stage of the campaign, the ephem-erality of the painted V's was matched by the equally short-lived and transient nature of the associated material culture. People cut V's out of pieces of news-paper and scattered them in the streets; some red paper V's still survive in the archives of Jersey War Tunnels museum (ref 2002/486/5). People also broke matches in the form of a V and threw them in the road or left knives and forks on tables in the shape of a V after a meal in a café (Jersey Archives ref R/06/4).

The Germans were, of course, aware of the V-campaign and wasted no time in passing orders against it and announcing penalties in the form of radio confiscation and civil guard duty for people living within a kilometre's radius of the offending graffiti. Within days, in high profile cases, two Jersey sisters in their early twenties (Lillian Kinnard and Kathleen Norman) and a Frenchman from Guernsey in his fifties (Xavier de Guillebon) were sentenced to imprisonment in Caen Prison, France, for nine months and one year respectively, for 'V propaganda' (Sinel 1945: 50; Bell 1995: 102). Just before the date for the 'V-Army mobilization', the Germans appropriated the letter V for themselves to denote a German victory. In this context, the V stood for 'Viktoria', which they claimed was an old German victory cry (Rolo 1943: 140). They argued that they were the only ones who could legitimately make the V-sign, as they were the only ones who had been victorious so far. They were vigorous in painting V's on their cars, on the houses which they occu-pied, and on brassards (armbands) which they wore over their uniforms. The German V, however, was ringed by oak or laurel leaves, and this became a clear way of differentiating ownership. Despite the penalties, the islanders were not content to let the Germans have it all their own way. In a couple of locations, somebody added the letter 'E' before a 'V', thus denoting an English victory (Falla 1981: 56; Bell 1995: 103–4; Harvey 1995: 83).

Because of the penalties and the German appropriation of the publicly visible V-sign campaign, a small number of Guernseymen decided to move the V into the private realm. This involved transferring V's from the ephemeral and transient into a more durable and portable material realm. This meant that it could be passed from hand to hand and could be quickly hidden. The prime example of this manifested itself as V-badges made by two young men, Alf Williams and Roy Machon. Using pennies, sixpences, shillings, florins or half-crowns, and especially coins of George V (for obvious reasons) the men would neatly clip and file around the King's head and cut a V-shape underneath. A safety-pin was soldered to the back and men would wear these badges underneath the lapel of their jackets; there is artefactual evidence that women wore them on slides in their hair or under their coat. When worn (or 'performed'), the wearer could flash the badge (or pointedly adjust their hair) in front of trusted friends when they passed in the street. These badges became quite popular and it is estimated that the men made three hundred to four hundred examples between them (Carr 2012). Machon was eventually caught in June 1943, but did not betray Williams. He was sentenced to five months' forced labour in Stadelheim Prison in Munich and was later transferred to Laufen civilian internment camp until the end of the war.

Around a dozen of these badges still survive in Guernsey museums (Fig. 6.1). They were popular symbols of defiance because they combined a number of sentiments in the one item. They spoke of patriotism, identity, faith in an Allied victory, and an unashamedly anti-German stance. It took some courage to wear one because of the consequences. The badges were even remarked upon by island diarists, of which two examples will suffice. On 23 October 1942, Violet Carey wrote in her diary, 'I met Mabel Kinnersly who gave me my Kings Head. She knows a mysterious boy who cuts out the King's head in an English shilling and also cuts out a beautiful V under the King's head and mounts a pin on it. He does it with a fretsaw. It is lovely; I wear my marquisite crown and G.R. on top of it. We have to provide the shilling and pay him a mark. We all wear them under our coats. Mabel wears hers openly, but it is rather silly because if the Gestapo spot it they will take it from her' (Evans 2009: 107).

On 16 November 1942, the diarist Reverend R. Douglas Ord wrote that 'Brooches are being sold for a Mark. They are fashioned out of a shilling by cutting out the King's head in relief and the rest of the coin to make a V. The Gestapo are on the watch for any who wear them and for the maker. If they caught a wearer they would, if necessary, use third degree methods to track down the maker. This job is ruinous to the little saws used. Like everything else they wear out and cannot be replaced' (Ord unpublished). This comment suggests that it is likely that the Reverend Ord saw the badges being made and spoke to Machon or Williams. Although the badges are the best-known artefact type bearing the V-sign, other items of jewellery were made from coins. The author has a bracelet made of George V sixpences, found in a Guernsey antiques fair. In her diary entry for 10 November 1941, diarist Violet Carey remarked in passing, 'I am told that they have made necklaces and bracelets out of shillings and sixpences'. This is very likely to be a reference to this exact type of artefact.

There is also an interesting pendant once given to Alf Williams and now in the German Occupation Museum in Guernsey. It is made up of two coins, soldered end to end, with a Guernsey coin on top and a German one below. The two are held in place with little Vs. Hanging from the V-shaped loop on top of the pendant is a plaited length of red, white, and blue wool. It is likely that Williams was given this pendant on the (mistaken) assumption that he, more than anyone, would understand its symbolic meaning. It is likely that this pendant plays upon a defiant piece of graffiti dating from the occupation. The algebraic fraction '22/G' was used to mean 'victory over Germany', as V is the 22nd letter of the alphabet. It is possible that the Guernsey coin 'over' the German coin, and surrounded by V's, symbolizes the victory of the Guernsey people over the Germans. The inventiveness of this artefact would have helped to protect the original wearer from prosecution if it was discovered. Its meaning is obscure enough to have precluded interpretation, and this in itself would have encouraged others to be equally inventive in their methods of defiance.

This inventiveness mixed with patriotic fervour gave birth to another type of defiant material culture: the cigarette lighter made of copper or brass tubing or knobs, decorated with coins which had been pressed into the side or the base (Carr 2012). Using the patriotic images on coins such as Britannia or the King's head (especially those of George V) from English coins, the islands' crests from island coins, and even the face of Marianne, symbol of the Republic, from French coins, it is clear that some island men were fashioning home-made lighters closely similar to those made in the trenches by Allied soldiers in WWI. Channel Island men volunteered in vast numbers to fight in the trenches, and it is here that many would have seen this type of trench art being made. It is likely, therefore, that the makers can be pinned down to a certain age group of island men. Because the use of the imagery on coins was not explicitly forbidden, this type of artefact, too, would have escaped German censure. These objects would have been 'performed' in front of others when lighting a cigarette or pipe.

Interestingly, the few examples which survive in occupation museums in Guernsey and Jersey are thought by the curators to have come from a German context. The curators of private amateur occupation museums in the islands, of which there are many, are collectors who use their museums primarily as a way of showing off their collections to the public (see Carr 2014b, ch. 2). Occupation museums have a long pedigree in the islands: the first one opened in 1946, just a year after the occupation ended. The collectors have acquired their items over a lifetime, and many of them hold the stories of their objects in their heads, as told to them over the decades by people who have given or sold artefacts to the museum. It is unusual for the owners to have any kind of written catalogue with details of provenance.

Given the Allied trench art style, and assuming that the German provenance is correct, it seems probable that, as well as trading or using them among fellow veterans, Island men were also bartering the cigarette lighters with German soldiers who wanted them as souvenirs; lighters with the islands' crest were particularly popular in this regard (Fig. 6.1). It is an attractive hypothesis to think that island men were making lighters with defiant symbols and then trading or selling them as part of an elaborate joke that only they and their friends appreciated. To the German soldiers, these objects would have been seen as apparently harmless yet attractive souvenirs. It is also possible that Island men were compelled to barter such attractive items with soldiers out of desperation and hunger. Unfortunately, no diary reference has been found to tell the real story of these objects.

The number of cigarette lighters decorated with coins featuring the Guernsey or Jersey crest (a shield featuring three leopards *passant gardant*) makes it clear that these items were coveted above other designs by German soldiers. The appropriation of the crest (the example of 'superficial hybridity' I gave at the start) is something seen on a wide variety of other items of German trench art from the Channel Islands. While the wooden bowl or wooden carved candlestick were favourite items to receive an engraving of the crest (e.g. Fig. 6.1), this symbol also features on items as diverse as on book plates, tobacco pots, pen holders, and ash trays. Many of the wooden or metal items made by German soldiers while in the islands were stamped or engraved with an island crest as if it was a trophy to display now that they had 'won' the islands. In the creation of

Fig. 6.1. V-sign badge, La Valette Military Museum (top left); cigarette lighter, La Valette Military Museum (top right); German bread bowl featuring Guernsey crest, La Valette Military Museum (bottom left); (d) crested badge, La Valette Military Museum (bottom right).

metal trench art, they used crests cut out of local coins which they soldered onto their objects. With the Germans carving, stamping, or soldering a crest on seemingly every item they made, it is inevitable that the islanders became aware of this. Such theft of the crest would have angered them, and with no means of persuading the occupiers to desist, the only way to battle for and reclaim this symbol of their own identity was to do so through material culture.Using the very same coins featuring the crest, islanders clipped and filed around the prime symbol of island identity to make badges, rings, and brooches (Fig. 6.1). These they wore silently on the body, and there is no record of anyone being caught in possession of such an item. Given the arrests over the V-sign badges, the

Germans were alert to such tiny symbols of defiance and identity. It is quite possible that these items, too, were made by former veterans. The crested badges are highly reminiscent of the Royal Guernsey Militia cap badges and lapel badges worn during the First World War. It is probable that crested coin badges were gendered objects, worn by veterans to signal their former membership of the military in a way that would have invoked Saunders's (2001) 'memory bridge', indicating the continuation of the 1914–18 fight with the Germans through material culture. The very small number of these items in occupation museums today suggests that they were not made in large numbers. Nonetheless, by reclaiming their identity in this way, an unarmed and undocumented battle for the crest took place in the garden sheds, private homes, and streets of the islands as they were manufactured and performed.

By the summer of 1943 it had become a lot more dangerous to deploy such symbols. Small symbols of defiance infuriated the Germans, leading to arrests and deportation to prison camps for those caught red-handed. On 30 June 1943, the Reverend Ord recorded in his diary that the Gestapo 'have been arresting people for wearing patriotic insignia, particularly the "V"-sign brooches...'. It is apparent that the grip of the occupation became more severe between June 1942 and June 1943 as the Germans attempted to stamp out ever-smaller details of defiance. By the beginning of July 1943, Ord wrote about a display in a shop window in St Peter Port, Guernsey's capital which, 'in direct defiance of the Gestapo', was decorated 'in red, white and blue.... This required great courage and has spoken a message to all who pass by. Nor has it been ignored.' Ord implied that the use of patriotic colours, visible to all, acted to incite others to greater, more courageous, and perhaps more risky acts of resistance. This, and the boosting of morale, was perhaps the greatest value of symbolic and patriotic defiance enacted through material culture. In this sense, we can see the agency afforded by these objects of resistance—they had the power to provoke people to carry out further acts as resistance as well as being objects of resistance themselves.

Resistance, defiance, and weapons of the weak

Roy Machon, Xavier de Guillebon, Kathleen Norman, and Lillian Kinnard are four of the most well-known examples of islanders charged with making 'V propaganda', as the Germans called it. Many others were imprisoned or deported for their acts of symbolic resistance. Yet how much good did this kind of defiance do? Was there any value in it at all? The V-sign campaign led

THE BIOGRAPHIES OF RESISTANT MATERIAL CULTURE   169

to reprisals for those who lived in the same parish as the V's, in the form of radio confiscation and civilian guard duty. Despite these reprisals, the act of painting up a V acted as a release for pent-up frustration and anger. They undoubtedly boosted the morale of many who saw them, who probably perceived them as a tiny victory scored against the enemy. They were also an excellent visible way to communicate a subversive message and encourage defiant behaviour among a large number of people. The real value of symbolic resistance was thus solidarity; it gave a feeling of security in numbers. As the V's multiplied, the more people became assured that others shared their anti-German feeling. Symbolic resistance, especially as expressed through clothing or badge-wearing, was a way of signalling to others that one belonged to an anti-German, patriotic club. While the perceived threat of denunciation was always present, it would have receded if all around appeared like-minded.

In his seminal study of everyday resistance among rural peasants in Malaysia, Scott (1985: xvi–xvii, 29) identified a mode of non-confrontational resistance and defiance against those who would extract taxes, labour, and rent from them, or who would expect them to adhere to onerous new laws. This included 'a struggle over the appropriation of symbols', 'foot dragging, dissimulation, desertion, false compliance, pilfering, feigned ignorance, slander, arson, sabotage, and so on'. Scott labelled these sorts of actions as 'weapons of the weak'—the 'ordinary weapons of relatively powerless groups'. The 'weapons' that these people wielded were critiques of power designed to nibble away at the authority of those in positions of power over them.

Despite the obvious differences in time and space between Malaysia in the late '70s (when Scott carried out his fieldwork) and the Channel Islands during the '40s, Scott's work strikes a strong chord with the different forms of resistance known to have taken place in the islands and with those identified here. Scott (1985: 38) believed that an important aspect of peasant defiance was a shared worldview of the meaning and value behind their acts. Certainly, in the Channel Islands, the display or 'performance' of V's or patriotic colours or symbols was to express wordlessly one's patriotic stance and anti-German world view to others; it was an appeal to solidarity. If the jacket lapel under which a V-sign badge was hidden was lifted in the street, the 'correct' response would have been to flash one's own badge or to make a V with the fingers, or just to smile. Scott (1985: 301) also emphasized the anonymity of many acts of defiance, for therein lay their safety. Again, this chimes with the opening stages of the V-sign campaign.

In analysing more closely the various weapons of the weak and behaviours of the dominated in different arenas, Scott (1990: xii, 4, 111) developed his concept of the 'hidden' and 'public transcripts'. The 'hidden transcript' he defined as the 'critique of power spoken behind the back of the dominant', a 'discourse that takes place "offstage", beyond direct observation by power holders', fuelled by 'anger, indignation, frustration and swallowed bile'; the public transcript is a 'subordinate discourse in the presence of the dominant'. It is clear that each transcript is produced for a different audience. Again, public and private transcripts are to be found in abundance in the anecdotes, memoirs, diaries, and archives of the Channel Islands relating to the occupation. With regards to the examples of symbolic resistance and defiance under discussion here, the use and bartering of patriotic cigarette lighters, the battle for the crest, the performance of V-badges, the chalking up of V-signs: these movements along the artefact biography/itinerary in and out of public and private transcripts can begin to be charted in a combination of Scott's and Kopytoff's concepts. Together, they give us a greater insight into interpretation and meaning over a period of time when artefact form changed rapidly yet maintained stability in the meaning of the symbols employed—at least, while within the sphere of islanders. When taken into the German sphere, meaning became about pride over appropriation, ownership, and occupation. These superficially 'hybrid' objects comprising island symbols in German ownership or within German-made artefacts were nothing of the sort. Certainly the symbols employed on cigarette lighters were chosen for their ability to slide with ease between different groups—but this 'double ownership' or movement from former WWI Allied soldiers to WWII German soldiers does not make them hybrid objects, even if both parties saw them as 'theirs', with symbols that appealed to both groups.

This swift movement of the same symbols into different forms of objects may be an example of what Rainbird (1999: 214) called 'entangled biographies', whereby artefacts may be modified over time 'in ways that take some aspects of their life history with them while discarding others'. Yet, where we see changes in both form and meaning when symbols move into a different sphere (such as, in this example, when German soldiers carved wooden objects featuring the islands' crests), they had biographical referents (the resistant items made by islanders). Such wooden objects are not wholly unique innovations, despite their traditional German form. Only when placed in a wider context is their biographical trajectory clear.

When studying the political landscape of power relations or audiences in the Channel Islands, we must be careful not to always use binary oppositions of Germans and islanders. The situation was more complex: in a small island, different government officials, for example, might simultaneously inhabit the

THE BIOGRAPHIES OF RESISTANT MATERIAL CULTURE   171

categories of family, friend, and acquaintance all at once. The same government officials might also be (and were) working with the German administration one day, and deported to Nazi prisons the next. Trusted friends, work colleagues, casual acquaintances, strangers, informers, policemen, those in positions of authority, members of the civil government and anti-Nazi or friendly Germans all formed part of a non-linear, overlapping, and shifting cloud-like network of relationships; all people who one might encounter on a daily basis. This makes identifying 'hybrid' Channel Island-German objects in the archaeological record almost a fool's errand. Alf Williams, one of the makers of the V-sign badges, even sold one or two of his creations to trusted German soldiers. The audience (and, indeed, the owners of objects) was certainly not a binary Island 'us' and German 'them' whose identities could be boiled down and identified in the search for hybridity, but if any such crude differentiation is to be made, then it would be, in Alf's words, into groups of 'people who could be trusted and people who could not'.

Scott proposed yet a third realm of 'subordinate group politics'. Lying somewhere between the public and private transcript, this was a politics of disguise and anonymity that took place in public view but was designed to have a double meaning or to shield the identity of the actors' (1990: 19). We might place the cigarette lighter, decorated with patriotic coins and symbols and bartered with German soldiers, into this category. Because of the ever-decreasing ways in which one could publicly express one's true feelings towards the occupier, ways of 'speaking in code' were deployed through material culture.

The increasing need for transformation of artefact form as the occupation wore on helps us to date the defiant items of material culture as they passed along their object itinerary. First, in June 1941, came the ephemeral V-signs—the pieces of newspaper and the broken matches—appearing just after the 'V-sound' was launched, which left no artefactual trace except in words written in diaries. The V-sign badges, brooches, and bracelets that followed them were made no earlier than late July 1941, after the Germans had appropriated the V for themselves and driven the campaign underground. I would postulate that the cigarette lighters would have been made some time after this, but probably before Roy Machon's high profile arrest in July 1943, after which trading subversive symbols with Germans became too risky. The German objects featuring the islands' crests escape easy dating, but quite possibly date from the height of the symbolic battle onwards (at their earliest), until the end of the occupation. In fact, many examples in museums date to 1944, as if showing off (or 'performing') the surplus stocks of wood which were available

172   GILLY CARR

for them to carve, compared to prohibition on islanders cutting down trees for firewood during that last cold winter of the occupation. Alf Williams's pendant, with its very sparing use of solder, was probably the last of the artefact types to be made, and could even have been made at or after liberation. The second half of the occupation was a time of great shortages of everything and extreme hunger, and it is unlikely that coins would have been sacrificed in this way if they could have been put towards food, although a barter system was also in operation at this time. Nonetheless, the food that was available reached incredible prices on the black market, and money was needed for this.

Discussion: archaeology and defiant material culture

This case study has considered a limited group of artefacts made at various points during a period of five years of German occupation of the British Channel Islands. We can certainly find direct parallels between the islands and other parts of occupied Europe during WWII. In his study of non-military forms of resistance against the Germans, Semelin (1993: 162) noted the importance of symbolic resistance. 'Symbols are the prime "weapon" of civilian resistance... [they] are the language through which an occupied society still expresses its independence of spirit. Whether in the form of a flower, a sign, or colours, symbols were a permanent challenge to the Nazi order... [they] are the rallying points for all those who refuse to bow their heads.' Archaeologists who study more ancient periods, lacking any form of written records let alone luxuries such as diaries, memoirs, or oral testimony to inform their work, face greater difficulties than those who work in historical periods. Added to this is the difficulty in identifying resistance at all because, as Semelin (1993: 186) has observed, 'the resister himself [sic] had to learn not to leave any traces'; and yet examples of the materiality of resistance have survived.

Unfortunately, the interpretation of material culture is not always as straight-forward as one might hope; context is not always helpful. The Germans who bought the cigarette lighters from local men took them into a new sphere of use, and it is possible that many examples found their way back to Germany after the war. Others may have been swapped with other German POWs or even their English guards after the war, before the former occupiers were allowed to return to their homeland in the late 1940s. The biographies or itineraries of such objects can be complex. Post-war souveniring of artefacts by collectors has also removed the objects discussed here from their original

THE BIOGRAPHIES OF RESISTANT MATERIAL CULTURE   173

context. Most are in stasis in museums, although some V-sign badges are still with the families of those who made, bought, and wore them, where they are kept as memory objects. Close analysis of photos taken on Liberation Day, 9 May 1945, has revealed that patriotic colours, symbols, and V-signs were given a new lease of life at this time, and on many Liberation Days thereafter. This new context was simply part of the continuing biography of the objects, during which new opportunities appeared annually for the drama of their performance.

This paper has highlighted how potential exists for misinterpretation. As described earlier in this chapter, many items made by German soldiers stationed in the islands were engraved, carved, or stamped with the islands' crest. We know definitively, however, that some of the objects presented here were examples of cultural theft or appropriation of symbols of identity rather than hybridity. As Silliman also admits, his definition given at the start of this chapter lacks any acknowledgement of power inequality, which is so crucial to understanding the occupied situation. Had the Channel Islands been occupied for, say, four hundred years, as was Britain by the Romans, for example, the interpretation (and, indeed, the form) of many of these objects might have been very different. Five years is a very short period of time; however, this case study has allowed us to identify material culture change which took place over days, weeks, and months—something almost impossible for most changes in the archaeological record.

A case study like this can not necessarily comment on the cultural essentialisms of 'Channel Island material culture' and 'German material culture' per se, as 'pure' states, not least because Channel Island material culture has English, Norman, and Breton influences, as well as being something unique, and these different identities were drawn upon in the material culture. No doubt 'German material culture' exemplified in the Channel Islands was also similarly mixed. Rather, this case study can be used as a lens to observe a particular military state of occupation. In our search for hybrid objects, we may well be aware that hybridity is as much a process as it is a description of objects in their moment(s) of creation, and the process here was one of careful game-playing and negotiation; of silent battles and one-upmanship; and of individual agents making choices and political decisions. Many of the objects examined here are unique; they are one-offs; but it is only when seen within the range of similar objects that their biographical entanglements and possible meanings to those who used them becomes clear. They represent, to paraphrase Silliman (2013: 496), a 'cultural production... with complex mimicry and camouflage'. Hybridity may well be, as Silliman has more recently suggested, 'a function of our own overwrought classification schemes rather than something fundamentally felt, meant or practised in the past' (2015: 291).

At the same time, we must remind ourselves that we are dealing with a small number of objects, indicating that only a small percentage of the civilian and military populations were interested in playing this game. Within the occupation situation, not everyone was busily engaged in making resistant material culture or appropriating symbols. What did the material culture of the majority look like? We might ask whether 'mainstream' (or non-resistant) material culture, when viewed through an archaeological lens, was more about continuity rather than change. However, the unequal power relations affected all aspects of everyday life, and people were forced to make new tools to create ersatz food out of non-foodstuffs and alternative methods of manufacture to cope with a lack of raw materials (e.g. Carr 2009). In short, occupation affected everybody, but did not result in the production of either hybrid or appropriated material culture from everybody. The objects discussed in this paper represented a minority practice. Even after the occupation ended, these objects were not put away; we see a fascinating 'reverse (pseudo)-hybridity' in the Channel Islands, where some of these appropriated symbols of identity were given back to the islanders by the occupiers (Carr 2012). Many of these items, and the ones used during the occupation, are still held by families as mementoes and in that sense are still 'current' today, thus existing in the same 'archaeological horizon' as those used seventy years ago. This has implications for the 'ending' of the period of hybridity discussed by Silliman (2013: 491) and any concept of biographical 'death'.

In summary, the value of this case study of the material culture of symbolic resistance is as a cautionary tale for archaeological practices and interpretation. It not only challenges our understanding of context, but what might first appear to archaeologists as hybridity—even in the postcolonial sense of 'cultural creativity and agency... subversion, nuance, and ambiguity' in the face of colonialism (Silliman 2015: 281)—may simply be plain appropriation or theft. Swift change in the form of material culture might hint at an attempt at evasion of such appropriation rather than any acquiescence to the fusion of cultural symbols and practices. This is particularly likely in a situation of relatively short military occupation. If anything, this chapter finds sympathy with Silliman's conclusion that hybridity may have run its course as a concept (2015: 278, 283)—at least, for the context of modern military occupation, where exploration of object biographies and their entanglements lead to a better understanding of material culture.

THE BIOGRAPHIES OF RESISTANT MATERIAL CULTURE   175

This case study also gives an insight into the inventiveness of powerless people to fight back using weapons of their own in ways which effectively encouraged solidarity and boosted morale. An unlooked-for additional outcome was probably that these little non-verbal acts of bravery helped to create a feeling of safety which would have spurred others to perform more dangerous yet, courageous acts. In such a way, one act of resistance can trigger another. Such observations are likely to be applicable to material culture in any situation of unequal power relations, most especially in theatres of war. They are testimony to a coping strategy, a way of living side by side with a powerful enemy when there is no alternative. This was a place and a time where men could solder badges instead of throwing punches, paint V's rather than shouting patriotic slogans, and could turn their 'swallowed bile' into symbolic swords.

Acknowledgements

The research for this chapter was based on fieldwork conducted between 2007 and 2010, funded by the British Academy, McDonald Institute for Archaeological Research, and Société Jersiaise, and was written in 2009 with an update made in 2020. I would like to thank my many friends in the Channel Islands for letting me examine and photograph their collections, especially Richard Heaume (German Occupation Museum, Guernsey), Peter and Paul Balshaw (La Valette Military Museum, Guernsey), and Chris Addy (Jersey War Tunnels). I would also like to thank staff at the Priaulx Library (Guernsey), the Island Archives (Guernsey), and Jersey Heritage.

References

Bell, W. 1995. *I Beg to Report: Policing in Guernsey During the German Occupation.* Guernsey: Guernsey Press Company Ltd.

Blades, J. 1977. *Drum Roll: A Professional Adventure from the Circus to the Concert Hall.* London: Faber and Faber.

Carr, G. 2009. 'Landscapes of occupation: a case study from the Channel Islands'. In N. Forbes, R. Page, G. Perez, and A. Tuzza (eds), *The Heritage of Europe's Deadly Century: Perspectives on 20th Century Conflict Heritage Presented in the Seminars of the Culture 2000 Landscapes of War Project.* Swindon: English Heritage Publications, pp. 35–43.

Carr, G. 2010. 'The archaeology of occupation and the V-sign campaign in the Channel Islands during WWII'. *International Journal of Historical Archaeology* 14(4): 575–92.

Carr, G. 2012. 'Coins, crests and kings: symbols of identity and resistance in the occupied Channel Islands'. *Journal of Material Culture* 17(4): 327–44.

Carr, G. 2014a. 'Heritage, memory and resistance in the Channel Islands'. In G. Carr, P. Sanders, and L. Willmot, *Protest, Defiance and Resistance in the German Occupied Channel Islands, 1940-1945*. London: Bloomsbury Academic, pp. 307–38.

Carr, G. 2014b. *Legacies of Occupation: Heritage, Memory and Archaeology in the Channel Islands*. Cham: Springer International.

Carr, G. 2019. *Victims of Nazism in the Channel Islands: A Legitimate Heritage?* London: Bloomsbury Academic.

Carr, G. and R. Heaume. 2004. 'Silent resistance in Guernsey: the V-sign badges of Alf Williams and Roy Machon'. *Channel Islands Occupation Review* 32: 51–5.

Carr, G., P. Sanders, and L. Willmot. 2014. *Protest, Defiance and Resistance in the German Occupied Channel Islands, 1940-1945*. London: Bloomsbury Academic.

Cruikshank, C. 2004. *The German Occupation of the Channel Islands*. 2nd edn. Stroud: Sutton Publishing.

Evans, A. 2009. *Guernsey under Occupation: The Second World War Diaries of Violet Carey*. Chichester: Phillimore.

Falla, F. 1981 [1968]. *The Silent War: The Inside Story of the Channel Islands under the Nazi Jackboot*. Guernsey: Burbridge Ltd.

Gosden, C. and Y. Marshall. 1999. 'The cultural biography of objects'. *World Archaeology* 31(2): 169–78.

Hahn, P. H. and H. Weiss. 2013. 'Introduction: biographies, travels and itineraries of things'. In H. P. Hahn and H. Weiss (eds), *Mobility, Meaning and Transformations of Things: Shifting Contexts of Material Culture through Time and Space*. Oxford: Oxbow Books.

Harvey, W. 1995. *The Battle of Newlands: The Wartime Diaries of Winifred Harvey*. Guernsey: Rosemary Booth.

Joy, J. 2009. 'Reinvigorating object biography: reproducing the drama of object lives'. *World Archaeology* 41(4): 540–56.

Kopytoff, I. 1986. 'The cultural biography of things: commoditization as process'. In A. Appadurai (ed.), *The Social Life of Things: Commodities in Cultural Perspective*. Cambridge: Cambridge University Press, pp. 64–91.

Le Ruez, N. 2003 [1994]. *Jersey Occupation Diary: Her Story of the German Occupation 1940-45*. Bradford-on-Avon: Seaflower Books.

Ord, R. D. Unpublished Occupation Diary. Guernsey: Priaulx Library.

Rainbird, P. 1999. 'Entangled biographies: western Pacific ceramics and the tombs of Pohnpei'. *World Archaeology* 31(2): 214–24.

Rolo, C. J. 1943. *Radio Goes to War*. London: Faber and Faber.

Sanders, P. 2005. *The British Channel Islands under German Occupation 1940–1945*. Jersey: Société Jersiaise and Jersey Heritage Trust.

Saunders, N. J. 2001. 'Apprehending memory: material culture and war, 1919–39'. In P. Liddle, J. Bourne, and I. Whitehead (eds), *The Great World War 1914–45*. Vol. 2: *The Peoples' Experience*. Hammersmith: HarperCollins, pp. 476–88.

Saunders, N. J. 2003. *Trench Art*. Oxford and New York: Berg.

Scott, J. C. 1985. *Weapons of the Weak: Everyday Forms of Peasant Resistance*. New Haven: Yale University Press.

Scott, J. C. 1990. *Domination and the Arts of Resistance: Hidden Transcripts*. New Haven: Yale University Press.

Semelin, J. 1993. *Unarmed against Hitler: Civilian Resistance in Europe, 1939–1943*. Westport: Praeger.

Silliman, S. W. 2013. 'What, where, and when is hybridity'. In J. J. Card (ed.), *The Archaeology of Hybrid Material Culture*. Carbondale: Southern Illinois University Press, pp. 486–500.

Silliman, S. W. 2015. 'A requiem for hybridity? The problem with Frankensteins, purées, and mules'. *Journal of Social Archaeology* 15(3): 277–98.

Sinel, L. 1945. *The German Occupation of Jersey 1940–1945*. Jersey: Jersey Evening Post.

7

Unblended America

Contesting Race and Place in Nineteenth-Century New England

Karen Ann Hutchins-Keim and Mary C. Beaudry

Introduction

The archaeology of enslaved and free African Americans in New England does not sit easily within frameworks that stress, on the one hand, 'cultural survivals' and on the other, cultural fusion (Ferguson 1992; Deetz 2006). Understanding the lives of African Americans in New England requires an unblinkered perspective on the long-term struggle for citizenship and equality in the face of racism, discrimination, segregation, and restricted access to resources. In what follows, we provide an overview of the historical context of slavery and emancipation in New England and discuss the approaches archaeologists have taken at three very different post-emancipation domestic sites to issues of African-American culture and identity. In assessing this work, we consider the pitfalls of employing, uncritically, the concept of creolization to interpret the materials recovered from sites where free African Americans once lived.

The nature of slavery and African-American life in New England

African Americans have been part of the cultural, racial, and economic fabric of New England since the seventeenth century. While the numbers of African and West Indian-born slaves in New England never reached the levels of the plantation colonies in the South, they did increase in the eighteenth century, and more importantly, slavery became deeply rooted in and crucial to New England's economic success (Melish 1998: 16, 18; Chan 2007: 70–1).

Karen Ann Hutchins-Keim and Mary C. Beaudry, *Unblended America: Contesting Race and Place in Nineteenth-Century New England* In: *Archaeologies of Cultural Contact: At the Interface*. Edited by: Timothy Clack and Marcus Brittain, Oxford University Press. © Oxford University Press 2022. DOI: 10.1093/oso/9780199693948.003.0008

UNBLENDED AMERICA   179

Between 1690 and 1800 the number of people of African descent in New England increased from 950 to 17,958. Within Massachusetts the number increased from 400 to 7,101. During this period, however, people of African descent never comprised more than 3 percent of the total population of New England (see Piersen 1988).

The African descendant population was most numerous in urban, coastal areas. Of the four thousand or more Blacks who lived in Massachusetts in 1750, over one-third lived in the city of Boston, and the city itself was over 10 percent Black. Blacks comprised 17 percent of the population in Newport County, Rhode Island (Piersen 1988: 15, table 6). Following the Revolutionary War the Black population—free or enslaved—decreased in proportion to the white population. In Boston free Blacks made up 4.2% of the population and in Providence and Newport, Rhode Island, the percentages of free and enslaved Blacks were 7.5 and 9.5, respectively (US Bureau of the Census 1790d, e, f). Black people in rural communities were more isolated from larger descendant African communities. Rural communities near Boston, such as Plymouth, Braintree, and Weymouth, had 1.2% (n = 54), 0.6% (n = 18), and 0.5% (n = 8) free Blacks, respectively (US Bureau of the Census 1790a, b, c). In such places, Black families may easily have found themselves isolated from other people of African descent and more often in direct contact with white neighbours and employers.

Despite the differences in numbers of Blacks, free or enslaved, in urban and rural areas, the demographics of the slave trade that brought people of African descent to New England were the same and differed from the practices that populated the American South. The enslaved Africans imported into New England in the seventeenth century came mostly from the Caribbean and were not generally African-born. Long voyages and high mortality rates made the African slave trade a risky investment; 'seasoned' slaves from the West Indies better served the needs of New England slaveholders and merchants who required that Africans be versed in colonial society, able to work closely with Europeans, and speak the language (Piersen 1988: 3; Chan 2007: 68).

By the eighteenth century, slave traders drew heavily from both the African coast and the West Indies. After 1750, as England became more involved in the African slave trade long dominated by the Portuguese, Dutch, and Spanish, the numbers of African-born slaves increased in the American colonies, including New England (Chan 2007: 69). Northeastern and New England traders from the major ports of Boston, New York, Philadelphia, and Newport made up a majority of the colonials trafficking slaves to the West Indies and the South (ibid. 69). The number of Africans shipped to the American colonies increased to over 100,000 from 1741 to 1760 (Horton and Horton 1997: 4). The vast majority of these slaves went to the South and the Chesapeake (Piersen 1988: 7; Chan 2007: 70). Historians argue that by understanding the nature of the slave trade in Africa and in the Americas, we can track different cultural and language groups as they arrive in the New World (Chambers 1996: 105; Thornton 1998: 192–6; Hall 2005: 55–6). While this has been done to some success in the American South, confirming that many regions may have selected for slaves from specific areas, the same cannot be said for New England (Berlin 1998; Walsh 2001; Hall 2005). Slaves imported into New England came from all over the Atlantic world—various locations in Africa and the West Indies. In an analysis of advertisements in several Boston newspapers, Robert Desrochers demonstrates that from 1704 to 1740, nearly 30 percent of advertisers offered slaves from the West Indies. And while that number dropped to 15 percent from 1740 to 1781 as the volume of African-born slaves imported into New England increased, the enslaved population of New England remained a diverse group (Desrochers 2002: 645–7).

The slave-for-sale advertisements offered slaves from the 'Gold Coast' (Donnan 1969: 27, 29), 'from the coast of Africa', 'from the coast of Guinea', or 'just arrived' (*Boston Post Boy*, 22 June 1761; *Boston Gazette*, 22 June 1761; Donnan 1969: 40, 50, 65–8; Desrochers 2002: 644–7). The 'coast of Africa' and even 'the coast of Guinea' refer to a wide geographical area that included at least eighty-one different states. Even when those states are narrowed into cultural groups based on common language families, the Senegal region of Upper Guinea contains three language-culture groups and the Lower Guinea contains two (Thornton 1998: x–xiv, 185–8). The demographics of the slave trade created a diverse slave community that likely lacked the cultural and linguistic cohesion seen on the large plantations of the American South and the Caribbean.

The growing slave populations resided primarily in urban ports and in the rich agricultural areas of Connecticut and Rhode Island (Piersen 1988: 14–15; Melish 1998: 15; Chan 2007: 73). Although some have argued that slavery in New England was a peripheral institution, in reality by the eighteenth century both the slave trade and slavery had worked its way into the fabric of the New England economy. The trade created immense New England fortunes. The triangular trade—sugar, slaves, and rum—was facilitated by the New England shippers and shipbuilders. The port towns of Boston and Newport thrived off the shipping industry, the sale of slaves, and the distillation of rum (ibid. 72). In addition, the bulk of agricultural goods and foodstuffs produced in New England for export—horses, beef, pork, flour, wheat, oats, maize, and rice—were shipped to the Caribbean (ibid. 73).

UNBLENDED AMERICA   181

Not only were the pockets of New England merchants and farmers lined by the trade in human beings, but the same merchants and farmers also benefitted from owning slaves. Although enslaved Africans never made up more than 3 percent of the entire population of New England, their heavy presence in coastal and urban areas made their economic and social impact greater in those areas (Piersen 1988: 14–15, tables 5 and 6). Enslaved individuals touched nearly all aspects of the economy. They performed a wide range of specialized tasks including 'carpenters, shipwrights, sail makers, printers, tailors, shoemakers, coopers, blacksmiths, bakers, weavers, and goldsmiths' (McManus 1973 quoted in Chan 2007: 74). Skilled slave labourers provided expensive services for their owners at a much-reduced cost, and owners could hire out their slaves to others for additional profit. While this practice is not unique to New England, the vast majority of enslaved individuals in New England were skilled labourers (ibid. 74). Those who were not skilled were often 'jacks of all trades' who performed a wide variety of tasks for their owners who capitalized on their slaves' economic value (ibid. 76).

These demographics along with the integrated nature of the New England economy meant that enslaved peoples came into routine contact with both other people of African descent and the greater New England society. The New England slave population lived among 'two linked communities of families'—their white-master family, of which the enslaved members were crucial, if forced, members, and their chosen Black families (Melish 1998: 45). Slaves often formed families outside of their master's household and continued to maintain those families as one or more members was sold, emancipated, or moved (ibid. 43–4). Beyond the family, enslaved African Americans joined in larger social groups for religious and political purposes. As early as 1693, a meeting of the 'Society of Negroes' in Boston served as a place for Blacks to pray and study their faith together (ibid. 47–8). Prayer meetings grew in number through the eighteenth and nineteenth centuries as informal and self-organized meetings (ibid. 48). Additionally, numerous local histories refer to a celebration that enslaved Africans in New England engaged in every spring. The African-American communities in New Hampshire, Massachusetts, Connecticut, and Rhode Island participated in the election of a king or governor throughout the late seventeenth, eighteenth, and early nineteenth centuries (ibid. 45–6; see also Wade 1981: 211–12; Piersen 1988: 117–18). Following the elections held by white New Englanders, enslaved New Englanders would hold their own elections complete with parades and celebrations. Historians disagree as to the purpose of these elections: 'black empowerment, white control, reinforcement of Africanity' (Melish 1998: 46). While allowing slaves to participate in these events likely provided owners with some benefit—or they would not have condoned the practice—it is clear that these events served valuable social and political functions for the African-American community. The elections enabled the often dispersed, Black community to facilitate social relationships as well as to mete out its own justice. The elected kings or governors often took the opportunity to punish offenders; in one case a man accused of stealing an axe was punished with several lashes (Brewster 1873: 212–13).

Free Blacks had long lived among enslaved populations in New England, but by the end of the eighteenth century, slavery in New England was coming to a slow end. Connecticut and Rhode Island passed gradual emancipation laws in 1783 that called for the children of slaves to be declared 'free' at the age of 25 in Connecticut, and age 18 for females and 21 for males in Rhode Island (Melish 1998: 68). In Massachusetts and New Hampshire, ambiguous judicial and constitutional decisions indecisively ended slavery 'as to merit consideration as a form of "gradual emancipation"' (ibid. 68). A judicial decision in 1783 officially signalled the end of slavery in Massachusetts, but in practice, and as a result of the ambiguous language of the decision, many individuals remained enslaved for several years after (ibid. 65, 95–6). By 1790, however, the Federal Census lists no enslaved persons living in Massachusetts; well into the nineteenth century, on the other hand, Connecticut and Rhode Island still listed some people as enslaved (ibid. 76).

Following emancipation, African Americans were not easily integrated into society and accepted as citizens. The process of gradual and ambiguous emancipation 'offered a kind of expulsion from [the structure of slavery] without providing a new place...to accommodate the new category of free people' (Melish 1998: 88). Instead, emancipation in Massachusetts, and more widely in New England, led to increased racism and the racialization of society. 'Whiteness' became defined as diametrically opposed to the 'Blackness' of recently emancipated African Americans and all other Blacks in society (Horton and Horton 1997; Melish 1998, 1999; Stewart 1998, 1999; Horton 1999). Historians argue that during the first half of the nineteenth century, violence against and mockery of the African-American community became commonplace actions for the white community (Stewart 1999: 699). Newspapers, almanacs, and broadsides began to deride the African-American dialect, to ridicule Black fashion as excessive, and to insinuate that Black holidays and celebrations were bastardized imitations of white festivities (Melish 1998: 171–8). By the 1820s and 1830s, white mobs made frequent visits to Black neighbourhoods to inflict violence and terror (Stewart 1999: 700–2).

Roughly forty years after emancipation in Massachusetts, 'the white North had emerged into an age of racial modernity, an era...resembling the white supremacist tyranny of the late nineteenth century' (ibid. 693).

Finding themselves excluded from full participation in American citizenship, African Americans often created their own parallel institutions to provide what was denied them by white society. Black mutual aid organizations developed in Boston around the turn of the nineteenth century with the purpose of providing assistance to the poorest members of their community. The Black church became one of the social centres of the African-American experience—informal meetings developed into more organized and formalized institutions. The demography of northern slavery meant that maintaining African-derived religious traditions was difficult, and Christianity developed quickly as the dominant form of worship. The Second Great Awakening of the early nineteenth century, which drew upon spirituality and the democratic nature of religion and preaching, fit well with the African-American community, and the Methodist and Baptist churches were initially welcoming to Black participants. Eventually, all-Black churches like the Bethel Church and the African Methodist Episcopal Church (AME) would spread all over the North and throughout the United States. The church became a place where the Black community cared for the well-being of its own; additionally the church often functioned as a town hall or government, keeping disputes and issues out of white-controlled courts (Horton and Horton 1997: 125–48). Educating its children, despite the exclusion from all-white schools, became a priority for the African-American community. The African-American community in Boston created its own African School in 1798, which moved to the African Meeting House in the early 1800s, when the town government thwarted its efforts to create a public school (Horton and Horton 1997: 149–50).

Archaeology of African Americans in New England

The nature of slavery in New England has made it difficult to link archaeological materials with enslaved Africans (but see Chan 2007), but there have been many excavations at sites with well-documented histories of occupation and use by free African Americans. Much of this work involves institutional/community sites such as the African Meeting House and Abiel Smith School in Boston (Mead 1995; Landon 2009) and the African Baptist Church on Nantucket (Beaudry and Berkland 2007), but archaeologists have also given attention to African-American home sites. We discuss three prominent

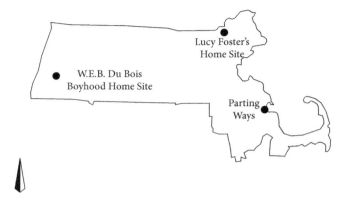

Fig. 7.1. Map of Massachusetts showing location of sites discussed in the text.

examples of domestic sites occupied by free African Americans in post-emancipation Massachusetts as background for considering ways of theorizing about and interpreting processes of creolization and syncretism in a hostile and racially charged context (Fig. 7.1).

Adelaide and Ripley Bullen conducted the first excavation in the United States at an African-American domestic site in the 1940s, at the Lucy Foster home site in Andover, Massachusetts (Bullen and Bullen 1945). Lucy Foster was the slave and, later, servant for the Foster family in Andover. In 1812 Lucy's former mistress bequeathed her 'a cow, one acre of land…to have and to hold…for and during her natural life' (Will of Hannah Foster Chandler, in ibid. 27). Archaeological evidence in the form of ceramics and building materials establish the construction of a small house around the year 1815; the property was occupied until 1845, when Lucy died at the age of 88 (ibid. 21–7). The Bullens's brief report was the only substantive work on the excavated materials from the site until the late 1970s when Vernon Baker (1978) analysed the ceramic vessels recovered from the site. Baker placed Lucy Foster's site within the contemporary archaeological discussion of African-American sites by attempting to distinguish consumption patterns linked to poverty and race (Baker 1980). He argued that Lucy Foster's site reflected three major patterns that struck him as distinctively African American: use of hollow ceramic vessel forms (e.g. bowls, for stews and pottages); chopped rather than sawn animal bones; and the 12 × 12-feet (3.66 m × 3.66 m) footprint of the house, in contrast to the 16-feet-square (4.88m^2) Anglo-American pattern observed elsewhere (note that Bullen, Baker, and Deetz—see below—based their estimates of house dimensions on cellar holes only, not accounting for the possibility that houses may have been only partially cellared under).

UNBLENDED AMERICA   185

Similar patterns associated with African Americans had been identified by archaeologists like Otto (1977) in the plantation South and by Deetz (2006) at Parting Ways in Plymouth. Baker cautioned, however, that only through further analysis of poor white sites could the patterns he observed be positively linked to African-American consumption patterns (Baker 1980: 33–6).

The archaeological collection resulting from the excavations conducted at Parting Ways, a small early nineteenth-century African-American community on the outskirts of Plymouth, Massachusetts, provides an opportunity to explore many of the issues presented above. In the 1970s, James Deetz conducted excavations on the property, which had been occupied by former slave Plato Turner and his descendants from 1779 to the early 1900s.

The full history of the Parting Ways settlement, which is coming to light through Hutchins-Keim's research (Hutchins 2013), reveals the complex struggles and negotiations its inhabitants experienced following emancipation. After years of enslavement, four men, beginning with Prince Goodwin and Plato Turner, came to a rocky area on the outskirts of Plymouth and set down roots that would, for Turner's family, last over a century (US Bureau of the Census 1790–1880; *Boston Globe*, 8 December 1895). This land had been a sanctuary for society's outcasts for twenty-five years prior to the arrival of African-American occupants—at least two white families 'warned out' of neighbouring towns for their poverty made Parting Ways their home in the middle of the eighteenth century (Jones 1975; Bethel 1997: 38–41).

For Plato Turner and the other Parting Ways inhabitants, life in their new home involved a mix of asserting independence and relying on the Plymouth community's good will. Immediately upon gaining his freedom, Plato Turner made several important moves forward: employment, getting married, and settling down. Plato Turner made a remarkable purchase of a house standing at Parting Ways in 1779, just eight years after achieving freedom (SCPR 1771, Docket 14: 966; PCRD 1779: 165). At the time he purchased the house, his profession was listed as mariner (PCRD 1779: 165) and he was in between military enlistments—he served several enlistments in the Continental Army from 1776 to 1783 (Department of Veterans Affairs 1819a, b). Unlike the other Parting Ways residents—Cato Howe, Quash Quande, and Prince Goodwin—who were labourers, Turner's work as a mariner may have afforded him a measure of economic freedom (Bethel 1997: 49).

As enterprising as Turner was following his emancipation, the town of Plymouth appears to have kept a close and paternal eye on the residents of Parting Ways from the beginning of their tenure on the property and throughout its occupation. Although Plato Turner purchased the house and other improvements owned by Job Cushman, the land remained in the hands of the town of Plymouth throughout its occupation and they lived on the property at the will of the town (PCRD 1767: 260; 1773a: 186–7; 1779: 165). When Congress passed a law in 1818 allowing destitute or impoverished war veterans who were not disabled to receive benefits, town leaders assigned Plato Turner, Cato Howe, Prince Goodwin, and Quomony Quash a guardian, who applied for the war pensions for them—8 USD a year—and then proceeded to deduct a 1 USD fee from each (PCPC 1818, 1821a, 1821b, 1823). Towns in Massachusetts carefully weighed the burden its poor placed on their governments, trying to limit the burden; the treatment of the Parting Ways residents is not unusual. On the other hand, 'freedom and citizenship were considered incompatible with dependence' (Foner 1996: 99–127; Horton 1999: 646). As discussed above, the early nineteenth century saw the rise of dehumanizing portrayals of African Americans designed to discredit their claims for citizenship and place them at the periphery of the new republic. As long as African Americans were a dependant class, they could not be a full free class of people.

While the town of Plymouth may have lent its paternalistic help to the Parting Ways inhabitants, the small community was probably a source of social and community strength as well. In areas with a denser African-American population, like Boston or Nantucket, organized African-American–run institutions developed to serve the communities' needs. Long before organizations like the Bethel-African Methodist Episcopal Church came to Plymouth in 1861, Parting Ways likely served to unite the four African-American families and their extended families. Although the numbers of African Americans living in Plymouth remained small at the turn of the nineteenth century— fifty-four in 1790—Plato Turner's family exemplifies how much larger and far-reaching the African-American community was than the demographics imply. Turner lived in Roxbury with his master James Mears and in 1764, while enslaved, he married Rachel Colley of Bridgewater (Town of Bridgewater 1916b: 87). Once emancipated Turner moved with his wife and young son to Plymouth where they made their home at Parting Ways. Later Turner's son, Plato Turner, Jr, moved to Bridgewater and raised his family there (Bridgewater 1916a: 320, 321; Bridgewater 1916b: 376). Two of Turner's daughters moved to Boston and lived on Beacon Hill with their husbands. Clearly the family's social ties spread all over the greater Boston area and Plymouth County. Members of Plato Turner's family—his son, granddaughter, and grandson— continued to live at Parting Ways until the early 1900s, maintaining the importance of the place. After a lifetime away from his family's ancestral home working as personal servant to important figures such as William Lloyd

Garrison and James T. Burr, Plato's grandson returned to live with his first cousin Rachel Johnson and her children (*Boston Globe*, 8 December 1895).

Paynter et al. (1994: 287) observed that 'a strategic pause is needed to consider how "race" may mark an interpretive divide in the way one approaches material records'. Parting Ways, with an occupation spanning the initial post-emancipation period through the end of the nineteenth century, is well situated in time to explore the impact of the development of 'race' and the racialization of society in rural Massachusetts. A wealth of material culture provides opportunities to explore the role material culture played in defining, negotiating, and combating the expectations of the day.

Deetz, in his book *In Small Things Forgotten* (first published in 1977, rev. edn 1996), focused his discussion of Parting Ways on identifying evidence of African cultural retentions—housing style, ceramics, and foodways. Deetz (2006: 201–3) argued that two of the dwellings on the property had foundations that measured 12 feet × 12 feet, reflecting an 'African-American mindset' because Anglo-style homes traditionally measured 16 feet × 16 feet. He also identified several coarse earthenware jars as possible tamarind jars that may have once contained a traditional West African fruit found in the West Indies (ibid. 199–200). The jars, discarded in cellar holes on Plato Turner's property, have wide shoulders and narrow bases, closely resembling syrup or molasses jars used in the processing of sugar and the storage and shipment of molasses (Brooks 1983); such vessels were often reused for water storage. Deetz (2006 :199) concluded that the Parting Ways jars were made somewhere in the West Indies and uses their presence on an African-American site in New England as an opportunity to speculate on African cultural retentions at the site.

In his focus on 'African' cultural retentions, Deetz essentialized the material culture of Parting Ways residents and failed to grapple with the site's complex occupation history or indeed with the issue of race. By emphasizing ethnicity instead of race and offering static interpretations of a few artefacts based on the notion that objects are direct representations of culture, he, like many other scholars of the time, failed to account for the agency of African Americans in the creation and negotiation of their new-found freedom (Singleton 1999: 5). Charles Orser characterizes Deetz's approach, with its emphasis on 'mind sets' and 'world view', as a prime example of the 'reification of creolized societies as whole-cultures' (Orser 2004: 21). This contrasts starkly with more nuanced models of creolization as a suite of processes distinguished by fluidity of form (Dawdy 2000: 2; Mullins and Paynter 2000); we discuss this further below.

Archaeologists investigating the W. E. B. Du Bois Boyhood Home Site in Great Barrington, Massachusetts, emphasized the importance of both race and gender in the interpretations of African-American archaeological sites. When considering how to interpret the material remains recovered from the site, home of the Burghardts, Robert Paynter and his colleagues posed several thought-provoking questions regarding the place race should take in archaeological investigations. They asked: 'does the use of European housing forms and mass-marketed commodities point to the social or cultural assimilation of African Americans into white New England society?' (1994: 287; see also Paynter 1992). They challenged archaeologists to explore whether the purchase, use, and deposition of the similar items by white and Black people held the same meanings and encourage archaeologists to consider the multivalency of ubiquitous artefacts. To that end, they considered the patent medicine bottles recovered from late nineteenth-century middens. Patent medicine bottles, they argued, lead to the inference that some residents of the homesite suffered ill health, but such an inference does not lead directly to an understanding of the role such products played in the lives of African Americans. Women were their family's caregivers, and middle-class white women were the target audience for patent medicine advertisers (Paynter et al. 1994: 311–12). The Black women living at the Du Bois home site in the late nineteenth century were the likely purchasers of patent medicines, even though they were marketed chiefly to white women. Paynter et al. (1994: 313) suggested that we should interpret the presence of mass-produced patent cure-alls at this site as evocative of the Black experience of 'double consciousness' that Du Bois in his writings described as the sense of seeing oneself through the eyes of others. They also made it clear that historical archaeologists lack information about African-American women's perspectives on specific types of objects and thus are ill-equipped to do more than raise questions about their meanings (see Muller 1994 for a detailed discussion of the important roles played by the women of the Burghardt family).

Rethinking freedom

In *Black Feminist Archaeology*, Whitney Battle-Baptiste (2011) critiqued the ways in which archaeologists have approached African-American archaeological sites, in particular the interpretations of the Lucy Foster home site. She acknowledged that Baker's conclusions regarding the distinctive African-American patterns at that site—and by extension Deetz's concerning Parting

Ways—were 'cutting edge and innovative' for their time, but noted that archaeologists have moved away from static and essentialist interpretations of material culture and race in favour of critical discussions of race, gender, and poverty (ibid. 114–15). She challenged conclusions that the material evidence from African-American sites points past race and gender solely towards poverty because they allowed researchers to avoid confronting identity as complex and multi-faceted; she remarked that 'the reason for my discomfort...in my rethinking through the Lucy Foster site, I see her as listed on the Annual Dole record, but my question is how is poverty defined...?' (ibid. 129). She observed that a rich archaeological assemblage including a minimum of 113 ceramic vessels was recovered from the Lucy Foster site, but instead of using the evidence 'to tell the story of a woman of African descent from New England' (ibid. 116), archaeologists have focused on Foster's economic situation and implied that poverty trumps race and gender and would look the same regardless of whether the archaeological record was created by whites or by people of colour. To Battle-Baptiste, the objects reflect not just consumption patterns, but also provide an opportunity to ask critical questions about the material nature of poverty, how poverty manifests itself, how poverty changes through time and through a person's lifetime, and the ways in which 'race, gender and class overlap, intersect and contradict each other all at once' (ibid. 116–17).

Lucy Foster, Plato Turner and the other occupants of Parting Ways, and the residents of the W. E. B. Du Bois site all owned their houses—whether they built them or not—and Foster and the Burghardt women owned the land on which their houses stood. As property owners, they had achieved an important step towards citizenship, undoubtedly an element in the construction of their identities. At the Foster site and at Parting Ways, the bulk of the excavated materials were European, mainly British, mass-produced ceramics and glass. The 15,000 or so fragments of Euroamerican ceramics, glassware, and small finds from Parting Ways do not explicitly reveal the African-descendant identities of the residents of Parting Ways any more than similar goods found at Lucy Foster's home site reflect her self-identification. Baker and Deetz were both so convinced that Lucy Foster and the residents of Parting Ways were defined more by being poor than by any other factors—being an older woman in Foster's case and Black or property owners in either case—that they interpreted the Euroamerican goods, especially the ceramics, as being too high in quality (and hence too costly) for African Americans to afford. Deetz (2006: 199) dismissed them as hand-me-downs from wealthy white patrons, while Baker sought to render them African by linking them to foodways of enslaved

Blacks in the American South. This approach has justifiably been subject to critique because it understands objects as reflecting culture and overlooks the role of material culture and material practices in cultural processes and in the 'generation and regeneration of social worlds' (Stahl 2010: 154).

Increasingly, historical archaeologists have embraced more nuanced and contextual models for interpreting material culture that attend to the active role material culture plays in the creation and manipulation of identity (White and Beaudry 2009). In Paynter et al.'s treatment of the W. E. B. Du Bois boyhood home site and in Battle-Baptiste's reconsideration of the Lucy Foster site, we see a constructive, alternative approach that acknowledges the colour line and acknowledges that the finds should be contextualized within the occupational and personal histories of the residents of the sites as well as within the local and larger histories of the region. Racial ideologies have different histories and vary with the social and cultural conditions in different places (Lucas 2006: 182); creolization is far from a uniform or simple process. Gundaker (2000: 131) has pointed to the importance of time and timing in creolization processes, noting that some scholars see creolization 'as the transgenerational process through which a population of disparate newcomers coalesces into a cultural group'. However, creolization does not produce hybrid styles or behaviours because 'they do not fuse but remain differentiated' (ibid. 131). She reminds archaeologists that 'this seems most obvious with reused and re-contextualized objects like pins, buttons, shells and mirrors that may well remain what they were—so they retain the potency that objects accrue through previous use—and what they have become as part of a new configuration...' (ibid. 132).

Steps archaeologists might take to recognize the fluidity, creativeness, and differentiated character of creolization in their analyses of 'intercultural situations' include close attention to historical, cultural, and archaeological contexts. Historical archaeology differs from prehistoric archaeology in many ways, most significantly because the documentary record makes it possible in most instances to learn a great deal about the people who lived at the sites we investigate, even if those people were part of a marginalized minority; we can develop biographies of individuals and families much as we are able to reconstruct site formation processes and the life history of a site. This is case-specific and site-specific, transferable only through critical application, and allows us to attend closely to sequence and to link the timing of events with generational shifts through which processes of creolization operate. We need to develop similarly contextual approaches to artefact analyses, acknowledging that goods are consumed not just by their purchase, but through their operation in everyday practices and broader projects of self-fashioning that entail ensembles or suites and combinations of objects of different materials (Antczak and Beaudry 2019). It is crucial to push our analyses beyond consideration of singular influences on individual subjectivities and on group formation to include the multiple elements of personhood: race, class, age, gender, economic rank, social role, and family structure. Working towards such nuanced understandings is not straightforward, and patterns lie 'not on the surface, but hidden in the details' (Battle-Baptiste 2011: 165). In the context of sites occupied by free African Americans in New England, what has begun to emerge from the material record is a picture of people engaged not in cultural fusion, but in a struggle between exclusion from civic society and participation in the emerging American society.

References

Antczak, K. A. and M. C. Beaudry. 2019. 'Assemblages of practice: a conceptual framework for exploring human-thing relations in archaeology'. *Archaeological Dialogues* 26: 1–24.

Baker, V. G. 1978. *Historical Archaeology at Black Lucy's Garden, Andover, Massachusetts: Ceramics from the Site of a Nineteenth Century Afro-American*. Andover: Robert S. Peabody Foundation for Archaeology, Phillips Academy.

Baker, V. G. 1980. 'Archaeological visibility of Afro-American culture: an example from Black Lucy's Garden, Andover, Massachusetts'. In R. L. Schuyler (ed.), *Archaeological Perspectives on Ethnicity in America: Afro-American and Asian American Culture History*. Farmingdale: Baywood Publishing, pp. 29–37.

Battle-Baptiste, W. 2011. *Black Feminist Archaeology*. Walnut Creek: Left Coast Press.

Beaudry, M. C. and E. P. Berkland. 2007. 'The archaeology of the African Baptist meeting house of Nantucket, Massachusetts'. In A. Ogundiran and T. Folala (eds), *Archaeology of Atlantic Africa and African Diaspora*. Bloomington: Indiana University Press, pp. 395–412.

Berlin, I. 1998. *Many Thousands Gone: The First Two Centuries of Slavery in North America*. Cambridge, MA: Belknap Press of Harvard University Press.

Bethel, E. R. 1997. *The Roots of African-American Identity: Memory and History in Antebellum Free Communities*. New York: St. Martin's Press.

Boston Gazette. 1761. 'Advertisements'. 21 June. Boston, MA.

Boston Globe. 1895. 'Jim Burr's Life'. 8 December. Boston, MA.

Boston Post Boy. 1761. 'Advertisements'. 22 June. Boston, MA.

192 KAREN ANN HUTCHINS-KEIM AND MARY C. BEAUDRY

Brewster, C. W. 1873 [1857]. *Rambles about Portsmouth, First Series: Sketches of Persons, Localities, and Incidents of Two Centuries: Principally from Tradition and Unpublished Documents*. 2nd edn. Portsmouth: Lewis W. Brewster.

Bridgewater, Massachusetts. 1916a. *Vital Records of Bridgewater, Massachusetts to the End of the Year 1850*. Vol. 1. Boston: New England Historic Genealogical Society.

Bridgewater, Massachusetts. 1916b. *Vital Records of Bridgewater, Massachusetts to the End of the Year 1850*. Vol. 2. Boston: New England Historic Genealogical Society.

Brooks, C. M. 1983. 'Aspects of the sugar-refining industry from the 16th to the 19th century'. *Post-Medieval Archaeology* 17: 1–14.

Bullen, A. K. and R. P. Bullen. 1945. 'Black Lucy's Garden'. *Bulletin of the Massachusetts Archaeological Society* 6(2): 17–28.

Chambers, D. 1996. '"He Is an African but He Speaks Plain": Historical Creolization in Eighteenth-Century Virginia'. In A. Jalloh and S. E. Maizlish (eds), *The African Diaspora*. College Station: Texas A & M University Press, pp. 100–33.

Chan, A. 2007. *Slavery in the Age of Reason: Archaeology at a New England Farm*. Knoxville: University of Tennessee Press.

Dawdy, S. L. 2000. 'Preface'. In S. L. Dawdy (ed.), *Creolization. Historical Archaeology* 34(3): 1–4.

Deetz, J. 2006. *In Small Things Forgotten: The Archaeology of Early American Life*. 2nd edn. New York: Anchor Books.

Donnan, E. 1969. *Documents Illustrative of the History of the Slave Trade to America*. Vol. 3: *New England and the Middle Colonies*. New York: Octagon Books.

Department of Veterans Affairs. 1819a. 'Survivor's Pension Application File S. 33832, Plato Turner'. NARA Microfilm Publication M804, Roll 2426, RG 15. National Archives: Washington, DC.

Department of Veterans Affairs. 1819b. 'Survivor's Pension Application File W. 2354, Cato Howe'. NARA Microfilm Publication M804, Roll 1344, RG 15. National Archives: Washington, DC.

Desrochers, Jr, R. E. 2002. 'Slave-for-sale advertisements and slavery in Massachusetts, 1704–1781'. *William and Mary Quarterly* 59(3): 623–64.

Ferguson, L. 1992. *Uncommon Ground: Archaeology and Early African America, 1650–1800*. Washington, DC: Smithsonian Institution Press.

Foner, E. 1996. Free Labor and Political Ideology. In M. Stokes and S. Conway (eds), *The Market Revolution in America: Social, Political, & Religious Expressions, 1800–1880*. Charlottesville: University of Virginia Press, pp. 99–127.

Gundaker, G. 2000. 'Discussion: Creolization, Complexity, and Time'. In S. L. Dawdy (ed.), *Creolization. Historical Archaeology* 34(3): 124–33.

Hall, G. M. 2005. *Slavery and African Ethnicities in the Americas: Restoring the Links*. Chapel Hill: University of North Carolina Press.

Horton, L. E. 1999. 'From class to race in early America: Northern post-emancipation racial reconstruction'. *Journal of the Early Republic* 19(4): 629–49.

Horton, J. O. and L. E. Horton. 1997. *In Hope of Liberty: Culture, Community, and Protest among Northern Free Blacks, 1700–1860*. New York: Oxford University Press.

Hutchins, K. A. 2013. 'In Pursuit of Full Freedom: An Archaeological and Historical Study of the Free African-American Community at Parting Ways, Massachusetts, 1779–1900'. PhD dissertation, Department of Archaeology, Boston University. Ann Arbor: UMI Dissertations Publishing—ProQuest.

Jones, D. L. 1975. 'The strolling poor: transiency in eighteenth-century Massachusetts'. *Journal of Social History* 8(3): 28–54.

Landon, D. B. 2009. *Archaeology of the African Meeting House*. Boston: Museum of African American History and Fiske Center for Archaeological Research, University of Massachusetts, Boston.

Lucas, G. 2006. *An Archaeology of Colonial Identity: Power and Material Culture in the Dwars Valley, South Africa*. New York: Springer.

McManus, E. J. 1973. *Black Bondage in the North*. Syracuse: Syracuse University Press.

Mead, L. A. 1995. *Report of Excavations at the Smith School Site at the African Meeting House, Boston, Massachusetts*. Lowell: National Park Service, Northeast Regional Cultural Resources Center.

Melish, J. P. 1998. *Disowning Slavery: Gradual Emancipation and 'Race' in New England, 1780–1860*. Ithaca: Cornell University Press.

Melish, J. P. 1999. 'The "condition" debate and racial discourse in the antebellum North'. *Journal of the Early Republic* 19(4): 651–72.

Muller, N. 1994. 'The house of the black Burghardts: an investigation of race, gender, and class at the W. E. B. Du Bois Boyhood homesite. In E. M. Scott (ed.), *Those of Little Note: Gender, Race, and Class in Historical Archaeology*. Tucson: University of Arizona Press, pp. 81–94.

Mullins, P. and R. Paynter. 2000. 'Representing colonizers: an archaeology of creolization, ethnogenesis, and indigenous material culture among the Haida'. *Historical Archaeology* 34(3): 73–84.

Orser, C. E., Jr. 2004. *Race and Practice in Archaeological Interpretation*. Philadelphia: University of Pennsylvania Press.

Otto, J. S. 1977. 'Artifacts and status differences: a comparison of ceramics from planter, overseer, and slave sites on an antebellum plantation'. In S. South (ed.), *Research Strategies in Historical Archaeology*. New York: Academic Press, pp. 91–118.

194 KAREN ANN HUTCHINS-KEIM AND MARY C. BEAUDRY

Paynter, R. 1992. 'W. E. B. Du Bois and the material world of African-Americans in Great Barrington, Massachusetts'. *Critique of Anthropology* 12(3): 277–91.

Paynter, R., S. Hautaniemi, and N. Muller. 1994. 'The landscapes of the W. E. B. Du Bois boyhood homesite: an agenda for an archaeology of the color line'. In S. Gregory and R. Sanjek (eds), *Race*. New Brunswick: Rutgers University Press.

Piersen, W. D. 1988. *Black Yankees: The Development of an Afro-American Subculture in Eighteenth-Century New England*. Amherst: University of Massachusetts Press.

Plymouth, Massachusetts. 1824. *Town Records*. Vol. 4 1793–1828: 477, 480.

Plymouth County Probate Court (PCPC). 1818. 'Guardianship proceedings of Plato Turner, Quamony Quash, Cato Howe, and Prince Goodwin, Plymouth'. Vol. 49: 249–52.

Plymouth County Probate Court (PCPC). 1821a. 'Guardianship Accounts of Plato Turner, Plymouth'. Vol. 53: 310.

Plymouth County Probate Court (PCPC). 1821b. Guardianship Accounts of Cato Howe, Plymouth. Vol. 54: 164.

Plymouth County Probate Court (PCPC). 1823. Guardianship Accounts of Quomony Quash, Kingston. Case #16316. Vol. 57: 536.

Plymouth County Registry of Deeds (PCRD). 1773a. 'Samuel Bartlett to Archippus Fuller, October 5, 1773'. Book 57: 186.

Plymouth County Registry of Deeds (PCRD). 1773b. 'Archippus Fuller to Elijah Leach, October 5, 1773'. Book 57: 186.

Plymouth County Registry of Deeds (PCRD). 1767. 'Seth Fuller to Samuel Bartlett, November 18, 1767'. Book 53: 260.

Plymouth County Registry of Deeds (PCRD). 1779. 'Job Cushman to Plato Turner, July 6, 1779'. Book 60: 165.

Singleton, T. A. 1999. 'An introduction to African-American archaeology'. In T. A. Singleton (ed.), *I, Too, Am America: Archaeological Studies of African-American Life*. Charlottesville: University Press of Virginia, pp. 1–17.

Stahl, A. B. 2010. 'Material Histories'. In D. Hicks and M. C. Beaudry (eds), *The Oxford Handbook of Material Culture Studies*. Oxford: Oxford University Press, pp. 150–72.

Stewart, J. B. 1998. 'The emergence of racial modernity and the rise of the white North', 1790–1840. *Journal of the Early Republic* 18(2): 181–217.

Stewart, J. B. 1999. 'Modernizing "difference": the political meanings of color in the Free States, 1776–1840'. *Journal of the Early Republic* 19(4): 691–712.

Suffolk County Registry of Deeds (SCRD) 1771. 'Will of James Mears'. Case #14966.

Thornton, J. 1998. *Africa and Africans in the Making of Atlantic World, 1400–1800*. 2nd edn. Cambridge: Cambridge University Press.

US Bureau of the Census 1790a. 'US Census, population schedule, Braintree, Norfolk County, Massachusetts.'

US Bureau of the Census 1790b. 'US Census, population schedule, Weymouth, Norfolk County, Massachusetts.'

US Bureau of the Census 1790c. 'US Census, population schedule, Plymouth, Plymouth County, Massachusetts.'

US Bureau of the Census 1790d. 'US Census, population schedule, Boston, Suffolk County, Massachusetts.'

US Bureau of the Census 1790e. 'US Census, population schedule, Newport, Newport County, Rhode Island.'

US Bureau of the Census 1790f. 'US Census, population schedule, Providence, Providence County, Rhode Island.'

Wade, M. 1981. ' "Shining in borrowed plumage": affirmation of community in the Black coronation festivals of New England (c.1750–1850)'. *Western Folklore* 40(3): 211–31.

Walsh, L. 2001. 'The Chesapeake slave trade: regional patterns, African origins, and some implications'. *William and Mary Quarterly* 58(1): 139–70.

White, C. L. and M. C. Beaudry. 2009. 'Artifacts and personal identity'. In T. Majewski and D. Gaimster (eds), *The International Handbook of Historical Archaeology*. New York: Springer, pp. 209–25.

8

'Such Was the End of Their Feast'

Violence, Intimacy, and Mimetic Practice in Early Modern Ireland

Audrey Horning

Scholarly emphasis upon investigating the archaeological signatures for hybridity and syncretism in the early modern world are often framed in opposition to considerations of insecurity, violence, and cultural destruction, yet they are inextricably linked. Far from being a visceral overreaction to the unfamiliar, violence is often the product of the same proximity and intimacy that leads to the emergence of hybrid identities and syncretic as well as mimetic practices. To engage in violence is to exercise just one of many possible actions inherent to social life and amplified through the operation of unequal power relations. Nowhere is this clearer than in considering the role of violence in the encounter between the English and Irish in the late sixteenth and early seventeenth centuries. Unlike recent considerations of cultural entanglements in the New World, which have emphasized indigenous agency and stressed creativity, continuity, and survival (e.g. Silliman 2005, 2009; Gallivan 2011), historical examinations of the encounter between English and Irish have always emphasized and indeed prioritized conflict and atrocity, linking the warfare of the early modern period directly to the violence associated with the Troubles of the twentieth century and into the present. The aim of this discussion is *not* to perpetuate this myopic historical vision, which has worked to the detriment of considering non-violent forms of cultural interaction and mutual affect, but rather to consider the context for one particular episode of intercultural violence—the 1574 death of Sir Brian MacPhelim O'Neill—for what it tells us about the processes of syncretism and mimesis in early modern Ireland.

Audrey Horning, *'Such Was the End of Their Feast': Violence, Intimacy, and Mimetic Practice in Early Modern Ireland*
In: *Archaeologies of Cultural Contact: At the Interface*. Edited by: Timothy Clack and Marcus Brittain, Oxford University Press.
© Oxford University Press 2022. DOI: 10.1093/oso/9780199693948.003.0009

Background

Since the Anglo-Norman invasions of the twelfth century, England had retained a foothold in Ireland as represented by the centre of English power in Dublin. However, English involvement in Irish affairs intensified during the sixteenth century, a reaction to the forces of Reformation and England's rivalry with Spain. Catholic Ireland represented a clear threat to England, serving as it did as a useful 'back door' for a Spanish invasion. Efforts to extend and consolidate English control in Ireland were first spearheaded by Henry VIII, who declared himself King of Ireland in 1541, having already assumed the head of the Irish Church in 1536. Enhanced English control in Ireland was to be achieved through a range of government-sponsored and individual strategies. Crown efforts focused upon building new fortifications, the granting of lands to loyal followers, and the confiscation and redistribution of monastic property. Furthermore, under a policy known as 'surrender and regrant', Gaelic and Old English lords (Old English is the designation used for the descendants of the twelfth-century Anglo Norman invaders) were to be compelled to give up title to their lands, in exchange for a regrant under English law, terms, and conditions. In a further effort to shore up the defences of Dublin, new communities of loyal settlers were to be 'planted' in counties Offaly and Laois in the 1550s. While colonial in intent, in practice these new plantations relied upon the loyalty of native landholders. Anyone, regardless of cultural identity, was eligible to take up a grant provided they professed their loyalty to the English Crown. The Laois and Offaly plantations were poorly administered and doomed from the start, succumbing to a series of localized rebellions (Loeber 1991).

Under Queen Elizabeth I, English policy shifted to an emphasis on military action. If Ireland could not be controlled through diplomacy, legislation, and land reform, it would have to be controlled through warfare and conquest. English forces in Ireland were increased from a few hundred in the 1530s to 21,000 by 1596 (Canny 2001: 66). Military efforts were accompanied by intensified efforts to destabilize Gaelic culture, and undermine the standing of the resolutely Catholic Old English leadership. Part and parcel of the shift to military conquest was a hardening of attitudes towards the Irish. The language used to describe Gaelic (and some extent, Old English) culture became increasingly unflattering and inflammatory, as efforts to 'other' rather than understand Irish society predominated. In the estimation of the poet Edmund Spenser (1997 [1598]), who variously referred to the Irish as 'warlike', 'unruly', and 'wild', reformation of the Irish character could only be accomplished 'by the sworde; for all those evilles must first be cutt awaye with a stronge hande, before any good cann bee planted; like as the corrupt branches and unwholsome lawes are first to bee pruned, and the fowle mosse clensed or scraped awaye, before the tree cann bringe forth any good fruicte'.

Following an abortive rebellion by the Old English Earl of Desmond, Gerald Fitzgerald, from 1579–83, the Crown confiscated the Desmond lands in the province of Munster and implemented a new plantation scheme in the 1580s. Unlike the Laois and Offaly Plantation, the Munster Plantation relied on the importation of New English settlers, of which Spenser was one of the best known. Planters were to fortify their lands, and introduce English habits and manners (MacCarthy-Morrogh 1986). While the plans for implementing this plantation were more exclusive than those drawn up for the Midlands efforts, the scheme suffered from the non-contiguous nature of the lands, made up of confiscated Desmond territories. The scattered nature of the plantation lands rendered adequate defence aspirational rather than achievable.

The conflict between English and Irish culminated in the Nine Years' War of 1594–1603, which saw the Ulster Gaelic lord Hugh O'Neill unite Irish forces in opposition to the English. O'Neill's men won a series of notable victories over the English, for example at the Battle of the Yellow Ford near Armagh in 1598 (Logue and O'Neill 2009). In the same year, localized rebellion decimated the Munster Plantation. Even Spenser's home, Kilcolman castle, was burned (Breen 2007: 108–9; Klingelhofer 2010: 108–29). Despite these successes, Irish forces suffered an unrecoverable defeat at Kinsale, County Cork, in 1601. En route to join their Spanish allies in the County Cork port, O'Neill's men were taken by surprise and routed by the English (Morgan 2004). Unable to regain strength in the face of a concerted English policy of massacre and starvation focused upon the northerly province of Ulster, O'Neill surrendered to the English at Mellifont, County Louth, in 1603. Armed resistance ended. The Munster Plantation was resurrected, and in 1609 a new colonial scheme was launched in the north of the island: the Ulster Plantation.

The death of Brian MacPhelim O'Neill

A closer examination of the death of Ulster chieftain Sir Brian MacPhelim O'Neill provides a mechanism for reconsidering the intimate yet ambiguous character of cultural relations in early modern Ireland, before the widespread implementation of the seventeenth-century plantation schemes. The episode in question took place in 1574, in a tower house on the shores of Belfast Lough, in the northern Irish province of Ulster. This particular castle was one of several controlled by Sir Brian MacPhelim O'Neill, Gaelic lord of Clandeboye and one-time loyal supporter of Queen Elizabeth I. O'Neill's loyalty, demonstrated through his allegiance to the Crown and symbolized by his knighthood, suffered a severe blow when the queen granted tracks of O'Neill's own lands to an English planter, Sir Thomas Smith, in 1570. In response to this humiliation, O'Neill defended his lands and Gaelic standing by burning out the newcomers, ordering the murder of Smith's son, and ensuring that the plantation venture was an embarrassing debacle (Dewar 1964; Canny 1976: 88–9, 130; Lennon 2005: 282–4). By autumn 1574, O'Neill had regained his lands and his local respect, but faced new opposition from Walter Devereux, the Earl of Essex. The queen had granted to Essex more of O'Neill's lands with the proviso that Essex subdue the Irish lord in order to take possession. It was to O'Neill's Belfast tower house that Essex marched in the autumn of 1574. While the structure is no longer extant, we can safely assume that like other Ulster tower houses, it was a defensible structure, encompassed by a fortification or bawn, and protected through architectural features such as machicolations and arrow slits or, more likely, up-to-date gun loops. A depiction on a map of 1602 (National Maritime Museum P/49(25)) shows the structure as defended by a square bawn with at least one corner flanker, with three small houses outside of the defences. On arrival, Essex did not seek to attack. Rather, he requested entry and hospitality for himself and his men, which was granted.

On the interior, the space would have been hierarchically structured, with the most private space situated at the top and accessible only by a spiral staircase. A description from 1620 provides a flavour of the welcome that may have been provided to Essex and his men:

> The hall is the uppermost room, let us go up, you shall not come downe agayne until tomorrow. The lady of the house meets you with her trayne...salutations paste, you shall be presented with all the drinks in the house, first the ordinary beere, then the aquavitae, then sack, then old ale, the lady tastes it, you must not refuse it. Then the fyre is made in the middle of the hall, where you may solace yourselfe until suppertime, you shall not want for lack of sack and tobacco.   (Gernon 1620)

Three days passed in which Essex and his men enjoyed the company and hospitality of the O'Neill household, as recorded in the *Annals of the Four Masters* (M1574):

200 AUDREY HORNING

Peace, sociality, and friendship, were established between Brian, the son of Felim Bacagh O'Neill, and the Earl of Essex; and a feast was afterwards prepared by Brian, to which the Lord Justice and the chiefs of his people were invited; and they passed three nights and days together pleasantly and cheerfully. At the expiration of this time, however, as they were agreeably drinking and making merry, Brian, his brother, and his wife, were seized upon by the Earl, and all his people put unsparingly to the sword, men, women, youths, and maidens, in Brian's own presence. Brian was afterwards sent to Dublin, together with his wife and brother, where they were cut in quarters. Such was the end of their feast. This unexpected massacre, this wicked and treacherous murder of the lord of the race of Hugh Boy O'Neill, the head and the senior.

Essex's version of the events in the tower house on the shores of Belfast Lough was rather less colourful:

> ... with the advice and consents of all the captains in the camp, I gave order to lay hold of Brian in the castle of Belfast where he lay. Resistance was offered by his men lodged in the town and 125 of them were slain. Sir Brian and his wife, Rory Óg and Brian Mac Revelin were taken.
>
> (Essex to Lord Deputy Fitzwilliam, 14 November 1574 in *Calendar of State Papers Ireland 1571–75*: 688)

Given the enmity between the two men and the broader context of the conflict between Ireland and England, why on earth did Brian McPhelim O'Neill invite Essex into his home? And how did Essex maintain the pretext of a friendly visit over three days of intensive socializing? The answer lies in Gaelic culture, and the proximity and intimacy between the Irish and the English that facilitated Essex's violation of Gaelic codes of hospitality. If the account from the Annals is correct, Essex's plan succeeded because he understood that the cultural importance of hospitality meant that O'Neill would be compelled to entertain his English guests. Lavish displays, involving feasting and toasting, served to demonstrate and enhance the power and status of the chiefly elite, as chronicled in Bardic poetry (Simms 1978). Competition between Gaelic nobles over the respective munificence of their hospitality is reflected in the ubiquitous invitations extended to the bards, who rewarded their patrons with verses celebrating the liberality of the host. Consider the late sixteenth-century poetry of Tadhg Dall Ó Huiginn, on the generosity of Cú Chonnacht Óg Maguire: 'I sat on the right-hand of the champion of Tara, till the circling of goblets was over; although it had its due of nobles the king's elbow never disdained me' (Ó Huiginn 1923 [*c.*1589], in Maxwell 1923: 337). Power was reflected in the ability of the host to attract noble guests and to demonstrate generosity through abundant food and drink, duly chronicled and proclaimed by the bard, given a seat of honour next to the lord.

Through violating the rules of hospitality, Essex not only inflicted maximum humiliation on O'Neill through disdaining Irish custom while appearing to be a willing participant, he also sent an aggressive message to the Gaelic leadership more generally. Essex understood the cultural expectations guiding the proffering of hospitality and its role in the maintenance of elite power and identity. Beyond that, the willingness of Essex and his men to break bread, sup wine, and engage in the rituals of entertainment including the recitation of stylized bardic poetry and the performance of music and dance reflects a deeper mimetic process. Mimesis involves the interpretation and imitation of behaviour. Crucially, it is a strategy employed not only by the 'colonized other', but also by those in authority engaging with and endeavouring to understand the behaviour of those over whom they wielded power (Taussig 1993; McLean 1998). In the case of Essex and O'Neill, each would have self-perceived as being in control of their intercultural dealings. Beyond being bound by tradition, O'Neill must have felt that he had the upper hand. Perhaps he was flattered by the attentions of one of the queen's trusted emissaries, a relationship that he could use to further his own political importance. O'Neill's strategy of 'duplomacy' or (after Bhabha 1994: 93–101) 'sly civility'— in other words, presenting himself as loyal to the English Crown while continuing to subvert English efforts to gain control—was repeated by the Gaelic elite throughout Ireland. By way of example, the leader of the Ulster military forces during the Nine Years' War, Hugh O'Neill, had been raised in the Dublin Pale and had once been a frequent visitor to the court of Queen Elizabeth (Morgan 1993).

For his part, the Earl of Essex seems to have employed his cultural knowledge as a self-aware means to an end. There were limitations to his knowledge, however. Essex did not understand the Irish language nor is it likely that Brian MacPhelim O'Neill understood English, so their conversations were either mediated by the liminal figure of a translator, or were conducted in Latin (Palmer 2003). Essex would not have fully grasped the nuances of the performance of hospitality. The potential for miscommunication or the unintentional violation of a cultural norm was considerable, and may have tipped the balance towards violence rather than negotiation.

While Essex rejected Gaelic culture as proffered by the Clandeboye lord, other English military men selectively incorporated aspects of Irish culture

202 AUDREY HORNING

into their own repertoires, facilitated by nodes of convergence between elite practices in both lands. A 1602 narrative by Captain Josias Bodley, describing a visit with English servitor Sir Richard Moryson, in Lecale, County Down, illustrates this process. Bodley (1854 [1602]: 78–9) describes Moryson's effusive hospitality in terms evocative of bardic poetry:

> For at first we sat as if rapt and astounded by the variety of meats and dainties .... But after a short time we fall to roundly on every dish, calling now and then for wine, now and then for attendance, everyone according to his whim. In the midst of supper Master Morrison ordered to be given to him a glass goblet full of claret, which measured (as I conjecture) ten or eleven inches roundabout, and drank to the health of all and to our happy arrival. We freely received it from him, thanking him, and drinking, one after the other, as much as he drank before us. He then gave four or five healths of the chief men and of our absent friends .... Et est res valde laudabilis
>
> (And it is a very praiseworthy thing).

That Bodley wrote in a bardic style is all the more remarkable considering that the English generally condemned the bards. According to Barnaby Rich (1610, in Maxwell 1923: 340), '[t]here is nothing that hath more led the Irish into error, than lying historiographers, their chroniclers, their bards, their rhymers, and such other their lying poets'. Over the week that Bodley spent with Moryson, he was entertained by travelling Irish mummers and indulged with sweetmeats, wine, brandy, Irish usquebaugh, beer, ale, and New World tobacco, which he praised for its health-giving properties. As Moryson directed the festivities from his seat within a captured medieval tower house, he was replicating practices that he must have witnessed during his long military service in Ireland. At the same time, his own status was conferred and confirmed not through his abilities as a host, but crucially via his authority over the now conquered Gaelic lords and his standing as a successful military leader. As such, his mimetic use of Gaelic practice signalled his standing as a conqueror as much as it can be understood as evidence for syncretism. In Taussig's sense of mimesis, Moryson would not have consciously acknowledged his adoption of Gaelic habits so eloquently recounted in Bodley's discourse.

Similar evidence for mimesis comes from the plantation of Offaly in the Irish Midlands, which was revived in the seventeenth century. There, planter Matthew de Renzy chose to make his plantation home in an extant Gaelic tower house at Clonony More (Lyttleton 2009: 44). Furthermore, De Renzy studied the Irish language under the tutelage of the MacBruadeadha, the hereditary Gaelic historians for the O'Brien lordship. De Renzy's interest in the Irish language was not solely scholarly: he employed his new found knowledge of the Irish annals to justify plantation and to support and justify his efforts to increase his own landholdings. While de Renzy's motivations must have been at least partially transparent to his tutors, the MacBruadeadha nonetheless honoured his scholarly achievements in a eulogy that provided de Renzy with an Irish name, Mathghaimhain Ó Rensi, and provided him with an Irish genealogy and pedigree (MacCuarta 2011; Connelly 2007: 401). Despite enthusiastically embracing his role as planter and representative of English law and society, de Renzy clearly found much to admire and to mimic in Irish culture, beyond that which he could readily exploit. That he was unable to openly acknowledge his admiration does not lessen its significance.

Violence and syncretism in the Ulster Plantation

Moving beyond the elite level, violence as the underside of syncretism can be discerned in the proximity of relations between the incoming settlers and the displaced Irish of the early seventeenth-century Ulster Plantation. Unlike the Laois and Offaly Plantations, which relied upon loyal native landholders, and the Munster Plantation, with its largely non-contiguous grants of land, the Ulster Plantation encompassed all of the counties of Armagh, Cavan, Donegal, Fermanagh, Tyrone, and Londonderry (formerly known as O'Cahan's Country and briefly as County Coleraine), while unofficial plantation efforts were also being implemented in the remaining Ulster counties of Antrim, Down, and Monaghan. Critically, the formal Ulster Plantation relied upon a principal of displacement of the Irish and their replacement by loyal British settlers. Such regulations were particularly applied to the plantation lands granted to the London merchant companies. In an effort to finance the Ulster Plantation, James I (VI of Scotland) coerced the great medieval merchant guilds of the City of London into underwriting the scheme. In exchange, the Companies received grants of land in the newly created County Londonderry, upon which they were required to build fortified settlements and settle British tenants. While the Companies were ostensibly forbidden to rent to Irish tenants, in practice this was an impossible requirement. Demographics demanded that the Companies rely upon the Irish for rents and for labour, as the Companies and other planters struggled to find many willing to move to Ulster (Moody 1939; Curl 1986; Canny 2001; Horning 2001; Donnelly 2007).

Far from settling an unpopulated colonial wilderness, those few planters who made their way to Ulster were thrust into a populated Gaelic world where their survival depended upon a process of accommodation and adaptation; materially echoed in the assemblages from plantation-period villages that incorporate locally made Irish ceramics as well as imported English wares (Horning 2001, 2009; Donnelly 2007). These items facilitated domestic life inside a range of buildings that, despite regulations to be built only 'after the English manner', were as likely to reflect vernacular Irish traditions and incorporate Irish construction techniques. Examples include a sub-rectangular, wattle work Irish house excavated in the Mercers' Company village of Movanagher in the Londonderry Plantation (Horning 2001), and the frequent appearance of wicker centring rather than corbelled arches in Planter castles. Wicker centring was a distinctly Irish form of vault construction that rather than employing keystones or corbeling, employed wattle frameworks covered with rubble and mortar. When the wicker framework was removed, mortar impressions of the wattles often remained.

Outnumbered by and dependent upon their Irish neighbours, incoming settlers had no choice but to engage; finding ways to communicate across the language divide and incorporating unfamiliar practices and objects into their daily routines. A brief consideration of drinking behaviour at the non-elite level illustrates the levels of intimacy necessitated by the process of plantation. In 1618, a delegation of English tenants from the Drapers Company plantation village of Moneymore journeyed all the way to London to present allegations against the Drapers' Company agent, Robert Russell, accusing him of having 'built a great and very large and unnecessary brewhouse both to the hindrance and great disturbance of the whole towne' (Drapers' Company Records PRONI D3632/A105). Russell had diverted the town's piped water supply to service his brewhouse, forbade occupants from home-brewing, and opened the doors of the village pubs to the local Irish. The closeness of relations between the drinkers, whatever their cultural identity, gives much pause for thought in terms of considering how alcohol may have lubricated communication.

The sharing of alcoholic beverages was a key element in both Irish and English practices of (primarily male) sociability, albeit governed by different rules, customs, and expectations that could easily, if unintentionally, be violated (Horning 2009). This may be the explanation for the violence that erupted on the Mercers Proportion in 1615. Four men who were settled on the Mercers' lands were assaulted and stabbed to death by nine Irish woodkerne (rebels). The murders do not seem to have been premeditated acts of resistance, as the attack occurred after Englishman John Browne and his wife and three of their Irish neighbours had spent several hours imbibing 'beer, wine, and aqua vitae' together *with* the nine raiders in Browne's home, operated as an illicit alehouse by Mrs Browne (Canny 2001: 435; Canning 1616). Was this the result of a drunken brawl sparked by a violation of custom or an ill-thought-out comment? Did the violence erupt when Mrs Browne demanded payment for the drink consumed by the Irish? Her early modern English understanding of the provision of hospitality as a primarily economic exchange was incompatible with the customary Gaelic right to expect and even demand hospitality. This disconnect graphically illustrates Bhabha's observation that 'the problem of cultural interaction emerges at the significatory boundaries of cultures where meanings and values are (mis)read or signs are misappropriated. Culture only emerges as a problem, or problematic, at the point at which there is a loss of meaning in the contestation and articulation of everyday life' (Bhabha 1994: 34). Whatever the loss of meaning that precipitated the violence, such shared consumption of food and drink, be it in the Browne house, Agent Russell's alehouses, or O'Neill's Belfast castle highlights the intimacy as well as ambiguity at the heart of relations between the English settlers and the Irish whom they were supposed to be supplanting.

Despite clear archaeological and documentary evidence, such significant cultural entanglements in early seventeenth-century Ulster are routinely denied in historical memory. In present-day Northern Ireland, it is primarily memories of the violence that prevail. For example, the 'morality' of the Republican campaign of violence throughout the years of the Troubles, to which over 3,700 deaths can be attributed in the period since 1968, was explicitly related to the plantation by British journalist and Irish Republican Army (IRA) apologist Kevin Toolis:

> It would be simple here to hedge and qualify the issue of the morality of the IRA's struggle, but I won't. A great historic injustice was perpetrated in Ireland in the seventeenth century—the blueprint for all future campaigns of conquest, dispossession, and colonisation by the Crown. Ireland was the first English colony and it will be the last. The natives always resisted their subjugation violently, savagely; the land was always troubled. Ireland remains troubled today, not just through the burden of this history but by the failure of the Crown to relinquish its final hold on the provinces of Ireland. (Toolis 1997: 369)

Similarly, the title of the Ulster Museum's new 'Troubles' exhibit, 'From Plantation to Power Sharing' explicitly links the early seventeenth-century

Ulster Plantation to the violence of the late twentieth century, with Plantation commonly understood as a stark colonial episode. Yet in reality, early seventeenth-century Ireland makes for an awkward colonial model (Howe 2000). In total, perhaps 30,000 Protestants settled in Ireland as a direct result of the plantation schemes, a very small achievement considering that the overall population of Ireland at the mid-point of the seventeenth century was somewhere between 1.3 and 1.5 million (Barnard 1973: 13). Even the lands encompassed by the Ulster Plantation, with its pretensions to cultural replacement, were populated by an Irish majority. In 1641, Catholics (both Gaelic and Old English) retained ownership of 59 percent of profitable land in Ireland, and many of the elite had at least partially accommodated themselves to the new order (Barnard 1973: 29). It must be considered significant that the period from the 1610s, which saw the establishment of plantation, to the 1640s when Ireland became embroiled in the wider War of the Three Kingdoms, was characterized by a remarkable lack of violent conflict. That the Irish and the incoming planters were able to at least tolerate one another is evident from both the archaeological and documentary records that underscore proximity and intimacy.

The balance of power began to shift in 1641, when a small group of Irish and Old English elites launched an insurrection in a bid to protect their property rights and religious freedom, which were threatened by the policies of Irish Lord Deputy of Thomas Wentworth, the Earl of Strafford. The action began at a dinner party. On the 22 October 1641, Irish chief and Member of Parliament Sir Phelim O'Neill invited himself to a meal with his English neighbour and friend Sir Toby Caulfield at Charlemount Fort in County Armagh. Neatly echoing the events in Belfast Castle seventy-three years before, O'Neill and his men pulled out their knives and took control of Charlemount in one of the opening salvos of the 1641 Uprising (Gillespie 1991, 1993).

While their aims were for constitutional reform rather than outright rebellion, the conspirators' actions sparked more widespread violence. In Ulster, the same Irish and British neighbours who had peaceably shared food, drink, and labour raised arms against each other, yielding to the underlying anxieties integral to cultural discourse. Half-remembered slights fed the anger of combatants. Soon the internal Irish conflict expanded into one front in the wider War of the Three Kingdoms, subsumed within the constitutional crises that were sweeping Europe. Protestants in Ireland divided their allegiances between the Parliamentarian and Royalist forces, while Confederate Catholics forged an alliance with Charles I. Both sides relied in part upon Gaelic Irish conscripts to fight their battles (Connolly 2008: 100–1). The victory of Cromwell's forces in 1652 ushered in a period of reprisal against Irish Confederates, with lands confiscated from rebels and granted to a new wave of Protestant settlers. The Cromwellian land settlement represented a far more radical reordering of Irish landholding than the plantations had ever attempted, let alone ever achieved (Barnard 1973; Connelly 2008). Protestant hegemony was ultimately assured in the aftermath of the Williamite Wars which saw the accession of Prince William of Orange to the English throne.

Conclusion

Turning our scholarly attention towards addressing the analytical value of examining violence in the colonial encounters of the early modern Atlantic World should not be read as a rejection of approaches that have stressed creativity and agency, particularly on the part of indigenous societies and individuals in the Americas. The consideration of the myriad, self-aware strategies employed by these groups have significantly enhanced our understanding of the complexities not only of early modern colonial entanglements, but of processes of identity formation, maintenance, and change more broadly, while also (very belatedly) affording space for the voices of contemporary descendant communities. What this brief consideration of violence in the context of British expansion into Ireland has hopefully demonstrated is the simple reality that violence is *also* a consequence of the exercise of agency and is one of many outcomes of processes of cultural hybridization. Familiarity provides cover and opportunity, as demonstrated by the capture of Brian MacPhelim O'Neill; as demonstrated by the ability of the Powhatans to take the Virginia settlers completely by surprise on Good Friday in 1622, when Native forces strolled into English homes and killed over three hundred colonists; and as demonstrated on the 22nd of October 1641, when Irish chief Sir Phelim O'Neill invited himself to dinner with Sir Toby Caulfield. In each case, it was the ordinariness of the proffering and acceptance of hospitality that facilitated violence. That violence was the outcome of intimacy should not outweigh the significance of those interactions and shared practices that ultimately facilitated such betrayals. The decades of peace that marked the period between the launch of the Ulster Plantation and the eruption of the 1641 Rising were founded upon intercultural discourse and the emergence of syncretic practices. Tension and the potential for violence were as much inherent to those discourses as was the merging of material culture and the sharing of food, drink, and entertainment.

Emphasizing the 'positive' aspects of creativity in colonial encounters may seem more desirable in the present, as we continue to struggle with the legacies of early modern European expansion, but it is nonetheless fundamentally dishonest to the lived experiences of people in the past. Acknowledging that violence can be facilitated and indeed amplified through the very same processes of hybridization that underpin cultural identities in colonial and postcolonial zones may just help us to understand why—particularly in a Northern Irish context—violence persists as an option in the present.

References

Annals of the Four Masters 8 M1574.4. http://www.ucc.ie/celt/online/T100005E/text008.html (accessed 19 March 2012).

Barnard, T. C. 1973. 'Planters and policies in Cromwellian Ireland'. *Past and Present* 61: 31–69.

Bhabha, H. 1994. *The Location of Culture*. New York: Routledge.

Bodley, J. 1854 (1602). 'A visit to Lecale'. *Ulster Journal of Archaeology* 2: 78–9.

Breen, C. P. 2007. *An Archaeology of Southwest Ireland, 1570–1670*. Dublin: Four Courts Press.

Canning, G. 1616. 'Letter'. Guildhall Library MS 17,278, 15 January 1616.

Canny, N. P. 1976. *Elizabethan Conquest of Ireland: A Pattern Established 1565–76*. Sussex: Harvester Press.

Canny, N. P. 2001. *Making Ireland British: 1580–1650*. Oxford: Oxford University Press.

Connelly, S. J. 2007. *Contested Island: Ireland 1460–1630*. Oxford: Oxford University Press.

Connolly, S. J. 2008. *Divided Kingdom: Ireland 1630–1800*. Oxford: Oxford University Press.

Curl, J. S. 1986. *The Londonderry Plantation*. London: Phillimore.

Dewar, M. 1964. *Sir Thomas Smith: A Tudor Intellectual in Office*. London: Athlone Press.

Donnelly, C. J. 2007. 'The archaeology of the Ulster Plantation'. In A. Horning, R. Ó Baoill, C. Donnelly, and P. Logue (eds), *The Archaeology of Post-Medieval Ireland c.1550–1750*. Dublin: Wordwell, pp. 37–50.

Gallivan, M. 2011. 'The archaeology of native societies in the Chesapeake'. *Journal of Archaeological Research* 19: 281–325.

Gernon, L. 1620. *A Discourse of Ireland*. British Library, Stowe MS, vol. 28, folio 5. http://www.ucc.ie/celt/published/E620001/index.html (accessed 19 March 2012).

Gillespie, R. 1991. 'Excuse me, Sir Toby, I'm taking your Castle'. *Fortnight* 229: 23.

Gillespie, R. 1993. 'Destabilizing Ulster, 1641–42'. In Brian Mac Cuarta (ed.), *Ulster 1641: Aspects of the Rising*. Belfast: Institute of Irish Studies, Queen's University Belfast, pp. 107–21.

Horning, A. 2001. '"Dwelling houses in the old Irish barbarous manner": archaeological evidence for Gaelic architecture in an Ulster Plantation village'. In P. Duffy, D. Edwards, and E. FitzPatrick (eds), *Gaelic Ireland 1300–1650: Land, Lordship, and Settlement*. Dublin: Four Courts Press, pp. 375–96.

Horning, A. 2009. '"The root of all vice and bestiality": exploring the cultural role of the alehouse in the Ulster Plantation'. In J. Lyttleton and C. Rynne (eds), *Plantation Ireland*. Dublin: Four Courts Press, pp. 117–18.

Howe, S. 2000. *Ireland and Empire: Colonial Legacies in Irish History and Culture*. Oxford: Oxford University Press.

Klingelhofer, E. 2010. *Castles and Colonists: An Archaeology of Elizabethan Ireland*. Manchester: Manchester University Press.

Lennon, C. 2005. *Sixteenth Century Ireland: The Incomplete Conquest*. New Gill History Ireland 2, Dublin: Gill and MacMillan.

Loeber, R. 1991. *The Geography and Practice of English Colonisation in Ireland from 1534–1609*. Irish Settlement Studies no. 3. Athlone: Group for the Study of Irish Historic Settlement.

Logue, P. and J. O'Neill. 2009. 'The battlefield archaeology of the Yellow Ford'. In A. Horning and N. Brannon (eds), *Ireland and Britain in the Atlantic World*. Dublin: Wordwell, pp. 7–30.

Lyttleton, J. 2009. 'Acculturation in the seventeenth-century Irish midland plantations'. In A. Horning and N. Brannon (eds), *Ireland and Britain in the Atlantic World*. Dublin: Wordwell, pp. 31–52.

MacCarthy Morrogh, M. 1986. *The Munster Plantation: English Migration to Southern Ireland 1583–1641*. Oxford: Clarendon Press.

MacCuarta, B. 2011. 'Sword and word in the 1620s: Matthew De Renzy and Irish reform'. In B. MacCuarta (ed.), *Reshaping Ireland 1550–1700*. Dublin: Four Courts Press, pp. 101–30.

Maxwell, C. 1923. *Irish History from Contemporary Sources (1509–1610)*. London: George Unwin.

McLean, N. 1998. 'Mimesis and pacification: the colonial legacy in Papua New Guinea'. *History and Anthropology* 11: 75–118.

Moody, T. W. 1939. *The Londonderry Plantation*. Belfast: William Mullan and Son.

Morgan, H. 1993. 'Hugh O'Neill and the Nine Years War in Tudor Ireland'. *The Historical Journal* 36(1): 21–37.

Morgan, H. 2004. 'Historiography and heritage of the battle of Kinsale'. In H. Morgan (ed.), *The Battle of Kinsale*. Bray: Wordwell, pp. 9–44.

Ó Huiginn, T. D. 1923 (c.1589). 'Enniskillen'. In C. Maxwell (ed.), *Irish History from Contemporary Sources (1509–1610)*. London: George Unwin, pp. 335–7.

Palmer, P. 2003. 'Interpreters and the politics of translation and traduction in sixteenth-century Ireland'. *Irish Historical Studies* 33(131): 257–77.

Rich, B. 1923 (1610). A new description of Ireland. In Maxwell, C. (ed.), *Irish History from Contemporary Sources (1509–1610)*. London: George Unwin, pp. 340–1.

Silliman, S. 2005. 'Culture contact or colonialism? Challenges in the archaeology of Native North America'. *American Antiquity* 70(1): 55–74.

Silliman, S. 2009. 'Change and continuity, practice and memory: Native American persistence in colonial New England'. *American Antiquity* 74(2): 211–30.

Simms, K. 1978. 'Guesting and feasting in Gaelic Ireland'. *Journal of the Royal Society of Antiquaries of Ireland* 108: 67–100.

Spenser, E. 1997 (1598). *A View of the Present State of Ireland*. A. Hadfield and W. Maley (eds). Oxford: Blackwell.

Taussig, M. 1993. *Mimesis and Alterity: A Particular History of the Senses*. New York: Routledge.

Toolis, K. 1997. *Rebel Hearts: Journeys within the IRA's Soul*. London: St Martin's Griffin.

9

Tacit Knowing of Thralls

Style Negotiation and Hybridization among the Unfree in Eleventh- and Twelfth-Century Sweden

Mats Roslund

Introduction

In the area that is modern-day Sweden, household pottery underwent minimal change from the seventh century to the end of the tenth century CE. When innovation arrived, in the form of pottery originating among Slavic groups, it was therefore particularly noticeable. The contrast between the old tradition and the new late Slavic pottery was striking as regards manufacturing technique, decoration, and variations in shape. What happened then was even more interesting; the indigenous potters adopted the new tradition after centuries of monotonous production. Moreover, local copies of Slavic vessels were developed and manufactured on Scandinavian soil; this is known as Baltic ware (Fig. 9.1).

Based on the idea of freely travelling craftsmen, Baltic ware is still sometimes perceived as having been imported as containers for commodities or as commodities in themselves. Instead, it was a hybrid, developed through a process involving both indigenous Scandinavian and Slavic ceramic traditions, which expressed a completely new cultural identity. The question is what the change represented in the everyday dialogue between people.

The notion of hybridization reflects a special form of social processes behind cultural transfer, but it does not explain how it happened in practice. Cultural transfer can be understood on a human level through an analysis of who in society created the vessels, where these people were in the household hierarchy, and how the craft was passed on from one generation to the next. An awareness of the fact that people moved through structuring norms of the group and individual innovations has a methodological impact on

Mats Roslund, *Tacit Knowing of Thralls: Style Negotiation and Hybridization among the Unfree in Eleventh- and Twelfth-Century Sweden* In: *Archaeologies of Cultural Contact: At the Interface.* Edited by: Timothy Clack and Marcus Brittain, Oxford University Press. © Oxford University Press 2022. DOI: 10.1093/oso/9780199693948.003.0010

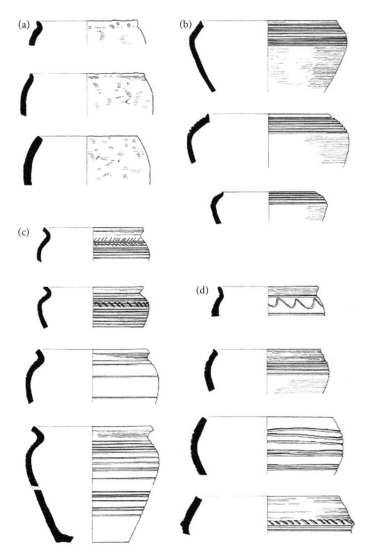

Fig. 9.1. (a) Indigenous late Viking Age pottery from Sigtuna, (b) Baltic ware from Lund, Skåne, (c) Baltic ware from Sigtuna, Uppland, and (d) Baltic ware from Skara, Västergötland. All dated to the eleventh century. Scale 1:4.

archaeology. This chapter reviews Michael Polanyi's actor-oriented model of knowledge transfer as an example (Polanyi 1983).

Since the late 1980s, studies of social identities have been geared to separate fields: Gender studies, perspectives on hierarchies, religious groups, and cultural identities are confined to different scholarly discussions instead of breaking the borders between them. How should we make this insight into the individual's diverse social identities operational for archaeological interpretation? As we shall see, in the case of the thralls (the Scandinavian name for slaves), women actors at the lowest level of society, initially originating from several ethnic groups, became creators of a new hybrid cultural identity. The dynamics over time and place are especially important, as regards both the speed of the transfer and the closeness to the style of the regions of origin.

The aim of this chapter is to explain the hybridization of material culture in the lowest social class in the towns of Sigtuna and Lund and their hinterland from *c.*970 to 1250 CE by seeing the producers as actors limited by their human qualities. In Scandinavian society during the Viking Age and High Middle Ages, heavy work was imposed on a group of unfree people, those who probably made vessels for cooking and storage. In order to expound upon their actions in two regions, I use explanations of stylistic transfer in material culture, through tacit knowing, with specific political and socio-economic conditions. The conclusions increase our understanding of the significance of 'context' and 'actors' for intercultural communication in the past.

Culture change: hybridization and creolization

There can be many causes behind the mixing of material cultures and their link to culturally encoded behaviour. Unlike a multi-cultural perspective, where lifestyles run parallel with little contact between them, concepts like hybridization, creolization, and transculturation challenge us to explain how new styles arise from the modes of material expression of two or more separate groups. In this chapter, emphasis is stressed on inter-human social relations. Case studies on agency in archaeology still needs empirical studies on the oscillation between societal norms and individual innovations, since agency is still considered elusive in hybridity studies. The fallacy is mentioned by Pappa: 'This results from a particular overlooking of agency's temporal dimensions, the specifics of time and the individual' (2013: 36). This chapter is a response to that call.

The basis for all definitions of cultural transfer is that there are clear differences between groups of people. Here we face a logical problem. On the one hand, insight into the shortcomings of the culture-history school in archaeology have forced us to abandon the idea of essential identities. On the other hand, the subjective and situational analysis of social identities has increased our knowledge of regional and local patterns of culture. Of course, there are problems with excessively stereotyped identity, but the dynamics of human societies stimulate shared forms of expression which make everyday dialogue easier. This is how we can define areas with similar material culture, even if borders are fuzzy. We therefore face a choice: either to see people as carriers of an essential identity or as constantly changing. In archaeology, this opposition has not yet been resolved, since scholars study either structures in the form of collective memory and primordial kinship or focus especially on dynamic traits, such as negotiation and identity change and culture transfer. One solution could be to study *the processes behind both cultural inertia and cultural change*. Both perspectives concerning identity are needed, since neither change nor the continuity of tradition emerge passively and without reflection. We are therefore bound between interaction and inertia.

Among anthropologists, the concept of creolization has drifted from having a specific linguistic, geographical, chronological, and social meaning in the Caribbean to becoming an analytical tool for studies of subaltern groups all over the world. In this new sense, there are also positive connotations of societies based on inclusive and dynamic principles. One problem with the term creolization is that it is both a model that describes and explains specific historical processes of cultural change and an analytical tool used for other places and times (Khan 2007: 653; see also Palmié 2006). Thomas Hylland Eriksen (2007: 172) argues that creolization is so close to other terms for change that we need rhetorical argumentation as a complement. He would limit creolization to comprise cultural amalgamations after profound contact through migrations of peoples. It therefore has a close link to displacement, individuals and groups physically removed from their original environment. The transformation of ruling groups' lifeways, and translation to shared local styles beyond those that previously existed, is guided by unequal relations.

For archaeology, the linguistic connotations of the term, creolization, have become problematic. The primary reference is to a mixture of languages, in colloquial speech and in literary style. Eriksen's observation about the contextual definition of concepts is therefore important. The terms hybridity and creolization have been juxtaposed as representing two different outlooks on cultural mixture. Hybridity has been described rhetorically as part of a biologistic outlook, with mixtures that make plants spectacular but sterile, and without actors driving the process. Creolization, at the same time, is held up as 'a process of self-awareness and self-assertion; it refers to the human hand, brain and sensibility being engaged in a process of creation, invention, critique and resistance' (Cohen and Toninato 2010: 14). Through the dichotomization of hybridization as a sterile observation imposed from without, and creolization as creative and fertile, a value-charged antagonism is created. I view this as being rhetorically interesting rather than a real difference. From an archaeological point of view, hybridity can instead express observable patterns of material culture which can be the effect of social processes that lead to creolization.

On the other hand, hybridity as a concept is criticized for being too indistinct and drained of its original meaning situated in a postcolonial context (Silliman 2015). However, hybridity in artefacts can be used outside the subaltern discussion. In many archaeological case studies, we have no information about the social hierarchies behind hybrid forms. Still, the term is useful to stress the process of social negotiations embedded in the artefact as 'cultural hybridity' (Burke 2009; Stockhammer 2012: 45–6). Whether the hybrid is an expression of a mixed identity or not, must be decided through a wider study on several material sources, such as sets of artefacts, settlement patterns, grave rituals, and food production.

Hybridity is also an opposite of purity. Since there are few, if any, pure cultural expressions constructed in isolation, purity in this text is seen in the light of degrees in cultural distinction. In the case of Baltic ware as a product of hybridization, there are no doubts about differences in the mental concepts and material practices between the two groups studied. Germanic Scandinavians and West Slavs represent distinct worldviews and cultural identities. Expressed in the production and use of ceramic vessels, the difference is unmistakable and, on comparison analytically, 'pure'.

In the words of Silliman, hybridity is a process of social practice, not a product (Silliman 2015: 286). We are given glimpses of that process in the material record, ideas and choices expressed in the combination of styles or materials in new spatial situations. To study process, we also need a series of altered artefacts over time. Both space and the pace of time are vital for the study of hybridization as constant material change. Style never sleeps, or if it does, conscious efforts to keep it in place are devoted to it. Therefore, in spite of the need for an explicit theoretical framework, the study of hybridization also is very empirical. We deeply need a well-dated and chronologically dispersed artefact set, organized in a taxonomy that is open to both contrast and similarities to avoid the creation of pure types (Roslund 2007: 153; Deagan 2013: 268ff.).

The specific context in time and space where my case study is situated has very little to do with a global system of slavery and plantations or with expansive empires. Nevertheless, the perspective of hybridity and creolization is fruitful, defined as processes for identity formation in a mixed population as expressed in everyday material culture (Loren 2005: 297). The people in focus in this study endured the same dislocation and subaltern position in Scandinavian society as did other creoles. However, one important difference affected the encounter: in the Scandinavian context we also find thralls of local origin in a centuries-old system of transfer.

Thralls in Scandinavian households

In the late Viking Age and the High Middle Ages on large estates in Scandinavia, tillage and animal husbandry were dependent on slave labour. Even smaller farms had thralls to do the heavy work in the household. The extent of slavery is controversial, and there were probably large regional differences. The formation of big estates through the amalgamation of lands, as in Denmark, required many hands to do the work, while the more dispersed agrarian settlement in central Sweden needed fewer. Through time, an economy based on slaves gave way to one based on free actors obliged to pay dues (Nevéus 1974; Lindkvist 1979; Karras 1988; Iversen 1994; Skre 1996).

Thralls were an important element in the Scandinavian economy. They were obtained through war, purchase, and childbirth among thralls. A free individual could also be forced by economic circumstances to place himself under the protection of another family. The relative proportions of these groups are impossible to determine, but a flow of captured individuals must have accounted for a significant share in areas where there were large estates. In particular, the constant arrival of such individuals must have affected the ethnic composition of the thrall group. Alien modes of expression must have been noticeable, at least among the slaves themselves. Repeated encounters with other patterns of culture would have given opportunities for stylistic transfer at this level.

Slaves captured in war during the High Middle Ages were probably brought from regions outside the growing community that Christendom constituted. The catchment area changed as countries tightened their security and the religious community expanded. People from Frankish territory on the continent, or from Ireland and Scotland, are documented as thralls in the West Norse area during the pagan Viking Age (Karras 1988: 47). Abduction of individuals within Scandinavia was another way to assemble people for sale.

During the period studied here, the Slavic areas in today's Mecklenburg-Vorpommern, Rügen, Pomerania, and the Baltic countries were probably victims of abduction. Further, people from central Sweden, from as early as the eighth century, frequently travelled eastwards. In the riverine areas, the active participation of Scandinavians in trade with Baltic and Finnish groups is recorded in Islamic sources. A picture emerges of the acquisition of slaves from a wide geographical area which changed through time. The common factor throughout is that the thralls became a part of household production.

Work on the farms was distributed on the basis of gender and position in society. In Norse sagas, in the provincial laws, and even among images in churches and documents we see the outlook that prevailed. In Scandinavian source material, the work performed in and near the house is portrayed as women's chores (Myrdal 2003). Milking, cooking, fetching water, grinding flour, and baking were heavy, monotonous chores that had to be done every day by the slave women in the household. Male slaves were tasked with digging, mucking out byres, and looking after livestock. Of course, there were social differences depending on the farm's carrying capacity, but it ought to have been possible to maintain this division of labour on most farms.

In historical perspective, then, thralls as a group are well known, but they left virtually no physical evidence of their existence. The main reason is, of course, their low status. They were of minimal interest to the free farmers or the elite and, seemingly, therefore not worthy of mention in documentary sources. In material terms, they were un-propertied and probably had very few personal possessions. For reasons that will be presented below, however, it is possible to conclude that it is feasible to find at least one group of unfree people who left material traces—pottery—that as a residue of household production allowed them to emerge from the obscurity of the houses.

Late Slavic ware, local late Viking Age ware, and Baltic ware as separate traditions

At the end of the tenth century there was a clear change in the production and consumption of household vessels, but where did the new ceramic tradition come from? Baltic ware was long considered to originate in the West Slavic areas south of the Baltic Sea, as reflected in the earlier designation 'Wendish black ware'. The vessels were primarily regarded as imports, suggesting trading connections with the West Slavic area before the breakthrough of the German Hansa. The origin has proved to be more heterogeneous in style, showing more regional and social variation than previously assumed (Roslund 2001, 2007; Fig. 9.2). To find an explanation for this process we

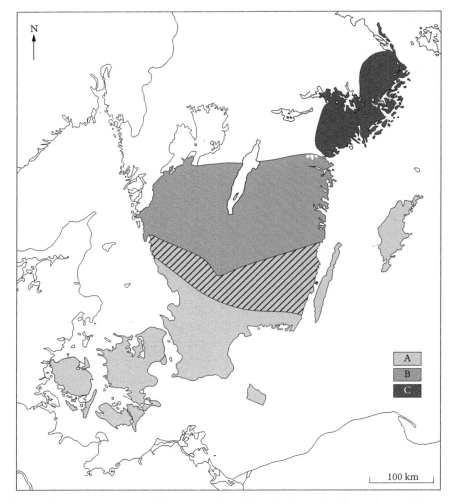

Fig. 9.2. Distribution of Baltic ware in Scandinavia. Occasional vessels have been found in other parts of the Nordic countries but were of little significance for pottery consumption. (a) In eastern Denmark and Gotland the production of indigenous late Viking Age pots ceased in the first half of the eleventh century when people switched to Baltic ware. (b) In northern Halland, Småland, Västergötland, and Östergötland the older tradition was continued parallel to the new Baltic ware. (c) In the eastern part of the Mälaren Valley Baltic ware was present in central places while a significant proportion of late Viking Age vessels continued to be manufactured there. Only a few vessels of simple Baltic ware were used in the countryside, which retained the older tradition. Between Götaland and eastern Denmark was a zone with a varied pattern of consumption, which is indistinct because of the lack of source material. The manufacture of Baltic ware stopped around 1,200 CE in eastern Denmark and in the mid-thirteenth century in the other areas. Map by Henrik Pihl (Roslund 2007).

must proceed from all three traditions produced at the time: indigenous late Viking Age ware, imported late Slavic ware, and Baltic ware.

Based on the late Slavic style, Baltic ware should be viewed as a Scandinavian reception of a foreign technique and idiom, created by social processes. It is difficult to determine the identity of the people who made the pottery, and we should not look for a direct link between style and ethnic identity. On the other hand, it is clear in Sigtuna and Lund that the first makers of Baltic ware came from Slavic areas. The tradition should thus be regarded as a process in varying social and political contexts rather than an essential ethnically defined type of pottery. Baltic ware can therefore be defined as a tradition with its roots in late Slavic pottery, but manufactured in Scandinavia from the time around 1000 CE onwards. As regards technique, the vessels were built on a turntable, decorated, and then fired in an open hearth or a pit. Slavic potters made these vessels in their new environment, but the transfer of the skill to their own children and to Scandinavian actors is the most important part of the process. This methodological orientation is a good point of departure for the discovery of hybrids in the source material.

A few areas were exposed to direct influence from Slavic potters. The three core areas—the town of Sigtuna in the Mälaren Valley, parts of medieval eastern Denmark, and Gotland—stand out during the second half of the tenth century. There were various reasons why people in Scandinavia accepted the new style, depending on earlier connections and the social framework of the transfer. Sigtuna's long-term relations with northwestern Kievan Rus' differed radically from other Scandinavian contacts. Development in eastern Denmark had a completely different background of power politics played between Danish and Obodrite rulers on the one hand, and Ranians and Luticians on the other. For the Gotlanders, the sailing route to the wealth of Kievan Rus', via the Gulf of Riga and along the Daugava to Smolensk, was important, as was the route via the island of Saaremaa (Ösel), the Gulf of Finland, and on to Novgorod. Despite differences in the processes that affected politics and patterns of culture, the encounters had a similar effect on households. Slavic potters arriving in Sigtuna, eastern Denmark, and Gotland came into contact with people who adopted the new style and made it their own. From these three core areas, the tradition spread further.

To understand the further spread of Baltic ware among indigenous potters, we must view its manufacture as a concern of the Scandinavian households. It is difficult to accept it as a commodity within the socio-economic framework of the time. We cannot talk about serial production for a market, which would have resulted in uniformity in shapes and ornamentation. Instead, the

220 MATS ROSLUND

appearance of the vessels varies both within the region and within the settlement. The potter had a general picture of what the vessel ought to look like, but could impose an individual appearance on it. The result was a heterogeneous set of vessels in southern Scandinavia.

Division of labour, active *ambátts*, and tacit knowledge

If we assume that people made food containers to cover their own household needs, the next question is: who made them? Ethnoarchaeological studies of low-technology societies show that making pots was chiefly a seasonal job connected with the female sphere (Wright 1991). The division of labour between women and men in the High Middle Ages must have resembled what we encounter in the late medieval and early modern period. Women could move outside the household sphere, but several of the everyday tasks were performed in the houses on the farmstead. These included the responsibility for preparing and storing food, which required containers of various materials. Other reasons why women were responsible for making pots concerned reproduction: pregnancy, as well as the need to be close to the children and supervise them. The simple pottery making that took place in Scandinavia in the eleventh and twelfth centuries could be adapted to fit in with other household chores. Besides the gender-related division of labour, other social identities determined who worked with pottery. Widows, old women, and childless women were other individuals who were not as closely involved in reproduction and could thus be released for other tasks.

It was probably women, then, who ensured that the Scandinavian household could prepare food and cooked it over the hearth. Can we get any closer to determining their social status? The conditions for status lie in the division of labour. People on the farms produced what was required for the house and for their immediate daily needs. The great variation in the forms of the pots reflects the work of several hands. If specialists had been employed in their manufacture, it would likely have been more homogeneous. The association with the household and the simple technique makes it likely that it was the family slaves who worked with the pots. In the conceptual terminology of the time, a female slave was called an *ambátt*, etymologically meaning 'one who runs for someone' (Brink 2003: 104). This resembles the low position of professional potters that we see in more advanced societies of the time (Roslund 2007: 144).

Close interaction between women and children meant that technical know-how about raw materials and a normative perception of suitable forms was handed on. This was important for the transfer of knowledge and experience between the generations. Crafts are usually learned through social and spatial intimacy. The transfer results in objects that display both the style and skill of the master and the individual ability of the apprentice. The transfer of craft know-how mostly takes place without any verbalization of the steps involved in the work. Instead the apprentice is encouraged or criticized by the older bearer of the knowledge and is led towards a higher level of insight and practical skill. The transfer of craft knowledge is both practical and abstract. The practical side lies in the *chaîne d'opératoire* that the potter must know to be able to visualize a vessel in the lump of clay before her. The chain of activities takes place openly in the collective in which the actor moves (Dobres 2000: 155). The sequence of actions affects several people, since the manufacture of pottery involves different individuals extracting raw clay and shaping and firing vessels. This increases the intensity of the cultural dialogue generated by the practice.

The view of craft 'know-how' as a stage in a chain of events on the way towards a finished object is tempting. Yet this image is merely an analytical tool, not a description of how the manufacture happened. The work was a temporal chain of events, but the potter had the totality of the process in mind. To arrive at the finished pot, she made several decisions that were a part of the cognitive knowledge of what constituted a correct choice. On the other hand, she did not stop thinking backwards or forwards in the process. Rituals and practice gave stability and a social framework to the events. Both practice and abstract thinking were technically, socially, and culturally conditioned. The *chaîne d'opératoire* is thus insufficient as an analytical instrument if we are to understand different forms of transfer. The passively analytical logistics must be placed in a social context where the potter plays an active part.

The practical process of knowledge transfer interested the chemist and philosopher Michael Polanyi, who developed an actor-oriented theory in the 1950s and 1960s, taking the social dimension of knowledge into consideration (Polanyi 1983). In his outlook, knowledge is more than pure description or learning. To achieve a particular goal for knowing, essential factors are: commitment, 'passion', and the person's experience. Polanyi distinguishes two levels of knowledge: focal knowing and tacit knowing. The former means concentrating on the object with which one is currently working, while the latter entails using previously acquired knowledge implicitly in order to manage the task. Tacit knowing is the knowledge that arises in the company of a master over a long time. In this way experiences are transferred which cannot be verbalized by the master himself, who knows more than he (or she, as here) can tell.

A temporary focus on the object should not be allowed to take over the actions. If a potter needs to stop and think about every movement when building a vessel, she will lose the flow. The effect can be failure or an innovation in style if it is a beginner that is acting. We can thus perceive new styles and hybrids in the archaeological record as deviating from the norm. In the silent transfer, the teacher conveys the experience she has acquired since childhood, and her individual contribution to the style through years of personal action. The pupil acquires both a normative collective knowledge and the changes that the individual has achieved consciously or unconsciously. In the material result of the action we can therefore detect traces of cultural, chronological, and geographical differences. In archaeological terms we talk of type, but concepts such as style or tradition give a more active meaning, because these contain the actor's choices, not just the archaeologist's method (the typology).

From a human perspective, we can see changes of generation where styles dynamically wane and undergo innovation as older teachers die and younger ones take over. Since knowledge is carried by people, the individual experience disappears with the passing of the carrier. Yet there is nevertheless a certain conservatism in all crafts. People are assigned roles and quickly assume them, and they can later fall back on these roles. If a woman on the farm did high-quality work that brought a favourable response, her role recurred seasonally. This stabilized the style of the vessels and left room for repeated occasions when she could teach others how to do things. Intimacy, intensity, and repetition affected the degree of tacit knowing and had the function of conserving styles. The process of change in a low-technology society thus tended to be slow, with individuals as both stabilizing and innovative actors. An individual's inability to repeat the predecessors' movements in detail made it difficult to retain exactly the same style over several generations. Inertia acting against change required effort and could be as much an expression of will as an innovation.

This discussion about the sex and social status of the potters, and of the changes between generations, suggests how Baltic ware arose as a material hybrid out of creolization as a social process. The next step is to introduce a social and historical interpretation of a corpus of source material, with an orientation to hybridization in time and place. The case study describes two areas differing in their interregional contacts, social complexity, and political history during the time from 980 to 1250 CE. Sigtuna and its hinterland in the Mälar Valley is the first area, whilst the town of Lund and the surrounding countryside is the other.

Sigtuna and Lund: hybridity in two historical contexts

Sigtuna

In Sigtuna's predecessor, Birka, the late Slavic and late Viking Age indigenous traditions already existed in parallel. When the late Slavic Rus' pottery came into use in the first half of the tenth century in towns like Novgorod, it simultaneously came westwards. The transfer between Kievan Rus' and the Mälar Valley thus took place without any time lag, and the Scandinavians were open to the new style. Occasional late Viking Age vessels at Birka have decoration in imitation of the wavy lines and parallel lines of the original, but executed with less stringency. When the town was abandoned around 960 CE, people with the same pattern of consumption settled in Sigtuna, but with a new addition in the form of Baltic ware (Fig. 9.3). As much as 80 percent of the pottery was of indigenous late Viking Age type, just under 20 percent was Baltic ware, and true late Slavic pottery accounted for only a couple of percent (Fig. 9.4).

The inspiration and the producers of the first Baltic ware in Sigtuna came from northeastern Kievan Rus', where a mixed population of Slavs, Baltic Finns, Balts, and Scandinavians created a distinctive culture (Callmer 2000). In the late tenth century the Slavic political and cultural element in the kingdom increased. Throughout the eleventh century the rulers in Kiev strengthened their position vis-à-vis the northern areas with a more heterogeneous population. The potters thus came from a kingdom with increased division of labour and control over an economic surplus. It is not entirely clear what social position the Rus' potters had in their homelands. For towns like Novgorod and Pskov we can envisage an incipient professionalization, with makers attached to major estates. The Scandinavians, on the other hand, were probably thralls since there is no evidence of any comparable specialization.

The relative proportions of the three traditions in Sigtuna changed over time. At the foundation of the town, indigenous late Viking Age ware predominated, but the increasingly common Baltic ware gained the upper hand

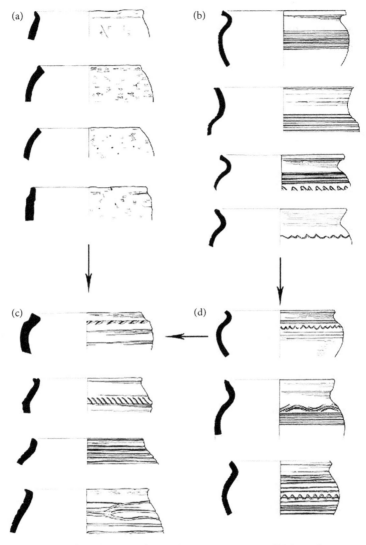

Fig. 9.3. Sigtuna. (a) Indigenous late Viking Age pottery, (b) late Slavic pottery imported from the Novgorod area, locally manufactured Baltic ware of (c) simple variant and (d) normal variant. Arrows indicate tradition influences. Scale 1:4.

from c.1050–75 CE. Until the mid-thirteenth century it accounted for the majority of household vessels, whilst the indigenous pottery declined sharply. Late Slavic pottery was imported along with guests from Rus' in the first decades of the town, but never in any large quantities. Yet despite its limited presence, it exerted a heavy influence. Two important quantitative leaps can be

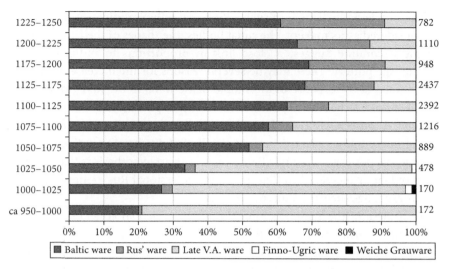

Fig. 9.4. Sigtuna. Percentage of early black earthenware in each period. A weak presence of Finno-Ugrian pottery (eleven units) during the first half of the eleventh century and weiche Grauware (thirteen units) around 1100 CE testifies to the presence of people from the Gulf of Finland and the southwest Baltic (n = 10,594).

observed in the last quarter of the eleventh century and from c.1125 CE. It was strongest just before the growing German influence in the mid-thirteenth century.

Particularly interesting is the division of Baltic ware into a normal, well-made variant and a simple, clumsier variant. Both were made of local clays, using the same technique, but they differ in the stylistic execution. Normal Baltic ware and the genuine late Slavic imports follow each other very closely in their stylistic development. When people in Novgorod, Pskov, and other urban centres in north-east Kievan Rus' in the period from 1000 to 1250 CE gave their vessels increasingly long rims, normal Baltic ware was still shaped in the same way. We may therefore assume that the normal Baltic ware was overwhelmingly made by potters from the Novgorod area but with a growing number of Scandinavians who learned how to shape and decorate vessels in a new way. Some may have learned to work with a turntable so that the form and decoration were given a distinct expression. Production of Baltic ware rose from 20 to 60 percent of the total amount of cooking pots in the course of the eleventh century. Influence from Rus' was strong throughout the twelfth century, and was particularly noticeable in the period c.1125 to 1175 CE when normal Baltic ware made up 85 percent of the forms, while simple Baltic ware consisted of 15 percent.

The simple Baltic ware is of such a kind that only Scandinavian thralls can be considered as its makers. The squat bodies, the shapes of the rims, and the simple decoration suggest a close link in proportions to indigenous late Viking Age pottery. There may be several reasons for the increase in normal Baltic ware, at the expense of the simple Baltic ware, in the mid-twelfth century. First of all, the Rus' population, including its potters, may have grown in Sigtuna. Another reason could have been a fall in the number of unfree people in the households, reflected in a drastically falling share of indigenous late Viking Age pottery and simple Baltic ware. A third hypothesis is that the division of labour increased so that the more professional Rus' potters began to sell or exchange their products on the market.

Regardless of the reason behind the process, we can conclude from the presence of normal Baltic ware that a large group of Slavic producers worked in the town during the entire period from 970 to 1250 CE. Their social position is difficult to pin down, but they must have been unfree members of the household or in some position of dependence rather than acting as free craftsmen, just as the individuals behind the simple Baltic ware. From the composition of the set of vessels it can be argued that no complete Rus' household was established in Sigtuna. The set of vessels show much equivalence between the towns, but in Sigtuna there are none of the large storage jars that we find in Novgorod (Fig. 9.5). The set that reached Sigtuna was homogeneous in size, intended for cooking on the ships during the journey and on hearths in the town. From about the last quarter of the eleventh century people also started making low, bowl-shaped oil lamps, common in the east. Working close to the potters from Kievan Rus' were Scandinavian thralls, who immediately adopted Rus' stylistic features. The process reveals a relationship that existed for a long time, intensive and regular, with a positive attitude towards the foreigners.

This close relationship declined in the second half of the thirteenth century. There had been German-speaking and Danish guests in the town since the beginning of the eleventh century. Around 1170/80 CE they came to Sigtuna in larger numbers, after Henry the Lion had negotiated a treaty on trade with the Swedish king, Knut Eriksson. With the new political situation, the way was prepared for increased participation in the important east–west trade. We can see the transition from Kievan Rus' influence to the influence of the Holy Roman Empire in the consumption of household pottery. In Sigtuna, we find none of the late Slavic vessel forms that were used in Novgorod, Pskov, and Suzdal after 1250 CE. At the same time, we see an increase in the quantity of round-based West European greywares for cooking (Kugeltöpfe, harte

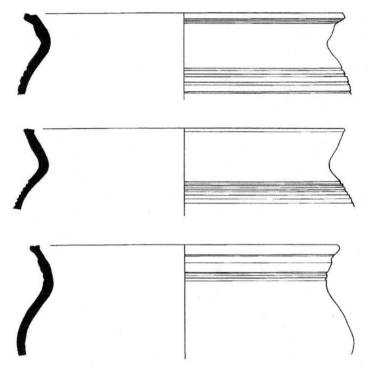

Fig. 9.5. Novgorod, the Troitski excavation. Large storage vessels from the twelfth century. Scale 1:4.

Grauware) in this transition period. Baltic ware of normal and simple type and the imported late Slavic pottery together were nevertheless still in an overwhelming majority at hearths in the town. This is remarkable in view of the incipient antagonism that arose between Swedes and Novgorodians in the struggle for wealth and souls in Finland at the end of the twelfth century. Trade was evidently so important that hostilities caused only temporary interruptions in the exchange.

In agrarian contexts in the Mälar Valley we see nothing of the close relationship with guests and diaspora from Kievan Rus'. No late Slavic vessels reached the countryside. Moreover, Baltic ware of both normal and simple type was very uncommon there. In the rubbish dumps on the farms they account for only 1 percent of the total pottery. The few examples of the ware that do occur show that simple forms were made by Scandinavian thralls who lived on a small number of farms. Instead, people on the farms retained the indigenous late Viking Age tradition intact for a very long time. It survived until the middle of the thirteenth century, both in the town and in agrarian settings. This ought to mean that there were differing socio-economic conditions in the household. The thralls in the town encountered foreigners doing work with the same low status as themselves, while the heavy chores in the countryside were entirely in the hands of Scandinavian thralls.

The inspiration from Kievan Rus' is obvious in Sigtuna. In normal Baltic ware we see potters from the east working in the town right from its foundation around 970 CE, transferring their tradition to Scandinavians. The source material, moreover, also includes the hybrid form of simple Baltic ware with its similar appearance to both the earlier indigenous black earthenware and the late Slavic tradition. These intermediate forms are a concrete expression of how Scandinavian potters gradually adopted the new tradition and transformed it together with their own local vessel style. In Sigtuna we therefore find the traces of a gentle transition reflecting protracted dialogue that resulted in a hybridization of material culture. Local potters watched and learned from the foreigners and from each other.

Lund

The first links between people in Skåne and western Slavs on the south coast of the Baltic Sea can be traced back to the late eighth century. West Slav pottery can be found at protected meeting places along the coast of Skåne in Löddeköpinge, Trelleborg, Ystad, and Åhus. They made no mark on the local tradition, however. The indigenous late Viking Age ware was virtually the only pottery in use in eastern Denmark until the end of the tenth century (Roslund 2007: 284ff.). The earliest dates for the late Slavic pottery in Skåne, that is the origin of Baltic ware, relate to this time. By then the West Slavic population had reached such a level of division of labour that specialists made pottery seasonally. This division of labour was unknown in Skåne. The situation looks very different when we consider the inhabitants in the town of Lund around 990 CE (Fig. 9.6). The oldest occupation layers in Lund are totally dominated by Baltic ware as cooking and storage vessels. The same applies to the countryside in the most fertile area in western and southwestern Skåne where the innovation was adopted fastest.

In Skåne, then, the centuries-old indigenous late Viking Age tradition was replaced with a foreign set of vessels in the course of a couple of decades. The speed of the change shows that the new style caught on very quickly on a widespread geographical scale, and with a very homogeneous range of forms. This must mean that a large group of people who carried the tradition arrived

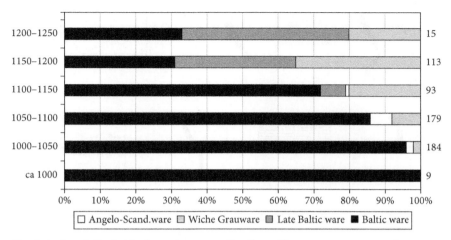

Fig. 9.6. Lund. Early black earthenware distributed by ware group over time. Percentage of units of each group in relation to the others within each period (n = 593).

from the same area and settled in both the town and the country. The potters who worked in Skåne were obviously from West Slavic territory on the south coast of the Baltic Sea. But where exactly did they come from? The most common forms that we find in early Lund and the surrounding countryside were used within a well-defined area among the Slavs (Fig. 9.7, side a). The vessels that are reminiscent in style and quantity with the forms in Skåne are gathered in a zone from the Warnow in the west to the mouth of the Oder in the east. In particular, many examples have been found on the island of Rügen (Roslund 2007: 218).

Political conditions encouraged movement from the area. Danish kings had long supported the Nakonids, a Slavic dynasty who ruled over the Obodrites in Schleswig-Holstein and western Mecklenburg. They were united by marriages, Christian missions, and joint military campaigns. Further to the east in Mecklenburg and on Rügen there were groups such as the Luticians and Ranians. They retained their old customs, in contrast to their Christian neighbours. Danes, Obodrites, the Piasts in Poland, and the Dukes of Saxony made repeated attempts to dominate them politically. Yearly attacks to capture booty and disrupt border zones were normative occurrences at this time. A major uprising among the Luticians in 983 CE had a political impact over a much larger area. During the decades from the end of the tenth century to the middle of the following century, we may assume that the Danish-Obodrite campaigns were intensified. It was at this time the West Slavic potters came to Skåne. The contrast is clear between the area with Danish-Obodrite

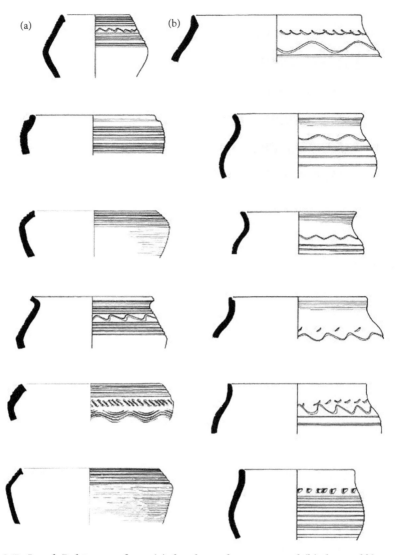

Fig. 9.7. Lund. Baltic ware from (a) the eleventh century and (b) the twelfth century. Scale 1:4.

sovereignty and the tradition bearers in the eastern part of Mecklenburg ruled by the Luticians and Ranians. The style must have come to Skåne from the hostile area along with unfree people who were brought back by force, chiefly to carry out agricultural labour on the farms there.

Since some of the West Slavic thralls were already potters in their homeland, they continued to act as such in Skåne. They repeated the forms with which they were familiar, but they were living in a completely new socio-economic context. They also adopted the forms of the new country. Importantly, the pottery from in and around Lund included vessels with functions not found in West Slavic territory. Hanging vessels used as cooking pots above hearths and oil lamps on pedestals were made at the request of new masters. The style and technique, however, remained Slavic. The combination of traditional function and new style became a hybrid contribution.

The impact was so total that we cannot discern any hybrid forms based on the late Viking Age or late Slavic traditions. An initial and rapid, social 'Big Bang' gave way to a slow hybridization process based on succeeding generations. The ceramic tradition gradually took a direction away from what had existed in the homelands. In the mid-eleventh century there were two tendencies. Inverted rims were conservatively kept as the norm, whereas people on the other side of the Baltic created new forms. Archaic forms were thus repeated, belonging to the time when the older generation had come to Skåne, since no new expressions could be passed on from the land across the Baltic Sea. This suggests that people had lost contact with their place of origin. The tradition bearers who had sat at the turntables on Rügen with Hinterland before they were forcibly brought to Skåne were disappearing. At the same time, new rim types became a part of the ceramic repertoire in Skåne, shaped by local skills (Fig. 10.7, side b). The late Slavic tradition of pottery production was slowly transformed to Baltic ware, a Scandinavian tradition with Slavic roots.

The change clearly exposes human physical limitations, and it can be linked to models for tacit knowing. Changes of generation usually involve gentle transitions to new forms, since no one can follow a style in detail. If this nevertheless happens, it is because someone is motivated to preserve a tradition and expends great energy in doing so. Conservatism requires immense effort. Small changes sneak into the everyday 'doing' because of individuals' inability to repeat a fixed pattern, or a desire to avoid doing so. Repeating a form exactly can be regarded as anxiously backward-looking. The speed of change and the willingness of people in the environment to undergo transformation are therefore also important elements in the understanding of hybridization.

At the beginning of the twelfth century this separate development was reinforced by further forms that were closer to German-Danish cooking vessels. The fabric became thinner and better fired in this late Baltic ware (Fig. 9.8). The earlier ware ceased to be produced at the start of the thirteenth century. By then the political and economic relations were directed towards areas dominated by German-speaking interests. The choice is clearly seen in

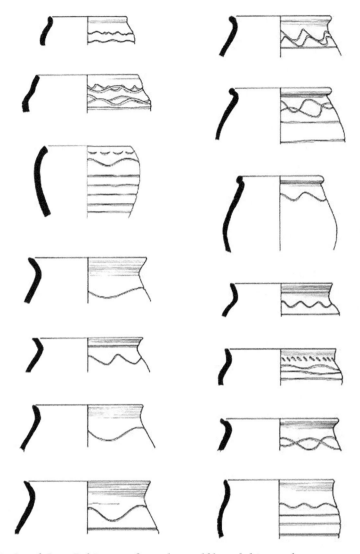

Fig. 9.8. Lund. Late Baltic ware from the twelfth and thirteenth century. Scale 1:4.

the households, as the round-based cooking pots of West European greywares for cooking (Kugeltöpfe, harte Grauware) increased heavily. At the same time, pottery production left the household level and became increasingly geared to the market.

Unlike the pattern of consumption in the Mälar Valley, where the use of late Slavic vessels and Baltic ware became a wholly urban concern, the traditions immediately caught on in the rural surroundings. The close contact between Lund and the hinterland is also noticeable in the fact that cooking vessels of Anglo-Scandinavian type and round-based vessels of the type 'Kugeltopf, weiche Grauware' were produced and consumed in the same way during the eleventh and twelfth centuries. Foreigners and their patterns of culture were spread to all social settings.

Conclusions: hybridization and creolization among the unfree in southern Scandinavia in the late Viking Age and High Middle Ages

If we accept a geographical and chronological extension of the concepts, it may be possible to use hybridization as model of the change in the production and consumption of pottery in Sigtuna and Lund from the late tenth century to 1250 CE. It is also possible to exemplify what was stated by Silliman: 'If hybridity is applied to moments of transition, as assumed by many who use it, we would need to know the duration of such transitions. These remain understudied if not outright neglected' (Silliman 2015: 286).

The two regions selected for the study show completely contrasting patterns of culture and different ways of receiving the Slavic ceramic tradition. The reasons, of course, were the different geographical locations, along with deliberate political and socio-economic conditions both in the country of origin of the Slavic producers and in the receiving regions in Scandinavia. The transfer is a very clear example of how a pattern of culture is changed through a hybridization process in which both groups affect the results. Whether they were unfree or dependent craftsmen or craftswomen, the Slavic and Scandinavian thralls were displaced and subordinate. The impact of the change was selective. One can view this as a creolization of a subaltern group of the society, but not all of it. At the same time, regional conditions affected the process.

The Mälar Valley displays a pattern of distribution for Baltic ware which suggests that pottery-making unfree people of Slavic origin or their children were not a part of the agrarian economy. Instead the use of the new hybrid and the genuine imported late Slavic pottery from the Novgorod area was restricted to the town of Sigtuna. The contacts were maintained for a long time, with continuous transfer of new producers up to the mid-thirteenth century. In Lund and eastern Denmark there was extensive transfer of unfree people from the West Slavic area from around 990 until 1050 CE. After that, contacts with potters in Slavic areas ceased. The traditions of the Slavic home-land died out with the grandmothers, and new forms were created by the younger women.

In the primary phase the transmission can be regarded as a transfer, but in the next stage it was a translation. The difference lies in the degree of close-ness, intensity, and continuity with respect to the innovators who came from Slavic territory. In Lund and Sigtuna there was daily contact through which the foreigners' craft was adopted. This was also the case in rural southwest Skåne and possibly Sjælland. In rural Södermanland and Uppland the people were even more isolated from the producers in urban settings. There, they stuck to the indigenous late Viking Age tradition and met just a few Scandinavian thralls who had adopted the hybrid form. On the other hand, it is obvious that Baltic ware gained a foothold in northern Skåne, Halland, Västergötland, and Östergötland, but it was then a translated style beyond direct contact with Slavs.

The hypothetical interpretation of the establishment of Baltic ware in Scandinavia as hybrid practice has important implications for the choice of method and the perspective of further studies of cultural change. Archaeological typologies must be constructed in such a way as to reveal transitional forms as signs of hybridization. Instead of simply classifying Baltic ware as Slavic, it is necessary to consider several different social iden-tities. Those who bore the knowledge of what Slavic pottery should look like came from different regions, they were women of different ages, and they had varying degrees of contact with the homelands. The places to which they came were urban and agrarian settings, in different parts of Scandinavia where their main role in life consisted of the everyday chores of *ambátts*, female thralls. The perspective shifts from structure to process. An important part of the analysis concerns how the stylistic transfer took place in everyday practice, with tacit knowing being transmitted between generations. Thus, the temporal perspective is crucial for our understanding. The examples show how archaeological sources can indicate whether the change was rapid or sluggish, whether it was a limited number of people who had the knowledge, or a large-scale displacement of people was involved.

Another important result of the study is that it sheds light on the obscurity in which the thralls found themselves. Since they have not left any archaeo-logical traces in other permanent material, the simple cooking pots are crucial evidence of their existence, origin, and social actions. The silent knowing of the thralls about pottery manufacture, transferred between generations of women and between people of differing ethnic background, is their only distinct vestige. With a close-up study of the style of artefacts, it is possible to highlight their actions and negotiations which resulted in a hybrid style.

Acknowledgements

The text was translated by Alan Crozier. Figures used by courtesy of Brill publishing house, Leiden.

References

Brink, S. 2003. 'Ambátt, seta, deigj: þræll, þjónn, bryti'. In T. Lindkvist and J. Myrdal (eds), *Trälar: Ofria i Agrarsamhället från Vikingatid till Medeltid*. Skrifter om skogs- och lantbrukshistoria. Stockholm: Nordiska Museets förlag, pp. 103–17.

Burke, P. 2009. *Cultural Hybridity*. Cambridge, Malden: Polity Press.

Callmer, J. 2000. 'From West to East: the penetration of Scandinavians into Eastern Europe ca. 500–900'. In M. Kazanski, A. Nercessian, and C. Zuckerman (eds), *Les centres proto-urbains russes entre Scandinavie, Byzance et Orient. Actes du Colloque International tenu au Collège de France en octobre 1997*. Réalités byzantines 7. Paris: Lethielleux. pp. 45–94.

Cohen, R. and R. Toninato. 2010. 'Introduction'. In R. Cohen and P. Toninato (eds), *The Creolization Reader: Studies in Mixed Identities and Cultures*. London: Routledge, pp. 1–21.

Deagan, K. 2013. 'Hybridity, identity, and archaeological practice'. In J. J. Card (ed.), *The Archaeology of Hybrid Material Culture*. Carbondale, Edwardsville: Southern Illinois University Press, pp. 260–76.

Dobres, M.-A. 2000. *Technology and Social Agency: Outlining a Practice Framework for Archaeology*. Oxford: Blackwell.

Eriksen, T. H. 2007. 'Creolization in anthropological theory and in Mauritius'. In C. Stewart (ed.), *Creolization: History, Ethnography, Theory*. Walnut Creek: Left Coast Press, pp. 153–77.

Iversen, T. 1994. *Trelldomen: Norsk Slaveri i Middelalderen*. Unpublished PhD dissertation, University of Bergen, Bergen.

Karras, R. M. 1988. *Slavery and Society in Medieval Scandinavia*. New Haven: Yale University Press.

Khan, A. 2007. 'Good to think? Creolization, optimism, and agency'. *Current Anthropology* 48(5): 653–73.

236   MATS ROSLUND

Lindkvist, T. 1979. *Landborna i Norden under äldre Medeltid*. Acta Universitas Upsaliensis 110. Stockholm: Almqvist & Wiksell International.

Loren, D. D. 2005. 'Creolization in the French and Spanish colonies'. In T. R. Pauketat and D. D. Loren (eds), *North American Archaeology*. Oxford: Blackwell, pp. 297–318.

Myrdal, J. 2003. 'Mjölka och mala, gräva och valla: Aspekter på trälarnas jordbruksarbete cirka år 1000–1300'. In T. Lindkvist and J. Myrdal (eds), *Trälar: Ofria i Agrarsamhället från Vikingatid till Medeltid*. Skrifter om skogs- och lantbrukshistoria. Stockholm: Nordiska Museets förlag, pp. 125–32.

Nevéus, C. 1974. *Trälarna i Landskapslagarnas Samhälle: Danmark och Sverige*. Studia Historica Upsaliensia 58. Uppsala: Uppsala University.

Palmié, S. 2006. 'Creolization and its discontents'. *Annual Review of Anthropology* 35: 433–56.

Pappa, E. 2013. 'Postcolonial baggage at the end of the road: how to put the Genie back into its bottle and where to go from there'. *Archaeological Review from Cambridge* 28(1): pp. 29–50.

Polanyi, M. 1983 [1967]. *The Tacit Dimension*. Gloucester, MA: Peter Smith.

Roslund, M. 2001. *Gäster i huset: Kulturell överföring Mellan Slaver och Skandinaver 900 till 1300*. Lund: Vetenskapssocieteten i Lund.

Roslund, M. 2007. *Guests in the House: Culture Transmission between Slavs and Scandinavians 900 to 1300 AD*. Leiden: Brill.

Silliman, S. W. 2015. 'A requiem for hybridity? The problem with Frankensteins, purées, and mules'. *Journal of Social Archaeology* 15(3): 277–98.

Stockhammer, P. W. 2012. 'Conceptualizing cultural hybridity in archaeology'. In P. W. Stockhammer (ed.), *Conceptualizing Cultural Hybridization*. Berlin, Heidelberg: Springer Verlag, pp. 43–58.

Skre, D. 1996. *Herredømet. Bosetning og besittelse på Romerike 200–1350 e. Kr.* Acta Humaniora 32. Unpublished PhD dissertation, University of Oslo, Oslo.

Wright, R. P. 1991. 'Women's labor and pottery production in prehistory'. In J. M. Gero and M. W. Conkey (eds), *Engendering Archaeology: Women and Prehistory*. Oxford: Basil Blackwell, pp. 194–223.

10

Cultural Interaction at Palmares

An Archaeology of South American Maroons

Pedro Funari and Aline de Carvalho

Syncretism is an interpretive concept originally linked to the study of religiosity in classical antiquity, particularly to address the politics of religious synthesis (Kraft 2002: 142). It was subsequently used to describe and understand processes of 'hybridisation or amalgamation of two or more cultural traditions' (Lindstrom 1996: 539). Classical antiquity, with a plethora of people mixing and interacting in different contexts, has been a favourable arena to discuss the cultural processes of interaction (Funari and Pollini 2005). Redefined time and again in anthropological, archaeological, and historical literature, the concept of syncretism has moved from classical antiquity to other cultural and geographical areas, beyond the original Mediterranean, and used to describe and understand religiosity in the Americas after European colonization.

From the late nineteenth century, the discussion of syncretism and hybrid social practices was particularly important in the New World. In Brazil, syncretism has been widely used to describe and interpret the interaction of religious practices of African, Native-Brazilian, European, and Catholic origins. As early as 1900, the influential social theoretician Nina Rodrigues related the Christian Cross to Orisha stones, mixing Catholic and African religiosity (Vainfas 2000: 532). From the 1930s, syncretism has been used not only to explain religious processes, but more widely applied to deal with national identities.

In Brazil, several scholars, such as Sérgio Buarque de Holanda, Edison Carneiro, Arthur Ramos, and Gilberto Freyre, asked themselves whether we Brazilians were as we have always been, and how important was the past in shaping our modern identities? What was the role of cultural heritage? How do the ways and features of our own Brazilian culture differ from the original European culture? Social theoreticians were thus concerned with understanding Brazilian mores, traits, and particularities with the aim of differentiating

Pedro Funari and Aline de Carvalho, *Cultural Interaction at Palmares: An Archaeology of South American Maroons*
In: *Archaeologies of Cultural Contact: At the Interface.* Edited by: Timothy Clack and Marcus Brittain, Oxford University Press.
© Oxford University Press 2022. DOI: 10.1093/oso/9780199693948.003.0011

238   PEDRO FUNARI AND ALINE DE CARVALHO

Brazil from the Old World colonial powers, most notably Portugal and Spain (Tuna 2000: 21). Syncretism was a key concept, used to describe a special blending of religious ideas and practices, fostering better interpretive schemes and explaining Brazilian national identity.

Other scholars in the Americas also enticed by the concept of syncretism included Siv Ellen Kraft, from the department of Religious Studies, University of Tromsø. Nonetheless, it took several further decades for a worldwide debate about cultural mixing, however polarized, to emerge from the 1960s and 1970s onward. Kraft (2002: 143) stresses that several conferences in North America, including leading anthropological ones, led to a perception that syncretism was among the concepts to be excluded from religio-historical research. Those debates focused on such concepts as syncretism, syncretization, meta-syncretism, and so forth. Discussions did not lead to a consensus, of course, but they were important for developing an understanding of several concepts relating to social interaction in a variety of historical, geographical, and anthropological contexts. Different disciplinary backgrounds provided a variety of approaches and emphases (Colpe 1987; Carlson 1993; Pye 1994; Stewart and Shaw 1994; Akinnaso 1995; Rothstein 1996; Werbner 1997; Kraft 2002).

A similar history applies to creolization, another key concept in cultural interaction studies. Creole is a Spanish term used to refer to Spaniards born in the Americas, referring to someone raised ('created', from the verb 'criar', to create and raise) in a foreign land. Originally, in the Spanish caste system, it referred to Spaniards; but in other contexts, such as in Brazil, it referred to Africans raised in the colony. In any case, the concept is linked to the late medieval concept of blood purity or *limpieza de sangre* (see Fernandes 2009: 162), 'where the absence of Jewish and Muslim blood defined an honorable Christian. In some instances, the term was used more to refer to groups of people of common origin' (Katzew pers. comm.).

From the early 1980s, creolization had become part of a general theory of culture change and was applied to a variety of cultural contacts and interactions, such as study of Nigerian popular culture (Hannerz 1987). Creole has been interpreted as a 'concept as an analytic to understand how forces of globalization produced diversity through interrelations instead of increasing homogeneity' (Munasinghe 2002: 551). This way, creole describes creative processes in a wide variety of situations. This broadening of the concept, beyond its original Latin American context, led some scholars, such as Viranjini Munasinghe, to warn that we cannot disentangle the different uses of the concept from contemporary contexts, thereby losing its potential to be

CULTURAL INTERACTION AT PALMARES   239

an interpretive tool. Creolization theory, by implication, is particularly relevant as a discursive device in specific historical contexts.

Considering the rich variety of understandings of interaction processes, including syncretism and creolization, in this chapter, we aim to explore how such concepts have been used to interpret maroons in what would become Brazil, and particularly the seventeenth-century runaway settlement (*quilombo*) known as Palmares. We start by describing the maroon and then outline how different readings of the evidence depending on specific understandings of syncretism, cultural interaction, mixing, and creolization have been put into action. We conclude by comparing Palmares with other archaeological studies of maroons in South America.

Palmares: a rebel polity

In order to understand the constitution of the Palmares *quilombo*, it is necessary to return to the fifteenth-century maritime expansionism pursued by Portugal in search of new routes to the Indies. In 1415, the Portuguese took over the island of Ceuta and initiated an expansion process through Africa. In subsequent decades, they crossed the Southern Atlantic and arrived at the territory which constitutes modern-day Brazil. During the second half of the sixteenth century and into the early seventeenth, when commerce with the Indies proved to be unprofitable for Europeans, the Portuguese implemented a new type of production in the newly discovered lands: the processing of sugar cane. Many sugar mills that used the slave labour of Africans and local Indians, known as 'Negroes of the land', were set up on the coast of Bahia and Pernambuco. Sugar cane processing returned a profit not only for Portugal, but also for Holland, which was responsible for refinement of the product. While the Portuguese dedicated themselves to the construction of the sugar mills, they also began to face the escape of Black and Indian slaves. Together, these slaves founded the Palmares maroon.

During the period of the Iberian Union (1508–1640), when Portugal was incorporated into the Spanish Crown under the power of Philip II, Palmares, located about 60 km inland from the Brazilian coast, received new inhabitants. According to the historiography of the maroon, which will be addressed below, not only Indians and Blacks lived in the maroon, but also Jews, Muslims, and witches. By 1612 Portuguese authorities began to acknowledge the settlement as a both powerful and dangerous refuge for slaves.

The religious disputes existing in Europe in the seventeenth century also had repercussions for daily life in the Brazilian colony, and thus for the Palmares maroon. Philip II, king of Catholic Spain, forbade Holland to enter into commerce with Brazil (which belonged to Spain through the Iberian Union). This proclamation was motivated by the loss of Spanish territories to the Netherlands. The Dutch, mostly Protestants, invaded Brazil in 1630 to search for sugar, but also in response to the actions of Philip II. The Dutch authorities, then dominating the region of Pernambuco, also recognized the danger of the Palmares settlement, but, despite all military efforts, were unable to destroy it.

With the end of the Iberian Union in 1640, and the 1654 expulsion of the Dutch from Brazil, colonial authorities and mill owners combined military forces in a drive to destroy the Palmares maroon. In response, the Palmarinos began to attack farms along the coast in order to obtain weapons, free slaves, and exact revenge on the mill owners and overseers. In one of the many conflicts, infantry captain Fernão Carrilho imprisoned about two hundred members of the maroon. In response to these developments, Ganga-Zumba, military chief of the Palmares maroon, sought to resolve the situation through negotiations. He proposed to the governor of Pernambuco, Aires de Souza e Castro, that the inhabitants of Palmares would disarm if, in exchange, they were granted ownership rights over the lands of Palmares, and personal freedom for all those born in the maroon.

As a result of Ganga-Zumba's proposition, discord arose inside the maroon. Another military leader, Zumbi, led the opposition against Ganga-Zumba, organizing Palmares's continued resistance to the colonial forces. In 1687, the governor of Pernambuco placed Domingos Jorge Velho, a pioneer or *bandeirante*, in command of the campaign against Palmares. After seven years of attempts Velho, leading an army of colonists, Indians, and *mamelucos* (mix of Indian and white ancestry), finally destroyed the settlement. Zumbi was not captured until 20 November 1695 (Funari and Carvalho 2008).

Palmares through archaeological lenses: syncretism and creolization at stake

Brazilian archaeology was deeply affected by the military dictatorship throughout the twenty-one years of discretionary rule, from 1964 to 1985. Funding and permissions were subjected to direct state control. Academia suffered severely and particularly archaeology for its humanistic defence of

CULTURAL INTERACTION AT PALMARES 241

Fig. 10.1. Map showing the location of Palmares. The maroons were situated between the states of Alagoas and Pernambuco.

native Brazilians. Prehistoric archaeology was broadly devalued, accepted only as an empirical import from the United States and devoid of political features. In contrast, colonial buildings and other elite material culture were put at the heart of nationalist and reactionary heritage policies.

Maroons, considered as resistance movements against oppression, were particularly devalued and seen as a way of challenging the official discourse. The archaeological study of maroons is thus political and linked to the opening up of the regime since the late 1970s. This is particularly visible in the 1979 amnesty of those expelled from the country and most notably with the restoration of civilian rule in March 1985 (cf. Guimarães and Lanna 1980; Guimarães 1990).

The Palmares Archaeological Project was set up in the early 1990s (see Fig. 10.1), directed by Charles Orser, Jr, Michael Rowlands, and Pedro Paulo Funari and later Scott Joseph Allen. As the most enduring case of slave resistance in the Americas (1604–95), the archaeological study of Palmares received scholarly and funding support from a wide variety of sources (see

Orser 1996). The archaeological results were published in scholarly outlets (e.g. Rowlands 1999; Funari 2003a) but also in a variety of popular science publications, addressing a wide audience, particularly in Brazil. Interestingly, even though the four archaeologists carried out field work in the same maroon, the narratives about the settlement differ quite significantly in their resulting interpretive models.

Creolization, as such, is not mentioned in the archaeological studies about Palmares, which is possibly explained by the Portuguese colonial use of the term *crioulo* to refer to slaves of African descent born in Brazil, to differentiate them from native Africans. *Crioulo* were usually well acquainted with the Portuguese language, Catholicism, and other social customs and mores. The term did not refer to Portuguese born in Brazil and had thus no relation to the different contemporary use of *criollo* by the Spaniards who controlled Portugal and Brazil from 1580 to 1640; however, the term was similarly used to differentiate the status of people.

Syncretism in Palmares: an ethnogenetic approach

In an ethnogenetic approach developed by Allen (1998), it was considered that Palmares settlement material culture is best interpreted within a syncretistic frame of study. Allen's study identified that three different pottery wares were in use: native Brazilian, European, and popular (ibid. 148). Native Brazilian wares were classified as *tupi-guaranis*; comparison of Palmares wares with examples elsewhere in region resulted in the postulation of a diffusion model (Prous 2005). European wares were related to similar ones found on the coast, some 60 km to the east, used during Dutch (1635–54) and Portuguese control. Popular wares were considered as those unrelated to Native Brazilian or European, and thus seen to be a local production, probably manufactured at the settlement itself (Allen 1998: 15–152). Local wares were potentially unique Palmares syncretistic entities, and thus a major opportunity to interpret the rebel community.

In order to verify the local manufacture of Palmares wares, comparisons were made not only with those from other sites in the Portuguese colony dated to between the seventeenth and nineteenth centuries and those from Dutch forts in Brazil, but also with other prehistoric wares from the Amazon Basin. However, they proved to be of singular occurrence as it was not possible to relate them to any other wares. For additional rigor, documents referring to the maroon from Dutch and local council sources were scrutinized

(Allen 1998: 154). Local wares became the focus of this archaeology of ethnogenesis. These wares were not Native Brazilian, African, or European and the producers were forgers of a new cohesive maroon identity. The ethnogenetic model described social and ethnic interactions in the rebel polity.

Such archaeologies of ethnogenesis catalysed discussions about African culture in the Americas and the emergence of a specific African-American culture (Allen 1998: 156). Comparing established theories of the African diaspora (e.g. Herskovits 1947; Frazier 1949; Bastide 1960; Mintz and Price 1976; Freitas 1978) with the evidence from Palmares, Allen (1998) considered that ethnogenesis was a useful model for considering how African-American practices compared to traditional African ones.

Herskovits (1947) suggested that it was possible to establish the degree of African traits in African-American societies. According to his model, the so-called 'survival' of African traits in religion, clothing, foodways, and other aspects of social life depended directly on the presence of people of African descent in the population and the distance from the dominant European society. Each trait could be counted in a classification table and divided into three main categories: more African, intermediate, and less African. Herskovits concluded that the less contact with the domineering white culture, the greater likelihood of keeping original African traits. In an opposing direction, Frazier (1949) emphasized that transfer from Africa has been essential in destroying the 'original' in African culture. The trauma and violence of slavery led Blacks to break with their original African cultural patterns, so that re-enacting their original identities was impossible. There was no other option except to emulate the European ways in organizing communities. As such, whilst Herskovits stressed the homogeneity of African culture, Frazier proposed a plethora of newly created cultures of African descent. Mintz and Price (1976) developed the analysis further proposing that historical conditions led Blacks to shape a new African-American identity. Under duress, slaves created new practices, avoiding traditional ones, in order to survive in the new context (Allen 1998: 152–72). The cultural fluidity proposed by Mintz and Price was complemented by the concept of the 'cultural mosaic', as described by Décio Freitas in the 1970s. This model has been popular with maroons and other Black social movements which aim to reinforce tradition and stability. A mosaic involves different colours in shaping an image and so the concept of 'mosaic culture' considers that different cultures, when in contact, form a new one.

All these models, despite their differences, share a common goal of spotting distinct cultural traits in maroon settlements and, as such, take for

244 PEDRO FUNARI AND ALINE DE CARVALHO

granted that there are fixed identities to be discovered, named, and compared (Azevedo 2000). Their differences are in developing a variety of possible ways of singling out distinct cultural traits. Then again, the challenge of Palmares pottery wares is unpacking the series of cultural elements in their shape and fabric. They are not only the result of Native Brazilian, African, and European traits, but they carry multiple meanings (Allen 1998: 156–74). In adopting an ethnogenetic approach how do we understand those cultural interactions expressed in the wares?

In reality, this challenge for the ethnogenetic approach is also a key archaeological discussion: how can archaeology address ethnicity, by analysing material culture (Schiavetto 2005: 79)? The ethnogenetic approach may use the concept of re-interpretive syncretism, as proposed by Bastide (1960), as a plausible way of engaging the cultural dynamics of Black communities in the Americas. With no relation to Herskovits, Frazier, Mintz and Price, or Freitas, Bastide proposed the 'fusion of cultural elements' as a key concept. Such elements have a variety of roots and are constantly re-negotiated within a given cultural system. Seen in every society, this ongoing, perpetual move towards re-creation is essential to understand how a new ethnic group may be interpreted by the ethnogenetic approach. The concept of re-interpretive syncretism was thus used to interpret material culture from Palmares and, accordingly, artefacts were used to prove the formation of a new ethnic group. The mix of Native Brazilian, African, and European elements in local wares was taken as clear evidence that Palmares people established in an unknown environment a new culture and identity.

Traditional and new elements mixed in innovative ways at Palmares, included clothing, names, and tools. At both material and intangible levels these elements shaped a new and cohesive identity (Allen 1998, 2000, 2001). From an ethnogenetic standpoint, all such mixings differentiated the new identity from slave society, including the Dutch, Portuguese, and colonists. In constant flux, new elements were continuously incorporated to previous configurations. From this perspective, Palmares forged a unique identity in opposition to colonial power. As such, Palmares is not only a symbol of the resistance in the seventeenth century, during its actual existence, but to modern, contemporary society.

Continuing within the theoretical horizon of syncretism, a different approach is the archaeology of the African Diaspora. This aims at understanding cultural relations and the shaping of new identities from roots in Africa, Europe, and the Americas (Orser 1998; Ferreira 2009). Beyond syncretism, global connections are emphasized, so that the Palmares *quilombo* did not form an isolated unit fighting as some fashion of 'pure' culture, because it was inserted into a complex web of direct and indirect relations with the inhabitants of the colony as well as with the Europeans. The colonists maintained a direct relationship with Palmares not only for trade and exchange purposes but also in the private spheres of daily life, because they shared an identity that was much closer to that of the dwellers of Palmares than to the farm owners and other local elites (see Orser 1996). In this interpretation, the Palmares settlement is part of a web of relations that facilitate the connection of several parts of the world. The Palmares *quilombo*, just like the plantations in the southern United States and rural areas in Ireland, is only understood as the result of capitalist forces; namely modernity, Eurocentrism, and colonialism. In this global approach, interconnection, starting in 1415 with the Portuguese conquest of Ceuta in Africa, explains local realities and enables us to appreciate the revolutionary force of worldwide capital (ibid.).

Palmares in other guises: ethnicity, gender, domination, and resistance

Syncretism has been a key interpretive advance, taking the maroon as a creative new endeavour, a unique polity. Archaeological syncretism does, though, imply the existence of some theoretical tenets: a cohesive and homogenous identity, reflected in a coherent and also cohesive material culture. Alternative approaches critique models of homogenous identities. Scott (2009: 129), for example, argues that 'identities do not exist prior to their political invocation and the strategic character of such invocation', and asserts that gender, race, and cultural heritage emerge unpredictably in practice rather than as preformed entities. Scott's standpoint stresses the intrinsic relationships linking science, identity, and power relations.

As Voss (2008: 13) notes, identity is a contested field, fraught with epistemological and political implications and which has long been understood as a normative concept, rooted in its Latin etymological meaning: 'the same' (*idem*). The notion of personal identity as a bounded concept emerged in tandem with the idea of nation states as bounded, coherent entities composed of similar-minded people (Grosby 2005). Moreover, it is connected with the spread of colonialism and to the opposition between different and homogeneous identities, particularly grounded by racial distinctions (Gosden 2004; Rattansi 2007: 36–7). The enforcement of norms of everyday identification was via indoctrination of people into 'discovering' what they really were, or what they should be (Bourdieu 2001: 181).

Reacting to definitions of identity as singular and stable, archaeologists have increasingly explored identity as plural, fluid, transient and unstable, and grounded in diversity (e.g. Jones 1999, Rago and Funari 2008). This move from normative identity models to less rigid and oppressive discourses that take into account identity, nationalism, and ethnicity has been important to archaeology in general, and in historical archaeology in particular (Funari et al. 1999; see also Hall and Silliman 2006; Hicks and Beaudry 2006).

If we consider identity as a political concept—an active invention—used with intentions (Funari 2008), then it is possible to interpret Palmares through an archaeology of ethnicity in which the *quilombo* was a place where people of various ethnic and cultural backgrounds would have lived together. This multi-ethnic setting originated from the historical and strategic situation of the *quilombo*. The Palmarians established themselves in a region where there were indigenes, colonial village dwellers, farmers, the Dutch, and other groups who were frequently outcast. Hence, the *quilombolas* were not isolated; they survived not only in conflict with these groups but also, and necessarily, through interaction with them. These contacts transformed Palmares not into a modified summary of a reliable copy of previous experiences (i.e. exclusively African); on the contrary, the residents of Palmares consolidated the *quilombo* as a unique cultural experience (Funari 2003b).

This perspective of ethnicity presents the settlement as a space of debate where the identities, fluid as they were, can only be determined with an analytical end or, better, with a didactic goal. The settlement can be seen as an example of interactions between different social elements and thus understood as testimony to the possibility of peaceful living and tolerance among people with fluid and diverse identities in current society. Such an approach linked to the archaeology of ethnicity does not attempt to build an explanatory model that can be applied to *quilombola* settlements all over America, but rather it values the historical context—of exchange, domination, and resistance—in which the Palmares *quilombo* appeared.

Considering gender relations as a key concept in social life, archaeological narratives about Palmares must study identities and sexualities, in terms of the polity itself and its leader, Zumbi. Palmares is widely acknowledged and revered as an anti-colonial, anti-slavery settlement. However, sexuality, intimacy, gender roles, and interpersonal relations are neglected subjects in the context of Palmares. Power relations at the micro-level, it seems, are still not accorded importance or relevance as subjects for serious scholarly inquiry. This is partly due to a lack of adequate attention to material evidence. Historical narrative built upon written sources is prone to several biases. First and foremost, such written sources systematically disregard ordinary daily life, including the realm of intimacy. This is the result of the limitations of written documents, which are the product of an elite male outlook. The primary value of archaeology is that it enables us to connect material remains with social relations, overcoming the biases of documentary narratives (see Funari et al. 1999: 10). However, owing to social and disciplinary constraints, the full potential of archaeology is not always explored.

In relation to Palmares, documents refer to gender relations in the rebel settlement in relation to polygamy and polyandry, particularly challenging to traditional normative interpretive models, and also the role of women in military negotiations. Even though those issues are present in seventeenth-century narratives of Palmares, they did not arise in the archaeological studies until recently. This is in sharp contrast to the archaeological study of gender issues at other maroons, for example at River Caura, where the key role of Black Panther, a runaway heroine, is to be described (Zuchi, pers. comm.). Why did gender issues enter so late in maroon archaeology? The answer concerns our own scholarly practices and narratives.

Beyond multiple identities and gender issues, Palmares has been studied though the lens of domination and resistance (e.g. Rowlands 1999). From this standpoint, the main focus is on the idea of Palmares as a plural structure where there was, for example, the important regional context of enslavement activities. In this perspective, the *quilombo* is seen as a society very close to the one existing elsewhere in the colonial world at the time. For example, there were divisions between the Palmarian elite and the other inhabitants of the *quilombo*; in other words, there were distinctions of class and established differences of gender and ethnicity. These were commonly used by Europeans to justify the existence of slavery.

Palmares is perceived to be a result of a combination of contexts: the existence of slavery, of sugar cane plantations, of Indians, of European dealers, of the Dutch, and other factors. The Portuguese colony, and later Dutch Brazil, had a very specific social structure that was, in part, reproduced in the Palmares *quilombo*. The settlement could be evidence that the concept of resistance can mean more than the escape of enslaved labourers or the defence of a 'pure' cultural identity. Palmares, as an extension of colonial society, situates negotiation and interaction within the concept of resistance. The archaeologies practiced in the Palmares *quilombo* emphasize different aspects of the settlement and, for this reason, when they are analysed together, allow different representations of the *quilombo*.

According to Woodward (2002: 74), systems of representation are cultural processes that 'construct the places from where the individuals can position themselves and from which they can speak'. Archaeological narratives about Palmares and representations of the *quilombo* structure unique locations of identification. Drawn through archaeologies, these places can be conceived as emergent through a series of political choices, implicit or otherwise (Shanks and Tilley 1987); their study fosters dissonance and elicits discussion and contestation among readers, public audiences, and interested parties. Each archaeological intervention in the Serra da Barriga has created a unique Palmares *quilombo*, images of which provoke a variety of reactions inside and outside of the academic sphere.

Public archaeologies of Palmares

According to Handler (2003), collective identities—as any other cultural process—are not considered by scholars to be objective. Indeed, identities are the result of processes of semiotic interaction, as acts of social interpretation—so much so that nurture and upbringing, both social and intellectual, shape the way scholars invent their own subjects. How, therefore, may archaeology promote positive changes in our own society?

Museums constitute themselves as essential elements in constructing identities. The institution's practice is to select social groups worthy of public remembrance, and in doing so, at the same time, contribute to the exclusion of other possible memories. According to Handler (2003: 359), 'the decisions we make to canonize certain objects as "culture", or worthy of preservation, always depend on contemporary ideological concerns'. It should therefore be possible to trace a parallel between the archaeological and museum discourses. Both of them engage directly with social memory and each employ narrative 'rules': the choice of the language and the presentation of one area of knowledge in place of another, etc. Archaeological discourse and museum narrative may each be viewed as instruments guided by power relations that mould certain memories in place of others. With the power of exclusion and inclusion, and the impact that discrimination plays within the construction of collective and individual identity, comes a duty of care and responsibility (Thomas 1995; Jones 1999).

CULTURAL INTERACTION AT PALMARES 249

Brazilian archaeology has recognized a need to be socially relevant. This has been manifested in critical approaches and interaction with society and social agents, even if traditional empiricism is still common currency (de Oliveira 2000; Zarankin 2000). Archaeological narratives about Palmares stem from a variety of theoretical and political standpoints through which different narratives of the settlement emerge. When we compare these narratives, it is clear that there is no single, true Palmares, but on the contrary a plethora of social groups together in action: Africans, Indians, Europeans, Muslims, witches, traders, poor, persecuted, LGBT+, and many more. There is thus dispute about the archaeological past in the present.

In this light, Palmares may play a role in fostering diversity and social inclusion in Brazil. Interpretative diversity enables a variety of people to employ Palmares in their own struggles for empowerment and freedom from constraint. Fostering diversity and freedom is no small accomplishment and the study of Palmares may continue to contribute to such endeavours. Palmares may again become a land of dreams.

Acknowledgements

We owe thanks to the editors, Scott Joseph Allen, Célia Marinho Azevedo, Joan Scott, Luiz Estevam Oliveira Fernandes, Lúcio Menezes Ferreira, Carlos Magno Guimarães, Martin Hall, Siân Jones, Jorge Eremites de Oliveira, Charles Orser, Jr, Airton Pollini, André Prous, Margareth Rago, Michael Rowlands, Solange Schiavetto, Michael Shanks, Stephen Silliman, Christopher Tilley, Julian Thomas, Gustavo Henrique Tuna, Barbara Voss, Andrés Zarankin, and Alberta Zucchi. We must mention the institutional support of the Center for Environmental Studies, World Archaeological Congress, São Paulo Science Foundation (FAPESP), and the Brazilian National Science Foundation (CNPq). Responsibility for the ideas presented here is our own.

References

Allen, S. J. 1998. 'A "cultura mosaic" at Palmares? Grappling with the historical archaeology of a seventeenth-century Brazilian Quilombo'. In P. P. A. Funari (ed.), *Cultura Material e Arqueologia Histórica*. Campinas: Unicamp (IFCH), pp. 141–78.

Allen, S. J. 2000. 'Preliminary directions in the historical archaeology of Palmares'. *Nova Revista de História da Arte e Arqueologia*. Campinas: Unicamp (IFCH), pp. 39–52.

250 PEDRO FUNARI AND ALINE DE CARVALHO

Allen, S. J. 2001. *Zumbi Nunca Vai Morrer: History, Race, Politics, and the Practice of Archaeology in Brazil*. Unpublished PhD thesis, Brown University, Providence.

Akinnaso, F. N. 1995. 'Bourdieu and the diviner: knowledge and symbolic power in Yoruba divination'. In W. James (ed.), *The Pursuit of Certainty: Religious and Cultural Formulations*. London: Routledge, pp. 234–58.

Azevedo, C. M. M. 2000. 'A nova história intelectual de Dominick La Capra e a noção de raça'. In M. Rago and R. Gimenez (eds), *Narrar o Passado, Repensar a História*. Campinas: Editora IFCH, pp. 123–34.

Bastide, R. 1960. *As Religiões Africanas no Brasil*. São Paulo, Companhia Editora Nacional.

Bourdieu, P. 2001. *Langage et Pouvoir Symbolique*. Paris: Éditions Fayard.

Carlson, M. 1993. *No Religion Higher than Truth: A History of the Theosophical Movement in Russia*. Princeton: Princeton University Press.

Colpe, C. 1987. 'Syncretism'. In Jones, L. (ed.), *The Encyclopedia of Religion*. London: Macmillan, pp. 218–27.

Ferreira, L. M. 2009. 'Arqueologia da escravidão e arqueologia pública: algumas interfaces'. *Vestígios Revista Latino-Americana de Arqueologia Histórica* 3: 7–23.

Fernandes, L. E. O. 2009. *Patria Mestiza: Memória e História na Invenção da Nação Mexicana entre os Séculos XVIII e XIX*. Tese de doutorado. Campinas: História IFCH/Unicamp.

Frazier, E. F. 1949. *The Negro in the United States*. New York: Macmillan.

Freitas, D. 1978. *Palmares: A Guerra dos Escravos*. Rio de Janeiro: Graal.

Funari, P. P. A. 2003a. 'Conflict and interpretation of Palmares, a Brazilian runaway polity'. *Historical Archaeology* 37(3): 81–92.

Funari, P. P. A. 2003b. 'Heterogeneidade e conflito na interpretação do Quilombo dos Palmares'. *Revista de História Regional* 6(1): 11–38.

Funari, P. P. A. 2008. 'O papel da Arqueologia na demarcação das terras indígenas e quilombolas'. *E-Premissas* 3: 1–15.

Funari, P. P. A. and A. V. Carvalho. 2008. 'Political organization and resistance on the other side of the Atlantic: Palmares, a maroon experience in South America'. In A. Ruiz-Martínez (ed.), *Desencuentros Culturales: Una Mirada Desde la Cultura Material de las Américas*. Barcelona: Universidad Pompeu Fabra, pp. 83–9.

Funari, P. P. A. and A. Pollini. 2005. 'Greek perceptions of frontier in Magna Graecia: literature and archaeology in dialogue'. *Studia Historica Historia Antigua* 23: 331–44.

Funari, P. P. A., S. Jones, and M. Hall. 1999. 'Introduction: archaeology in history'. In P. P. A. Funari, M. Hall, and S. Jones (eds), *Historical Archaeology: Back from the Edge*. London: Routledge, pp. 1–20.

CULTURAL INTERACTION AT PALMARES 251

Gosden, C. 2004. *Archaeology and Colonialism: Cultural Contact from 5000 BC to the Present*. Cambridge: Cambridge University Press.

Grosby, S. 2005. *Nationalism*. Oxford: Oxford University Press.

Guimarães, C. M. 1990. 'O Quilombo do Ambrózio: lendas, documentos e arqueologia'. *Estudos Ibero-Americanos* 16(1–2): 161–74.

Guimarães, C. M. and A. L. Lanna. 1980. 'Arqueologia de Quilombos em Minas Gerais'. *Pesquisas: Série Antropológica* 31: 147–64.

Hall, M. and S. Silliman. 2006. *Historical Archaeology*. Oxford: Blackwell.

Handler, R. 2003. 'Cultural property and culture "theory"'. *Journal of Social Archaeology* 3(3): 353–65.

Hannerz, H. 1987. 'The world in creolisation'. *Africa*. 57(4): 546–59.

Herskovits, M. J. 1947. *Man and His Works: The Science of Cultural Anthropology*. New York: Alfred A. Knopf.

Hicks, D. and M. Beaudry. 2006. *The Cambridge Companion to Historical Archaeology*. Cambridge: Cambridge University Press.

Jones, S. 1999. 'Historical categories and the praxis of identity: the interpretation of ethnicity'. In P. A. Funari, M. Hall, and S. Jones (eds), *Historical Archaeology: Back from the Edge*. London: Routledge, pp. 219–32.

Kraft, E. 2002. '"To mix or not to mix": syncretism/anti-syncretism in the history of theosophy'. *Numen* 49(2): 142–77.

Lindstrom, L. 1996. 'Syncretism'. In A. Barnard and J. Spencer (eds), *Encyclopedia of Social and Cultural Anthropology*. London: Routledge, pp. 539–41.

Mintz, S. and R. Price. 1976. *An Anthropological Approach to the Afro-American Past: A Caribbean Perspective*. Philadelphia: Institute for the Study of Human Issues.

Munasinghe, V. 2002. 'Creating impurity out of purity: nationalism in hybrid spaces'. *American Ethnologist* 29(3): 663–92.

Oliveira, J. E. 2000. 'Editorial'. *Revista de Arqueologia* 12/13: 5–6.

Orser, C. E. 1996. *A Historical Archaeology of Modern World*. New York: Plenum Press.

Orser, C. E. 1998. 'The archaeology of the African Diaspora'. *Annual Review of Anthropology* 27: 63–82.

Prous, A. 2005. 'A pintura em cerâmica Tupiguarani'. *Ciência Hoje* 36(213): 22–8.

Pye, M. 1994. 'Syncretism versus synthesis'. *Method and Theory in the Study of Religion* 6: 217–29.

Rago, M. and P. Funari, eds. 2008. *Subjetividades antigas e modernas*. São Paulo: Annablume.

Rattansi, A. 2007. *Racism*. Oxford: Oxford University Press.

252 PEDRO FUNARI AND ALINE DE CARVALHO

Rothstein, M. 1996. *Belief Transformations: Some Aspects of the Relation between Science and Religion in Transcendental Meditation.* Aarhus: Aarhus University Press.

Rowlands, M. 1999. 'Black identity and sense of past in Brazilian national culture'. In P. P. A. Funari, M. Hall, and S. Jones (eds), *Historical Archaeology: Back from the Edge.* London: Routledge, pp. 328–44.

Schiavetto, S. N. O. 2005. 'A questão étnica no discurso arqueológico: a afirmação de uma identidade indígena minoritária ou inserção na identidade nacional?'. In P. P. A. Funari, C. E. Orser, and S. N. O. Schiavetto (eds), *Identidades, Discurso e Poder: Estudos da Arqueologia Contemporânea.* São Paulo: Annablume-Fapesp, pp. 77–90.

Scott, J. W. 2009. *Théorie Critique de l'Histoire: Identités, Experiences, Politiques.* Paris: Fayard.

Shanks, M. and C. Tilley. 1987. *Social Theory and Archaeology.* Londres: Polity Press.

Stewart, C. and R. Shaw, eds. 1994. *Syncretism/Anti-Syncretism: The Politics of Religious Synthesis.* London: Routledge.

Thomas, J. 1995. 'Where are we now: archaeology theory in the 1990s'. In Peter J. Ucko (ed.), *Theory in Archaeology: A World Perspective.* London: Routledge.

Tuna, G. 2000. *Gilberto Freyre: Entre Tradição e Ruptura.* São Paulo: Cone Sul.

Vainfas, R. 2000. 'Sincretismo'. In R. Vainfas (ed.), *Dicionário do Brasil Colonial.* Rio de Janeiro: Objetiva, pp. 532–4.

Voss, B. L. 2008. *The Archaeology of Ethnogenesis: Race and Sexuality in Colonial San Francisco.* Berkeley: University of California Press.

Werbner, C. 1997. 'Introduction: the dialectics of cultural hybridity'. In P. Werbner and T. Modood (eds), *Debating Cultural Hybridity: Multi-Cultural Identities and the Politics of Anti-Racism.* London: Zed Books, pp. 46–57.

Woodward, K. 2002. 'Identidade e diferença: uma introdução teórica e conceitual'. In T. T. da Silva (ed.), *Identidade e Diferença.* Rio de Janeiro: Ed. Vozes, pp. 7–72.

Zarankín, A. 2000. 'El pensamiento moderno y el pensamiento posmoderno em arqueología'. In M. Rago and R. A. de Oliveira Gimenes (eds), *Narrar o Passado: Repensar a História.* Campinas: IFCH—Unicamp, pp. 341–60.

11

Creole Identity and Syncretism in the Archaeology of Islam

Andrew Petersen

Within strict linguistic terms, creolization is a process by which a new language is developed from prolonged contact between two or more languages (see for example Blevins 1995). One anthropological definition states that creolization 'describes cultural phenomena that result from the displacement and the ensuing social encounter and mutual influence amongst/between groups...eventually leading to new forms with varying degrees of stability' (Eriksen 2007: 172). In archaeology, creolization is generally used as a way of discussing the physical evidence of the colonial encounter between Europeans, indigenous societies, and imported labour (usually slaves) in the New World. Whilst creolization is used to apply to the culture and peoples involved in the process of amalgamation, syncretism is a more specialized term used to refer to the merging of religions or worldviews to produce new belief systems. At this point, it is worth differentiating syncretism from anti-syncretism. Whereas the merging of different religious ideas to create a new worldview might be described as syncretist, a local variation of a world religion is anti-syncretist as it implies an inferior or impure set of beliefs compared with the 'original' religion.

As the youngest of the three monotheistic religions, Islam is syncretist by nature, sharing much of its beliefs and history with the earlier faiths of Judaism and Christianity. In many ways, this is not surprising, nor unique, as every religion is syncretistic and it is not just the synchronicity of syncretic elements that defines particular religions (Clack 2011: 230). From the perspective of a devout believer, Islam has always existed as a revealed religion and dates from the early seventh century and the preaching of the Prophet Muhammad in Mecca and Medina in present-day Saudi Arabia. Christianity, as an organized religion, had already been in existence for at least four

Andrew Petersen, *Creole Identity and Syncretism in the Archaeology of Islam* In: *Archaeologies of Cultural Contact: At the Interface.* Edited by: Timothy Clack and Marcus Brittain, Oxford University Press. © Oxford University Press 2022.
DOI: 10.1093/oso/9780199693948.003.0012

hundred years, whilst Judaism can trace its origins back a further three thousand years.

Although secular historians and devout Muslims may disagree over details of the development of Islam as a religion, it is generally agreed that Islam adopted religious practices from both groups (Christians and Jews) whilst insisting on certain practices which were not found in either of the two earlier religions in order to re-enforce its own unique identity. One of the ways in which Islam resembles Judaism is the way in which a particular culture and identity (in this case Arab culture and identity) is given a particular prominence within the religion. For example, the Quran is revealed through the language of Arabic and can only be truly understood in this language. Similarly, most of the examples and much of the setting for the narratives of the Quran come from an Arabian context. Seen through this perspective, many of the laws and customs of Islam are a projection of seventh-century Arabian society into distant lands and epochs. In this sense, Islam can be seen as a religion which privileges Arabian values and identity above all others in the same way as Judaism is based on a particular people. However, Judaism, in its Orthodox sense, is generally restricted to those who can trace their origins to the Jewish people through the female line. Islam, on the other hand, was from its origins, a missionary faith actively seeking converts from pagans and adherents of other faiths whatever their ethnic origin. If one looks at Islam this way, it could be seen as an imperial or colonizing religion imposing a uniform set of cultural values on people of diverse origins. Although most adherents would not subscribe to this view, it does suggest one (all be it extreme) way in which Islam can be seen as non-creolizing and anti-syncretic. At the other end of the scale, there are forms and interpretations of Islam (for example, various forms of Sufism) that are so widely inclusive of diverse beliefs and customs that the Arabian origins are almost entirely lost. Both these views are, of course, unusual and, for the majority of Muslims, the Arabian origins of the religion are important but do not dominate either their religious practice or their daily activities.

Arab and others in early Islam

Against this general background, it is worth reviewing the early history of the Muslim faith and its outward spread from the Arabian Peninsula (see Fig. 11.1). At its earliest stage from the sixth century, Islam posed a challenge to Arabian society, which was firmly constituted according to tribal affiliation. Muhammad called for a general truce amongst the perpetually warring tribes

CREOLE IDENTITY AND SYNCRETISM IN THE ARCHAEOLOGY

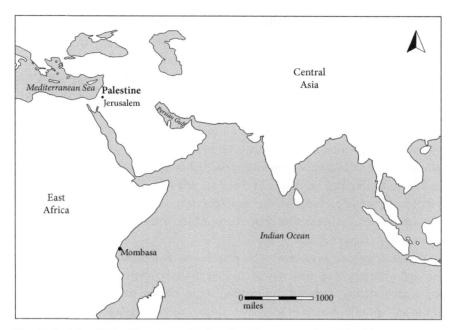

Fig. 11.1. Map of the Islamic world showing places mentioned in the text.

and sought to replace tribal affiliation with allegiance to a universal God (Allah). Following the unification of the Arab tribes under a general truce, the Muslim Arabs expanded outwards towards Syria, Egypt, and Iran. The expansion was carried out as an armed invasion (*jihad*) of neighbouring territories whereby conquered peoples were allowed to maintain their own religion and customs subject to a tax which was paid to the Arab armies and then distributed amongst the tribes of the believers. At first the majority of the conquered people chose to retain their own religion, though as time went on more and more people sought to convert to the new religion. The non-Arab converts were known as *mawali*, and although they professed Islam they were not only excluded from the cash payments made to Muslim Arabs, but were obliged to continue paying the taxes *kharaj* paid by non-Muslims. From the middle of the eighth century (end of the Umayyad period) this position was no longer tolerated and the non-Arabs became not only accepted but the main political force within the Islamic world. By the eleventh century, Arabs were no longer the dominant ethnic group amongst Muslims and were outnumbered by Turks, Iranians, Berbers, and others. Nevertheless, descent from an Arab tribe, particularly from the family of the Prophet Muhammad, still carried a certain cachet.

The role of archaeology

Archaeology can present some tangible examples of how Islam emerged as a trans-national and trans-cultural society. In particular, archaeology can act as a counter to the linguistic approach which sees the matter in black and white, i.e. areas where Arabic has been adopted and those where the pre-Islamic language has survived. In this contribution, it will be argued that whilst in many areas (e.g. Mesopotamia, the Levant, Egypt, and North Africa) Arabic was adopted as a first language, other aspects of Islamic cultures displayed distinct creolizing tendencies. Similarly, in the areas where Arabic was not adopted as a first language (e.g. Anatolia, Central Asia, Iran, India, Malaysia, Indonesia, and sub-Saharan Africa) this does not preclude a significant creolizing tendency within these regions.

Archaeology can investigate the process of syncretism and creolization through a variety of approaches, including analysis of environment and landscape, architecture, material culture, and approaches to death and burial. One of the few specific studies of identity in Islam using archaeology is the collection of papers edited by Donald Whitcomb (2004) which examines the development of Islam in different parts of Asia and Africa. In this paper I will be following Whitcomb's example using case studies from different parts of the Islamic world (Palestine, Central Asia, and East Africa) to examine creolization and syncretism. Considerable archaeological fieldwork has been carried out in all three areas so that in each case the transition from pre-Islamic to Islamic culture is well documented. Each area has its own trajectory of Islamicization which leads to the development of distinct Muslim cultures with their own particular social, cultural, and religious frameworks.

Palestine

The identification of Jerusalem as the destination of Muhammad's night journey to the furthest place, 'al-Aqsa, ensures Palestine's central place within Muslim religious teaching and within Islamic culture. The fact that Palestine was already the Holy Land for Judaism further enhanced the sanctity of the region and, subsequently, re-enforced Islam's claim to be the perfected form of the monotheistic religions. The importance of Palestine to Islamic culture is further enhanced by the fact that it was one of the first places to be conquered by the newly formed Arab Muslim armies when they ventured out of Arabia.

CREOLE IDENTITY AND SYNCRETISM IN THE ARCHAEOLOGY   257

Given the importance attached to the 'Holy Land', the process by which the Palestinian population became Muslim illustrates many features of creolization in terms of language, identity, and religion. When the Arab armies first arrived in Palestine they were evidently at a cultural disadvantage. The local inhabitants had a long tradition of settled urban life and adherence to either one of the monotheistic religions. In contrast, the Arabs had very little experience of a sedentary urban life and a newly acquired and still developing monotheistic religion (Islam). Unlike most colonial encounters, the conquerors were considerably less developed and, with the exception of their religion, were forced to learn and adopt many of the customs and traditions of the conquered peoples. This reminds us of the intimate connection between power and syncretism summarized aptly by Clack's (2011: 234) statement that 'power is a vital dynamic of syncretism'. In a strange reversal of the usual concept of an indigenous or displaced people developing a creole culture in response to a dominant conquering group, in this case the in-comers were forced to make considerable adaptations to their new social environment.

Much of the interest in the early Islamic archaeology of the region has focused on the acculturation of the Arabs and the formation of a new identity neither fully Arab nor simply a continuation of the Hellenistic/Byzantine traditions of Palestine (see for example Pentz 1992).

One of the most eloquent expressions of the new society is the coinage used prior to the reforms of the caliph 'Abd al-Malik in 696–7 CE. For the first few years (630–90s) the new rulers continued to use the Byzantine coinage which had been in use before the conquest. However, Arabs issued new coin mints which approximate to the general pattern of Byzantine coins, and yet the symbols were used in a new way (Bates 1994: 382; see also Walmsley 2007: 59–64 for a summary). For example, the gold coinage substituted the cross on three steps for an image of uncertain meaning (Bates 1994: 382). The main difference is the Arab writing, which appeared with the message: 'There is no god but God alone, Muhammad is the messenger of God.' Within silver coins the cultural mix was even more pronounced and was modelled on Sassanian (Iranian) coins (see Fig. 11.2) with the picture of the Iranian emperor on one side (obverse) and an image of a Zoroastrian fire temple with two attendants on the other side (reverse). It should be noted that these coins were minted for use within the western part of the early Islamic empire (i.e. former Byzantine territory) and that the use of Sassanian-type coins in this area has interesting cultural connotations. On the one hand, this reflects historical precedent as the Arabs had previously used both Byzantine gold coinage (*solidi*) and Sassanian coinage (*drahms*) in Mecca and Medina. However, on the other

Fig. 11.2. Arab Sassanian coin. This silver dirham was minted on the orders of Ziyad ibn Abi Sufyan, the Arab governor of Southern Iran. It bears a portrait of Khusrau II (Sassanian emperor 590–628) as well as inscriptions in Middle Persian. However, on the edge of the coin there is an Arabic Islamic inscription 'in the name of Allah the Lord' indicating that this is an example of the Sassanian-style coins that continued to be produced for more than a hundred years after the Arab Islamic conquest of Iran.

hand, the presence of silver Sassanian-type coinage in Palestine would have carried a clear cultural message of an emerging new identity.

A similar merging of identities is signalled within novel architecture. The most famous examples of early Islamic architecture are the buildings known collectively as 'desert castles' which are found throughout Syria, Jordan, and Palestine (for a discussion of these structures see Walmsley 2007: 99–104). Whilst the precise form and function of these structures differ from one to another the underlying principle is the adoption of Late Roman military architecture for the creation of palatial residences (Genequand 2006). Within Palestine the best example is Khirbet al-Minya, which is a rectangular enclosure (66 m × 73 m) with four round corner towers and semi-circular interval towers. The interior of the building contains a variety of rooms including a mosque and a triple-aisled basilica-style hall which has been interpreted as a throne room. In many of the castles there was elaborate stucco decoration, mosaics, bath houses, and other indications of a luxurious lifestyle. The Umayyad 'desert castles' were a short-lived phenomenon and were not built after the mid-eighth century (see Fig. 11.3). Although clearly built by and for elite Arab patrons, the eclectic mixture of styles and re-use of an architectural form for a different purpose are all indicative of a creolized identity—part Bedouin, part Byzantine.

Fig. 11.3. Bronze lion excavated at Shanga, Kenya (photo: Mark Horton).

Central Asia

If we turn further east to Central Asia the situation becomes more complex as the distance from the Arabian heartland increases and the proportion of Arab Muslims within the population decreases. To a certain extent, this can be measured linguistically—from Mesopotamia eastwards, Arabic did not replace the native languages, thus today Farsi remains the dominant language in Iran. Central Asia was an area already strongly influenced by Iranian culture with Persian used as the urban language whilst the native population were of Turkic origin. In one sense, there was already some form of creolized society in Central Asia prior to the Muslim conquests in the seventh and eighth centuries (see for example the discussion of the Kusho-Sassanian kingdom in Dani and Litvinsky 1996). The geography of Central Asia between the Middle East and China meant that it already had a developed hybrid culture drawn through trade and travel via the Silk Roads.

The Muslim conquest of this region was carried out initially by Arabs from garrison towns (*amsar*) in Iraq (primarily Basra and Kufa). Later, the Arab troops settled in the region in centres such as Merv, Afrasiab, and Nishapur. We cannot be sure of the ethnic identity of the Arab Muslim armies in Central Asia, although it is known that of the 5,000 troops in the army of Ahnaf ibn Qais at least 1,000 were Persian Muslims (al-Baladhuri in Kolesnikov 1996:

260   ANDREW PETERSEN

463). Another indication of the fragmentation of Arab Muslim power was the fact that many local governors and rulers were allowed to keep their positions without converting to Islam as long as they acknowledged their allegiance to the Muslim state and collected taxes on their behalf. The coinage of the period reflects the sometimes considerable power of these local rulers; Sassanian-type silver drachms therefore continued to be issued but with an Arabic religious inscription on the obverse and the name of the local (often non-Muslim) governor (Kolesnikov 1996: 465). There is also considerable evidence of the survival of pre-Islamic religion. An archaeological survey in the region of Sistan revealed an extensive series of fortifications, ceramics, and coins which indicate a continuity of Sassanian culture and in particular the cult of Zoroastrianism (Ball and Gardin 1982, I, nos. 145, 206, 270, 369, 900 et seq.; II, 484–5). Also, in Bamiyan in the seventh century there were a number of Buddhist monasteries and more than 1,000 monks. Definitive evidence of religious syncretism is found in the coinage of the *kaghan* of the Western Turks which includes iconography related to Iranian Zorastrianism and Indian Shivaism. Other coins in use in nominally Muslim Central Asia have local counter-stamps which include depictions of mythical beasts such as the *simurgh* as well as camels and elephants (Kolesnikov 1996: 467–8). Continuity and merging of traditions is also evident in architecture, for example the four-iwan-plan madrassa bears a strong resemblance to Buddhist monastic buildings and there may be a direct link (Litvinsky 1996: 486–7). Other forms of architecture show strong continuity, in particular houses, palaces, and tombs.

Whilst the continuity and merging of traditions is to be expected within the first decades and even centuries of Islamic rule, in Central Asia there was a persistence of pre-Islamic culture and religion into recent times. This is particularly evident in the approach to Muslim saints and shrines where Sufism combined with shamanism are used to mediate between people's daily lives and the spiritual world. For example, Kenneth Lymer has recently shown how Kazakh Muslims continue to revere sacred sites which have petroglyphs dating to the Bronze Age (*c*.1400–1000 BCE) (Lymer 2004). At Tamgaly there are petroglyphs which include depictions of 'solar-headed gods'. Lymer (2004: 162–3) describes how:

> On a high ledge overlooking the bushes is one of the most celebrated scenes of the 'solar-headed gods' and Kazakh pilgrims have tied rags to the small scraggy bushes growing directly in front of it. In the north 'entrance' to the Tamgaly valley there are more hillsides covered with petroglyphs and rags have been even tied on small jutting rocks near petroglyph scenes.

CREOLE IDENTITY AND SYNCRETISM IN THE ARCHAEOLOGY   261

East Africa

The association between Africans and creoles in the Caribbean has meant that considerable attention has been paid to the concept of creolization and syncretism in West Africa. For example, Insoll (2004: 101) has observed that 'throughout sub-Saharan Africa the agency of syncretism has been adopted as a mechanism to reconcile Islam with older traditions in an ongoing process of reconstructing social and religious identities'. In contrast, Horton and Middleton (2000: 2) reject the idea of a creolization in the Swahili culture of East Africa, stating that 'Historiography and archaeology...have assumed, on remarkably little evidence other than wishful thinking, that the Swahili have formed a creole society whose civilisation has been implanted on the African coastline by invaders from Asia, mostly Arabia'. They further argued that the idea of Swahili as a creole society has negative connotations both because of its associations with slavery in the nineteenth century and because of its association with European ideas of colonialism. However, the term creole does not necessarily imply that there were large numbers of Arab invaders or that the society was intimately involved in nineteenth-century slavery or British Colonial rule (although both of the latter have been the case at certain times). Even Horton and Middleton (2000: 15–16) agree that the concept of Swahili identity is complex and that there are in fact a number of components to Swahili identity which include elements from Asia. Certainly, if one looks at the archaeological evidence there is strong support for a composite ethnically diverse Muslim society from as early as the eighth century (Horton and Middleton 2000).

Archaeological excavations at Shanga in Kenya have shown that in the eighth century the coastal people probably had a culture similar to the Mijikenda who in the present day occupy the area inland from the coastal strip (Horton 1996). Excavations in the earliest levels of Shanga revealed a rect-angular area (100 m × 80 m) built around a central well with the remains of a large tree and remnants of iron working. Around the edge of the enclosure a series of post holes were found together with domestic refuse (e.g. animal and fish bones) indicating a habitation area of round thatched huts. All of these features are typical of the *kaya* (central enclosure) found in the settlement of the neighbouring Mijikenda people. Evidence from Muslim burials indicates that Islam became established by the beginning of the ninth century. The earliest mosque appears to have been built over a tree stump and iron-working area that may have been a ritual centre during the pre-Islamic period. The presence of imported pottery from the Persian Gulf and China indicates that

262   ANDREW PETERSEN

these pre-Islamic African settlements already had contacts with the Indian Ocean trading system and, in particular, with the Islamic Middle East. Throughout the various subsequent levels there continued to be a mixture of African and imported Muslim tradition. In addition to the African-Arabian axis, Shanga also provides evidence of another aspect of Swahili culture which concerns contacts with the wider cultures of the Indian Ocean (e.g. China, India, and Southeast Asia). Probably the best example of this hybrid culture is a bronze lion (see Fig. 11.4) excavated from eleventh-century levels at Shanga. Stylistically, the lion figurine is similar to Hindu figurines made in western India (the Deccan) however the type of lion depicted is African whilst the metal composition is different from Indian examples. One plausible explanation suggested by the excavator is that the lion was made by Indians resident in East Africa, again adding another component to the developing Swahili society (Horton 2004: 65–6).

Conclusions

The initial observation from these three case studies is that Muslim societies in all areas have a complex history which incorporates elements of pre-Islamic cultures as well other contemporary cultures. Whilst in some cases there are evident examples of creolized societies, this description is generally avoided because of supposed negative connotations and associations with a slave society and also because as a religion Islam generally prefers to propagate the idea that there is one culture and one religion. In practice formal Islam is divided into many confessional groups (e.g. Shi'a, Sunni, 'Ibadi, Ismaili, Sufi, Ahmedi), whilst informal folk Islam has multiple forms tied closely to local and ethnic identities and connections with other religions.

Looking more specifically at the three case studies, it can be seen that each indicates different ways of positing a creole Muslim identity. In the first case, Palestine is used as an example from the Islamic Middle East—a country which should form the core of Muslim Arab identity. However, it is evident that the creation of a Muslim identity involved the integration of Arab Islamic ideas into the late Roman Mediterranean social and state structure. In ethnic terms, this meant the accommodation of Arabs within the cities and also in camps outside the cities. The process by which local people were converted to Islam and by which Muslim Arabs acculturated to late Antique culture is a complex and interesting one that has been the subject of considerable scholarly interest (see for example Cameron and King 1994). However, this was

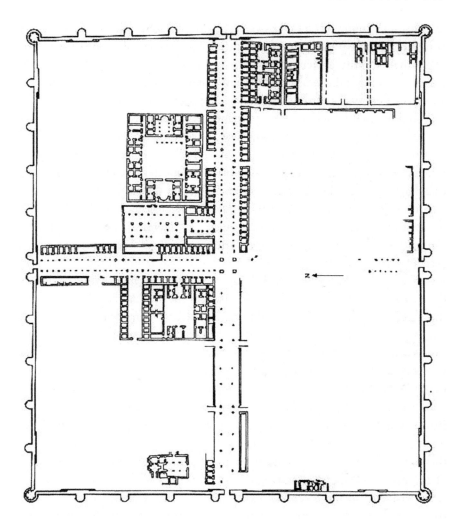

Fig. 11.4. Plan of the Umayyad city of 'Anjar in Lebanon. This site, which has many similarities to a Roman town, was built by the Umayyad caliph al-Walid in 714–15.

only the first stage in a process of Islamicization that was not really completed until the twelfth century. In the years between the first Muslim conquest of Palestine in the seventh century to the Crusader occupation of the twelfth century, the ethnic mix was increased by the arrival of various Turkic tribes, each with their own traditions and varying degrees of attachment to the Muslim faith. Throughout this period, the concept of orthodox Islam in the area fluctuated from Sunni to Shi'a and back to Sunni with an added overlay of Sufism. Despite this complex overlapping of religious and ethnic identities, continuity can be traced in many of the basic structures of Palestinian society (e.g. urban identity, agricultural practices). In many ways it could be said that the pre-existing culture absorbed Islam just as it had absorbed Christianity and that there was a strong continuity of culture; after the first few decades this could therefore no longer be described as a creole society.

In Central Asia, the situation was more complex owing to the greater number of ethnic groups and religions involved and also because it covered a much larger area. Central Asia was additionally located at the junction of several major cultural blocks—East Asia and China to the east, India to the south and Iran and Western Asia to the west—connected by the Silk Road that brought into contact not only goods but ideas, religions, and people. In this sense, Central Asia already had a partially creolized identity prior to the arrival of Islam, and it has already been noted that many of the cities in the western part of Central Asia had an overlay of Persian identity derived from the Sassanian conquests in the region. The advent of Islam certainly added to the cultural religious mix and added a new ethnic component: Persianized Arabs and Abrabized Persians. The persistence of shamanistic, Buddhist, and Zoroastrian beliefs along with an adherence to Islam suggest that conditions were favourable to the development of syncretic belief systems. Despite these multiple and overlapping identities, it appears that rural Central Asia was not a 'creolized society'; ethnic groups retained their specific identities even if territorially they sometimes overlapped. However, the situation was different in towns, where diverse ethnic groups and cultures would have been mixed through generations of intermarriage and trade demanding common forms of communication, including languages.

In East Africa, the Swahili provide a convincing example of a creolized society. In spite of the objections of Horton and Middleton (2000), it seems clear that the Swahili identity has incorporated many ethnicities into a cultural synthesis defined by its allegiance to Islam and language of communication: *Kiswahili*. Archaeology, as well as modern ethnography, indicates that Swahili society is not simply an amalgam of Arab identity imposed on local African groups, but has much wider roots with Indian and possibly Chinese elements becoming part of the society. It is worth pointing out that the Swahili people are almost entirely urbanized (cf. Central Asia above) with the town being the basic unit of social and cultural life, production, and government (Horton and Middleton 2000: 11). To identify Swahili society as creole is not to denigrate it, but to acknowledge its inclusive nature. In a time when modern communications impose increasingly uniform ideas of Islam and culture on people throughout the world, the concept of a creole society that includes multiple different ethnicities and interpretations of religion seems particularly attractive. The role of archaeology and other historical disciplines is to show that creole identities have always existed and are part of the history of Islamic civilization. Furthermore, this illustrates an opportunity to demonstrate diverse approaches to religious belief that are not mutually exclusive.

References

Ball, W. and J.-C. Gardin. 1982. *Archaeological Gazetteer of Afghanistan*. 2 vols. Paris: Editions Recherche sur les civilisations.

Bates, M. 1994. 'Byzantine coinage and its imitations: Arab-Byzantine Coinage'. *Aram* 6(1–2): 311–403.

Blevins, J. P. 1995. 'Syncretism and paradigmatic opposition'. *Linguistics and Philosophy* 18: 113–52.

Cameron, A. and G. R. D. King. 1994. *The Byzantine and Early Islamic Near East: Land Use and Settlement Patterns*. Princeton: Darwin Press.

Clack, T. 2011. 'Syncretism and religious fusion'. In T. Insoll (ed.), *Oxford Handbook of the Archaeology of Ritual and Religion*. Oxford: Oxford University Press, pp. 226–42.

Dani, A. H. and B. A. Litvinsky. 1996. 'The Kusho-Sasanian kingdom'. In B. A. Livintsky (ed.), *History of Civilizations of Central Asia. The Crossroads of Civilizations: A.D. 250 to 750*. Vol. III. Paris: UNESCO, pp. 103–8.

Eriksen, T. H. 2007. 'Creolization in anthropological theory in Mauritius'. In C. Stewart (ed.), *Creolization: History, Ethnography, Theory*. Walnut Creek: Left Coast Press, pp. 153–76.

Genequand, D. 2006. 'Umayyad castles: the shift from late antique military architecture to early Islamic palatial building'. In H. Kennedy (ed.), *Muslim Military Architecture in Greater Syria: From the Coming of Islam to the Ottoman Period*. Leiden: Brill, pp. 3–25.

Horton, M. C. 1996. *Shanga: The Archaeology of a Muslim Trading Community on the Coast of East Africa*. London: British Institute in Eastern Africa.

Horton, M. C. 2004. 'Artisans, Communities and commodities: medieval exchanges between North Western India and East Africa'. *Ars Orinetalis* 34: 62–80.

Horton, M. C. and J. Middleton. 2000. *The Swahili: The Social Landscape of a Mercantile Society*. Oxford: Blackwell.

Insoll, T. 2004. 'Syncretism, time and identity: Islamic archaeology in West Africa'. In D. Whitcomb (ed.), *Changing Social Identity with the Spread of Islam:*

266 ANDREW PETERSEN

Archaeological Perspectives. The University of Chicago Oriental Seminars Number 1. Chicago: The Oriental Institute, pp. 89–101.

Kolesnikov, I. 1996. 'Social and political consequences of the Arab Conquest'. In B. A. Livintsky (ed.), *History of Civilizations of Central Asia. The Crossroads of Civilizations: A.D. 250 to 750*. Vol. III. Paris: UNESCO, pp. 461–8.

Litvinsky, B. A., ed. 1996. *History of Civilizations of Central Asia. The Crossroads of Civilizations: A.D. 250 to 750*. Vol. III. Paris: UNESCO.

Lymer, K. 2004. 'The landscapes of holy site pilgrimage in the Republic of Kazakhstan'. *World Archaeology* 36(1): 158–72.

Pentz, P. 1992. *The Invisible Conquest: The Ontogenesis of Sixth and Seventh Century Syria*. Copenhagen: National Museum of Denmark.

Walmsley, A. 2007. *Early Islamic Syria: An Archaeological Assessment*. Bath: Duckworth.

Whitcomb, D. (ed.), 2004. *Changing Social Identity with the Spread of Islam: Archaeological Perspectives*. The University of Chicago Oriental Seminars Number 1. Chicago: The Oriental Institute.

12

Syncretism and Cognition

African and European Religious and Aesthetic Expressions in the Caribbean

Jay B. Haviser

Incipient aspects of syncretic processes among Africans and Europeans had begun on the African continent by the fifteenth century, particularly in relation to religious practices (Heywood and Thornton 2007). Considering the relatively isolated participation of the two groups within the early interactive sphere of West Africa, as well as the in situ contexts of the African cultures, these syncretic expressions were evident, yet due to the disproportional ratio of populations, were subtler on the continent. However, once the various African populations were forcibly transported to the Caribbean, eliminating a strong homogeneity of cultural traditions, the degree of interactive exchange between Africans and Europeans increased dramatically, resulting in more complex and open forms of syncretism. A significant part of this process was driven by the interpersonal relations and cognitive formations of European children being predominately raised by female African caretakers. This chapter seeks to provide a discussion about how African-European syncretic processes manifested themselves in successful forms, such as in benign cognitive compromises relating to religious practices, as well as how these syncretic processes were also rejected, such as with conflictive cognitive aspects in forms of aesthetic expression. It is proposed here that variable degrees of syncretic effectiveness were based on fundamental variations of African and European social-psychological cognitive approaches.

A general overview of the contexts of African and European interactions in the Caribbean is provided. Two archaeological case studies are presented to understand the cognitive basis of interaction: one of successful syncretism and the other of rejected syncretism, both on the Dutch Caribbean island of St Maarten.

Jay B. Haviser, *Syncretism and Cognition: African and European Religious and Aesthetic Expressions in the Caribbean*
In: *Archaeologies of Cultural Contact: At the Interface.* Edited by: Timothy Clack and Marcus Brittain, Oxford University Press.
© Oxford University Press 2022. DOI: 10.1093/oso/9780199693948.003.0013

Syncretism and cognition in African-European interactive contexts

It seems relevant to first discuss the understanding of what syncretism is, how cognition affects its manifestation, and how these are presented according to variable social or political agendas and perspectives.

In defining syncretism, one is most often first presented with the Greek root for the word, having reference to the Cretan peoples who were noted to have mixed, or closed ranks with others, when confronted by a mutual enemy. Syncretism is a dynamic process, which presupposes encounter and confrontation between systems, and subsequently is applied to the integration of various beliefs into new forms of religion. However, syncretism has relevance to more than religious transformation and reorganization; it is indeed consistent with broader aspects of creolization processes. However, here one is cautioned against a Eurocentric bias that limits definitions of the word to non-European religions; the universality of syncretism is a fact in all major religions (Fernandez Olmos and Paravisini-Gebert 2003). As such, in overemphasizing only the syncretic elements, one is missing the essence of independent legitimacy for the effective evolution of African religions in the Americas (Mosquera 1992). Moreover, enslaved Africans took possession of the religion of the 'masters', and repossessed themselves as active spiritual subjects; revising, transforming, and appropriating Christianity's power for their own discourse (Apter 1991). The intertwined elements of syncretic religion and creolization are strong. As Thornton (1998) suggests, European Christianity may well have served the same function in the development of African-Creole religions as European languages served in the formation of Creole languages; providing a form of lingua franca that joined various religious traditions, without necessarily replacing them. Thus, Creole religions are seen at the very core of the transculturation process that produced the essence of African-Creole societies in the Caribbean.

Beneath these processes of syncretism and creolization are the even more fundamental aspects of human cognition and the variable cognitive approaches that form the basic maps of understanding for the different groups participating in the syncretic process. For a general comparison of European and African cognition, we see that social organization affects cognitive processes in two basic ways: indirectly by focusing attention on different parts of the environment, and directly by making some kinds of social communication patterns more acceptable than others (Nesbit et al. 2001). It has been demonstrated that African cognitive maps are more holistic, attending to the entire environment and assigning causality to it, making relatively little use of categories and logic, and relying on 'dialectical' or 'experiential' reasoning, while European cognitive maps are more analytic, paying attention primarily to the object and the categories to which it belongs, and using rules including formal logic to understand behaviour (Haviser 2006a). In the study of syncretic formations, one must not be overly focused on the content of differences and similarities, but rather examine the context of the often desperate need by the active participants to create boundaries that serve the purpose of differentiation or assimilation. On the cognitive level, ethnic or group attitudes have their origins with an individual's infantile experiences of self-other differentiation; it has been shown that by 4–6 years of age most children have acquired a vocabulary and concepts reflecting ethnic attitude (GAP 1987: 63). Thus, in this regard, religion can also be seen to originate in the family unit and serve as a bridge conjoining the individual (and family) and society. For the present argument, the European concept of 'Africanness' does not consist solely of what Africans are, but also contains some of their own unwanted European cognitive elements which have been externalized and projected onto Africans in psychological patterns. Thereby negotiating with 'them' entails negotiating with parts of 'us' (GAP 1987: 127). This often unconscious symbiosis between adversaries is a powerful factor in human negotiations, and will be shown to have played a key role in the contexts of African and European acceptance or rejection of syncretic elements.

In the contexts of the African continent before the trans-Atlantic slave trade, Heywood and Thornton (2007) have identified that both African and European religions were in the early process of syncretism. Thornton (1998) further notes that the two religious positions were structured in very similar ways, with a belief in a Supreme Being and through the philosophical interpretation of revelations. He notes that the Africans did not formulate their religious interpretations with a structured orthodoxy, due to the absence of a recognized power of the priesthood, and a constant flow of revelations from many individuals that could not support a rigid cosmology with the ongoing addition of new insights (1998: 246). By contrast, the Europeans, who also structured their philosophical interpretations based on revelations and miracles, did develop a strong clergy infrastructure with political power. However, the prospect of continuous revelations was perceived by these Europeans as a danger. Revelation interpretation was therefore reserved for the clergy and any views inconsistent with the positions of the clergy were deemed to be derived 'of the devil'.

Contextual shifts between the New World after the trans-Atlantic slave trade began and the heterogeneity of African origins forged localized religious traditions. The creative foundation for new African revelations and the increased potential for the introduction of Christian elements was heavily influenced by the ubiquitous presence of Christianity shaped by both African Christians of the continent and European missionaries in the colonies. However, Thornton (1998: 271) makes it very clear that religious conversion in the New World was not simply a process of forcing acceptance of an alien religion; nor were continued African revelations and practices forms of cultural resistance. Rather, conversion was a spontaneous and voluntary act on the part of Africans. These Africans were convinced by the same types of revelations that formulated their own gods, i.e. that the 'other world' was in fact inhabited by beings who were almost identical to the deities of the Europeans. With these insights, and considering the general lack of orthodoxy among the Africans, it becomes clear that by giving Catholic cachet to ceremonies which were clearly not Catholic, the Africans were not trying to fool the authorities or the Church, but rather they were convinced of the efficacy of the Catholic liturgy and therefore wished their own practices to benefit from it (Metraux 1960). In response, the Catholic Church tolerated many popular African-Creole practices in the hope of eventually transforming those beliefs by eradicating them slowly and non-violently, a skill acquired and honed over 2,000 years of Christianity's survival. The result has not been what the church expected. Indeed, the African-Creole religious practices of the Caribbean have actually enthusiastically embraced Catholicism, as illustrated by the use of baptism, Holy Sacraments, calendar dates, sacred objects, etc.

Most African-Creole religions transformed their beliefs within the new contexts of slavery and colonial domination. The strongest influences came primarily from the Yoruba, Fon, and Kongo culture areas and Bantu linguistic group. The larger African-Creole religions of the Caribbean are very formalized with established liturgy and community rituals as well as specific syncretism elements with the Roman Catholic Church. Such examples include the Vodou of Haiti, Santeria, and Regla de Ocha of Cuba, and Orishas of Trinidad. Other African-Creole religious practices of the region are less characteristic of formalized (i.e. institutional) 'religion' and belong more to a system of beliefs in spirituality with individualistic practices focused on ritual invocations, fetishes, and charms with African ancestry. Such examples include the Obeah, Myal, and Quimbois (Fernandez Olmos and Paravisini-Gebert 2003). Schular (1991: 296) points out that the earliest notion of 'Pan-African' cooperation was spawned with the spirit of collaboration among enslaved Africans of various ethnic backgrounds for these African-Creole religious practices.

Accepted syncretism: Obeah healing and child cognition

Obeah is a West African-influenced healing practice, which Handler and Bilby (2001: 91) suggest may be associated with the Niger Delta, the Igbo term *di abia* meaning 'healer' or 'herbalist', and, it is noted, most prevalent in the Anglophone and Dutch colonial areas. The focal point of Obeah is the person who conducts practices as 'Obeahman' or 'Obeahwoman', and who treats clients secretly on a one-to-one basis, avoiding public or community attention. Physical deformities are often associated with Obeah practitioners and beliefs; those born with physical irregularity are believed to have been endowed with special powers (Fernandez Olmos and Paravisini-Gebert 2003: 134). The primary authority recognized for Obeahmen is their knowledge of African-derived healing practices, using herbal and animal medicinal properties. The secondary function of Obeah is to direct relations between the human and spirit worlds, by casting spells for both good and evil purposes, on an individually commissioned basis. These spells and invocations include: (1) protecting self, property, and family; (2) harming real or perceived enemies; (3) bringing fortune in love, employment, or personal or business pursuits; and (4) veneration of ancestors.

Objects related to specific Obeah practice have been identified in historical documents since the seventeenth century (see Fernandez Olmos and Paravisini-Gebert 2003). Olmos and Paravisini-Gebert (ibid. 135–7) identified the primary objects of Obeah as candles, cigars, coins, bird feathers, egg shells, honey, nails, cat skulls, dog teeth, rags, twine, bottles, rum, compiled bundles of twine and rags, sealed bottles of blood and other liquid concoctions, food offerings, animal sacrifices, and various forms of charms and dolls. However, recently Handler (2011) has complied a more thorough understanding of the 'instruments of Obeah', based on anti-Obeah laws in the Caribbean from the eighteenth century. It is interesting to note the intentional use of vague legal wording, often shared across the various European colonies of the region, to allow for categorization of anything used or intended to be used for Obeah practice. Nonetheless, it is necessary to keep some of these general 'Obeah practice' artefacts in mind for the next section, whilst observing the specific artefacts collected from a Catholic priest burial site containing African-Creole religious objects on St Maarten.

Within the contexts of African and European interactions in the Caribbean, a critical cognitive aspect that has been overlooked in most historical reconstructions is the significant role of the African domestic workers serving as

Fig. 12.1. Nanny and her charge, Barbados, 1880 (left); Nanny 'Yaya' with children on Curacao, 1907 (right).

the primary childcare provider in the colonial household setting (Fig. 12.1). As Higman (1984: 189) has well documented, 70 percent of all domestic workers in Caribbean plantation households were female, of which their primary chores were childcare, sewing, cooking, and laundry. Shepherd (1999: 55) has further noted that enslaved women working in the plantation household as domestics enjoyed a higher status than field workers. In the personal interactive sphere of the Caribbean colonial plantation household, whilst the (white) European women were concerned with domestic management in day-to-day life, very few did actual housework or childcare, which was undertaken by their domestic servants (Brereton 1998).

As described above, the earliest years of childhood have the greatest impact on self-other cognitive differentiations. Parents introduce ideas to a growing child, many of them of the 'us' and 'them' type, which are readily and uncritically incorporated by a mind in transition and receptive to ideas that conform to an innate tendency to dichotomize (GAP 1987: 41). However, and ironically in the colonial Caribbean context, the person who was communicating most intimately on a daily basis with these formative European children was the African domestic worker, endearingly known as the 'Nanny' in the Anglophone Caribbean and 'Yaya' in the Papiamentu-speaking Dutch

Caribbean. For the European children, this created an overlapping set of loyalties, whose contradictory elements presented multiple, and at times conflicting, cognitive approaches. Identity boundaries separate those to whom one feels a sense of kinship and obligation from those to whom one feels unrelated. Thus, this colonial context of the nannied European child was one of conflicting personal identity. From the intimacy of this early nurturing relationship, the child participated in a projected identification, by which part of her/his 'self' was split and projected onto the nanny, with whom s/he then felt identified and who had become a reservoir of her/his own qualities as a target of externalization. The experience of being 'part' of the nanny enhanced the European child's personal connection with other African elements in their world, via song, food, language, observed behaviours, and the nanny's associated kin. In contrast, African children of the same colonial plantation context had absolutely no intimate personal connections with European adults in their formative early childhood years, and thus readily developed a strong 'us' and 'them' type of relationship with Europeans.

It is proposed that, when looking to the syncretism of African and European religious practices in the Caribbean, a critical and over-looked cognitive aspect has been the very personal and intimate sympathies held by those raised as European children with African nannies. These sympathies were often manifested in the 'blind eye' turned by Christians—the dominant social group—towards African-Creole religious practices. These religious aspects are manifestations of successful and effective syncretism among Africans and Europeans in the colonial Caribbean. The archaeological manifestation of effective syncretism will comprise the first case study whilst the second will demonstrate non-effective or rejected syncretism in a similar context.

The illusion of control is a vital element of European (indeed Western) philosophy. This view of the control of objects in the environment provisions a strong sense of confidence. In comparison, the African cognitive view makes it difficult to separate objects in the environment from the environment itself (Haviser 2006a: 32). The European desire for control of the environment, through capitalist endeavours such as colonial plantations, was, in essence, the very foundational stimulus of the trans-Atlantic trade of African slaves. Understanding that Africans and Europeans inhabited different assumptive and representational worlds, based on the consideration that their own world was correct and rational, and all others are intrinsically wrong (see GAP 1987: 127), it is presented here that aesthetic expression is a prime example of the conflicting cognitive maps for these two groups in the colonial Caribbean.

274   JAY B. HAVISER

From the earliest of European global travels, tales of bizarre creatures and alien cultures were the staple of descriptive journals, most often with considerable exaggeration and moralistic overtones. If the customs or cultural behaviours of African cultures did not fit the European norm of moral or aesthetic quality, they were presented as demonic, evil, or pathetic. Europeans corrupted the early concept of African religious practices, such as Obeah, by initiating negative reference terms and consistently describing the practices as for evil intent. Handler and Bilby (2001) have been able to reconfirm the original concepts of normal, positive, and socially beneficial purposes for Obeah practices both in Africa and the Caribbean. Nonetheless, the European colonial view of African-Creole religious practices as negative was, at the same time, a response to the potential threat practitioners posed in terms of ritualistic power being translated into political leadership and resistance/ aggression against white authority (see Handler 2000: 87).

In the Caribbean colonies, and of great importance to the African slave workers, was the consistent application of colonial laws against non-Christian beliefs and practices, particularly the punishments for practitioners (Turner 1997; Handler 2011). Indeed, by the nineteenth century, all Anglophone Caribbean territories had legislation to ban or limit African-Creole practices. Legislation limiting 'Obeah practices' specifically was also enacted (Bilby and Handler 2004; see Fig. 12.2). These practices carried the potential punishment of death; however, these laws were inconsistently applied (Handler 2000). Two ironies emerge if we consider that these laws were intended to suppress African-Creole practices. First, written regulations served to 'officialize' and 'diffuse' the term 'Obeah' at a regional level, thereby inadvertently expanding its use beyond local contexts (Allsopp, in Handler and Bilby 2001: 99). Second, punishments legitimized the political significance of African religions and claims to supernatural powers among the enslaved population (see Turner 1997); and indeed emphasized the perceived deleterious influences of Obeah practitioners by the Europeans (Handler 2011). As a further covert challenge to European hegemony, enslaved Africans did have certain public rights, such as funerals, in which they could manifest religious expressions, such as ancestor worship, without prosecution.

Case study: African-European religious syncretism on St Maarten

In 2006, the remains of a nineteenth-century Dutch priest of the Dominican Order were excavated from the Frontstreet cemetery on St Maarten, a Dutch

Fig. 12.2. African-descendant prisoners for Obeah violations in the Caribbean, Antigua, 1905 (UK National Archives, CO 152/287, Knollys to Lyttelton no. 208, 12 May 1905, London).

island in the northeast Caribbean. During the course of this excavation, African-Creole religious artefacts were found in both the direct burial contexts and also as subsequent activities at the burial site location. Identified below is a specific African-Creole religious artefact assemblage from the St Maarten excavations that further demonstrate aspects of distinction among various African-Creole religious groups, as well as the syncretism between the Catholic Church and local African-Creole religious practices on the island over the last 120 years. The research itself was initiated by the St Maarten Catholic Church, in order to have the remains exhumed for reburial at the main cathedral (Haviser 2006a). Interestingly, one of the primary concerns for the church was the desecration of the grave site by African-Creole religious practices over the years, which had resulted in numerous artefacts being deposited at the site. From these specific artefact collections came the opportunity to define an African-Creole religious material culture assemblage from St Maarten, with the further potential to also suggest the specific form of African-Creole religious practice that was manifest at the site.

The Dutch priest and the Catholic cemetery

Father Jordanus Onderwater was born Engelbertus Antonius Onderwater in Leiden, the Netherlands, on 9 November 1850 (see Fig. 12.3). He was raised in an orphanage of Dominican Sisters and became a Dominican Priest, changing his name in 1869. In 1881, he was sent to Curaçao to serve the Dominican mission there and in 1887 he was moved on to St Maarten for service of the three Windward Islands, including Saba and St Eustatius. By 1890, Father Onderwater was a highly respected member of the community, introducing Dominican nuns as teachers. He was also a signatory benefactor for many emancipated Africans to acquire land on the island. On 13 October 1891, aged just 41 and just days before his intended date to leave St Maarten for the Netherlands, he died of unknown causes, with rumours of poisoning. On 14 October 1891, he was buried at the main Catholic cemetery on Frontstreet, with remarkable eulogies of appreciation and loss expressed by the African-descendant population in the local newspapers (van Veen 1999).

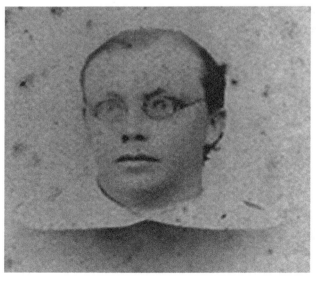

Fig. 12.3. Photograph of Father Onderwater.

In 2006 there were over one hundred graves in the Catholic Frontstreet cemetery, all dated after 1848, but with only eight dated before 1891. There is a large stone cross monument at the centre of the grounds, and all of the oldest graves were in proximity to this central monument, including Father Onderwater who was immediately adjacent to it. It is important to note that only a few graves in this cemetery have African-Creole religious artefacts associated with them. In contrast, Father Onderwater's grave was covered with such artefacts, placed there apparently in homage to the priest or his representation of authority. The headstone of Father Onderwater was made of a unique metal alloy material, clearly imported, which had been moved about a metre from its original location atop a small stone-mortar base.

Excavations of the priest

Three small excavations were conducted at the site (120 × 180 cm; 130 × 160 cm; 80 × 90 cm) in the immediate area of the Onderwater grave, all dug in 20 cm spit intervals and to a maximum depth of 210 cm below the ground surface. Noted in the soil stratigraphy of loose fine sand was evidence that about 40 cm of sand had accumulated over the site since 1891. The specific fill of burial pit was full of large beach-worn boulders, with three separate-depth layers of mortar poured over the stones. The deepest of these mortar layers, at about 135–40 cm, also contained five large conch shells, just above the head of the coffin. General artefacts associated with the burial pit were all nineteenth-century ceramics and glasses. Also recovered in the upper 40 cm of the excavations were numerous small African-Creole religious bundles which had been intentionally buried into the grave site (see Fig. 12.4).

The primary material remains in direct physical relation within the grave were the priest's complete skeleton, brass tacks, iron nails in the soil colour outline of the coffin box, and several personal artefacts (see Fig. 12.5). The personal artefacts consisted of bone buttons, brass clothing clasps, a brass crucifix (12.5 cm long), and black glass beads with white dots on the left of his waist. The beads were from his rosary, with the Dominican Order black-white colours. His skeleton revealed that he was a slight man, with probable chronic knee and back pain, and as having a distinctive birth defect on the left side of his face. Post-excavation tests for poisons on samples of the bone material were inconclusive.

Thousands of artefacts associated with African-Creole religious practices were recovered from this location, in both surface and sub-surface contexts, apparently as homage to the priest himself or what he represented. On the

278   JAY B. HAVISER

Fig. 12.4. Father Onderwater excavation with in situ African-Creole fetish objects from the early to mid-twentieth century.

Fig. 12.5. Bone buttons and a brass clasp, direct association with the priest skeleton (left); rosary beads and crucifix, direct association with the priest skeleton (right).

Fig. 12.6. One of many altar contexts at the grave site; note the candles, cigars, coins, and food offerings (top right); coins found in both surface and sub-surface contexts at the site (523 total, 65.6 percent copper coins) (top left); rag-thread bundles and honey-bottles with offerings in both surface and sub-surface contexts at the site (bottom).

surface, there were makeshift altars on all four sides of the monument, each covered with food offerings, small animal sacrifices, artefact bundles, candles, cigars, and coins (Fig. 12.6).

The multiple placements of these objects indicate repeated religious practices at the site. Among the buried artefact bundles were conch shells, bottles filled with objects and wrapped with thread, as well as three handmade dolls with pins in them and also wrapped with thread (Fig. 12.7). The majority of these objects date from the 1960s or later.

Excavation unit #1, level 1 (0–20 cm including surface)

- 523 coins (343 copper); 442 USA, 53 Netherlands Antilles, 28 other;
- 19 wax candles (white);

Fig. 12.7. Handmade dolls with pins and bound with thread, found buried at the site, note the painted round-eye shape on the dolls (bottom); handmade dolls placed at the gravesite after removal of skeletal remains, note the sewn slit-eyes on the dolls (top).

- 8 cigars, 3 cigar wrappers;
- 1 woven basket, 1 ball of black thread;
- 22 glass bottles/bottle fragments (4 identified as rum);
- 12 razor blades;
- 9 iron nails, 15 iron fragments, 1 steel wire, 14 bottle caps (9 rum), 1 steel knife, 1 aluminium cooking pot with lid;
- 2 whiteware ceramic bowls, 3 coarse earthenware sherds;
- 1 melted plastic bottle, 1 black shoe polish plastic bottle, 1 plastic lighter, 1 melted plastic drinking cup, 1 vapour-rub plastic bottle, 16 plastic pin heads;
- 10 chipped basalt fragments, 1 burned limestone, 7 beach pebbles, 2 polished marble fragments;
- 9 whelk shells, 12 clam shells, 2 arca shells, 1 oyster shell, 16 land snail shells;
- 1 cat mandible, 3 bird bones, 4 goat bones;
- 4 egg shells.

SYNCRETISM AND COGNITION   281

Excavation unit #1, level 1 (discreet deposit feature)

- 3 wax bundles with numerous steel sewing pins;
- 1 wax bundle wrapped in red thread;
- 1 cloth bundle (with zipper inside) wrapped around many square nails;
- 1 bundle of white string;
- 1 plastic bag with cloth and square nails wrapped inside;
- 1 Goya honey bottle with thick wax on top, inside paper with writing;
- 3 plastic powder drink bottles filled with dirt and objects.

Excavation unit #1, level 1 (discreet deposit feature)

- 3 cloth doll bundles;
- 1 white doll (at front) and 1 red doll (at back) with pins joining them (on red side pins in random pattern, white side in a cross); painted white-green eyes on white side; head tie on white doll;
- 2 identical front-back dolls of black cloth with blue shirts and same white-green painted eyes; wrapped and tied together with black thread; no pins; head ties present;
- 1 single doll, black with flower-print dress, head bound with black thread, hands and feet bound with red thread; no pins; head tie present.

Excavation unit #1, level 2 (20–40 cm)

- 1 large whole conch shell, with machete cut mark, at the old surface level;
- 1 rum bottle wrapped in white thread, filled with liquid and cigar.

Surface deposits (after the 2006 removal of the human remains)

- 1 small wooden coffin (22 cm length), black with white letters 'E.P.D.' on the lid; single black cloth doll inside with pins in arms and genitalia, red thread and black ribbon pinned on; cloth-body filled with cotton; sewn white slit eyes;
- 1 dual black-cloth dolls wrapped in white thread and connected with many coloured plastic-head pins, headpiece on one also with black

282   JAY B. HAVISER

thread body wrap and red thread leg wrap; cloth bodies filled with dirt; sewn red slit eyes;

- 1 dual black-cloth dolls wrapped in red thread; cloth filled with dirt, sewn red slit eyes; no pins.

Reburial ceremony and evident syncretism

In anticipation of the reburial, Father Onderwater's remains, in addition to the excavation report and an altar cloth, were sealed in a stainless-steel box by Father Thomas Krosnicki and the author. On the day of the reburial, a ceremony was performed at the old grave site with the stainless-steel box present. This was followed by a walking procession with the box, from the cemetery to the main cathedral, which included enthusiastic singing and chanting. It is of no small importance that the largest ethnic group present at this reburial ceremony was the Haitian Catholic Community of St Maarten. During the official reburial ceremonies within the cathedral, the Haitian group performed energetic songs and dances. This emphasizes the particular practice of the Haitian community on St Maarten for expressions of religious syncretism within formal Catholic contexts, and their sympathetic demonstration that some African-Creole beliefs were involved in the reburial ceremony (see Fig. 12.8).

Interpretations of the Father Onderwater burial

Father Onderwater was a slight man, with an obvious deformity in his lower right face, a feature noted as significant to Obeah practitioners by anthropologists (Fernandez Olmos and Paravisini-Gebert 2003). It is not evident that the priest was an Obeah practitioner, but rather that he was a focal person, someone perceived as significant by local Obeah practitioners. The widespread public appreciation of this priest is evident in the newspaper eulogies, as well as by the placement of conch shells at the time of burial and after. Together, these activities are indicative of the great affection felt for him by African descendants as per the nineteenth-century African-Creole symbolic tradition of conchs on graves, which carried over into the twentieth century.

Serious efforts were made in the original sealing of the grave. Three mortar layers were used to seal the burial, perhaps in response to the fear of disease, spirit-release, or the exhumation of remains by Obeah practitioners. Although

Fig. 12.8. Father Onderwater's reburial procession, led by the Catholic priest and followed by chanting Haitian Catholic community members.

unconfirmed, poisoning or even the rumour of poisoning reflects a common practice within African-Creole religious contexts, and is also noted in various literature references across the Caribbean. The headstone placed at his grave, a unique non-local metal alloy material, was, perhaps, additionally attractive to African-Creole religious practices. Multiple episodes of Obeah practice are noted at the grave through numerous artefact deposits. Stylistic change of eyes found on the fetish dolls may indicate that more than one practitioner was involved over some duration of time where a continuity of practice may otherwise be observed.

Modern Obeah activities have focused extensively and exclusively on the grave of this individual priest. This is due to his aforementioned attributes and also, perhaps, because he was the sole Catholic priest (and male spiritual leader) buried on the island. Obeah practices had increased at the site since the 1960s, perhaps relating to increased immigration from Anglophone areas. This demonstrates the popularity of Obeah practices on the island during the later twentieth century. Increased Haitian and Dominican Republic populations also arrived in the 1960–70s, yet the specific type/presentation of artefacts at this site suggest continuity of individualistic Obeah belief practices, rather than fresh influences from Vodou or other African-Creole formal religious symbolisms. Yet, the serious interest shown in the actions of the Haitian community in connection with the reburial of Father Onderwater suggests a broader sympathy for the association of African-derived contexts of religious syncretism. Indeed, this specific grave site has continued as a site of Obeah-derived practices, even following the removal of the priest's physical remains. This exemplifies the strong sense of traditional focus on specific localities linked to these practices on St Maarten.

This case study provides an African-Creole material culture assemblage for Obeah practices on St Maarten, which can be used for reference in future archaeological and anthropological investigations on the island and elsewhere. The greater lesson for the archaeological community researching African-Creole religious themes are the opportunities and challenges of distinguishing between artefacts of the individualistic Obeah-like practices from the remains of the more formalized religions, e.g. Vodou and Santeria.

Rejected syncretism: dental modification

Physical intimidation produces a cognitive response and, in the majority of humans, direct and conscious reactions of fear. Compared to the more passive threats posed by African-Creole religious practices, in which, as noted before, there could even have been particular cognitive sympathies on the part of the Europeans, the perception of potential physical harm, expressed through some African aesthetic body modifications such as dental-modification and scarification, surpassed the boundaries of European cognitive acceptability. Therefore, the case study for rejected syncretism presented for this comparison relates to three African skeletons from the late seventeenth century recovered on St Maarten, all with extensive dental modification (Haviser 2010b; Haviser and Schroeder 2011).

The earliest known evidence of dental modification in West Africa has been documented at the Karkarichinkat Nord site, Mali, with a date of 4500–4200 BP (Finucane et al. 2008). Continued practice has been noted in the Hausa region of Nigeria into the early second millennium CE (Haour and Pearson 2005). The earliest evidence of African dental modification in the Americas has been reported at Campeche, Mexico, between the late sixteenth to early seventeenth centuries (Handler and Lange 2006). More extensive work on African dental modifications in the New World from the seventeenth to nineteenth centuries includes, amongst others, Newton Plantation on Barbados (Handler et al. 1982) and African burial grounds in New York

(Blakey 2001), New Orleans (Owsley et al. 1987), and Philadelphia (Angel et al. 1987).

Of particular relevance for our discussion of non-effective syncretism are issues concerning African cultural traditions of dental modification and their continuation into the colonial contexts involving enslaved Africans. Handler (1994) has viably argued that dental modification was not an African tradition carried over to the Caribbean, whilst it was regularly maintained on the African continent at least until the early twentieth century. Fig. 12.9 depicts several examples of African dental modification and scarification from the early twentieth century, from the Congo c.1904–12, including the most unique case of Ota Benga, a Congolese pygmy. Ota Benga was transported from the Congo and put on display at the 1904 World's Fair in St Louis, USA, under the title of 'Louisiana Purchase Pygmies' (Frazer [1910] 2006). He became the favourite attraction, due to the extensive dental modifications performed on him as a young boy in Africa. Following the fair's closure, he lived in the Bronx Zoo Monkey House from 1904–6. He lived in a cage, with only a chimpanzee to accompany him, and was regularly photographed as the 'wild savage'. It seems that dental modification was the finishing touch for a latent Euro-American cognitive fear-fantasy concerning 'ferocious savages from the Dark Continent'. With these fantasy sentiments lingering into the early twentieth century, with many more examples dating back to the eighteenth century, it should not be impossible to concede that the discontinuance of the African cultural tradition of dental modification in the colonial contexts was a rejected syncretism forced, primarily, from the intimidation felt by the

Fig. 12.9. Examples of dental modification and scarification (left) Utopo men from Congo (c.1912) and from Congo (Ota Benga, c.1904); Ota Benga lived in the Bronx Zoo Monkey House 1904–6 (right).

286 JAY B. HAVISER

Europeans at the sight of such mutilations. Essentially, discontinuance was demanded by European colonial authorities.

In the colonial contexts of the Caribbean there are also numerous examples of incidental tooth modification. For example, relatively common are the 'pipestem notches'—distinctive gaps between the teeth resulting from the extensive use of hard kaolin clay tobacco pipes—evident on both African and European skeletons. However, this incidental form of tooth modification resulting from pipe-smoking is fundamentally different from the intentional modification discussed here. Intentional tooth modification is extremely rare in the European population in colonial contexts. In the only case known to this author, identified during archaeological excavations associated with a nineteenth-century practising dentist on the island of Saba, enamel was purposefully removed in preparation for molar extraction (Espersen and Haviser 2019).

Case study: rejected African-European aesthetic syncretism on St Maarten

Three human burials were recovered at Zoutsteeg, Philipsburg, St Maarten, in 2010. All three skeletons were identified as African, two males and a female, and all had culturally modified teeth. The artefacts associated with these skeletons date from the late seventeenth century (Haviser 2010b: 5). To understand their personal relationship, as well as their origins in Africa, skeletal samples were submitted for mtDNA and strontium isotope analysis (Haviser and Schroeder 2011). This case study presents a brief overview of these results. It also discusses the potential of certain historical indications, interpreted from these results, with regard to the non-effective syncretism of aesthetic expressions between Africans and Europeans based on conflicting cognitive boundaries.

Zoutsteeg site: background and skeletal remains

In 2010, construction work on Zoutsteeg, Philipsburg, Saint Maarten, revealed three articulated human skeletons which had been buried at about 150 cm depth, and into the deepest white sand stratum of the Philipsburg peninsula. Artefacts associated directly with the skeletal remains, in the deepest stratum soils, indicate burial took place in the late seventeenth century.

Skeletal features, and in particular their culturally modified teeth (Figs 12.10 and 12.11), suggested that they were Africans, probably enslaved and brought to St Maarten for the exploitation of salt from the Great Salt Pond. Indeed, the Dutch name Zoutsteeg translates as 'Salt Street', and this particular street, from which the remains were recovered, was a direct access route from the coast to the pond. As recently as 1918, some of the largest salt accumulation piles were recorded in the immediate area of these burials. In 1968, Philipsburg was expanded with the extensive filling of the Great Salt Pond, at the pond-side of the peninsula. The result was that the original sandy shore-line of the pond in the seventeenth century became the centre of the city.

Due to the initial discovery of these remains by mechanical construction work, portions of the burials were disarticulated and damaged. However, upon rescue excavation, it was clearly determined that all three skeletons were buried articulated, lying on their backs, heads to the east, and parallel to each other about a metre apart, with no coffin boxes/nails evident. These burial

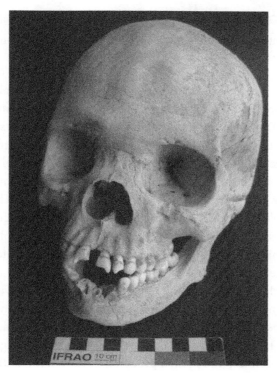

Fig. 12.10. Zoutsteeg skeleton #1 with modified upper incisors and post-mortem loss of lower incisors.

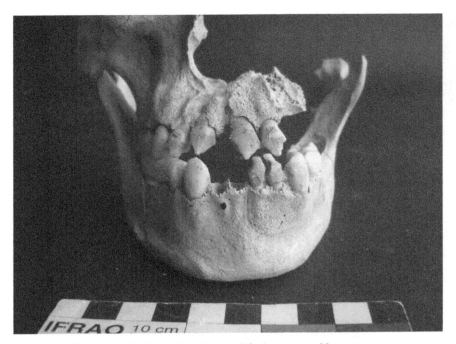

Fig. 12.11. Zoutsteeg skeleton #2 with modified upper and lower incisors.

characteristics are consistent with the earliest African burial evidence in Barbados, from the mid-seventeenth to early eighteenth century (Handler et al. 1982: 300). Due to the close proximity of the bodies, it is suggested that the Zoutsteeg three were probably buried at the same time, into the sandy shoreline of the salt pond and out of visibility from the ships on the coast.

Among the three individuals, there were identified two males and one female, all of whom were aged between 25 and 45 years old. The younger of the males (Skeleton #1) and the female (Skeleton #3) in particular had clear indications of some form of treponema infection (such as syphilis) on their respective crania and long bones. The older of the males (Skeleton #2) was an unusually large person, with a calculated stature of about 190 cm, with pronounced muscle attachments on the humerus and femur (Haviser 2010b: 3). The mtDNA analysis concluded that the three skeletons were not maternally related, and they had come from various areas of West Africa (Haviser and Schroeder 2011: 9). This suggests that, rather than family linkages or regional ethnic relations underpinning their grouping, social and/or aesthetic bonding based on appearances was apparent. The strontium isotope analysis confirmed that the three had been born in Africa, albeit in various different regions, possibly including the Senegambia, southern Nigeria, and the Gold Coast (ibid. 10). These results are consistent with findings of earlier studies that revealed similarly elevated Sr-87/86 values for individuals with artificially modified teeth (e.g. Schroeder et al. 2009) and therefore lends support to the idea that dental modification can be used to identify African-born individuals (Handler 1994).

Three colonial-period African burial grounds of the eighteenth and nineteenth centuries have been previously excavated on St Maarten. None of the more than forty skeletons observed have shown intentional dental modification; this has been recorded in many cultures around the world (see Labajo Gonzalez et al. 2010), with diagnostic forms of dental modification from the African continent and West Africa in particular (Jones 1992). Although sporadic examples of African dental modification have been recorded in the Americas (Stewart and Groome 1968; Handler et al. 1982; Angel et al. 1987; Handler 1994), it is rare, as at Zoutsteeg, to find three specimens together in one burial context. In addition, at the St Maarten Museum there is one further example from the island, an adult male with ground upper incisors, found in the 1970s at Marigot on the French-side. Since the 1990s, professional discussion about dental modification as diagnostic of African continental birth has flourished. Haviser and Schroeder (2011) were able to confirm the potential of such methods through the strontium isotope and DNA analyses of the Zoutsteeg remains. It is of further interest that all three of the Zoutsteeg skeletons exhibit extremely healthy teeth, aside from these modifications, indicating desire for a specific and intentional aesthetic.

Of the types of dental modification identified as diagnostic for West Africa (Goose 1963), all are found in the four skeletons from St Maarten. From research in Africa, it is known that dental modification is performed on both males and females, generally beginning at about 15 years of age. Some ethnic groups in Africa have specific conditions for the modification of teeth, such as the Upoto of central Congo, where men file only the upper teeth, while women file both upper and lower teeth (Frazer [1910] 2006: 193). In most African cases, the modification of teeth is done primarily for specific purposes of clan, tribal, or group identity, yet producing a desired lifelong aesthetic of dramatic impression. It is interesting to note that with the three Zoutsteeg and one Marigot examples of modification, three display a similar grinding/filing technique (i.e. Skeletons #1, #3, and Marigot) with one (i.e. Skeleton #2) modified by chipping. The mtDNA analysis helped to show that these individuals were from different areas and thus likely represent different ethnic expressions from West Africa. Singer (1953: 118) has suggested that

290 JAY B. HAVISER

filing is a later aesthetic refinement, a development of the earlier chipping technique. However, Stewart and Groome (1968), having recorded a diversity of filing and chipping techniques in larger African population groups, maintain that specific groups tend to use only one technique or the other. The presence of both upper and lower dental modification on the male Skeleton #2 indicate that he was not following practices known from the central Congo region (Frazer [1910] 2006).

As for socio-cultural interpretations of the specific Zoutsteeg skeletons, it is suggested that it was more than coincidence that three African-born persons with the same unique and aesthetically distinctive physical attributes were buried close together in one place. Dental modification is an uncommon trait on skeletons of enslaved Africans investigated from the region; the clustering of these three individuals exhibiting this trait at the same time and place could therefore indicate either a sense of collective social cohesiveness or their isolation by European colonizers. Evidence from two skeletons also indicates that contagious disease may have played a role in their death either directly or indirectly—execution may, for example, have been instigated as an outcome of their menacing appearance—as well as their grouped burial.

A reason that dental modification traditions did not carry over into colonial African-descendent populations is convincingly explained by Price and Price (1972; see also Handler et al. 1982) who argue that dental modification was a far too visible African characteristic, which would thus inhibit the 'code-shifting' or social camouflage behaviour of the enslaved African descendants born in the colonies. These descendants needed to opportunistically play the 'master's game' in certain circumstances, whilst enacting their 'traditional values' in more private circumstances. Social adaptability was restricted by the visibility of dental modification, thereby rendering it a less attractive practice for Africans to continue in contexts requiring engagement with Europeans. Handler et al. (1982: 310) further suggest that dental modification was also a very obvious, personally identifiable characteristic, thus restricting the ability for runaway slaves to hide elsewhere in society. Nevertheless, this obvious trait may also have been a badge of identity for free African populations (ibid. 311). Although we know from historical records that St Maarten had a proportionally large ratio of free Africans to slaves compared to the eastern Caribbean region in the early nineteenth century, the seventeenth-century dates of the Zoutsteeg finds disassociates them from such contexts, unless the remains are taken as an indicator of the beginnings of such free African populations on the island. What can be stated more clearly, however, is that deliberate dental modification was rarely carried into colonial

Caribbean contexts from the African continent. Further, due to a strong rejection of syncretism by the Europeans, perhaps for reasons of intimidation, dental modification was consciously discontinued by the Africans perhaps in response to the disruption of their adaptive social strategies.

Conclusion: interpretations of syncretism and cognitive boundaries

In both case studies the success or failure of the syncretic process was controlled directly by either sympathy or encroachment on the cognitive boundaries of the dominant group in the colonial Caribbean. Two key factors may be identified in the successful African-European syncretism within religion. First, there was a sense of common agreement on the basic principles of a Supreme Being and the theological value of revelations (even when specific interpretations of the revelations may not be in agreement). Second, a degree of intimate personal association was established between Africans (via domestics, especially in the role of nanny) and Europeans (via nanny-reared children), which in adult life opened many Europeans (and eventually European-Creoles) to both a sense for and empathy with certain African customs and behaviours, most notably ritual practices. Alternatively, African children in colonial contexts were not afforded equivalent intimate association with European adults, and thereby as adults developed more segregated 'us' and 'them' cognitive perceptions of European customs and behaviours. This encouraged actions of camouflage within their religious practices, whilst allowing for the usurpation of the liturgical structure of European religion.

With regards to rejected syncretism among Africans and Europeans, the case studies clearly illustrate the primal cognitive impact of fear and physical intimidation. The physical appearance of Africans with intentionally mutilated teeth and scarification surpassed the cognitive boundaries of colonial European sensibilities. Within a European cognitive grasp in the colonial contexts, if an African could intentionally mutilate themselves with such brutal practices, there is a perceived implication that they could as easily inflict physical harm on others—in particular their European adversaries. This aesthetic was direct intimidation, and the Africans themselves were surely aware of what emotional stimulation was brought forth by their physical aesthetics. The physical thus served as a psychological threat, in this case to European colonizers, when physical reprisals were neither possible nor effective. In the context of the colonial Caribbean, the European domination over most aspects of the lives of Africans rapidly put a stop to this intimidating aesthetic practice, rejecting any maturation of syncretic forms in the colonial sphere. A context therefore developed wherein only recognizably born Africans displayed modifications. As adaptation to their disadvantaged new social setting of the colonial Caribbean contexts, the Africans themselves also eventually rejected this practice, discontinuing dental modification and related aesthetics, as these practices threatened their code-sharing strategies for survival.

This chapter has shed light on the significant role of social-psychological elements of cognition in the success and failure of some syncretic processes. In the colonial Caribbean context, particular overlaps of African and European cognitive perspectives allowed for multiple facets of blended religious expression on the one hand, while on the other, primal cognitive fears suspended reason and rejected syncretic elements and aesthetic expressions.

Acknowledgements

I would like to thank Hannes Schroeder and Paul Fullagar for their continued cooperation with the skeletal mtDNA and strontium isotope analyses of the 'Zoutsteeg three'. I would also like to thank Jerry Handler and R. Grant Gilmore for their valuable comments on a draft of this paper.

References

Angel, J. L., J. O. Kelley, M. Parrington, and S. Pinter. 1987. 'Life stresses of a free black community as represented by the First African Church, Philadelphia, 1823–1841'. *American Journal of Physical Anthropology* 87(2): 213–29.

Apter, A. 1991. 'Herskovits's heritage: rethinking syncretism in the African Diaspora'. *Diaspora: A Journal of Transnational Studies* 1(3): 235–60.

Bilby, K. M. and J. S. Handler. 2004. 'Obeah: healing and protection in West Indian life'. *The Journal of Caribbean History* 38(2): 153–83.

Blakey, M. 2001. 'Bioarchaeology of the African Diaspora in the Americas: origins and scope'. *Annual Review of Anthropology* 30: 387–422.

Brereton, B. 1998. 'The white elite of Trinidad'. In H. Johnson and K. Watson (eds), *The White Minority in the Caribbean*. Kingston: Ian Randle Publishers, pp. 32–70.

Espersen, R. and J. Haviser. 2019. 'Cist graves on Saba: funerary traditions in the colonial Caribbean'. *Antiquity* 93(371): 1322–38.

Fernandez Olmos, M. and L. Paravisini-Gebert. 2003. *Creole Religions of the Caribbean*. New York: New York University Press.

Finucane, B., K. Manning, and M. Toure. 2008. 'Prehistoric dental modification in West Africa: early evidence from Karkarichinkat Nord, Mali'. *International Journal of Osteoarchaeology* 18(6): 632–40.

Frazer, J. G. [1910] 2006. *Totemism and Exogamy: A Treatise on Certain Early Forms of Superstition and Society*. New York: Kessinger Publishing.

GAP. 1987. *Us and Them: The Psychology of Ethnonationalism*. Group for the Advancement of Psychiatry 123. New York: Brunner/Mazel Publishers.

Goose, D. H. 1963. 'Tooth-mutilation in West Africa'. *Man* 63: 91–3.

Handler, J. S. 1994. 'Determining African birth from skeletal remains: a note on tooth mutilation'. *Historical Archaeology* 28(3): 113–19.

Handler, J. S. 2000. 'Slave medicine and Obeah in Barbados circa 1650–1834'. *New West Indian Guide* 74(1–2): 57–90.

Handler, J. S. 2011. 'Anti-Obeah laws of the Anglophone Caribbean, 1760s to 2010'. Paper presented at the 35th Annual Conference of the Society for Caribbean Studies, Liverpool, UK.

Handler, J. S. and K. M. Bilby. 2001. 'On the early use and origin of the term "Obeah" in Barbados and the Anglophone Caribbean'. *Slavery and Abolition* 22(2): 87–100.

Handler, J. S., R. Corruccini, and R. Mutaw. 1982. 'Tooth mutilation in the Caribbean: evidence from a slave burial population in Barbados'. *Journal of Human Evolution* 11: 297–313.

Handler, J. S. and F. Lange. 2006. 'On interpreting slave status from archaeological remains'. *African Diaspora Archaeology Network Newsletter* June. http://www.diaspora.uiuc.edu/news0606.html.

Haour, A. and J. Pearson. 2005. 'An instance of dental modification on a human skeleton from Niger, West Africa'. *Oxford Journal of Archaeology* 24(4): 427–33.

Haviser, J. B. 2006a. *Archaeological Excavation of a 19th Century Dutch Priest of the Dominican Order, Buried on St. Maarten, Netherlands Antilles*. St Maarten: SIMARC Archaeological Reports.

Haviser, J. B., 2010b. *Observations Relating to the Emergency Recovery of Human Skeletal Remains at Zoutsteeg, Philipsburg, St. Maarten*. St Maarten: SIMARC Technical Police Reports.

Haviser, J. B. and H. Schroeder. 2011. 'Bio-archaeological analysis of African skeletal remains exhibiting significant dental modification, recovered from Zoutsteeg, Sint Maarten'. Paper presented at the 24th International Congress for Caribbean Archaeology, Fort-de-France, Martinique.

Heywood, L. and J. Thornton. 2007. *Central Africans, Atlantic Creoles, and the Foundation of the Americas, 1585–1660*. Cambridge: Cambridge University Press.

294 JAY B. HAVISER

Higman, B. 1984. *Slave Populations of the British Caribbean 1807–1834*. New York: Johns Hopkins University Press.

Jones, A. 1992. 'Tooth mutilation in Angola'. *British Dental Journal* 173: 177–9.

Labajo Gonzalez, E., B. Perea Perez, J. A. Sanchez Sanchez, and M. Mar Robledo Acinas. 2010. 'Dental aesthetics as an expression of culture and ritual'. *British Dental Journal* 208: 77–80.

Metraux, A. 1960. 'A selection from Voodoo in Haiti'. In C. Leslie (ed.), *Anthropology of Folk Religion*. New York: Vintage Books, pp. 391–448.

Mosquera, G. 1992. 'Africa in the art of Latin America'. *Art Journal* 5(4): 30–8.

Nesbit, R., K. Peng, I. Choi, and A. Norenzayan. 2001. 'Culture and systems of thought: holistic versus analytic cognition'. *Psychological Review* 108(2): 291–310.

Owsley, D., C. E. Orser, Jr, R. W. Mann, P. Moore-Jansen, and R. L. Montgomery. 1987. 'Demography and pathology of an urban slave plantation from New Orleans'. *American Journal of Physical Anthropology* 87(2): 185–97.

Price, R. and S. Price. 1972. 'Kammba: the ethnohistory of an Afro-American art'. *Antropologica* 32: 3–27.

Schroeder, H., T. O'Connell, J. Evans, K. Shuler, and R. Hedges. 2009. 'Trans-Atlantic slavery: isotopic evidence for forced migration to Barbados'. *American Journal of Physical Anthropology* 139: 547–57.

Schular, M. 1991. 'Myalism and the African religious tradition in Jamaica'. H. Beckles and V. Shepherd (eds), *Caribbean Slave Society and Economy*. Kingston: Ian Randle Publishers, pp. 295–303.

Shepherd, V. 1999. *Women in Caribbean History*. Kingston: Ian Randle Publishers.

Singer, R. 1953. 'Artificial deformation of teeth: preliminary report'. *South African Journal of Science* 50: 116–22.

Stewart, T. D. and J. R. Groome. 1968. 'The African custom of tooth mutilation in America'. *American Journal of Physical Anthropology* 28: 31–42.

Thornton, J. 1998. *Africa and Africans in the Making of the Atlantic World, 1400–1800*. Cambridge: Cambridge University Press.

Turner, M. 1997. 'Religious beliefs'. In F. Knight (ed.), *General History of the Caribbean*. Vol. III. Paris: UNESCO Publishing, pp. 287–321.

van Veen, G. 1999. *Colorful Religion*. St Maarten: House of Nehesi Publishers.

PART III
CONCLUDING THOUGHTS

13

Observations of a Diverse Discussion on Power and Diversity

Jeb Card

Scale and interpretation

As an archaeologist, I feel the temptation to either start at the very beginning or the very end of things. In the case of this volume, the very beginning (in terms of chronology) provides an exception that proves the rule. I dislike using that phrase, but in this case, the distant circumstances of Upper Palaeolithic Europe make it appropriate. The beginning of the Upper Palaeolithic might seem a far cry from the primarily historical cases in this volume, but Gravina, d'Errico, and Bachellerie's 'Disentangling Neanderthal-Modern Human Interactions in Western Europe: A Heuristic Odyssey' and Clack's 'Other than Human Hybridity?' illustrate through temporally and genetically extreme examples a number of the difficulties surrounding discussions of hybridity, acculturation, culture contact, and other ways of dealing with change within and between groups of individuals from different species.

Even ignoring any issues of biological or cultural difference between Neanderthals and modern Humans, the Châtelperronian controversy is about contact and transformation between small-scale hunting and gathering societies, and not the states of colonial culture contact and imperialism. The contributions amply demonstrate the importance of detail and the limitations of the sparse evidence in attempting to understand this earliest case of material culture change being attributed to culture contact. The notions of boundaries and 'contact' seem more applicable to state societies, whereas genetic evidence for the Upper Palaeolithic transition increasingly suggests a fluid situation over thousands of years. Yet at the same time, these people clearly interacted, even if genetic evidence provides the only unambiguous trace, making non-interaction unappealing as a null hypothesis. Despite the spotty archaeological evidence, the question has become not if these people interacted but how this occurred.

Jeb Card, *Observations of a Diverse Discussion on Power and Diversity* In: *Archaeologies of Cultural Contact: At the Interface.* Edited by: Timothy Clack and Marcus Brittain, Oxford University Press. © Oxford University Press 2022. DOI: 10.1093/oso/9780199693948.003.0014

298 JEB CARD

Perhaps the polar opposite case in this volume, certainly temporally, is Gilly Carr's 'The Biographies of Resistant Material Culture in Occupied Landscapes: The Channel Islands and World War II'. For a relatively small island, a wealth of physical and historical evidence is available for a complex situation of power dominance occurring over a short period of time. Yet many of the issues of hybridity or acculturation found in other cases are found here as well. Despite fixed dates beginning and ending the German occupation, Silliman's (2013) question of when hybridity ends is valid, as is if and when it begins at all. Carr notes that many of the modified symbolic items created during the occupation were likely made by veterans of the First World War. Do roots in a previous war between Germany and Britain, one that many have argued was in fact a continuation of the first struggle, negate these objects as hybrid or new? Further, these objects were not only valued by the occupied British but by the occupying Germans who may have purchased the objects as keepsake souvenirs of their military travel and service. Yet these objects were also designed to be subversive defiant symbols of resistance against these same Germans.

One possible comparison to this paradox might be the collection of *zemi* objects by Spanish conquistadors and colonists in the early sixteenth-century Caribbean. At La Isabella, the first Spanish settlement in the Americas, indigenous ornamental and ritual objects including *zemi* images and beads were found with greater frequency in Spanish middens than those associated with indigenous contexts (Deagan and Cruxent 2002: 40). These objects could have been treated by Spaniards as dangerous vessels for indigenous political resistance and literal supernatural demons, and a common pattern in early Spanish colonial indigenous material culture is a decline in non-Christian figural imagery as potentially being political and religious symbols (Garcia-Arevalo 1990: 276). However, their collection by Spaniards has also raised the possibility that like the German soldiers, these forbidden symbols of the conquered became curios or mementos of value to the conquerors.

Facets of the relationship between the past and the present are manifested clearly in 'Cultural Interaction at Palmares: An Archaeology of South American Maroons' by Pedro Funari and Aline de Carvalho. The archaeology of Palmares resonates with the interactive struggles of others relating to empowerment and freedom from persecution and control. As such, the sociopolitical theory and case study informs a number of wider disciplinary questions. Can fluid identity in the past be testimony to the possibility of peaceful living in the present? What is the role of public archaeology in this area? How can archaeological understandings of the past inform today's discourse on diversity, social inclusion, and power relations?

An uncertain spectrum of identity

Do the Channel Island objects take on hybrid form when they enter German hands? Are they no longer hybrids when they enter German hands? We have the names of people who likely made and wore such objects and their documentary testimonies of this time, but use, motivations, and meaning still elude us. Questions of motivation and boundaries are present in Audrey Horning's '"Such Was the End of Their Feast": Violence, Intimacy, and Mimetic Practice in Early Modern Ireland'. Horning examines English colonialism in Ireland, a situation in which, as in Latin America, a small number of foreign colonists ruled large populations. Colonial settings for studies of hybridity are the norm, but the subjects of such studies are usually more enduring products (ceramic vessels, churches, artwork, architecture, languages) that are the indirect outcome of violent colonial encounters but not directly of violence itself. Can an act of violence be evidence of hybrid practices? As with the Channel Island objects, does the identity of the perpetrator of a violent act matter? What about the victims? Horning argues that an English military leader taking advantage of hospitality is a crafty use of cross-cultural knowledge of Gaelic hospitality. In other cases, such as when a band of Irish rebels surprise and kill their English colonial hosts in their illegal alehouse, one imagined scenario is that it was the English who had violated Irish cultural norms. Gaelic hospitality is discussed, but what of English hospitality practices? Do they substantially differ? What role might they have in either accidental cultural misunderstandings or tactical trickery?

Uncertain and tricky ground is the norm in discussing hybridity. As Silliman (2013) has pointed out, perhaps the defining difference between hybridity and other approaches to blending and change is subversion.

The complexity and permeability of identity is the key issue of 'Becoming One or Many: Material Mediation of Difference in Honduras' by Rosemary A. Joyce and Russell N. Sheptak. Their novel study, blending analysis of language, space, and artefacts of western Honduras, finds paradoxical patterns seen in other parts of Latin America. Archaeologically, churches produced the only European goods found in the survey of the colonial sites in the

San Pedro Sula area. Superficially, we might expect churches to act as powerful agents of change in favour of Spanish-imposed culture, yet across the larger region, churches form the core of many indigenous communities. This archaeologically confused situation is matched in the Spanish language of the region, a hybrid Honduran Spanish shaped by pre-Hispanic institutions and the colonial changes that transformed them.

As Card (2013b) has found across the modern border at Ciudad Vieja, the early sixteenth-century villa of San Salvador in El Salvador, movement of people and creation of new social roles and labels through ethnogenesis can affect the material record in subtle ways. Joyce and Sheptak find seemingly local pottery made with new techniques, possibly due to the introduction of African potters. This situation recalls the transformation of pottery production on the Sylvester Manor (Hayes 2013). At Ciudad Vieja, the more obvious products of hybridity are brimmed plates, locally made but adopting new forms from Mediterranean basin majolica. However, the tight chronological control these plates provide has highlighted more subtle shifts in pottery production suggesting generational changes in social networks that point to the roots of new identities (Card 2013b). The more obvious products of hybrid negotiations of colonial power are likely the more ephemeral, while subtle shifts in production are more important for understanding the creation of post-contact Latin America.

Mats Roslund also explores the complex interplay of trade, power, manufacture, and identity in 'Tacit Knowing of Thralls: Style Negotiation and Hybridization among the Unfree in Eleventh- and Twelfth-Century Sweden', but with an interesting difference in the power dynamic. American colonial cases feature a seemingly inevitable European colonization of indigenous peoples, though successful cases of resistance such as the Pueblo Revolt leave both subtle and dramatic material remnants of rebellion (Liebmann 2013). In the case of medieval Sweden, Roslund chronicles shifting technical and stylistic influences that result in different patterns and pacing of change, noted on Baltic ware as the outcome of fluid political fortunes. Also differing in this case is the emphasis on food containers. Some of the examples discussed throughout this volume are technological or 'utilitarian' but many have an element of display. As in the above Spanish colonial cases, these changes signal shifting social forces at a community level more than purposeful expression of identity, with resulting status and network changes consciously or unconsciously impacting production (Bowser and Patton 2008: 124–6; Gosselain 2008: 162–3). Such changes are likely tied, in part, to the movement of individual crafters and the effects on subsequent generations learning their

A DIVERSE DISCUSSION ON POWER AND DIVERSITY 301

craft in new social contexts, and may even purposely distinguish generational cohorts (Bowser and Patton 2008: 128).

Hybrid practices, traditional products

That varying products make sense of related phenomena in the Swedish case highlights a recurring theme in several of the chapters in this volume: that hybrid materials are less important than hybrid practices. This is a major point in 'Nodes of Interaction: Changing Rock Paintings in the Eastern Cape Mountains of South Africa' by Lara Mallen and David G. Pearce. They argue that the breakdown of hunter-gatherer life and the rise of multi-cultural cattle-raiding bands left a mark on nineteenth-century art. Practiced in various types of rock art, artisans mixed their techniques as they worked together in raiding bands. Only limited elements were shared in these groups, and were unshared as the groups broke up. This highlights another theme found in several of the chapters in the volume, that adoption of elements or practices from other people does not need to form a stable or 'blended' new form or identity in the sense generally associated with ideas of cultural creolization (Delle 2000). The notion of sectors of articulation reflects similar findings of material culture adoption by the Arikara (Rogers 1993), that novel practices were more likely to be adopted wholesale rather than syncretically.

The re-inscription and modification with historical change in the case of South African rock art brings to mind the re-inscription of sites elsewhere. Euro-American settlers in the United States explicitly re-inscribed indigenous sites, especially funerary sites, simultaneously appropriating and denying previous peoples. In Middletown, Connecticut, a cemetery was erected on 'Indian Hill' in the nineteenth century after indigenous burials were removed and the indigenous inhabitants described as a 'legend' that had gone extinct. The appropriation of indigenous people as fictive kin served as a charter myth for the new inhabitants (Kavanagh 2011). Marietta was perceived as the first American settlement in Ohio, a symbolic victory for former colonists whom the British Crown had previously forbidden from settling west of the Appalachian Mountains. To commemorate this victory, Marietta's Mound Cemetery became the resting place for a large number of Revolutionary War officers. It was placed in an indigenous mound site, possibly still actively under construction at the point of European contact. During the dedication of the cemetery, the ancient mounds were rhetorically associated with imagined human sacrifices and ties to Mexico (Cutler 1798: 34–6). In order for the Euro-Americans to take possession of them, the mounds were re-inscribed with Latin names worthy of the Neoclassical movement of the day (Woodward and McDonald 2001: 252–5). Indigenous burial grounds, real or imagined, became popular symbols of demonic evil in the twentieth century, playing an important role in folk spirituality in Euro-American culture (Caterine 2014). Are these modified burial grounds hybrid? Are they syncretic? With enough chronological distance, would our answer change?

Some of these issues are explored in Jay B. Haviser's chapter, 'Syncretism and Cognition: African and European Religious and Aesthetic Expressions in the Caribbean'. Using a cognitive approach, syncretism and anti-syncretism are described through a focus on European and African interactive circumstances of fusion in the Caribbean, in particular relating to burial. This case raises the issue of when a syncretistic form becomes recognizable as normative practice distinct from other religious practices. Moreover, through cognitive maps, syncretism is demonstrated to be a dynamic process with creativity and change constrained by 'cognitive acceptability'.

The notion of acceptance is also apparent in Andrew Petersen's chapter 'Creole Identity and Syncretism in the Archaeology of Islam'. Taking a broad geographic perspective, the chapter illustrates a core-periphery framework in which degrees of religious syncretism are maintained to a greater degree in Islam, the youngest of the monotheistic religions, irrespective of the geographical distance to Mecca, whilst in comparison creolized identities become more diverse. Indeed, different geographical areas have their own 'trajectory of Islamicization' leading to distinct Muslim cultures underpinned by different frameworks of sociality, culture, and belief. For example, in Palestine rather than the dominant group imposing change on locals, it was incomers who adapted to their new social environment. This 'bottom up' dimension to hybridity should not be overlooked.

Regarding questions of time and change, 'Unblended America: Contesting Race and Place in Nineteenth-Century New England' by Karen Ann Hutchins-Keim and Mary C. Beaudry critiques both the essentializing frame of cultural survival (see Voss 2015 for discussion of the 'continuity turn') and the universal application of creolization to the African Diaspora. Through examination of several archaeological investigations of nineteenth-century New England, Hutchins-Keim and Beaudry find that local context and diversity of experience are critical. It is issues of diversity in a smaller New England African American population with more diverse origins that make cultural survival and creolization less appropriate perspectives for understanding the history and culture of the region. People with a greater likelihood of at least

A DIVERSE DISCUSSION ON POWER AND DIVERSITY 303

belonging to a second generation in the Western hemisphere, those also more likely to be skilled laborers and far less isolated from white residents are, according to Hutchins and Beaudry, not the ones creolizing into a new subculture. Some of the communities under study here acted as non-white sanctuaries, yet were still economically and politically tied to white communities. Instead of a separate subculture, life for non-white New Englanders was a constant negotiation, partly effected through material culture.

One thread that was not discussed by Hutchins-Keim and Beaudry was interaction between non-white New Englanders of different origins, namely between African Americans and indigenous communities. The creation of blended multi-ethnic communities within colonial New England such as the Lighthouse Site in Connecticut (Feder 1994) or the seventeenth-century Sylvester Manor on Long Island (Hayes 2013) and the subsequent erasure of this history into essentialized 'Black' or 'Indian' labels points out the power of race in the hierarchy of New England society. The importance of race as a division and label over class is a major point made by Hutchins-Keim and Beaudry. Earlier archaeological approaches to African New England emphasized static creole subcultures characterized by poverty, making it difficult to see the multiple values and double consciousness associated with the consumption of 'white' goods such as patent medicines.

The contrast between mass global consumption and the blending of entities, discrete or not, is the key question in Nicole Boivin's 'The Domestication of Difference: Globalization, Hybridity, and Material Culture in Archaeological Perspective'. Elsewhere, various authors have examined questions about the boundaries and utility of hybridity (Card 2013a; Deagan 2013; Frieman 2013; Hauser 2013; Silliman 2013). Both these and Boivin note how different and earlier archaeological concerns have largely ignored the nuances of communication and change. A focus on time and space, or reflexive reactions to that focus, have either emphasized culture history or local-centric evolutionary or historical interpretive frameworks, none of which handle boundary-crossing very well.

Boundaries and definitions become more ambiguous with the emphasis on decentring and subversion emergent in discussions of hybridity. Boivin discusses the notion of technological philosophies. These might initially be taken for 'pure states'. One critique of hybridity is that it assumes pure 'befores' to contrast with a 'blended' after. But what a number of the chapters in this volume make clear is that pure states are an illusion. Boivin's technological philosophies are not immutable; they are by definition conceptions of practice, of how things are done. These philosophies may change through time, but even

304   JEB CARD

when they are somewhat stable they are constantly changing in how they use materials, in what is 'traditional'. Boivin describes deep traditions for boiling foods in East Asia that predate the Holocene; these are by no sense 'pure', as they accommodate new materials, change how things are boiled, how boiled foods are treated, and do not stop waxing and waning in the social value of boiled foods. Nonetheless, a deep, complicated, and fluid tradition can be detected, but not one that approaches any pure state that might sustain a biological metaphor for hybridity (another critique of the concept). As in other chapters in this volume, Boivin's emphasis is on the act of transformation, moving away from concern over 'hybrid' things and towards these things as traces of technological and social actions and contexts.

New labels and the old imperialism

One nuance that Boivin focuses on is an unpacking of the distinction between a traditional kind of hybridity that domesticates the foreign and a newer globalization that wields the corporate power of the neoliberal system to re-mould parts of the globe into a paradoxically homogenous cosmopolitan 'diversity'. Traditional hybridity, according to Boivin, puts a local stamp on the imported, emphasizing local control over consumption and identity. New material culture can be adopted whole, particularly when associated with behavioural complexes not previously existing before being introduced (Rogers 1993). But the emphasis on local transformation as key to understanding hybrids is important. The power of the local can even the flow back to distant producers. Boivin's fastidious African consumers bring to mind how Persian desires for blue and non-figural pottery decorations (based on both religious concerns and the distribution of cobalt) and the importance of the Middle East as a market drove Chinese porcelain makers to transform their products to the point that 'Chinaware' became synonymous with blue floral patterns (Lister and Lister 1987).

Boivin contrasts a more subversive hybridity with a newer form of commodified diversity, where transformation is at the will of multinational corporate forces, not local innovators, domesticating the globe for the sake of capital. Is this a new form of transformation or is it a new version of an older one—imperialism? Commodified difference is sold to urban elites who pride themselves on their ability to sample and to celebrate diversity. The superficial reworking of the exotic, the 'food court'-ification of the world in urban pockets of wealth, strikes me as another symptom of a New Gilded Age,

A DIVERSE DISCUSSION ON POWER AND DIVERSITY   305

a Neo-Victorian celebration of a world under new enlightened management. Rather than a global food court, are we looking at a global curiosity cabinet filled with electronically archived and micro-broadcasted (Twitter, Instagram, etc.) experiences rather than curated artefacts? The disturbing possibility is that our new globalized cosmopolitanism could be a subtle form of imperial nostalgia, a revived memory of another time when globalization created a burgeoning class of elites who paraded their international credentials through the display of command over the exotic, and when the centre of cities around the world predictably had a foreigner or European quarter. Observers on the left (Edsall 2016) and the right (Douthat 2016) offer almost identical diagnoses of a new elite that wears diversity commodified as a class or tribal marker.

The seeming difference between a diversity of practices making up 'traditional' Indian cuisine, and a 'diversity' of choices repeated in the world's elite urban enclaves brings us back to some of the same questions raised in the discussion and criticism of the concept of hybridity (Silliman 2013). Who/what/when is hybrid? Is hybridity imposed on the subjects of colonization and imperialism, as Voss (2015: 664) argues for ethnogenesis? Is it a value-neutral blending, or is subversion central to the framework or phenomenon? The cases and approaches in this volume seem to underline Bhabha's (1994) interstitial and boundary-questioning approach to hybridity. None of them cohere well to essentializing or authoritative frameworks, and those things or practices in question also question these frameworks.

A number of the chapters in this volume question the utility of creolization for archaeology, outside of the narrower linguistic use. While several cases explicitly discuss how new products emerge from the adaptation of practices and materials to new contexts, they also generally agree that these new products are 'traditional'. While they can be viewed as new discrete things, this is not how they are typically seen on the ground. Honduran *Spanish* may differ from Spanish *Spanish*, but from the perspective of eighteenth- (or twenty-first-)century Honduras, it is *español* or just *mi lengua*. The same seems to be the case with patent medicines or rock paintings. Differences are occurring, transformations are propagating, but other than for perhaps brief initial periods, they are novel primarily to the outside observer focused on intense periods of change. Not all of the cases in this volume are inherently unequal or rooted in violence and force, tension and power, but most are.

A similar pattern is found in considerations of ethnogenesis, though as with hybridity, syncretism, and other terms for understanding the 'new', a broad range of application threatens to make the concept useless (Voss 2015).

The creolization framework emphasizes new products, and to some degree, a new stability after these moments, while the hybrids here generally are subversive and unstable. Unsurprisingly, subversion and resistance are more important tools for those on the less powerful side of these violent periods of change or their aftermath, though this makes scholarly rhetoric about hybridity potentially fraught with political dangers for indigenous people (Voss 2015: 657). The exception that makes this point is found in the contributions of Clack and Gravina et al., when they rightly state that the inherent unequal nature of hybridity (or even creolization) interpretive frameworks simply does not apply to the social context of late Neanderthal technological practices. Boivin's globalized homogenous diversity is not new. It is a very visible indicator of dramatic transformations in power, the nature of power, and reactions to these changes, as are most of the hybrid things and practices discussed in this volume.

References

Bhabha, H. 1994. *The Location of Culture*. London: Routledge.

Bowser, B. J. and J. Q. Patton. 2008. 'Learning and transmission of pottery style: women's life histories and communities of practice in the Ecuadorian Amazon'. In M. T. Stark, B. J. Bowser, and L. Horne (eds), *Cultural Transmission and Material Culture: Breaking Down Boundaries*. Tucson: University of Arizona Press, pp. 105–29.

Card, J. J. 2013a. 'Introduction'. In J. J. Card (ed.), *The Archaeology of Hybrid Material Culture*. Center for Archaeological Investigations, Occasional Paper No. 39. Carbondale: Southern Illinois University Press, pp. 1–21.

Card, J. J. 2013b. 'Italianate pipil potters: Mesoamerican transformation of Renaissance material culture in early Spanish colonial San Salvador'. In J. J. Card (ed.), *The Archaeology of Hybrid Material Culture*. Center for Archaeological Investigations, Occasional Paper No. 39. Carbondale: Southern Illinois University Press, pp. 100–30.

Caterine, D. V. 2014. 'Heirs through fear: Indian curses, accursed Indian lands, and white Christian sovereignty in America'. *Nova Religio: The Journal of Alternative and Emergent Religions* 18(1): 37–57.

Cutler, Reverend Doctor, of Hamilton. 1798. 'The charge. In A sermon preached August the 15th, 1798, at Hamilton, at the ordination of the Rev. Daniel Story: to the pastoral care of the church in Marietta, and its vicinity, in the territory of the United States, north-west of the river Ohio, by I. Story', pp. 28–36. Thomas C. Cushing, Salem, Massachusetts. Gale, Cengage Learning. http://

galenet.galegroup.com/servlet/Sabin?af=RN&ae=CY3802848304&srchtp=a& ste=14 (accessed 10 August 2018).

Deagan, K. 2013. 'Hybridity, identity, and archaeological practice'. In J. J. Card (ed.), *The Archaeology of Hybrid Material Culture*. Center for Archaeological Investigations, Occasional Paper No. 39. Carbondale: Southern Illinois University Press, pp. 260–76.

Deagan, K, and J. M. Cruxent. 2002. *Archaeology at La Isabella: America's First European Town*. New Haven: Yale University Press.

Delle, J. A. 2000. 'The material and cognitive dimensions of creolization in nineteenth-century Jamaica'. *Historical Archaeology* 34(3): 56–72.

Douthat, R. 2016. 'The myth of cosmopolitanism'. *New York Times*, 2 July, SR9. Electronic document: http://www.nytimes.com/2016/07/03/opinion/sunday/the-myth-of-cosmopolitanism.html (accessed 10 August 2018).

Edsall, T. B. 2016. 'Is Trump wrecking both parties?'. *he New York Times*, 11 August. Electronic document: http://www.nytimes.com/2016/08/11/opinion/campaign-stops/is-trump-wrecking-both-parties.html (accessed on 11 August 2016).

Feder, K. L. 1994. *A Village of Outcasts: Historical Archaeology and Documentary Research at the Lighthouse Site*. Mountain View: Mayfield Publishing Company.

Frieman, C. 2013. 'Innovation and identity: the language and reality of prehistoric imitation and technological change'. In J. J. Card (ed.), *The Archaeology of Hybrid Material Culture*. Center for Archaeological Investigations, Occasional Paper No. 39. Carbondale: Southern Illinois University Press, pp. 318–41.

Garcia-Arevalo, M. 1990. 'Transculturation in contact period and contemporary Hispaniola'. In D. H. Thomas (ed.), *Columbian Consequences*. Vol. 2: *Archaeological and Historical Perspectives on the Spanish Borderlands East*. Washington, DC: Smithsonian Institution, pp. 269–80.

Gosselain, O. P. 2008. 'Mother Bella was not a bella: inherited and transformed traditions in southwestern Niger'. In M. T. Stark, B. J. Bowser, and L. Horne (eds), *Cultural Transmission and Material Culture: Breaking Down Boundaries*. Tucson: University of Arizona Press, pp. 150–77.

Hauser, M. W. 2013. 'Of earth and clay: Caribbean ceramics in the African Atlantic'. In J. J. Card (ed.), *The Archaeology of Hybrid Material Culture*. Center for Archaeological Investigations, Occasional Paper No. 39. Carbondale: Southern Illinois University Press, pp. 50–79.

Hayes, K. 2013. 'Small beginnings: experimental technologies and implications for hybridity'. In J. J. Card (ed.), *The Archaeology of Hybrid Material Culture*. Center for Archaeological Investigations, Occasional Paper No. 39. Carbondale: Southern Illinois University Press, pp. 425–48.

Kavanagh, S. S. 2011. 'Haunting remains: educating a new American citizenry at Indian Hill cemetery'. In C. E. Boyd and C. Thrush (eds), *Phantom Past,*

Indigenous Presence: Native Ghosts in North American Culture and History. Lincoln: University of Nebraska, pp. 151–78.

Liebmann, M. 2013. 'Parsing hybridity: archaeologies of amalgamation in seventeenth-century New Mexico'. In J. J. Card (ed.), *The Archaeology of Hybrid Material Culture*. Center for Archaeological Investigations, Occasional Paper No. 39. Carbondale: Southern Illinois University Press, pp. 25–49.

Lister, F. C. and R. H. Lister. 1987. *Andalusian Ceramics in Spain and New Spain: A Cultural Register from the Third Century B.C. to 1700*. Tucson: University of Arizona Press.

Rogers, J. D. 1993. 'The social and material implications of culture contact on the Northern Plains'. In J. D. Rogers and S. M. Wilson (eds), *Ethnohistory and Archaeology: Approaches to Postcontact Change in the Americas*. New York: Plenum Press, pp. 73–88.

Silliman, S. W. 2013. 'What, where, and when is hybridity'. In J. J. Card (ed.), *The Archaeology of Hybrid Material Culture*. Center for Archaeological Investigations, Occasional Paper No. 39. Carbondale: Southern Illinois University Press, pp. 486–500.

Voss, B. 2015. 'What's new? Rethinking ethnogenesis in the archaeology of colonialism'. *Latin American Antiquity* 80(4): 655–70.

Woodward, S. L. and J. McDonald. 2001. *Indian Mounds of the Middle Ohio Valley: A Guide to Mounds and Earthworks of the Adena, Hopewell, Cole, and Fort Ancient People*. Granville: The McDonald and Woodward Publishing Company.

Index

Note: Figures are indicated by an italic "*f*" following the page numbers.

For the benefit of digital users, indexed terms that span two pages (e.g., 52–53) may, on occasion, appear on only one of those pages.

Abd al-Malik 257–8
Abiel Smith School 183–4
acculturation 2–4, 14, 31–3, 94–5, 115–18,
    122, 126, 130–2, 134–7, 139–40, 257,
    262–4, 297–8
Acheulean 94, 110–11, 113–14, 136–7,
    see also Mousterian
Adams, M. J. 32
admixture 93–4, 110, 119–25, 134
  of personal ornaments 121–2
  of populations 86
adornment 134–5, *see also* jewelry
advertisements/advertisers 179–80, 188
aesthetic
  body modifications 284
  bonding 288–9
  expressions 267–92
  material forms 5–6
  practice 291–2
  processes 34
  quality 273–4
  refinement 289–90
  syncretism 286–91
  tastes 33–4
aesthetics 16, 289–92
Afrasiab 259–60
African
  aesthetics 33–4, 267–92
  ancestry 270
  burial 287–9
  children 272–3, 291
  coastline 261
  cognition 267–9, 273–4, 292
  consumers 304
  cultural retentions 187
  cultural traditions 285–6
  culture 243, 267, 273–4
  customs 291

  descent/descendants 63–4, 66, 72–6,
    78–80, 178–9, 181–2, 188–90, 242–3,
    275*f*, 276–7, 282, 290–1
  domestic workers 271–3
  groups 72, 264–5
  populations 62–4, 124–5, 267, 289–91
  potters 300
  religions 268–9, 274
  religiosity 237
  religious expression 267
  religious syncretism 16
  revelations 269–70
  rock art 44
  settlements 261–2
  traders 33–4
  traits 243–4
  see also East Africa, North Africa,
    South Africa, West Africa
African-American
  archaeological sites 188–9
  communities 181–3, 185, 303
  consumption 184–5
  culture 178, 243
  dialect 182–3
  domestic sites 183–5
  experience 183
  families 182
  identity 243
  life 178–83
  mind-set 187
  occupants 182, 185
  population 182, 302–3
  practices 243
  societies 243
African Americans 178–9, 183–91,
    see also Blacks
African-Arabian axis 261–2
African Baptist Church 183–4

310 INDEX

African-Creole
  beliefs 282
  fetish objects 278f
  material culture 274–6, 284
  practices 269–70, 274
  religions 268, 270
  religious artefacts 274–7
  religious bundles 277
  religious contexts 282
  religious groups 274–6
  religious objects 271
  religious practices 269–70, 273–9, 282–4
  religious symbolism 282–4
  religious themes 284
  societies 268
African-European
  aesthetic syncretism 286–91
  interactive contexts 268–70
  religious syncretism 274–84
  syncretic processes 267
  syncretism 291
African Meeting House 183–4
African Methodist Episcopal Church 183, 186–7
Africans 62–3, 66, 76, 78–80, 179–84, 238–9, 242, 249, 261, 267–70, 273–4, 276, 284–7, 290–2, see also Blacks
agency 3–4, 7–8, 26, 32–4, 94, 127–8, 168, 174, 187, 196, 207, 213, 261
agrarian
  contexts 227–8
  economy 233–4
  settings 227–8, 234
  settlement 216
agricultural
  fields 78
  goods and foodstuffs 180
  labour 229–30
  practices 28–9, 264
agro-pastoralists 44, 47–9
Ahmarian 136–7
Ahnaf ibn Qais 259–60
Åhus 228
Akey, J. 93–4
Akinnaso, D. N. 238
Alagoas 241f
Alberti, B. 11–12
alcohol 204–5
Aldhouse-Green, M. 92–3

Allen, S. J. 241–4
alliances 5–6, 76–7, 206–7
Allied
  soldiers 165–6, 169–70
  trench art 166
  victory 164
Allier 112–13, 130–1
altars 277–9, 279f, 282
Alves, I. 124–5
Amazon 241f, 242–3
America 37, 178–91, 238, 246
  citizenship 183
  clocks 34–5
  colonial cases 300–1
  colonies 179–80
  crocodile 86–7
  settlement 301–2
  society 190–1
  styles 25
  see also United States
American Revolutionary War 179, 301–2
American South 6, 179–80, 189–90
Americas 26, 62, 65, 70–1, 76, 131, 179–80, 207, 237–8, 241–5, 268, 284–5, 289, 298
Amerindians 62
AMH 89f, 136–7
analytical
  approach 2–3, 114
  concepts 1, 94–5
  logistics 221
  schemes 7–9
  tools 4–5, 27, 214, 221
  value 1, 9, 207
Anatolia 256
anatomically modern humans 90, 93–4, 111–18, 123–6, 131–2, 137–40, 169–70, see also modern humans
Andara, Eugenia Gertrudis 72–3, 76, 79–80
Andes 29–30
Andrews, S. C. 14–15
Angel, J. L. 284–5, 289
Anglo-American pattern 184–5
Anglo-Norman invasions 197
Anglophone areas 271, 283–4
Anglophone Caribbean 272–4
Anglo-Scandinavian cooking vessels 232–3
Anglo-style homes 187

INDEX   311

animals 11–12, 28–9, 46, 73–4, 76, 85,
    92–3, 100, 121–2
  bones 184–5, 261–2
  husbandry 13, 216
  medicinal properties 271
  sacrifices 271, 277–9
  teeth 127–8, 134–5
Anjar 263*f*
Annals of the Four Masters 199
Antczak, K. A. 190–1
anthropological
  circles 114
  contexts 238
  investigations 284
  literatures 237
  studies 3
anthropologists 85, 102, 162, 214, 282
anthropology 26–7, 85
Antigua 275*f*
Appadurai, A. 27
appropriation 7, 13–14, 98–9, 159, 162–4,
    166–74, 268, 301–2
Apter, A. 10–11, 268
Arab
  armies 254–7, 259–60
  coin 258*f*
  culture 254
  heartland 259
  ideas 262–4
  identity 254, 262–5
  invaders 261
  patrons 258
  society 254–5
  tribes 254–5
  values 254
  writing 257–8
Arabia 256, 261
Arabian Peninsula 254–5
Arabic 254, 256, 258*f*, 259–60
Arabs 254–60, 262–4
architecture 15, 28–9, 77–8, 256,
    258–60, 299
  features 198–9
  form 258
  materials 4–5
Arcy-sur-Cure 94, 114–15, 118–20, 127–8,
    129*f*, 135*f*, 140–1
Arikara 301
Armenia 25–6

artefacts 3, 66–7, 90–2, 94, 114, 119–20,
    122–3, 126–8, 130–5, 137, 140–1,
    161–2, 164–6, 169–73, 187–8, 190–1,
    215, 234–5, 244, 271, 274–9, 282–4,
    286–7, 299–300, 304–5
Asia 95, 261
  Central 6, 16, 32, 255*f*, 256, 259–60,
    264–5
  East 25, 30–2, 124–5, 264, 303–4
  South 25–6
  Southeast 25–6, 32, 110–11, 261–2
  Western 264
Asian immigrants 7–8
Asian populations 124–5
Asselin, G. 132–4
assemblages 4–5, 11–12, 14, 73–4, 90–1,
    94, 119–22, 132–4, 188–9, 204,
    274–6, 284
assemblage theory 11–12
assimilation 2–4, 7–8, 13, 44, 137–8,
    188, 268–9
Atlantic World 179–80, 207
Atwood, Margaret
  Oryx and Crake 84, 102–3
Aurignacian 91–2, 94, 112–24, 126–31,
    134–6, 139–40
Australopithecine fossil data 89
Australopithecus africanus 89*f*
autochthonous
  development 94
  hunter-gatherers 44–7
  Neanderthal populations 115–16
Azevedo, C. M. 243–4

Bachellerie, F. 117*f*, 119–20, 127, 132–6,
    133*f*, 140–1
Bacho Kiro 124–5
Baden-Württemberg 91–2, 91*f*
Bae, C. 110–11
Bailey, S. E. 114–15
Baker, H. C. 88
Baker, V. G. 184–5, 188–90
Bakhtin, M. 10–11, 67–8
Balkans 126
Ball, W. 259–60
Baltic Sea 217–19, 228–9
Baltic ware 211, 212*f*, 215, 217–20, 218*f*,
    222–8, 224*f*, 229*f*, 230*f*, 231–4, 232*f*,
    300–1

312 INDEX

Bamiyan 259–60
Bandura, A. 100
Banks, W. 114, 122, 126–7, 137–8
Bantu 47–52, 270
Barbados 272*f*, 284–5, 287–8
bardic poetry/style 200–2
Barnard, N. 31
Barnard, T. C. 205–7
Baron, R. 5–6
Barth, F. 49, 55–6
Bar-Yosef, O. 110–11, 118–21
Basra 259–60
Bastide, R. 243–4
Bates, M. 257–8
Battle of the Yellow Ford 198
Battle-Baptiste, W. 190–1
   Black Feminist Archaeology 188–9
Bayesian modelling/models 119–23, 126, 128–30, 129*f*
beads 28–9, 33–4, 77, 277, 298
Beaudry, M. 183–4, 190–1, 246
Bednarik, R. 90–1
Belfer-Cohen, A. 110–11
Bell-Cross, S. M. 47–8
Bell, W. 163–4
Benazzi, S. 123–4
Bentley, J. H. 28–9, 36
Berawan 32
Berbers 254–5
Berkland, E. P. 183–4
Berlin, I. 179–80
Berry, J. 137
Bethel Church 183
Bethel, E. R. 185
Bhabha, H. 11, 87–8, 95, 201, 204–5, 305
Bilby, K. M. 271, 273–4
Binneman, J. 47
biographies 159–75, 190–1
biological
   affiliation 114
   affinity 122
   applications 86
   approaches 102
   arena 86
   associations 85
   attributes 98–9
   determinism 116–18
   difference 297

domains 86–7
   models 86
   population 139–40
   significance 68–9
   species 86–7
biology 7, 28–9, 86–8
Bircher, J. 88
Birka 223
black earthenware 223–33, 225*f*
Black, N. 77
Black Panther 247
Blacks 78–9, 179, 181–3, 188–90, 239, 243–4, 303, *see also* African Americans, Africans
Blades, J 162–3
Blaisdell-Sloan, K. 64–5, 73–4
Blakey, M. 284–5
Blench, R. 25–6
Blevins, J. P. 253
Blundell, G. 45–6, 50, 52, 55–6
Bodley, J. 201–2
body painting 134–5
Boesch, C. 12–13, 85
Boesch-Acherman, H. 12–13, 85
Bohunician 136–7
Boivin, N. 25–6, 28–31
Bombay 25–6, 33–4
Bon, F. 114, 139–40
bone/bones 32, 73–4, 86, 93, 103, 115, 119–20, 122, 127–8, 135*f*, 184–5, 261–2, 280, 288–9
   buttons 277
   fragments 122
   industry 121
   manufacture 94
   points 127–8
   samples 129*f*
   tools 115–16, 121–2, 131–2, 134–7, 135*f*, 139
Bonnie, K. E. 96–7
Bordes, F. 113–15, 117*f*, 118
Bordes, J.-G. 114, 117*f*, 118–21, 123, 130–4, 140–1
Bordian facies 136–7
Borneo 32, 96
Boston 179–84, 186–7
Bourdieu, P. 245–6
Bowser, B. J. 300–1
Bradfield, N. 53

INDEX 313

brain 100–1, 214–15
  development 89–90
  evolution 88, 100
  lateralization 89
Braintree 179
Brandstetter, A.-M. 3
Brazil 6, 15–16, 238–42, 247–9
  archaeology 240–1, 249
  culture 237–8
  jiu-jitsu 25
  national identity 237–8
  religious practices 237
  society 16
  wares 242–4
Breen, C. P. 198
Brereton, B. 271–2
Breuil, H. 112–14
Bridgewater 186–7
Brink, S. 220
Britain 26, 173, 298
  ceramics 189–90
  colonial occupation/rule 3, 261
  Crown 301–2
  expansion 207
  neighbours 206–7
  settlers 203
  tenants 203
Brittain, M. 11–12
Britton, Colonel (Douglas Ritchie) 161
Brives, C. 95
Bronk-Ramsey, C. 126, 137–8
Bronx Zoo Monkey House 285–6
bronze
  casting 31
  lion 259f, 261–2
  metallurgy 31
  vessels 31
Bronze Age 31, 260
Brooks, C. M. 187
Brooks, J. F. 70
Browne, John 204–5
Bruner, E. 89–90
Bryceson, D. F. 28–9
Buddhist beliefs 264
Buddhist monasteries 259–60
Bulgaria 124–5, 136–7
Bullen, A. K. 184–5
Bullen, R. P. 184–5
Burghardt family 188–90

burial/reburial 93, 118–19, 256, 261–2,
    271, 274–7, 282–90, 283f, 301–2
Burke, P. 86–8, 215
Burr, James T. 187
Bushmen 50
bustles 53, 53f
Byzantine
  coins 257–8
  identity 258
  tradition 257

Cáceres Gomez, R. 63, 75–6, 78–9
Caen Prison 163–4
Cameron, A. 262–4
Campeche 284–5
Canada 4–5
Candelaria (Masca) 63, 64f, 65, 68,
    71–3, 78–9
Cañizares-Esguerra, J. 65–6
Canning, G. 204–5
Canny, N. P. 197–9, 203–5
Cape Colony 53
Cape Verde 6
capitalism 8, 35–8, 244–5, 273–4
Capps, B. 86
Captaincy General of Guatemala 63
Cara, A. C. 5–6
Card, J. J. 1, 76, 140–1, 300, 303
Carey, V. 164–5
Caribbean 6, 16, 179–80, 214, 261,
    267–92, 298, 302
  coast 66–7, 78–9
  colonies 274
  outpost 65
  plantation households 271–2
  ports 63
  sites 75–6
  territories 274
Carlson, M. 238
Carneiro, E. 237–8
Caron, F. 119–20, 135f
Carr, G. 26–8, 159–61, 164–6, 174, 298
Carrilho, Fernão 240
Carrion, J. 137–8
Caterine, D. V. 301–2
Catholic
  cemetery 276–7
  Church 269–70, 274–6
  contexts 282

314 INDEX

Catholic (*cont.*)
  Ireland 197
  leadership 197–8
  priest 271, 283–4, 283*f*
  religiosity 237
  religious observances 78
  Spain 240
Catholicism 77, 242, 269–70
Catholics 48, 205–7
Caulfield, Sir Toby 206–7
Caura River 247
Cavan 203
Central America 66, 72
Central Europe 136–7
Ceramic, *see also* bowls, cooking
    pots/vessels, earthenware, greywares,
    jars, pottery/potters
  form 76
  models 31
  processes 31
  production 15, 75–6
  technology 30–1
  traditions 211, 217–19, 231, 233
  vessels 184–5, 188–9, 215, 299
ceramics 29–30, 32, 73–4, 77, 184–5, 187,
    189–90, 204, 259–60, 277
Ceuta 239, 244–5
Challinor, E. 6
Challis, W. 44, 55–6
Chambers, D. 179–80
Chan, A. 178–81, 183–4
Chandler, Hannah Foster 184–5
Channel Islands 14, 159–75, 298–9
  Guernsey 159, 163–8, 167*f*
  Jersey 159, 163–4, 166, 168
  Jersey War Tunnels 163
  Liberation Day 172–3
  Sark 159
  V-sign badges/campaign 14, 161–73,
    167*f*
Charlemount Fort 206
Charles I, King 206–7
Châtelperron 112–13, 130–1
Châtelperronian 14, 94–5, 101, 111–18,
    117*f*, 123–4, 126–8, 130–2, 134–41
  blades 133*f*
  deposits 119–20, 122
  evidence 94
  layers 118–19, 121–2, 130

levels 114–15, 119–23, 128–30,
    129*f*, 135*f*
  points 112–15, 119–20, 132–4
Chesapeake 179–80
childcare 16, 271–2
child cognition 271–4
Child, D. 53
childhood 222, 272–3
children 16, 70, 72, 76, 86, 119–20, 182–3,
    186–7, 219–21, 233–4, 267–9,
    272–3, 291
chimpanzees 84–5, 88, 96–100, 285–6
  behaviour 98
  cognition 98–9
  communicative gestures 14
  communities 85, 99
  groups 12–13, 99
  social hierarchy 99–100
  societies 101–2
  see also great apes
China 32, 34–5, 259, 261–2, 264
  bronze casting 31
  bronzes 31
  culture 31
  elements 264–5
  noodles 30–1
  porcelain 304
Chomsky, N. 90
Christian, D. 28–9
Christian
  cross 237
  elements 269–70
  marriages 70
  missions 229–30
  practices 77
  theology 10
Christianity 183, 253–4, 262–4, 268–70
Christians 69–70, 238, 254, 269–70, 273
cigarette lighters 165–73, 167*f*
Ciudad Vieja 300
cognition 85, 101–2, 267–92
cognitive
  arguments 135–6
  capabilities 89–90, 93, 101
  capacity 90, 92–3, 100–1, 115–18, 137
  changes 88
  conditions 85, 98–9
  constraints 9–10
  differences 136–7

domains 92
evolution 88–93
fluidity 90–1
functions 90–1, 100–1
knowledge 221
modelling 100
modernity 90
response 284
worlds 98–9, 101
Cohen, R. 5–6, 110, 214–15
coinage/coins 159, 161, 164–8, 171–2,
257–60, 271, 277–9
collagen 122, 127–8
Colley, Rachel 186–7
colonialism 2–3, 7–8, 13, 16, 62, 174,
244–6, 261, 299
colonists 53, 69–70, 79, 207, 240, 244–5,
298–9, 301–2
colonization 4–5, 10, 27, 32–5, 38, 65–7,
77–8, 112–13, 137–8, 237, 300–1, 305
colonizers 3–4, 110, 290–2
Colpe, C. 238
Comayagua 63, 69
Combe-Cappelle 113
Combe Grenal 135–6
Congo 285–6, 289–90
Connecticut 180–2, 301–3
Connelly, S. J. 202–3, 206–7
Connet, N. 119–20, 123
conquerors/conquest 44, 197–8, 202, 205,
244–5, 254–60, 262–4, 298
Continental Army 185
continuity 8–9, 13, 54–5, 94, 132–7, 162,
174, 196, 213–14, 234, 259–60, 262–4,
282–4, 302–3
Cook, I. 37
Cook, J. 91–2
cooking/cuisine 25–6, 28–9, 31, 37, 213,
217, 220, 226–7, 271–2, 305
cooking pots/vessels 213, 225–8, 230–5, 280
Coolidge, F. 91–2, 100–1
Cooper, J. 34
Crais, C. 49, 56
Crang, P. 37
creativity 4–8, 10–11, 27–8, 84–5, 90,
100–1, 174, 196, 207–8, 302
creole identity 55–6, 253–65, 302
creolization 1–2, 4–11, 14–16, 25–8, 38–9,
55, 62, 65, 78–80, 139–41, 178, 183–4,

187, 190–1, 213–16, 222–3, 233–5,
238–42, 253, 256–7, 261, 268–9,
301–3, 305–6
Cretan peoples 268
Cro-Magnon man 113
Crosby, A. W. 25–6
cross-cultural
consumer 36
contact 140–1
interaction 48–50
knowledge 299
Cruikshank, C. 162–3
Crusader occupation 262–4
Cruxent, J. M. 298
Cuba 35, 270
Cuban cosmological belief systems 34
Cuculí, Blás 68–9
cultural change 1–2, 4, 8–10, 12, 131–2,
140–1, 213–14, 234
cultural contact 1–16, 26–9, 35, 37–9, 94,
115–16, 130–1, 140–1,
238–9, see also intercultural
Curaçao 272f, 276
Curl, J. S. 203
Currat, M. 124–5
Currie, E. 92–3
Cusick, J. 3
Cutler, Reverend Doctor 301–2
Czechia 124–5

Danes 229–30
Dani, A. H. 259
Danish
cooking vessels 231–2
guests 226–7
kings 229–30
rulers 219
see also Denmark
Danish–Obodrite campaigns 229–30
Dansgaard–Oeschger events 137–8
Dansgaard, W. 137–8
Daugava River 219
David, F. 120–1
Davies, W. 94
Dawdy, S. L. 187
Dayet, L. 135–6
Deacon, T. 90
Deagan, K. 215, 298, 303
de Carvalho, A. 240

316 INDEX

de Certeau, M. 13–14, 79
Dediu, D. 93
Deetz, J. 178, 184–5, 187–90
  In Small Things Forgotten 187
defiance 14, 160–75, 298
Delporte, H. 112–14
Demars, P.-Y. 114–16, 134
demographic
  contingency 113
  expansions 131–2
  history 110–11
  interactions 137
  patterns 138
  replacements 110
  shifts 138
  survival 79
  terms 160–1
demographics/demography 125–6, 137–8,
  179–83, 186–7, 203
Denham, T. 32
Denisova Cave 124–5
Denisovans 93–4, 124–5
Denmark 216, 218f, 219, 228, 233–4,
  see also Danish
Dennell, R. 110–11
dental modification 284–6, 285f, 288–92,
  see also teeth
de Renzy, M. 202–3
d'Errico, F. 90–1, 94, 110, 116–20, 122–3,
  127, 130–1, 134–5, 137–8
Derricourt, R. 47–8
Descola, P. 102
Desrochers, R. E. 179–80
Detroit, F. 84–5
de Waal, F. 96–7
Dewar, M. 198–9
difference 4–9, 11–13, 25–39, 49, 52–3,
  55–6, 62–80, 84, 86, 89–90, 96,
  119–22, 130, 132–7, 160, 169, 179,
  213–17, 219, 222, 234, 243–4, 247,
  257–8, 268–9, 297, 299, 304–5
Discamps, E. 120–1, 127–8, 132–4
Discoid-Denticulate Mousterian
  level IX 119–20
diversity 1, 6–8, 37, 62, 73–4, 78–9, 86–8,
  98–9, 125, 137, 238–9, 246, 249,
  289–90, 297–306
DNA 86, 90–1, 93–4, 124–5, 286, 288–90
Dobres, M.-A. 134–5, 221
dolls 271, 279, 280f, 281–4

domestic
  animals 28–9, 73–4, 86
  life 204
  management 271–2
  plants 28–9
  practices 76
  production 15
  refuse 261–2
  servants 271–2
  sites 178, 183–5
  workers 16, 271–3
domestication 25–39
Dominican Order 274–7
Donnan, E. 180
Donnelly, C. J. 203–4
Douthat, R. 304–5
Dowson, T. A. 44–6, 56
Drakensberg 44, 45f, 47–9, 55–6
Drapers' Company 204
Duarte, C. 93–4
Du Bois, W. E. B. 184f, 188–90
Dussubieux, L. 28–9
Dutch 179–80, 240, 242, 244, 246, 271,
  274–7, 286–7, *see also* Holland
Dutch Brazil 242–3, 247–8
Dutch Caribbean 267, 272–3
Dutch East India Company 53

earthenware 65, 74–6, 79, 187, 223–33,
  225f, 280
East Africa 6, 16, 28–9, 32–4, 97–8, 256,
  261–2, 264–5
Eastern Cape 44–57, 45f, 301,
  see also South Africa
ecological
  convergence 116–18
  differences 96
  niches 28–9, 138
  perspective 110–11
  reconfigurations 137–8
  shifts 94
  systems 26
economic
  activities 47, 50, 55
  analyses 132–4
  capital 14–15
  changes 47
  circumstances 216
  conditions 213, 233
  exchange 204–5

INDEX 317

foundations 8
framework 219–20
freedom 185
impact 181
practices 54
rank 190
relations 231–2
resistance 160
shift 54–5
significance 36
situation 188–9
success 178–9
surplus 223
value 181
economics/economy 4–5, 26, 56, 180–2,
  216, 233–4
Edsall, T. B. 304–5
Egypt 254–6
Eliade, M. 92–3
Elizabeth I, Queen 197–9, 201
Ellenberger, D. F. 48
El Pendo 130–1
El Salvador 300
emancipation 178, 181–7, 276
England 179–80, 197, 200–1
  coins 165–6
  colonialism 299
  colony 205
  cotton 33–4
  Crown 201
  elites 206
  forces 197–8
  guards 172–3
  homes 207
  influence 173–4
  language 25, 161, 201
  law 197, 202–3
  leadership 197–8
  manners 198
  military 201–2, 299
  people 196, 202
  planter 198–9
  policy 197–8
  power 197
  practices 204–5, 299
  settlers 198, 204–5
  shilling 164
  society 202–3
  tenants 204
  throne 206–7

victory 163–4
wares 204
environment 96, 99–102, 214, 219, 231,
  243–4, 256–7, 268–9, 273–4, 302
environmental
  adaptation 87–8, 95, 140
  factors 92, 97–8
  inhabitation 90
  pressures 94
  stimuli 90–1
Eriksen, T. H. 214–15, 253
Essex, Earl of 198–202
ethnic
  attitude 268–9
  background 234–5, 246, 270
  communities 303
  composition 216
  food court 37
  groups 212–13, 244, 254–5, 264,
    282, 289–90
  identification 134–5
  identities 219, 259–60, 262–4
  integration 4–5
  interactions 242–3
  labels 80
  origin 254
  relations 288–9
  roots 78
  terms 262–4
ethnicity 4–5, 187, 242, 245–8, 264–5
ethnogenesis 1–2, 4–10, 62, 65, 79–80, 243,
  297, 305–6
ethnogenetic
  approach 242–5
  projects 10
  record 116–18, 131, 137
ethnomusicology 26–7
etymology 7, 86, 220, 245–6
Eurasia 84–5, 93–4, 125, 139–40
Euro-American cognitive
    fear-fantasy 285–6
Euro-American culture 301–2
Eurocentric bias 268
Eurocentric roots 6
European
  aesthetic expression 267
  archaeological record 111–13
  children 16, 267, 272–3
  clocks 34–5
  cognition 268–9, 284, 291–2

318 INDEX

European (*cont.*)
  colonialism/colonization 10, 13, 53, 237,
    261, 271, 285–6, 290–2, 300–1
  culture 237–8
  dealers 247–8
  dress 53
  expansion 110–11, 208
  goods 299–300
  greywares 226–7, 231–2
  hegemony 274
  housing 188
  imperialist ideas 87
  institutions 77–8
  interactions 267, 271–4
  languages 268
  magistrates 49
  materials 77
  missionaries 269–70
  philosophy 273–4
  populations 62–3, 125, 131, 286
  religion 16, 267–92, 302
  settlers 48
  society 243
  tradition 73–4
  wares 189–90, 242–4
Europeans 62–3, 65–6, 179, 239, 244–5,
  247, 249, 253, 267, 269–70, 272–4,
  284–6, 290–2
Evans, A. 163–4
Evans, C. 6
excavations 64–5, 115, 121–4, 130–1,
  183–5, 227*f*, 261–2, 274–82, 278*f*, 286–8
Excoffier, L. 124–5

Falla, F. 162–4
farming/farms 25–6, 47–50, 70, 181,
  216–17, 220, 222, 227–30, 240, 244–6
faunal remains 120–1, 127–8, 130–1
Federal Census 182
Feder, K. L. 303
Feely, J. M. 47–8
Fenton, J. P. 14–15
Ferguson, L. 178
Fernandes, L.E. O. 238
Fernandez Olmos, M. 268, 270–1, 282
Ferrera, Juan Lazaro 72–3
Ferrera, Santiago 72–3
fetishes 27, 270, 278*f*, 282–3
figurines 90–2, 91*f*, 261–2

finger painting 51–2, 51*f*
Finland 216–17, 219, 225*f*, 226–7
Finlayson, C. 137–8
Finno-Ugrian pottery 225*f*
Fitzgerald, Gerald (Earl of Desmond) 198
Fletcher, W. J. 137–8
Flynn effect 88
Fon culture 270
Foner, E. 185–6
food 25–6, 29–31, 37, 73–4, 76, 79, 98,
  171–2, 174, 180, 187, 189–90, 200–1,
  204–7, 215, 220, 241, 243, 271–3,
  277–9, 279*f*, 300–1, 303–5
Fossey, Dian 96
fossils 89, 93–4, 110–11, 121–2,
  134–5, 135*f*
Foster, Lucy 184–5, 184*f*, 188–90
Fowler, C. 12
France 94, 112–15, 117*f*, 123–4, 127,
  130–4, 163–6, 289
Francis, P. 28–9
Frazer, J. G. 285–6, 289–90
Frazier, E. F. 36, 243–4
Freitas, D. 243–4
Freyre, G. 237–8
Fridman, E. 92–3
Friedman, J. 26–7, 35
Fuller, D. Q. 25–6, 28–31
Funari, P. 237, 240–2, 246–7, 298–9
Fu, Q. 124
Fynn, H. F. 50

Gaelic
  Catholics 205–6
  conscript 206–7
  culture 197–8, 200–2
  elite 201
  historians 202–3
  hospitality 200–1, 299
  leadership 201
  lords 197–202
  right 204–5
  world 204
Galdikas, B. 96
Galef, B. 85
Gallivan, M. 196
Gamble, C. 89
Ganga-Zumba 240
Gardin, J.-C. 259–60

INDEX 319

Garrison, William Lloyd 186–7
Genequand, D. 258
genes 87–8, 114–15, 124
genetic
  admixture 86–7, 93–4, 124–5, 134
  assimilation 138
  changes 28–9
  composition 87–8
  diversity 88, 125
  evidence 48–9, 93–4, 125–6, 297
  exchange 88, 124–5
  hybridization 28–9
  introgression 124–5
  mixing 55–6
  modification 86
  purity 86–7
  signature 124–5
genomes 124–5
geographical
  areas 52–3, 180, 216–17, 237, 302
  boundaries 49
  coherence 27
  contexts 238
  differences 222
  displacement 37
  locations 233
  meaning 214
  perspective 302
  range 116–18
  scale 228–9
  scope 2
  segregation 86–7
geography 96, 125, 259
German
  administration 170–1
  army 159
  bread bowl 167f
  censure 165–6
  coin 165
  cooking vessels 231–2
  Gestapo 164–5, 168
  Hansa 217–19
  influence 223–5
  material culture 173–4
  military forces 14
  objects 171–2
  occupation 159–60, 172, 298
  orders 161
  POWs 172–3

  soldiers 166–71, 173, 298
  trench art 166–8
  V-sign 163–4
German Occupation Museum 165
Germans 91f, 159–60, 162–73, 298
Gernon, L. 199
Ghirotto, S. 124–5
Gillespie, R. 206
global
  arbitrage 34
  colonialism 62
  communication 37
  connections 244–5
  consumer base 36
  consumption 303
  corporation 36–7
  cuisine 37
  currency 35
  food court 304–5
  goods 32–3
  images 36
  interactions 36
  marketing 37–8
  migration 88
  slavery 215–16
  trade 32–4
  travels 273–4
globalization 2, 25–39, 238–9, 304–6
gold 34–5, 63, 257–8
Gold Coast 180, 288–9
Gombe 97–8
Gombe Chimpanzee War 99–100
Goodall, J. 96, 98–100
Goodwin, Prince 185–6
Goody, J. 30–1
Goose, D. H. 289–90
Gosden, C. 161–2, 245–6
Gosselain, O. P. 300–1
Götland 218f
Granger, J. E. 47
grave sites 274–7, 279f, 282–4
Gravina, B. 94, 118–20, 130–4
great apes 85, 96, see also chimpanzees
Great Barrington 188
Great Depression 3
greywares 226–7, 231–3
Griqua 48–9, 55–6
Groome, J. R. 289–90
Grosby, S. 245–6

320 INDEX

Grossberg, L. 37
Grotte des Fées 112–13, 130–1
Grotte du Renne 94, 114–15, 118–23,
  127–8, 129*f*, 134, 135*f*
Grün, R. 110–11
Guillebon, Xavier de 163–4, 168–9
Guimarães, C. M. 241
Guinea 180
Gulf of Riga 219
Gundaker, G. 6, 190
Gunn, B. 28–9
Gunz, P. 89–90

Hahn, P. H. 162
Haile-Salassie, Y. 84–5
Hair, P. E. H. 47–8
Haiti 270
Haitian Catholic Community
  282–4, 283*f*
Halland 218*f*, 234
Hall, G. M. 179–80
Hall, M. 246
Hall, S. 6, 10–11, 44
Hammond-Tooke, D. 47–50, 56
Handler, J. S. 271, 273–4, 284–91
Handler, R. 248
Hanks, W. F. 67–8, 77, 80
Hannerz, H. 238–9
Haour, A. 284–5
Haraway, D. 12–13, 95
Harinck, G. 47
Harvey, W. 163–4
Hasemann, G. 64–5
Hauser, M. 75–6, 303
Haviser, J. B. 268–9, 273–6, 284,
  286, 288–9
Hawks, J. 88, 125
Hayden, B. 90–1, 138
Hayes, K. 300, 303
Heep, G. 127
Hellenistic tradition 257
Henn, B. M. 110
Henry VIII, King 197
Henry, L. 51–2
Henry the Lion 226–7
Hershkovitz, I. 110–11
Herskovits, M. J. 243–4
Herzog, T. 65
Heywood, L. 267, 269

Hicks, D. 246
Higham, T. 119–20, 122–3, 126–30,
  129*f*, 271–2
Hindi 25
Hindu dinner 25–6
Hindu figurines 261–2
Hobart, J. H. 47
Hobsbawm, E. 54
Hobson, J. 34
Hodgson, J. 47
Hohlenstein-Stadel Cave 91*f*
Holanda, S. B. de 237–8
Holland 239–40, *see also* Dutch
Holloway, R. 88–9, 100
Holy Land 256–7
Holy Roman Empire 226–7
hominin 90, 93–4, 124–5
  ancestors 102–3
  brain 88–9
  cognitive evolution 88
  endocasts 89*f*
  expansions 110–11
  groups 127–8
  species 89, 94
Homo erectus 89*f*
Homo sapiens 84–5
Honduran
  authorities 77
  colonial dialogics 68
  colonial history 66
  colonial practices 65–7
  colony 69, 80
  Spanish 67, 69
Honduras 4, 13–14, 62–80, 64*f*,
  299–300, 305
Hong Kong 25
Horning, A. 203–5, 299
Horton, J. O. 179–80, 182–3
Horton, L. E. 179–80, 182–3, 185–6
Horton, M. 28–9, 259*f*, 261–2, 264–5
Howe, C. 185–6
Howe, S. 205–6
Hublin, J.-J. 110–11, 114–16, 119–20,
  122–5, 127–30, 129*f*, 134–7
hunter-gatherers 44–50, 301
  art/paintings 44–5, 46*f*, 51–2, 51*f*
  communities 48–9, 54–5
  groups 112, 132, 138
  material culture 52

INDEX 321

populations 131
ritual 50, 56
Huntington, R. 32
Hutchins, K. A. 185
hybridity 1–2, 4–14, 25–39, 55–6, 62, 65,
  76–7, 80, 84–103, 139–41, 159–60,
  166–8, 170–1, 173–4, 196, 213–16,
  223–33, 297–300, 302–6
  biological hybridity 85–7, 93–4,
    102, 303–4
hybridization 7, 13–15, 26–9, 32–9,
  55, 66–7, 86–7, 92–4, 99, 102, 112,
  118, 137–41, 207–8, 211–35,
  237, 300–1
hybrids 8–11, 28–39, 86–7, 160, 219,
  222, 299, 304–6

Iberian administrators 66
Iberian Peninsula 70, 138
Iberian Spanish 69
Iberian Union 239–40
Igbo 271
imagery 52–4, 56, 93, 165–6, 298
images 13, 36–7, 51–2, 54–6, 77–8,
  160–1, 165–6, 217, 243, 248,
  257–8, 298
imitation 93–4, 98, 100, 134–6, 182–3,
  201, 223
imperialism 87, 297, 304–6
India 30–1, 256, 261–2, 264
Indian
  ancestry 240
  cuisine/food 25–6, 305
  dyed cloth 33–4
  labels 303
  Shivaism 259–60
  slaves 239
  towns 63
  villages 25–6, 76–7
Indian Ocean 2, 13, 28–9, 255f, 261–2
Indians 68, 239–40, 247–9, 261–2
Indonesia 256
Ingold, T. 12–13
innovation 5–6, 8, 13, 27–30, 74–6, 79,
  96–7, 99–101, 115–20, 122, 126,
  130–2, 134–40, 170, 188–9, 211–13,
  222, 228, 244
interaction 44–57, 62, 94–5,
  110–41, 237

intercultural
  communication 213
  contact 12–13, 38–9
  dealings 201
  discourse 207
  encounters 8–9
  identities 15
  interactions 26
  networks 13
  situations 190–1
  violence 196
interstratification 94, 130–1
intimacy 196–208, 221–2, 246–7,
  272–3, 299
Iran 256, 264
Iranian
  coins 257–8
  culture 259
  Zoroastrianism 259–60
Iranians 254–5
Iraq 259–60
Ireland 196–208, 216, 244–5
  Armagh 198, 203, 206
  Belfast 198–200
  Belfast Castle 204–6
  Belfast Lough 198–200
  Clonony More 202–3
  Coleraine 203
  Cork 198
  Donegal 203
  Down 201–2
  Dublin 197, 200–1
  Fermanagh 203
  Kinsale 198
  Londonderry 203–4
  Louth 198
  Munster Plantation 198, 203
  Offaly 197–8, 202–3
  Ulster 198–9, 201, 204–7
  Ulster Plantation 15, 198, 203–7
  Tyrone 203
Irish
  affairs 197
  ceramics 204
  chiefs 206–7
  conflict 206–7
  culture 201–3, 299
  custom 201
  elite 206

322 INDEX

Irish (*cont.*)
　forces 198
　genealogy 202–3
　landholding 206–7
　language 201–3
　lord 198–9
　majority 205–6
　mummers 202
　neighbours 15, 204–7
　rebels 299
　sociability 204–5
　society 197–8
　tenants 203
　traditions 204
Irish Church 197
Irish Republican Army (IRA) 205
Irish Rising (1641) 206
Islam 253–65, *see also* Muslims
Islamic
　archaeology 257
　architecture 258
　civilization 264–5
　culture 256
　empire 257–8
　identities 16
　inscription 258*f*
　Middle East 261–4
　religion 259–60
　rule 260
　sources 216–17
　world 254–6, 255*f*
Islamicization 256, 262–4, 302
Israel 124–5
Italian cuisine 30–1
Italy 30–1, 126
Iversen, T. 216

James I/VI, King 203
jars 32, 65–7, 74, 75*f*, 187, 226
Jaubert, J. 132–4
Jerusalem 256
Jetegua 78
jewelry, *see also* adornment
　bracelets 164–5, 171–2
　brooches 164–8, 171–2
　necklace 164–5
　rings 166–8
Jews 160, 238–9, 254
Johnson, Rachel 186–7

Jolly, P. 30–1, 44–5, 49
Jones, A. 11–12, 289
Jones, D. L. 185
Jones, S. 4–5, 246, 248
Jordan 258
Joyce, R. A. 62–3, 299–300
Joy, Jody 162
Judaism 253–4, 256
Julien, M. 121, 130

Kahlheber, S. 25–6
Kapchan, D. A. 34–5
Karkarichinkat Nord 284–5
Karras, R. M. 216
Kasoje 97–8
Katzew, I. 66, 238
Kaufman, A. 100, 102
Kavanagh, S. S. 301–2
Kazakh Muslims 260
Kenya 259*f*, 261–2
Khan, A. 214
Khirbet al-Minya 258
Khoekhoen 44, 47–8, 55–6
Khusrau II, Emperor 256
Kievan Rus' 219, 223, 225–8
King, G. R. D. 262–4
King, R. 48
Kinnard, Lillian 163–4, 168–9
Kinnersly, Mabel 164
Kiple, K. F. 25–6
Klein, N. 36–7
　No Logo 37
Klein, R. 89–90, 115–16
Klingelhofer, E. 198
Knut Eriksson 226–7
Kochiyama, T. 100–1
Koekhoen 47
Kolesnikov, I. 259–60
Kongo 270
Koplin, J. 86
Kopytoff, I. 161–2, 169–70
Kozarnikian 136–7
Kraft, E. 237–8
Kraidy, M. 11
Krings, M. 124
Kroeber, A. L. 115–16
Krosnicki, Thomas 282
Kufa 259–60
Kuhlwilm, M. 124–5

INDEX 323

Kusho-Sassanian kingdom 259
Kuzmin, Y. V. 30–1
KwaZulu-Natal 45*f*, 48, 55–6

Labrador Bay 4–5
Laidlaw, J. 9–10
La Isabella 298
Laland, K. 85, 96–7
Landon, D. B. 183–4
Lange, F. 284–5
Lankton, J. 28–9
Lanna, A. L. 241
Laois plantation 197–8, 203
Laplace, G. 114
La Roche-à-Pierrot 114–15, 118–19
Late Glacial Maximum 125
Latin America 62, 238–9, 299–300
Latour, B. 10–11, 102
Laurens, G. 44
La Valette Military Museum 167*f*
LaViolette, A. 28–9
Leakey, L. 96
Lebanon 263*f*
Lecale 201–2
Lechtman, H. 29–30
Le Moustier 135–6
Lenca 67, 77–8
Lennon, C. 198–9
Le Piage 111*f*, 130–1
Leroi-Gourhan, A. 114–15, 119–22,
    130, 137–8
Leroyer, X. 137–8
Le Ruez, N. 163
Lescureux, N. 102
Levallois
    flakes 117*f*
    points 117*f*, 119–20
    products 119–20
    reduction methods 132–4
Levant 110–11, 114, 256
Lévêque, F. 114–15, 118–19
Levinson, C. 93
Levitt, T. 36
Lewis-Williams, J. D. 44–6, 52, 90–3
Liebmann, M. 1, 3–4, 7–11, 300–1
Lightfoot, K. G. 3, 5–7, 26–8, 34–5, 62
Lincombien–Ranisian–Jerzmanowician
    111–12
Lindkvist, T. 216

Lindstrom, L. 237
Linduff, K. M. 28–9, 31
Lister, F. C. 304
Lister, R. H. 304
lithic
    artefacts 119–20
    assemblages 119–20, 134
    components 118–19, 135–6
    industries 94, 132–4
    objects 118–19
    refits 123
    remains 130–1
    technology 116–18, 132–5
Litvinsky, B. A. 259–60
Löddeköpinge 228
Logue, P. 198
Lokken, P. 66
Long Island 303
Lope 97–8
Loren, D. D. 10–11, 26–8, 215–16
Loubser, J. 44
Lowe, L. 7–8
löwenmensch (lion-man) figurine
    91–2, 91*f*
Lucas, G. 3–4, 190
Lund 212*f*, 213, 219, 222–34, 229*f*
Luticians 219, 229–30
Lymer, K. 260
Lyttleton, J. 202–3

Maasai 33–4
MacBruadeadha 202–3
MacCarthy-Morrogh, M. 198
Machon, R. 164–5, 168–9, 171–2
Mackintosh, N. 88
Macquarrie, J. W. 48, 50–1, 55–6
Maguire, Cú Chonnacht Óg 200–1
Mälaren Valley 218*f*, 219, 222–3, 227–8,
    232–4
Malaysia 169, 256
Mali 284–5
Mallen, L. 51–2, 301
Maloti-Drakensberg escarpment/region
    13, 47–9
Maloti-Drakensberg Mountains 44
mammoth ivory 91–2, 91*f*, 127–8
Manot Cave 124–5
Maran, J. 7–9, 11
Marietta 301–2

maritime
  expansionism 239
  links 25–6
  routes 28–9
  trade 32
Maritime Silk Road 28
maroons 15–16, 237–49, 241*f*, 298–9
Marshack, A. 91–2
Marshall, L. 45–6
Marshall, Y. 161–2
Martinez, A. 5–6, 26–8, 34–5
Martinez, I. 93
Martinòn-Torres, M. 34
Masca (Candelaria) 68–9, 78–9
Massachusetts 178–9, 181–8, 184*f*
material culture 3–5, 14–15, 25–39, 47,
    52, 90, 93–4, 98–9, 101–3, 110–12,
    116–20, 125–6, 130–1, 159–75,
    187–90, 207, 213–16, 228, 240–2,
    244–5, 256, 274–6, 284,
    297–8, 301–4
Mather, K. A. 28–9
Maya conversion 77
Mazel, A. 44, 47–8, 50–1
Mazière, M. 117*f*
MBelekwana 50
McGrew, W. 97–8
McManus, E. J. 181
Mdwebo 50
Mead, L. A. 183–4
Mears, J. 186–7
Mecca 253–4, 257–8, 302
Mecklenburg-Vorpommern 216–17,
    229–30
Medina 253–4, 257–8
Mediterranean 25–6, 237, 262–4, 300
Mei, J. 28–9, 31
Melish, J. P. 178–83
Mellars, P. 90–1, 94, 110–11, 113–16,
    132–4, 136–8
Mellifont 198
Mercers' Company 204–5
Merv 259–60
Mesolithic/Neolithic transition 131–2
Mesopotamia 256, 259
metal 29–30, 34, 74, 166–8, 261–2, 277,
    282–3
  knives 163, 280
metallurgy 31

Metcalf, P. 32
Métis 4–5
Mexica (Aztec) tribute state 69
Mexican languages 68–9
Mexico 284–5, 301–2
Mfecane 47–8
Middle East 6, 259, 261–4, 304
Middleton, J. 28–9, 261, 264–5
migration 7–8, 13–14, 25–6, 32–3,
    38, 47–8, 84–5, 88, 97–8, 122,
    214, 283–4
Mijikenda 261–2
Miles, H. 101–2
military 162–3, 166–8, 201–2
  action 197–8
  architecture 258
  campaigns 229–30
  conflicts 63
  conquest 197–8
  dictatorship 240–1
  enlistments 185
  forces 14, 201, 240
  junta 15–16
  leaders 240, 299
  negotiations 247
  occupation 159–60, 173–4
  populations 174
  resistance 63, 69–70, 160, 172
  service 202, 298
militias 65–6, 166–8
mimesis 15, 196, 201–3
mimetic
  play 15
  practice 196–208
  process 201
Mintz, S. 243–4
Miracle, P. J. 28–9, 44, 47, 49, 131–2
Mithen, S. 9–10, 90–1, 93
modern humans 84–5, 89–90, 94–6,
    98–101, 110–41, 297, *see also*
    anatomically modern humans
Moody, T. W. 203
Moorish kingdoms 70
Moreiras, A. 7–8
Morgan, H. 198, 201
Morin, E. 118–19
Morris, I. 99–100
Moryson, Sir Richard 201–2
Moshoeshoe, Nehemiah 48

INDEX   325

Mosquera, G. 268
Moths, P. 38–9, 50
Mousterian 112–13, 115–16, 118–22, 126,
    128–30, 134–6, 139–41
Mousterian (Acheulean Type B) 94,
    115, 132–4
Mousterian of Acheulean Tradition (MTA)
    113–15, 117f, 132–4, 136–7, *see also*
    Acheulean
Movanagher 204
Mpondo 47–8, 50–1
Muhammad 253–8
Muller, N. 188
Mullins, P. R. 26–8, 187
Multi-Regional Model 114–15
Munasinghe, V. 238–9
Munich 164
Muslims 239, 249, 254
    Arabs 254–5, 259, 262–4
    armies 256
    blood 238
    conquests 259–60, 262–4
    cultures 256, 302
    faith 254–5, 262–4
    identities 16, 262–4
    population 257
    power 259–60
    saints 260
    societies 261–2
    tradition 261–2
    youths 25
    see also Islam
Myal 270
Myrdal, J. 217

Nakonids 229–30
nanny 272–3, 272f, 291
Nantucket 183–4, 186–7
natural selection 87–8
Neanderthal
    agency 94
    ancestry 125
    authorship 116–18
    bands 138
    bone/bones 115, 122
    brain 89–90, 100–1
    cognition 101
    communities 96
    culture 85, 136–7

endocast 89f
features 169
genes 124
genetic contribution 125
genome 124
groups 111–12, 124, 134, 136–40
innovations 135–6
language 93
populations 94, 115–16
practices 305–6
proportions 93–4
remains 118–19, 121–2, 127–8
skeleton/skeletal material 114–15,
    118–20
teeth 119–20
Neanderthals 84–5, 88, 93–6, 98–100, 102,
    110–41, 297
Nederveen Pieterse, J. 25–7
Neolithic 25–6
    populations 125
    tradition 31
Neolithic/Mesolithic transition 131–2
Nesbit, R. 268–9
Neumann, K. 25–6
Nevéus, C. 216
New Archaeology 26
New England 6, 14–15, 178–91, 302–3
New Hampshire 181–2
New Orleans 284–5
Newport 179–80
newspapers 160, 163, 171–2, 179–80,
    182–3, 277, 282
    Boston Gazette 180
    Boston Globe 185–7
    Boston Post Boy 180
Newton Plantation 284–5
New World 25–6, 29–31, 160, 179–80, 196,
    202, 237, 253, 269–70, 284–5
New York 179–80, 284–5
Nguni 44, 47–50, 56
Niger Delta 271
Nigeria 238–9, 284–5, 288–9
Nine Years' War 198, 201
Nishapur 259–60
nodes of interaction 44–57
Nomansland 13, 44–56, 45f
Nordic countries 218f
Norman, Kathleen 163–4, 168–9
Norse sagas 217

326 INDEX

North Africa 2, 125, 256
Novgorod 219, 223, 224f, 225–7,
   227f, 233–4
Nqabayo 50
Nuestra Señora de la Encarnación 77–8
Nurse, G. T. 47

Obeah healing 16, 270–4, 275f, 282–4
Obodrites 219, 229–30
Óg, Rory 200
Ohio 301–2
Ó Huiginn, T. D. 200–1
Old World 26, 28–9, 31, 34, 237–8
Oliveira, J. E. 249
Omoa 64–5, 67–9, 71–2, 74–6
Onderwater, Father Jordanus 276–9, 278f,
   282–4, 283f
O'Neill, Brian McPhelim 196, 198–207
O'Neill, Felim Bacagh 200
O'Neill, Hugh 198, 200
O'Neill, J. 198
Opperman, H. 45
Ord, R. D. 164–5, 168
Ó Rensi, M. 202–3
ornaments 34, 93–4, 115–22, 127–8,
   131–2, 134–7, 135f, 139, 219–20, 298
Ornelas, K. C. 25–6
Orpen, J. M. 50–1
Orser, C. E. 187, 241–2, 244–5
Östergötland 218f, 234
Ota Benga 285–6, 285f
Otte, M. 115–16
Otto, J. S. 184–5
Owsley, D. 284–5

Pacheco-Sierra, G. 86–7
painting 45f, 46, 52, 54, 56, 134–5, 162–4,
   168–9, 175, 281, 301, see also body
   painting, finger painting, rock art/
   paintings
palaeoanthropology 110–11
palaeogenetics 123–32
palaeogenomics 123–32
Palaeolithic
   archaeology 110, 113, 126, 140–1
   contexts 134–5
   development 30–1
   human groups 114–15
   Middle 94–5, 111–12, 124, 126, 132–4,
      136–7, 140–1

origins 30–1
   sequence 112–13, 132–4
   systematics 113–14
   traits 136–7
   typo-technological elements 119–20
   Upper 90–4, 111–14, 124, 126, 132–4,
      136–7, 140–1, 297
Palestine 16, 255f, 256–9, 262–4, 302
Palka, J. 62
Palmares 237–49, 241f, 298–9
Palmares Archaeological
   Project 15–16, 241–2
Palmié, S. 6, 9, 26–7, 35, 70–1, 80, 214
Pappa, E. 213
Papua New Guinea 124–5
Paravisini-Gebert, L. 268, 270–1, 282
Parting Ways 184–90, 184f
patriotic
   cigarette lighters 169–70
   club 168–9
   coins 171
   colours 168–9, 172–3
   defiance 168
   determination 161
   fervour 165–6
   images 161, 165–6
   insignia 168
   slogans 175
   symbols 161
Patton, J. Q. 300–1
Paynter, R. 26–8, 187–8, 190
Pearce, D. G. 44–6, 301
Pearson, J. 284–5
Pech de L'Aze 135–6
Peires, J. B. 47
Pelegrin, J. 113–15, 132–4
Perigordian 113–14
Pernambuco 239–40, 241f
Persian
   desires 304
   identity 264
   language 256, 259
   Muslims 259–60
Persian Gulf 255f, 261–2
petroglyphs 260
Peyrony, D. 113–14
Philadelphia 179–80, 284–5
Philipsburg 286–7
Phuthi 34, 48
Piast 229–30

Piersen, W. D. 178–82
Pihl, H. 218*f*
Pilcher, J. M. 25–6
Pleistocene 110, 124–6, 131, 137–8, 140
Pleistocene–Holocene transition 125
Plymouth 179, 184–7
Poland 229–30
Polanyi, M. 211–12, 221–2
Pollini, A. 237
Pomerania 216–17
Portugal 237–8
Portuguese 179–80, 239, 244
  authorities 239
  colonies 242–3, 247–8
  conquest 244–5
  control 242
  language 242
  lineage 6
Posth, C. 125
pottery/potters 4–5, 74–6, 211, 212*f*, 217, 218*f*, 219–35, 224*f*, 242–4, 261–2, 300, 304, *see also* ceramic, ceramics
Powhatans 207
Prestholdt, J. 32–5
  Domesticating the World 33–4
Price, R. 243–4, 290–1
Price, S. 290–1
Primault, J. 117*f*
Prins, F. E. 47
Protestants 205–7, 240
Prous, A. 242
Providence 179
Pruetz, J. 98–9
Prüfer, K. 124–5
Pskov 223, 225–7
pueblos de indios 63–6, 64*f*, 68–9, 71–2, 74–80
Pusey, A. 99–100
Pye, M. 238

Quande, Quash 185
Quimbois 270
Quran 254

Racimo, F. 93–4
radiocarbon dating (¹⁴C) 45, 118–22, 126–31, 129*f*
radiometric age/dating 115, 119–20, 126–7
Rago, M. 246
Rainbird, P. 170

Ramos, A. 237–8
Ranians 219, 229–30
Rattansi, A. 245–6
Rawson, J. 28–9, 31
Redfield, R. 3
Reformation 197
Regla de Ocha 270
Reich, D. 125
Reynolds, V. 85, 97–8
Rhode Island 179–82
Rich, B. 202
Richards, M. 48–9
Rigaud, J.-P. 116–20, 132–4
Rio Ulua 63–5, 64*f*
rituals 9–10, 31–2, 34, 44–6, 48–50, 52, 54, 56, 85, 91–3, 201, 215, 221, 260–2, 270, 273–4, 291, 298
Robb, J. 131–2
Roberts, B. C. 31
Robertshaw, P. 28–9
Robertson, R. 37
Roc de Combe 111*f*, 130–1
Rocca, R. 119–20
rock art/paintings 13, 44–57, 301–2, 305
Rodrigues, N. 237
Roebroeks, W. 135–6
Rogers, J. D. 301, 304
Rolo, C. J. 162–4
Roman Britain 26, 173
Roman Empire 226–7
Roman Mediterranean 262–4
Romans 44, 258, 263*f*
Roslund, M. 215, 217–20, 218*f*, 228–9, 300–1
Ross, R. 48, 50–1
Rothstein, M. 238
Rougier, H. 93–4
Roussel, M. 132–4, 140–1
Rowlands, M. 3, 30–1, 241–2, 247
Rügen 216–17, 228–31
Russell, Robert 204–5
Russian Altai 124–5

Saint Césaire 111*f*, 114–15, 118–20, 122, 127
Sánchez-Gōni, M. 137–8
Sanchez-Quinto, F. 125
Sanders, P. 162–3
San Francisco 79–80
Sankararaman, S. 93–4

328 INDEX

San Pedro 13–14, 63–4, 64f, 66–72, 76–8, 299–300
San Salvador 300
Santa Barbara 77
Santeria 270, 284
Santiago de Guatemala 68
Sassanian coins 257–60, 258f
Sassanian conquests 264
Saudi Arabia 253–4
Saunders, N. J. 161, 166–8
Savage-Rumbaugh, S. 98
Scandinavia 211, 216, 218f, 219–20, 232–5
  ceramic tradition 211
  economy 216
  households 216–17, 219–20
  potters 228
  society 213, 215–16
  source material 217
  thralls 226–8, 233–4
  tradition 231
Scandinavians 215–17, 223, 225, 228
Schaik, C. 96
Schiavetto, S. N. O. 244
Schleswig-Holstein 229–30
Schoeman, M. H. 44
Schroeder, H. 284, 286, 288–9
Schular, M. 270
Scott, J. C. 169–71
Scott, J. W. 245
scrapers 94, 112, 117f, 119–20
Semelin, J. 172
Semino, O. 125
Senegal 180
Sepulchre, P. 137–8
Serre, D. 124–5
Sevilla 69–70
shamanism/shamans 44–6, 91–3, 260, 264
Shanga 259f, 261–2
Shanks, M. 248
Shaw, R. 238
Shephard, J. 50–1, 55
Shepherd, V. 271–2
Sheptak, R. N. 62–70, 73–4, 77–9
Sheringham, O. 5–6
Siberia 124
Sigtuna 212f, 213, 219, 222–34, 224f, 225f
Silayi 55–6
Silk Road 13, 28–9, 259, 264
Sillar, B. 29–30

Silliman, S. 2–5, 8–9, 62, 76, 87–8, 94–5, 160, 173–4, 196, 215, 233, 246, 298–9, 303, 305
Simms, K. 200–1
Sinclair, A. 134–5
Sinel, L. 163–4
Singer, R. 289–90
Sjælland 234
Skåne 212f, 228–31, 234
Skara 212f
skeletons/skeletal material 114–15, 118–20, 122, 124, 277, 278f, 280f, 284, 286–92, 287f, 288f
Skre, D. 216
Slatkin, M. 93–4
slavery/slaves 6, 14–16, 49, 62–3, 66, 75–6, 80, 86, 160, 178–87, 189–90, 212–13, 215–17, 220, 239–44, 246–8, 253, 261–2, 268–74, 285–7, 290–1, see also thralls
Slavic
  areas 216–19, 233–4
  ceramics 211, 233
  groups 211
  imports 225
  potters 219, 229–30
  pottery 211, 219, 223–8, 224f, 233–4
  producers 226, 233
  territory 228–31, 234
  thralls 230–1, 233
  traditions 211, 228, 231, 233
  vessels 211, 226–8, 232–3
  ware 217–20
Slavs 215, 223, 228–9, 234
Småland 218f
Smolensk 219
Society of Negroes 181–2
Södermanland 234
Soficaru, A. 93–4
Solutrean 112–13
Sørensen, M. L. S. 6, 12
Soressi, M. 113–14, 118–19, 132–6
Sotho 44, 48, 50
South Africa 2, 13, 44–57, 45f, 301–2, see also Eastern Cape
South America 2, 10, 237–49, 298–9
Spain 130–1, 179–80, 237–8, 240
  administration 65, 68
  allies 198

America 66
caste system 238
census 72–3
citizens 63, 71
colonialism 7–8, 62–3, 65–7, 69–70, 78–80, 298, 300–1
Crown 239
factions 63
governance 69
identity 64, 73–4
invasion 67–8, 197
language 68–9, 299–300, 305
liaisons 70–1
neologisms 67
policies 65–7
population 66–7, 70
pottery 65
territories 240
towns 64–6, 64*f*, 71, 80
traditions 76–7
Spenser, E. 197–8
Speth, J. 115–16
Spoor, F. 84–5, 115, 119–20
Stadel Cave 91–2, 91*f*
Stadelheim Prison 164
Stahl, A. B. 189–90
Staller, J. 92–3
Stanford, W. E. 55–6
Stepanoff, C. 95–6
Steppe Road 28–9, 31
Stewart, C. 1–2, 9–11, 112, 238
Stewart, J. B. 182–3
Stewart, T. D. 289–90
St Maarten 16, 267, 271, 274–84, 286–91
Stockhammer, P. W. 1, 8–9, 87–8, 98–9, 102, 215
stock raiding 13, 49–51, 54–6
stone tools, *see also* Levallois, lithic, Mousterian
blades/bladelets 29–30, 94, 112–13, 117*f*, 119–20, 133*f*, 134, 280
burins 94, 117*f*
flake/flake tools 73–4, 112–13, 115, 117*f*
knives 113–14, 117*f*, 132–4, 163, 280
Stross, B. 86–7
Strutt, D. H. 53
Sumatra 96
Sundkler, B. 10

Supernant, K. 4–5
Suzdal 226–7
Swabian Alps 126–7
Swahili 28–9, 32–3, 261–2, 264–5
Sweden 4, 15, 211–35, 300–1
High Middle Ages 213, 216, 220, 233–5
Sylvester Manor 300, 303
symbols/symbolism 13–16, 29–30, 34–6, 54, 56, 89–93, 95, 98, 115–16, 130–1, 136–7, 159–61, 164–75, 198–9, 244, 257–8, 282–4, 298, 301–2
syncretic
belief systems 264
elements 253–4, 268–9, 292
expressions 267
forms 28–9
practices 196, 207
processes 6, 52–3, 56, 267–9, 291–2
religion 4, 268
syncretism 1–2, 4–10, 15–16, 26–8, 44, 49, 55–6, 77–9, 183–4, 202–7, 237–45, 253–65, 267–92, 301–2, 305–6
anti-syncretism 253–4, 302
Syria 254–5, 258
Syrotinski, M. 7

Tamgaly 260
taphonomy 94–5, 113, 115–20, 123, 126, 128–31, 137, 140–1
teeth 91–4, 114–15, 119–25, 127–8, 134–6, 135*f*, 162, 271, 286–92, *see also* dental modification
Teyssandier, N. 132–4, 140–1
Thembu 47–8, 55–6
therianthrope 46*f*, 90–1
Thiébaut, C. 117*f*, 132–4
Thola 50
Thomas, J. 248
Thomas, M. 132–4
Thomas, N. 26–7, 35
Thornton, C. 31
Thornton, J. 16, 179–80, 267–70
thralls 15, 211–35, *see also* slavery/slaves
Thrupp, L. 88
Ticamaya 63–5, 70–6, 79–80
Tilley, C. 248
Tolmie, C. 94–5, 120–1
Toninato, R. 214–15

330 INDEX

Toolis, K. 205
Tostevin, G. B. 140
Transkei 47–8
Trelleborg 228
Trinkaus, E. 93–4, 137
Troitski excavation 227f
Troncoso, Jose Manuel 72–3
Turks 254–5, 259–60, 262–4
Turner, M. 274
Turner, Plato 185–7, 189–90
Turner Strong, P. 34–5

Ulluzian 111–12, 123–4
Umayyad 254–5, 258, 263f
Umzimvubu River 47–8
unfree people 4, 15, 211–35, 300–1
United States 3, 7–8, 183–5, 240–1, 244–5, 279, 285–6, 301–2, see also America
United States Bureau of the Census 179, 185
Uppland 212f, 234
Ust-Ishim 124
Utopo C12/D09f 289–90

Vainfas, R. 237
Van Calker, E. 48, 50, 55
Vandermeersch, B. 114–15
Van Doornum, B. L. 44
Vanhaeren, M. 121, 134–5
Van Pelt, W. P. 1
Van Riebeeck, Jan 53
Van Valkenburgh, P. 10–11
Van Veen, G. 276
Västergötland 212f, 218f, 234
Verna, C. 114
Vernot, B. 93–4
Vigne, J.-D. 95–6
Viking Age 213, 216, 227–9, 231, 233–5
pottery/ware 212f, 217–20, 218f, 223–6, 224f, 228
Vinnicombe, P. 49–51, 55
violence 4–5, 10, 15, 70, 79, 138–40, 182–3, 196–208, 243, 299, 305–6
Virginia settlers 207
Vodou 270, 283–4
Voss, B. 4–5, 62, 79–80, 245–6, 302–3, 305–6

Wade, M. 181–2
Wagner, D. 31
Walmsley, A. 257–8
Walsh, L. 179–80
Walter, M. 92–3
War of the Three Kingdoms 205–7
war/warfare 14, 27, 29–30, 70, 99–100, 159–75, 179, 185–6, 196–8, 201, 205–7, 216, 298, 301–2
weapons 31, 52, 175, 240
weapons of the weak 168–72
W. E. B. Du Bois Boyhood Home Site 184f, 188–90
Webster, J. 26–8
Weeks, J. 77
Weik, T. 4–5, 62
Weiss, H. 162
Wentworth, Thomas (Earl of Strafford) 206
Werbner, C. 238
West Africa 6, 97–8, 187, 261, 267, 271, 284–5, 288–90
West Indies 179–80, 187
Weymouth 179
Whitcomb, D. 256
White, C. L. 190
Whitehouse, H. 9–10
Whitelaw, G. 47, 49
Whiten, A. 85, 96
White, R. 94, 119–20, 134–5
Whitley, D. 92–3
Wildman, D. 85
Wilkie, L. 26–8
Wilkinson, D. 86
William of Orange, Prince 206–7
Williamite Wars 206–7
Williams, Alf 164–5, 170–2
Wilson, M. 99–100
Windward Islands 276
Winkelman, M. 92–3
Wolpoff, M. H. 114–15
Wood, N. 28–9, 31
Woodward, K. 248
Woodward, S. L. 301–2
World War I 165–70
World War II 14, 159–75, 298
Wrangham, R. W. 12–13, 85
Wright, J. B. 47–51, 55

Wright, R. P. 220
Wu, X. 30–1
Wynn, T. 91–2, 100–1

Yamala 64*f*, 77–8
Yang, M. A. 124–5
Yoruba 270
Young, R. 7
Ystad 228
Yucatan 67, 69, 77

Zanzibar 34–5
Zarankin, A. 249
Zilhão, J. 116–20, 123–6, 130–1, 135–8
Ziyad ibn Abi Sufyan 256
Zohary, D. 25–6
zooarchaeology 122
Zoroastrianism 257–60, 264
Zoutsteeg 286–91
Zoutsteeg skeletons 287*f*, 288*f*, 289–90
Zumbi 240, 246–7